Behind the Scenes!!

03

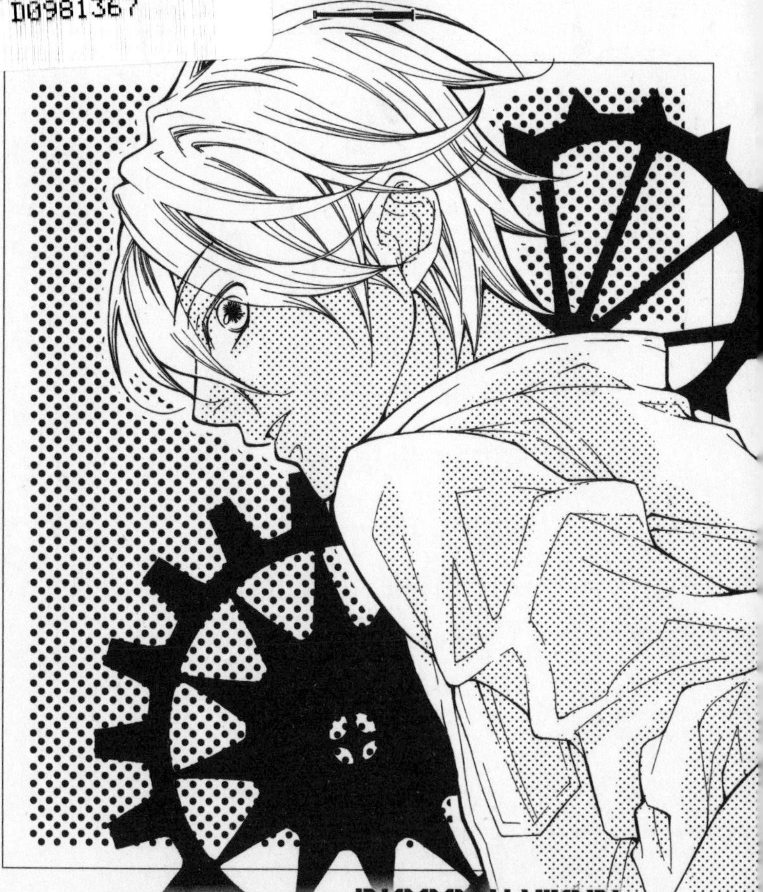

STORY AND ART BY BISCO HATORI

Behind the Scenes!!

03

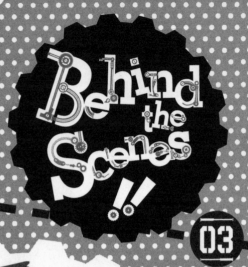

Contents

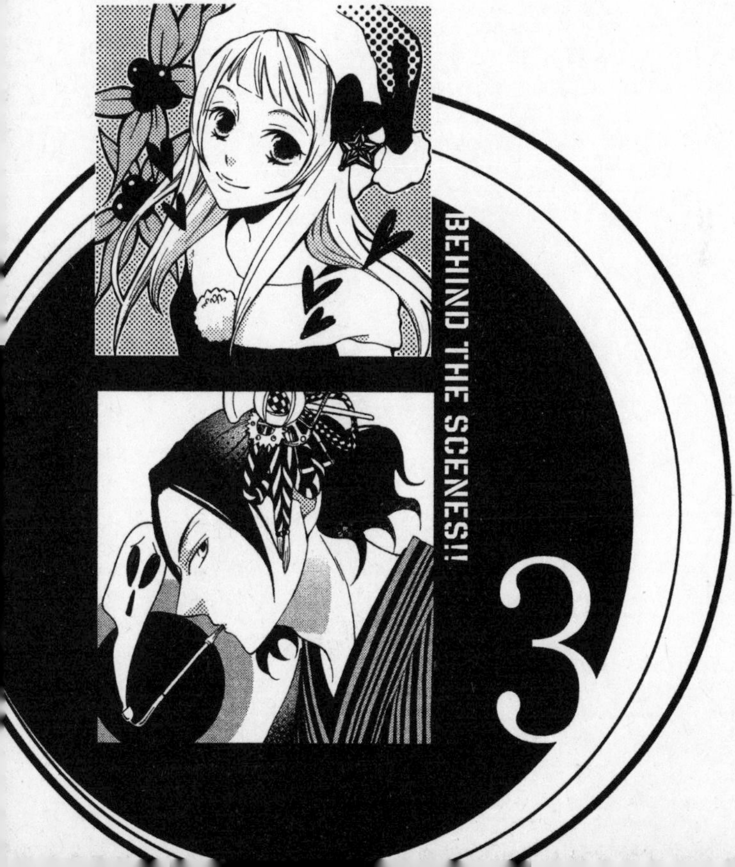
BEHIND THE SCENES!!
3

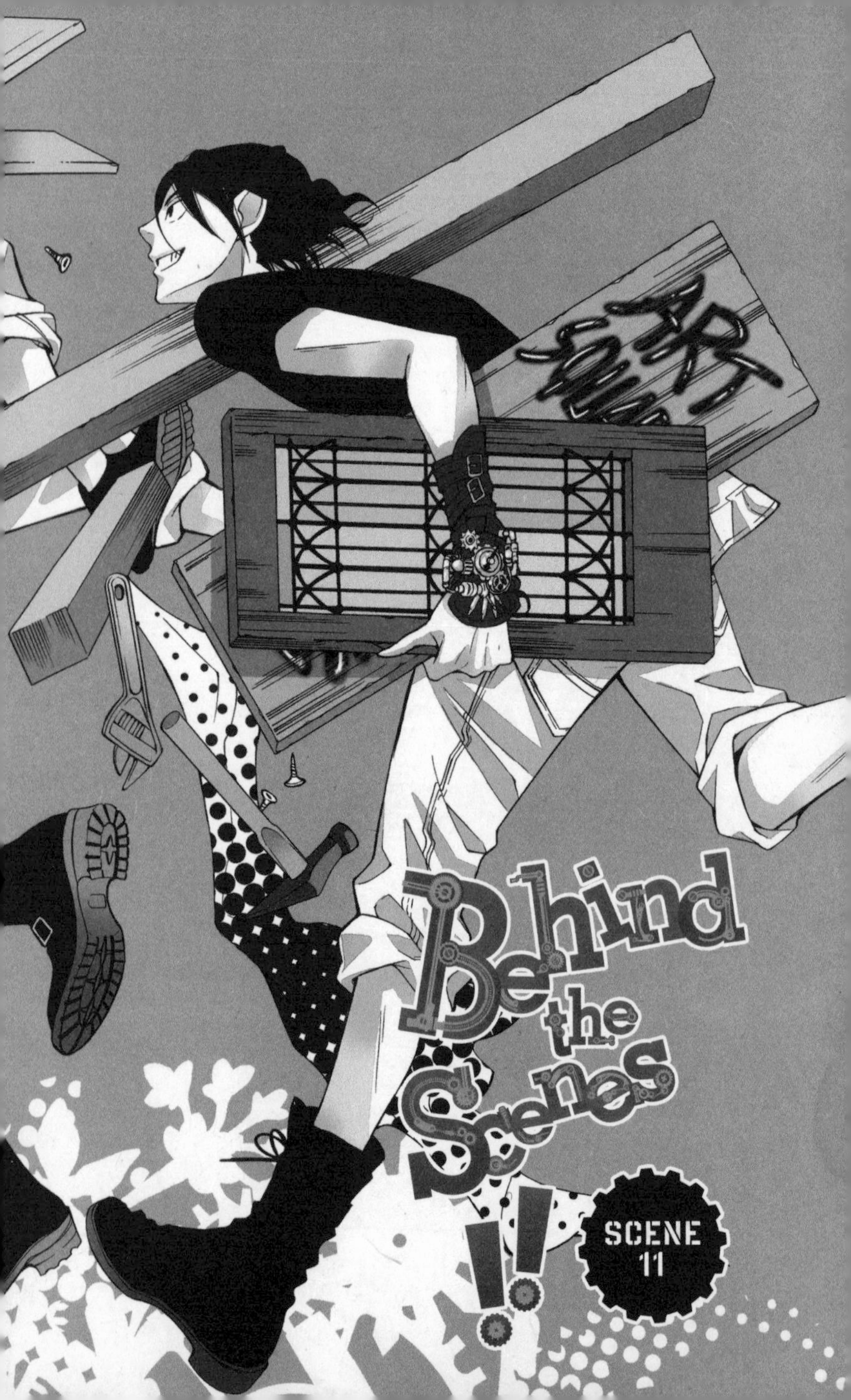
ART
Behind the Scenes!!
SCENE
11

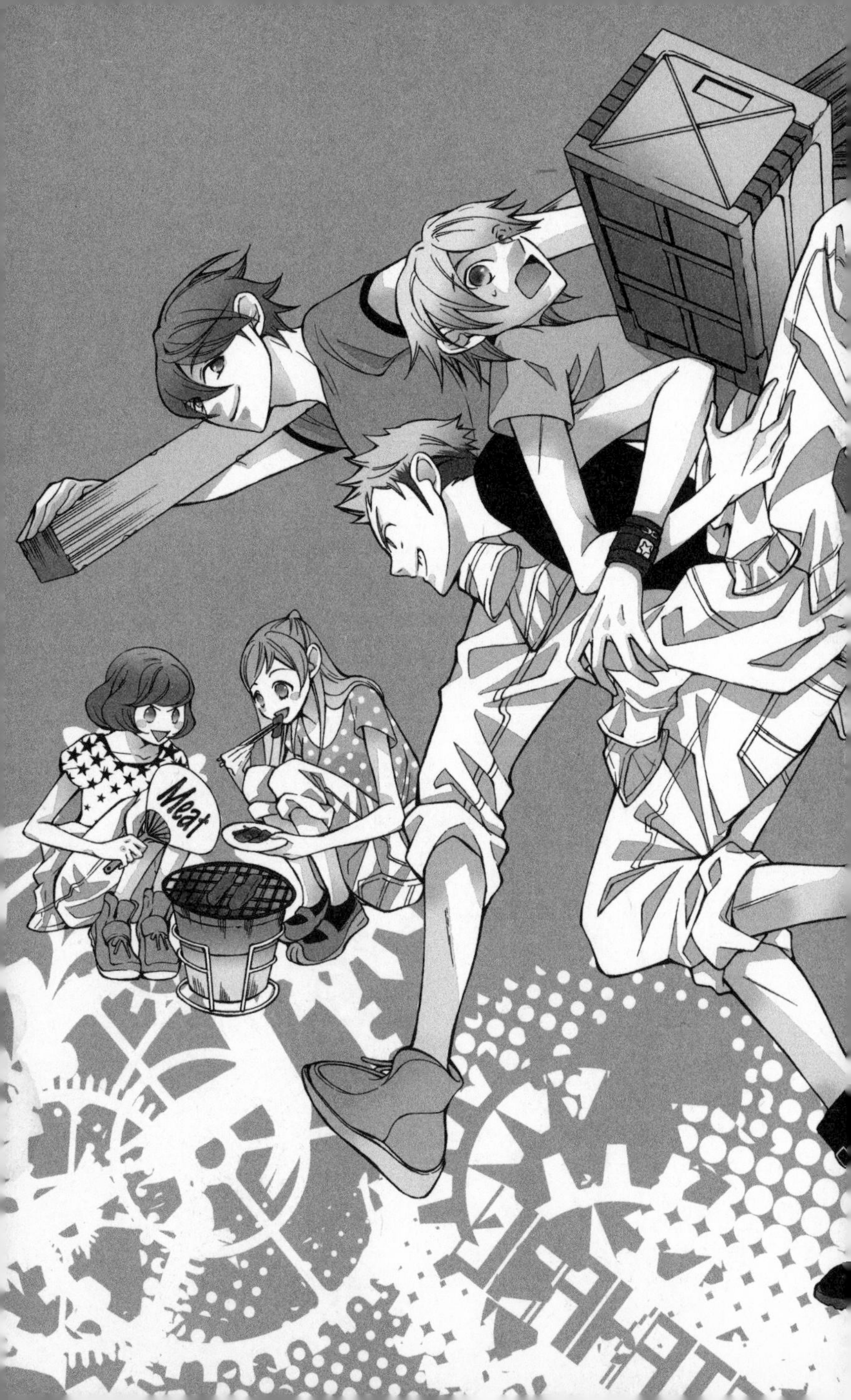
Meat

BEHIND THE SCENES!!

3

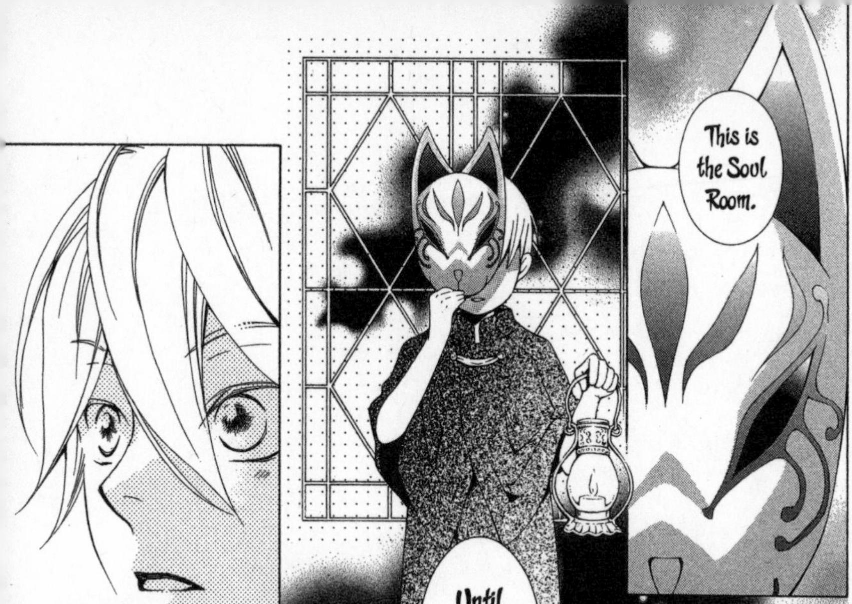
This is the Soul Room.
Until the rain ceases...
...your hearts will remain here.
THIS IS THE FIRST FILM CAMP THIS SUMMER.

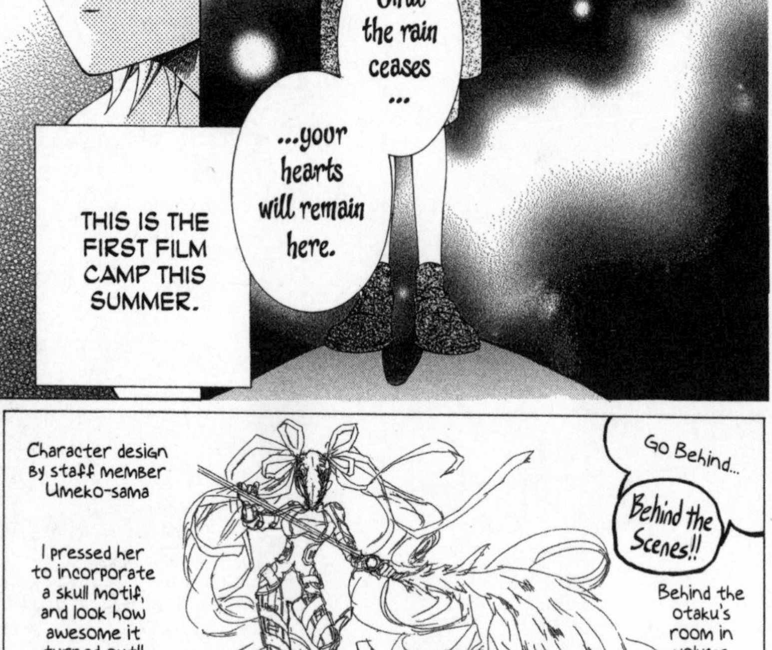
Go Behind...
Behind the Scenes!!
Behind the otaku's room in volume 2.
Character design by staff member Umeko-sama
I pressed her to incorporate a skull motif, and look how awesome it turned out!!

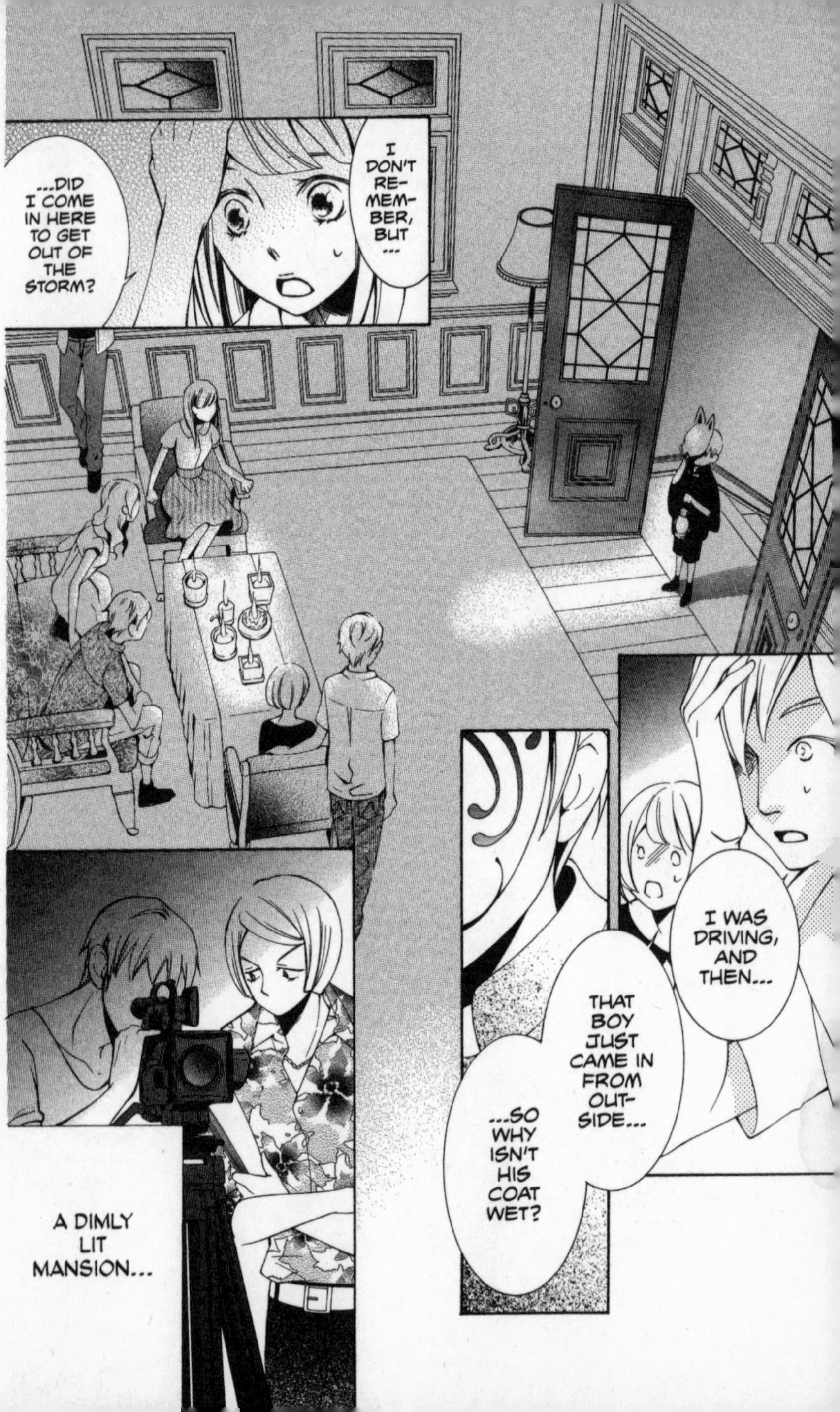
I DON'T RE-MEM-BER, BUT...
...DID I COME IN HERE TO GET OUT OF THE STORM?
I WAS DRIVING, AND THEN...
THAT BOY JUST CAME IN FROM OUT-SIDE...
...SO WHY ISN'T HIS COAT WET?
A DIMLY LIT MANSION...

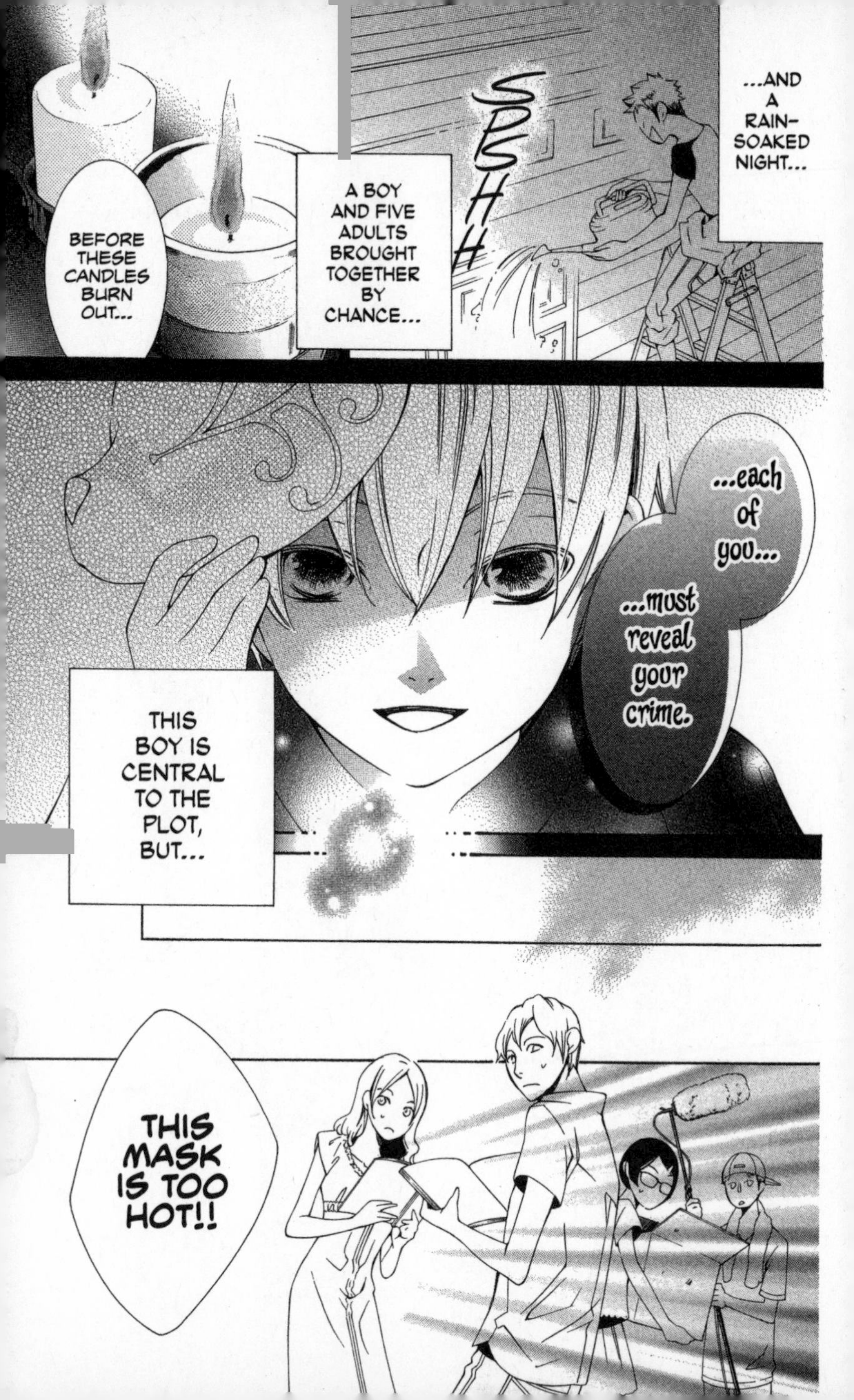

...AND A RAIN-SOAKED NIGHT...
SPSHH
A BOY AND FIVE ADULTS BROUGHT TOGETHER BY CHANCE...
BEFORE THESE CANDLES BURN OUT...
...each of you...
...must reveal your crime.
THIS BOY IS CENTRAL TO THE PLOT, BUT...
THIS MASK IS TOO HOT!!

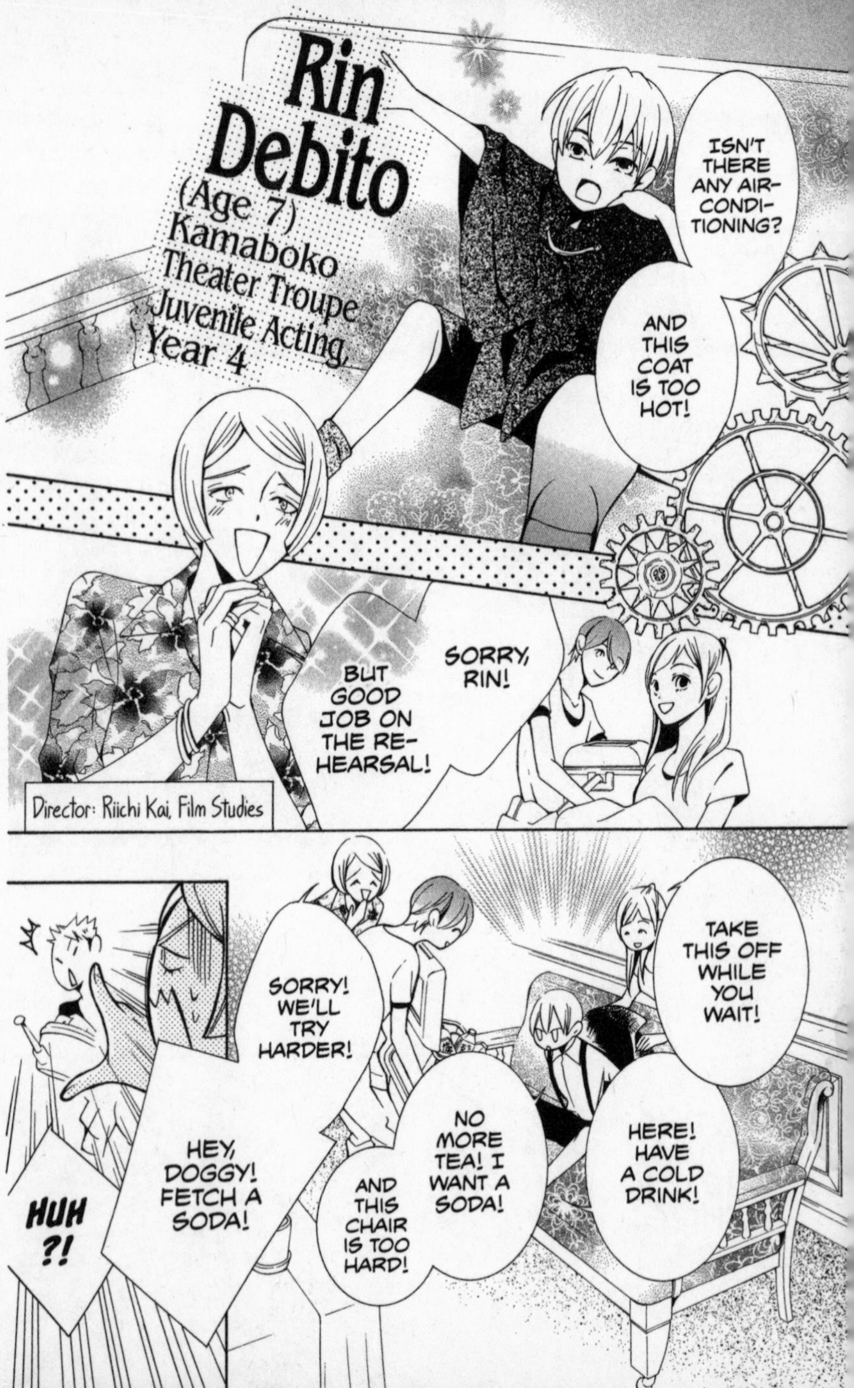
ISN'T THERE ANY AIR-CONDITIONING?
AND THIS COAT IS TOO HOT!
Rin Debito
(Age 7) Kamaboko Theater Troupe Juvenile Acting, Year 4
SORRY, RIN!
BUT GOOD JOB ON THE REHEARSAL!
Director: Riichi Kai, Film Studies
TAKE THIS OFF WHILE YOU WAIT!
SORRY! WE'LL TRY HARDER!
HERE! HAVE A COLD DRINK!
NO MORE TEA! I WANT A SODA!
AND THIS CHAIR IS TOO HARD!
HEY, DOGGY! FETCH A SODA!
HUH?!

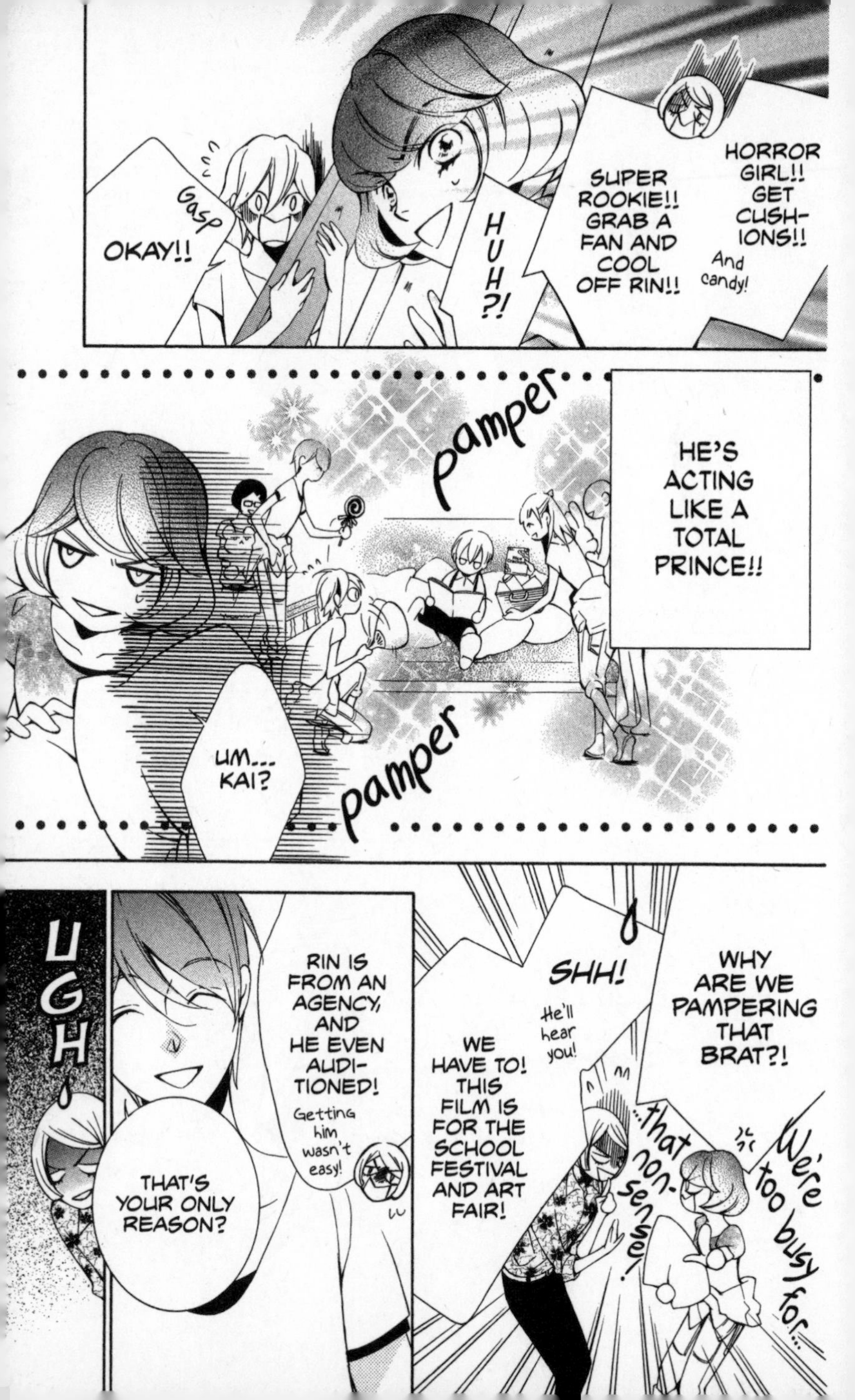
HORROR GIRL!! GET CUSHIONS!!
And candy!
SUPER ROOKIE!! GRAB A FAN AND COOL OFF RIN!!
HUH?!
OKAY!!
Gasp
HE'S ACTING LIKE A TOTAL PRINCE!!
pamper
pamper
UM... KAI?
WHY ARE WE PAMPERING THAT BRAT?!
We're too busy for...
...that nonsense!
SHH!
He'll hear you!
WE HAVE TO! THIS FILM IS FOR THE SCHOOL FESTIVAL AND ART FAIR!
RIN IS FROM AN AGENCY, AND HE EVEN AUDITIONED!
Getting him wasn't easy!
THAT'S YOUR ONLY REASON?
UGH

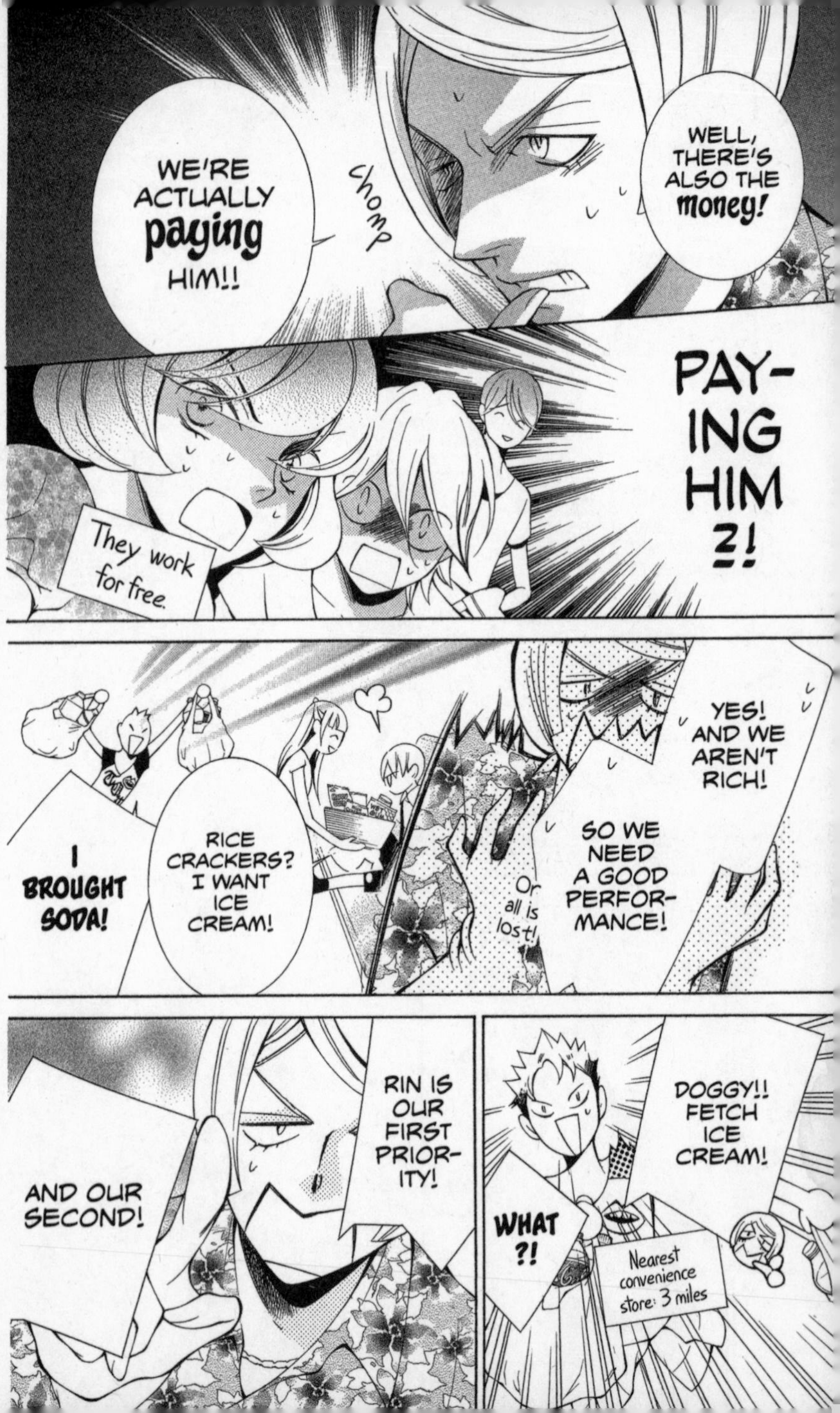
WELL, THERE'S ALSO THE money!
chomp
WE'RE ACTUALLY paying HIM!!
PAY-ING HIM?!
They work for free.
YES! AND WE AREN'T RICH!
SO WE NEED A GOOD PERFOR-MANCE!
Or all is lost!
RICE CRACKERS? I WANT ICE CREAM!
I BROUGHT SODA!
DOGGY!! FETCH ICE CREAM!
WHAT?!
Nearest convenience store: 3 miles
RIN IS OUR FIRST PRIOR-ITY!
AND OUR SECOND!

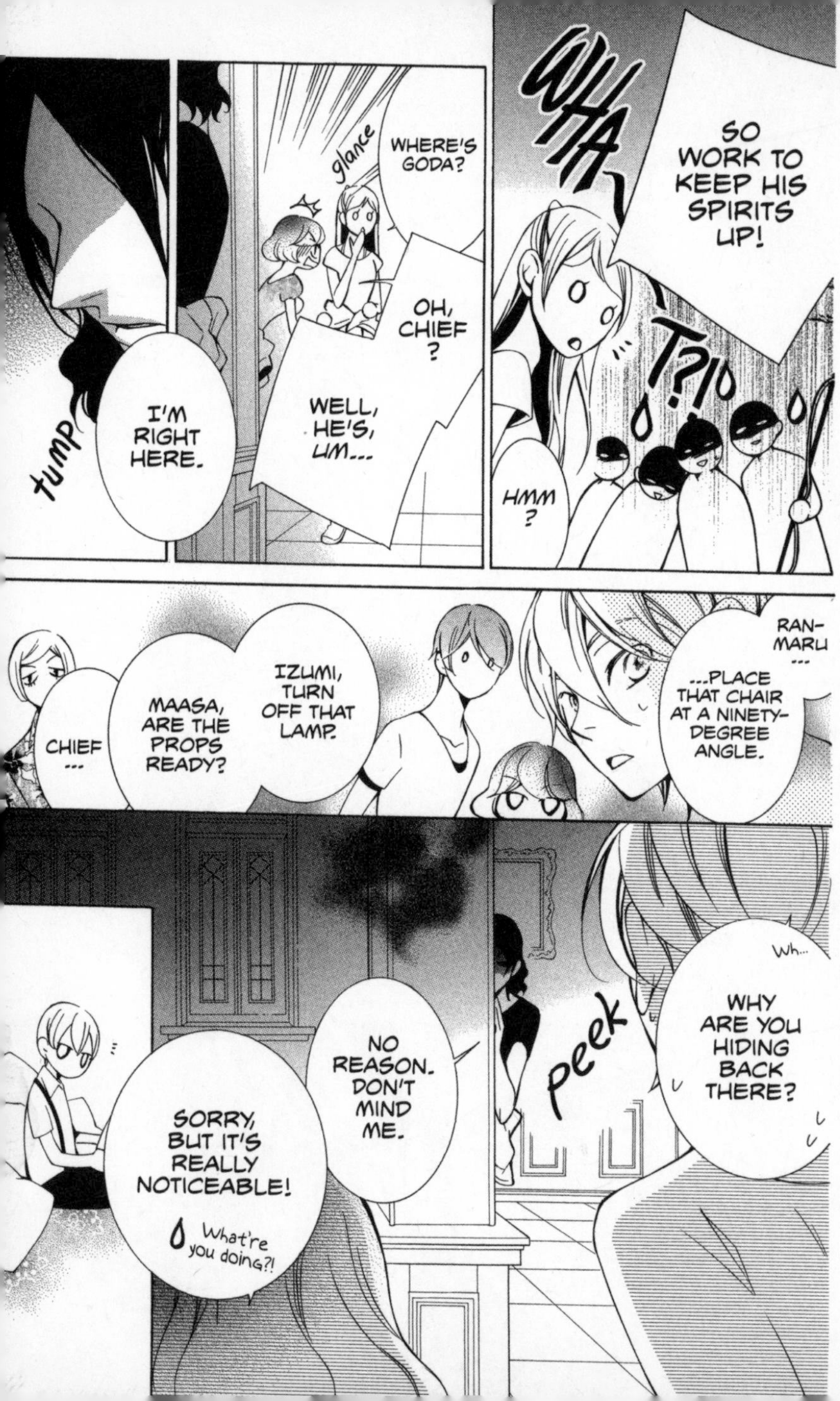
SO WORK TO KEEP HIS SPIRITS UP!
WHA
T?!
HMM?
glance
WHERE'S GODA?
OH, CHIEF?
WELL, HE'S, UM...
tump
I'M RIGHT HERE.
RAN-MARU...
...PLACE THAT CHAIR AT A NINETY-DEGREE ANGLE.
IZUMI, TURN OFF THAT LAMP.
MAASA, ARE THE PROPS READY?
CHIEF...
Wh...
WHY ARE YOU HIDING BACK THERE?
peek
NO REASON. DON'T MIND ME.
SORRY, BUT IT'S REALLY NOTICEABLE!
What're you doing?!

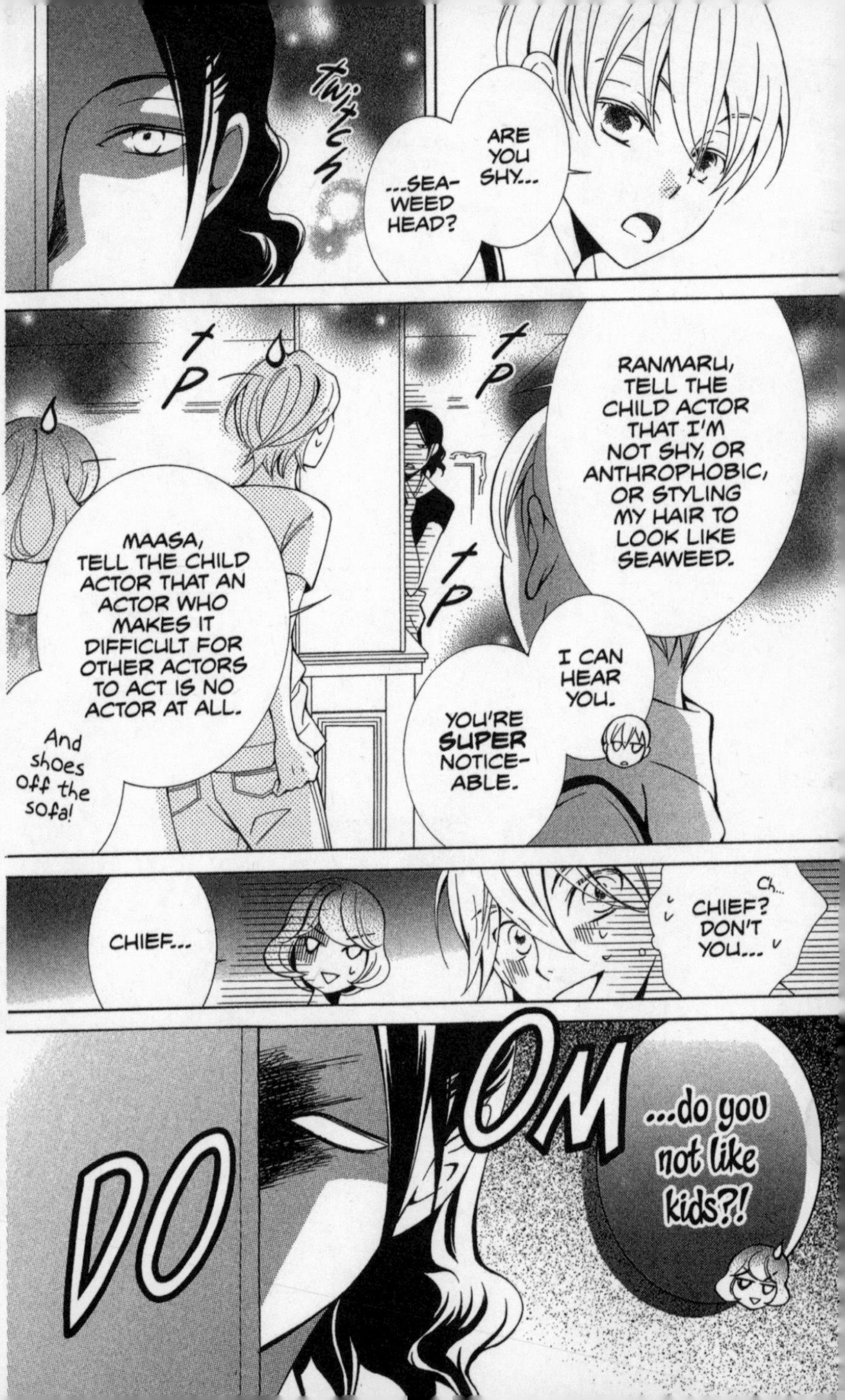

ARE YOU SHY... ...SEA-WEED HEAD?
twitch
RANMARU, TELL THE CHILD ACTOR THAT I'M NOT SHY, OR ANTHROPHOBIC, OR STYLING MY HAIR TO LOOK LIKE SEAWEED.
tp
tp
I CAN HEAR YOU.
YOU'RE SUPER NOTICE-ABLE.
tp
MAASA, TELL THE CHILD ACTOR THAT AN ACTOR WHO MAKES IT DIFFICULT FOR OTHER ACTORS TO ACT IS NO ACTOR AT ALL.
And shoes off the sofa!
Ch... CHIEF? DON'T YOU...
CHIEF...
...do you not like kids?!
DOOM

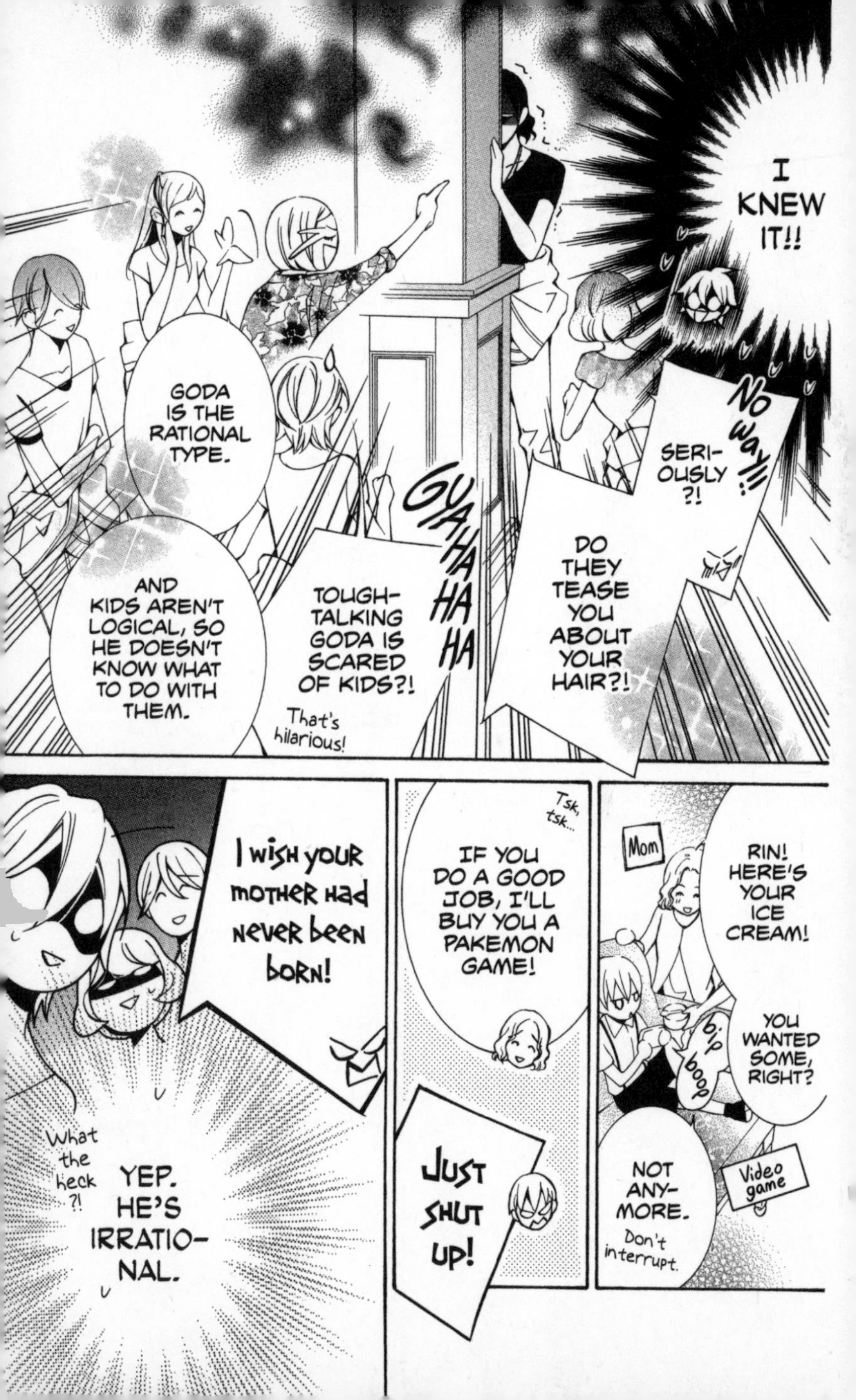
I KNEW IT!!
No way!!
SERIOUSLY?!
DO THEY TEASE YOU ABOUT YOUR HAIR?!
GYAHAHAHA
TOUGH-TALKING GODA IS SCARED OF KIDS?!
That's hilarious!
GODA IS THE RATIONAL TYPE.
AND KIDS AREN'T LOGICAL, SO HE DOESN'T KNOW WHAT TO DO WITH THEM.
Mom
RIN! HERE'S YOUR ICE CREAM!
YOU WANTED SOME, RIGHT?
bip boop
Video game
NOT ANYMORE.
Don't interrupt.
Tsk, tsk...
IF YOU DO A GOOD JOB, I'LL BUY YOU A PAKEMON GAME!
JUST SHUT UP!
I wish your mother had never been born!
YEP. HE'S IRRATIONAL.
What the heck?!

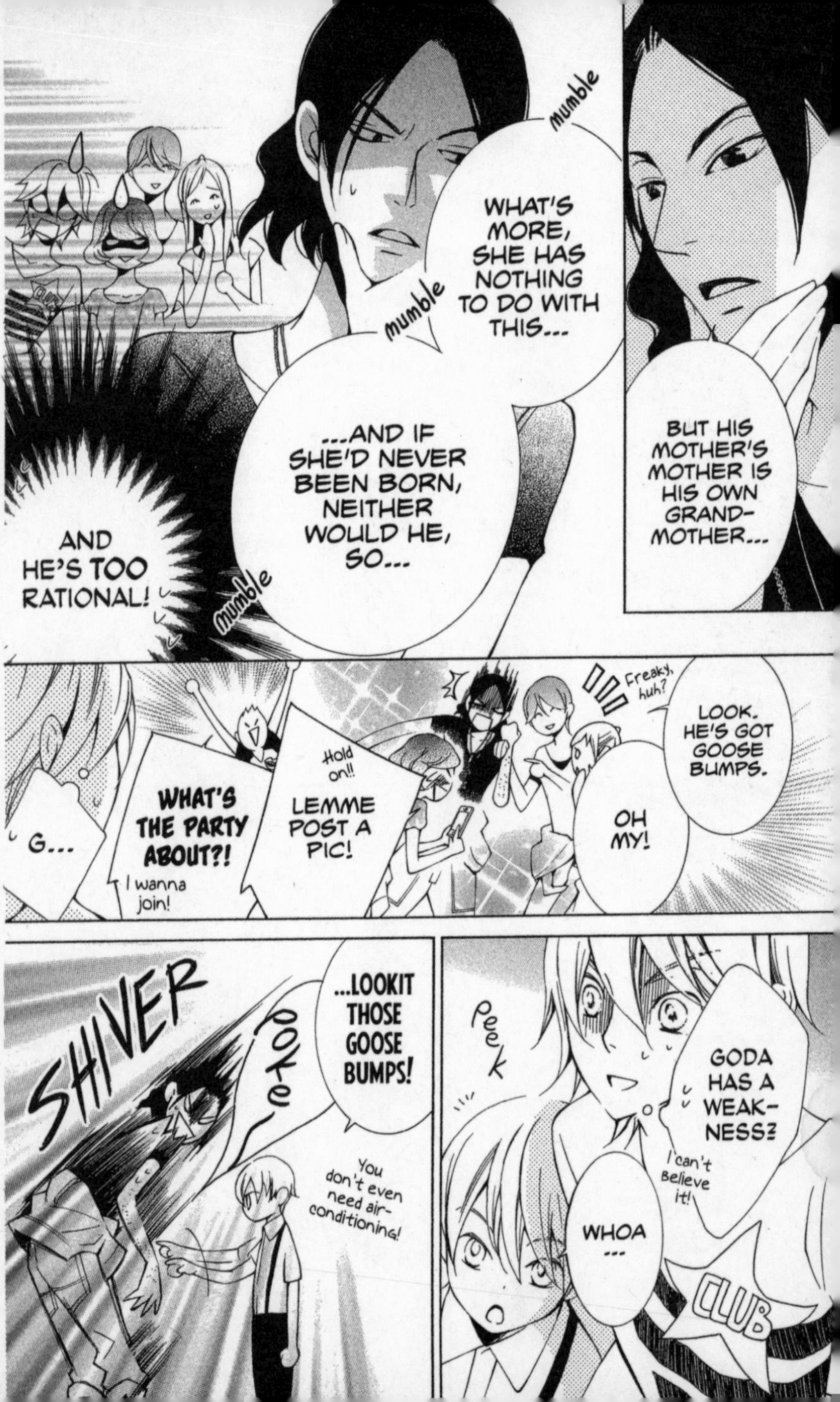

BUT HIS MOTHER'S MOTHER IS HIS OWN GRAND-MOTHER...
mumble
WHAT'S MORE, SHE HAS NOTHING TO DO WITH THIS...
mumble
...AND IF SHE'D NEVER BEEN BORN, NEITHER WOULD HE, SO...
mumble
AND HE'S TOO RATIONAL!
Freaky, huh?
LOOK. HE'S GOT GOOSE BUMPS.
OH MY!
Hold on!!
LEMME POST A PIC!
WHAT'S THE PARTY ABOUT?!
I wanna join!
G...
Peek
GODA HAS A WEAK-NESS?
I can't Believe it!
WHOA...
CLUB
...LOOKIT THOSE GOOSE BUMPS!
poke
SHIVER
You don't even need air-conditioning!

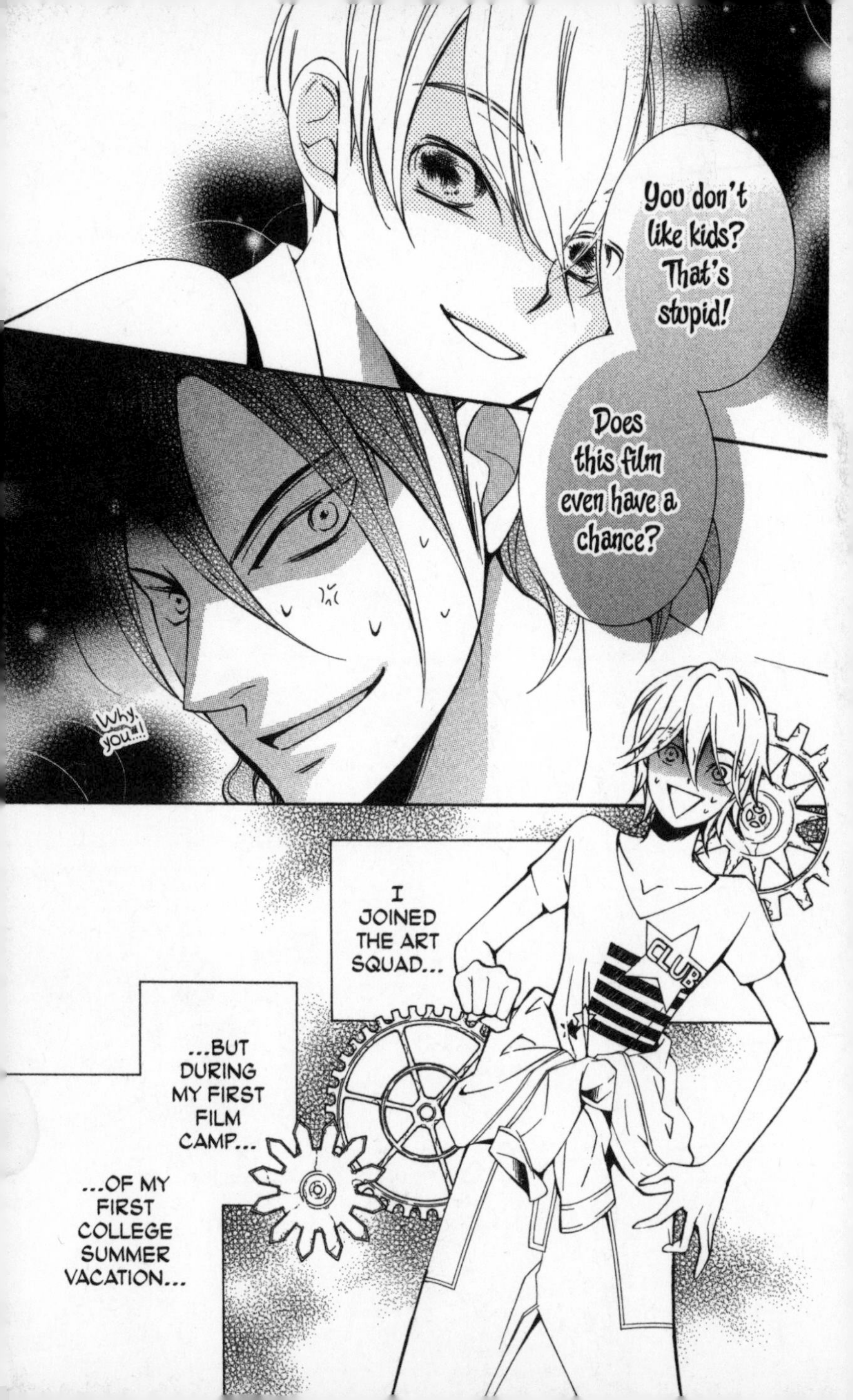
You don't like kids? That's stupid!
Does this film even have a chance?
Why you...!
I JOINED THE ART SQUAD...
...BUT DURING MY FIRST FILM CAMP...
...OF MY FIRST COLLEGE SUMMER VACATION...

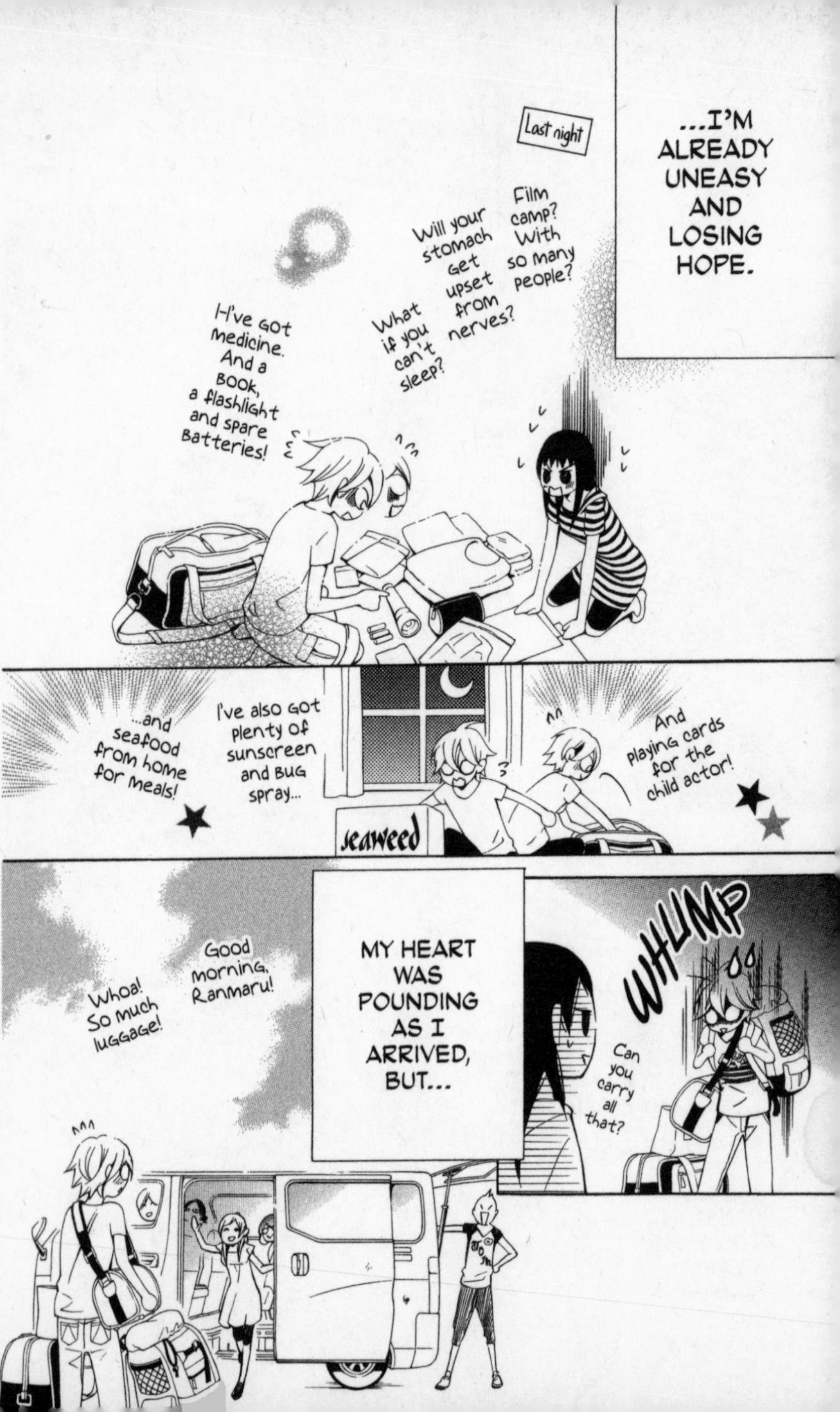
...I'M ALREADY UNEASY AND LOSING HOPE.
Last night
Film camp? With so many people?
Will your stomach get upset from nerves?
What if you can't sleep?
I-I've got medicine. And a book, a flashlight and spare batteries!
And playing cards for the child actor!
I've also got plenty of sunscreen and bug spray...
...and seafood from home for meals!
seaweed
WHUMP
Can you carry all that?
MY HEART WAS POUNDING AS I ARRIVED, BUT...
Good morning, Ranmaru!
Whoa! So much luggage!

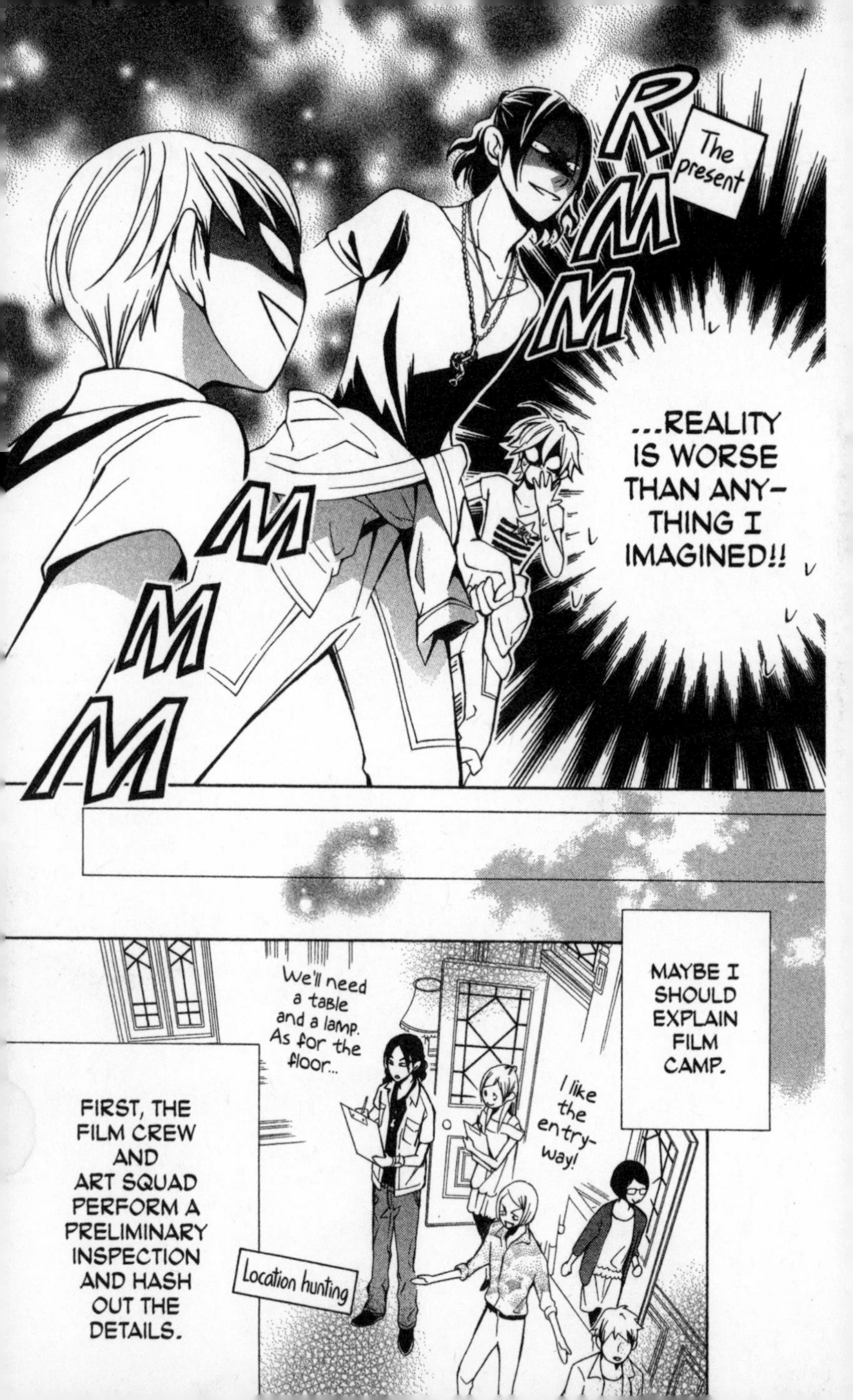

The present
RMM
...REALITY IS WORSE THAN ANYTHING I IMAGINED!!
MMM
MAYBE I SHOULD EXPLAIN FILM CAMP.
I like the entryway!
We'll need a table and a lamp. As for the floor...
Location hunting
FIRST, THE FILM CREW AND ART SQUAD PERFORM A PRELIMINARY INSPECTION AND HASH OUT THE DETAILS.

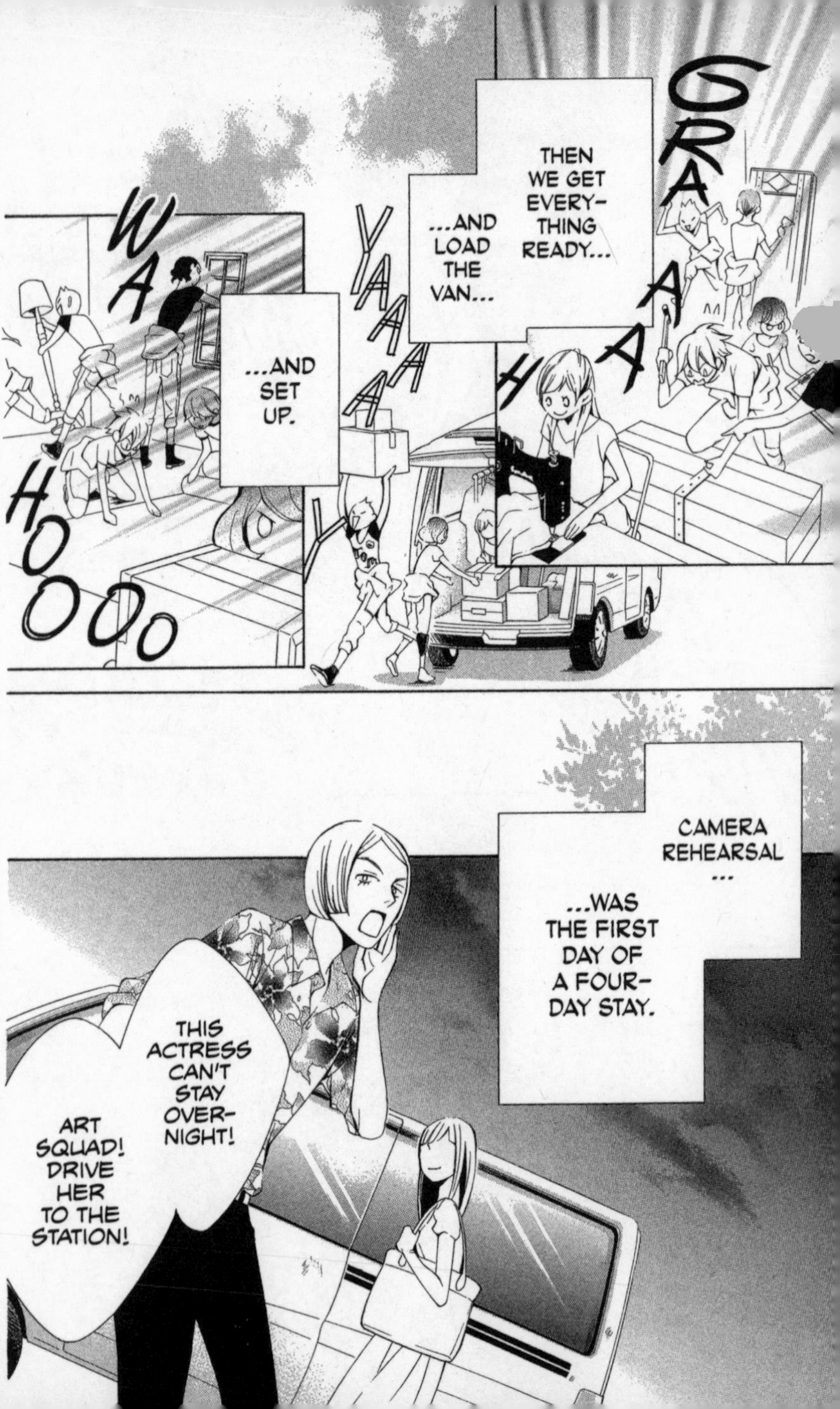
THEN WE GET EVERYTHING READY...
GRAAAH
...AND LOAD THE VAN...
YAAAAAY
...AND SET UP.
WAHOOOO
CAMERA REHEARSAL ...
...WAS THE FIRST DAY OF A FOUR-DAY STAY.
THIS ACTRESS CAN'T STAY OVERNIGHT!
ART SQUAD! DRIVE HER TO THE STATION!

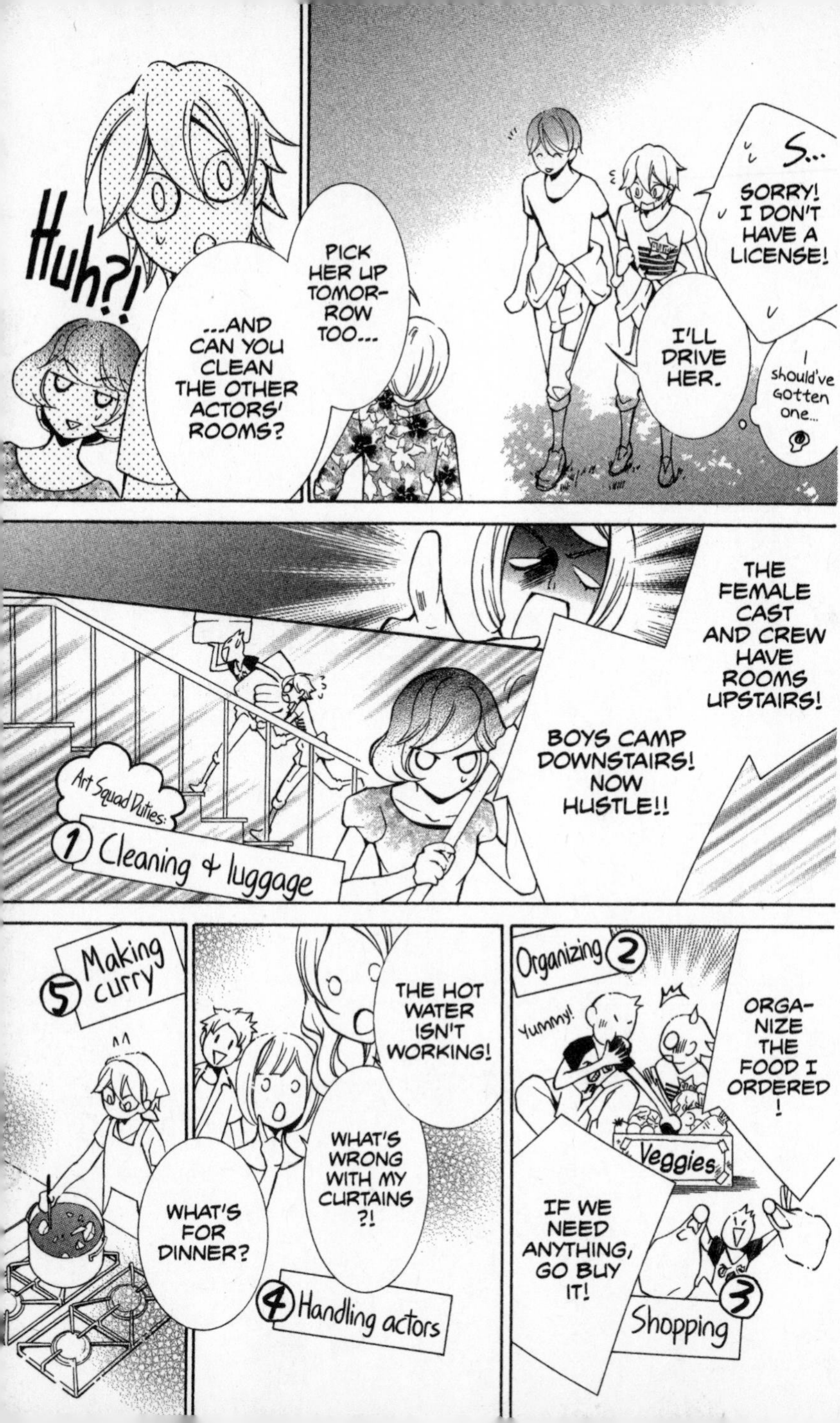
S... SORRY! I DON'T HAVE A LICENSE!
I'LL DRIVE HER.
I should've gotten one...
PICK HER UP TOMORROW TOO...
...AND CAN YOU CLEAN THE OTHER ACTORS' ROOMS?
Huh?!
THE FEMALE CAST AND CREW HAVE ROOMS UPSTAIRS!
BOYS CAMP DOWNSTAIRS! NOW HUSTLE!!
Art Squad Duties:
1 Cleaning & luggage
Organizing 2
ORGANIZE THE FOOD I ORDERED!
Yummy!
Veggies
IF WE NEED ANYTHING, GO BUY IT!
3 Shopping
THE HOT WATER ISN'T WORKING!
WHAT'S WRONG WITH MY CURTAINS?!
WHAT'S FOR DINNER?
4 Handling actors
5 Making curry

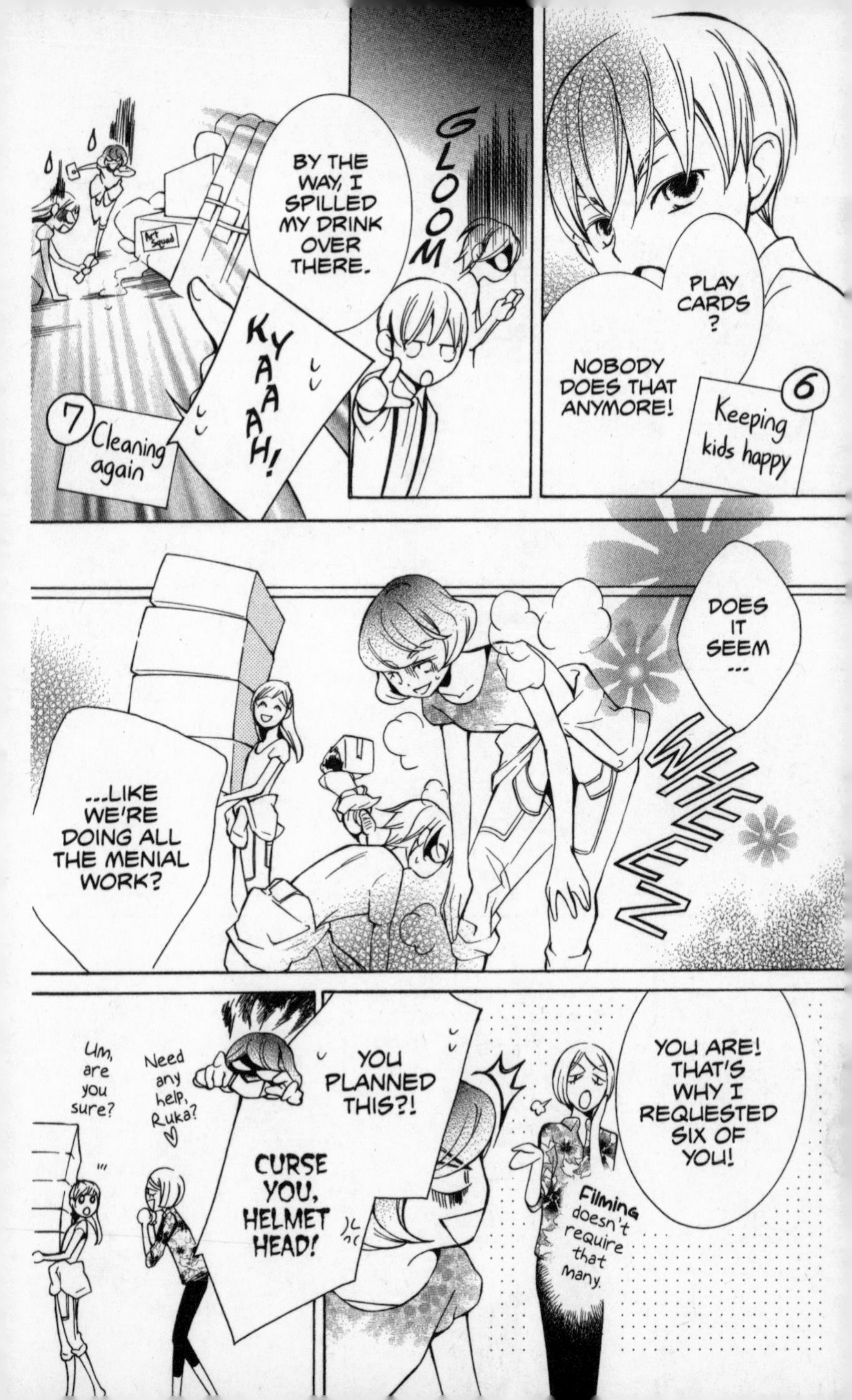
PLAY CARDS?
NOBODY DOES THAT ANYMORE!
6 Keeping kids happy
GLOOM
BY THE WAY, I SPILLED MY DRINK OVER THERE.
KYAAAH!
Art Squad
7 Cleaning again
DOES IT SEEM...
WHEEN
...LIKE WE'RE DOING ALL THE MENIAL WORK?
YOU ARE! THAT'S WHY I REQUESTED SIX OF YOU!
Filming doesn't require that many.
YOU PLANNED THIS?!
CURSE YOU, HELMET HEAD!
Need any help, Ruka?
Um, are you sure?

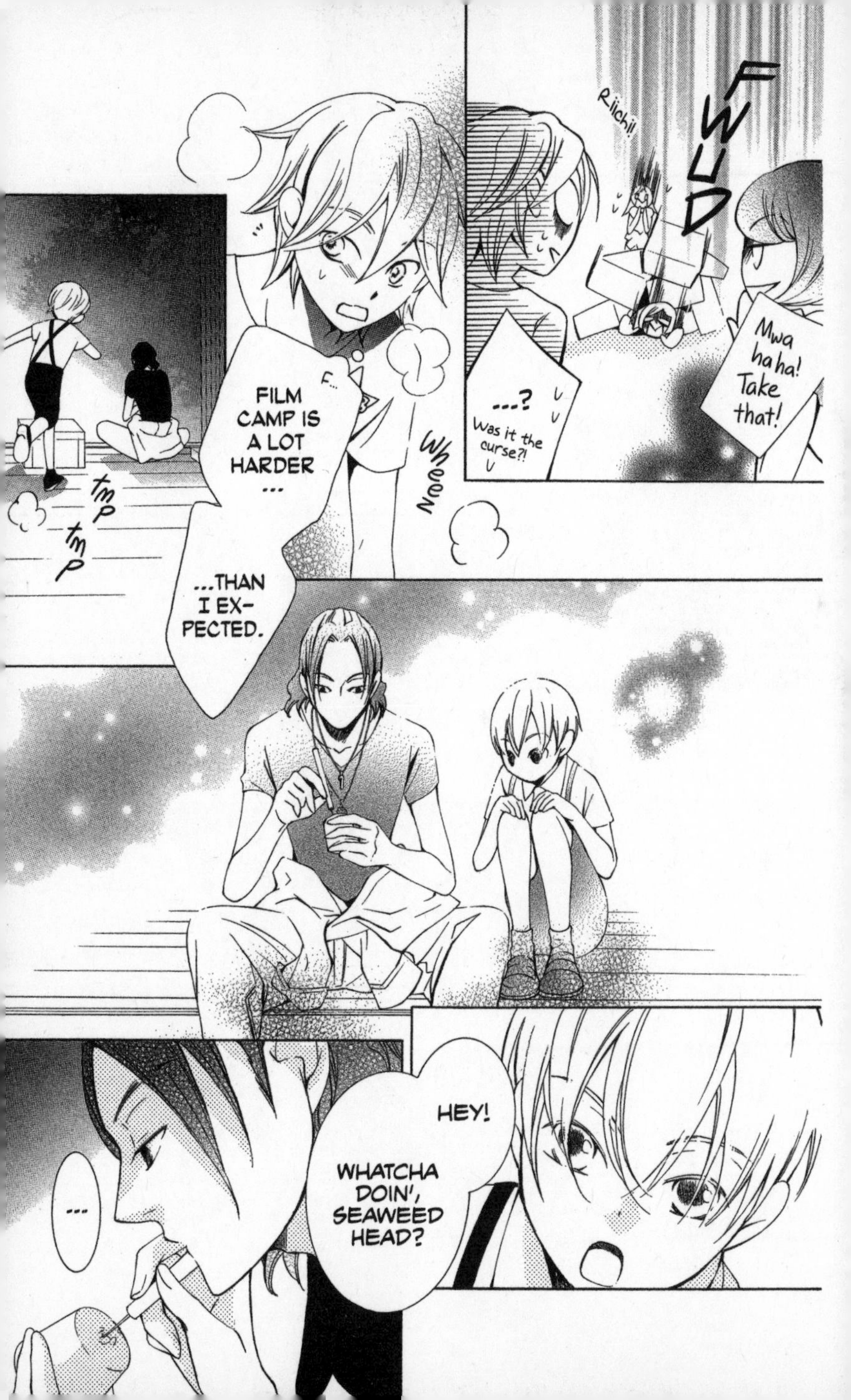
FWUD
Riichi!
Mwa ha ha! Take that!
...?
Was it the curse?!
F...
FILM CAMP IS A LOT HARDER...
Wheeen
tmp tmp
...THAN I EX-PECTED.
HEY!
WHATCHA DOIN', SEAWEED HEAD?
...

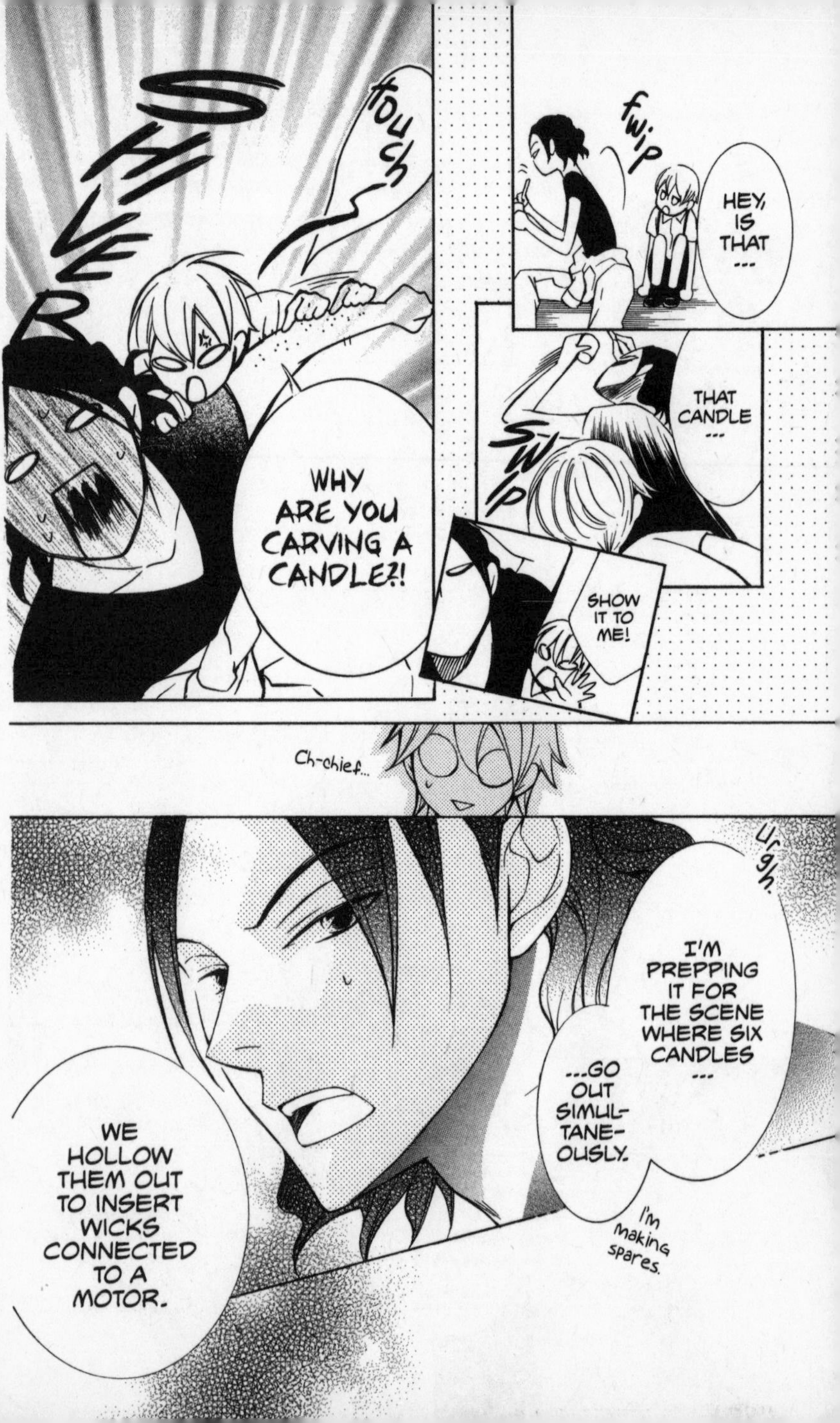
HEY, IS THAT ---
fwip
THAT CANDLE ---
SWIP
SHOW IT TO ME!
touch
SHIVER
WHY ARE YOU CARVING A CANDLE?!
Ch-chief...
Urgh.
I'M PREPPING IT FOR THE SCENE WHERE SIX CANDLES ---
---GO OUT SIMUL-TANE-OUSLY.
I'm making spares.
WE HOLLOW THEM OUT TO INSERT WICKS CONNECTED TO A MOTOR.

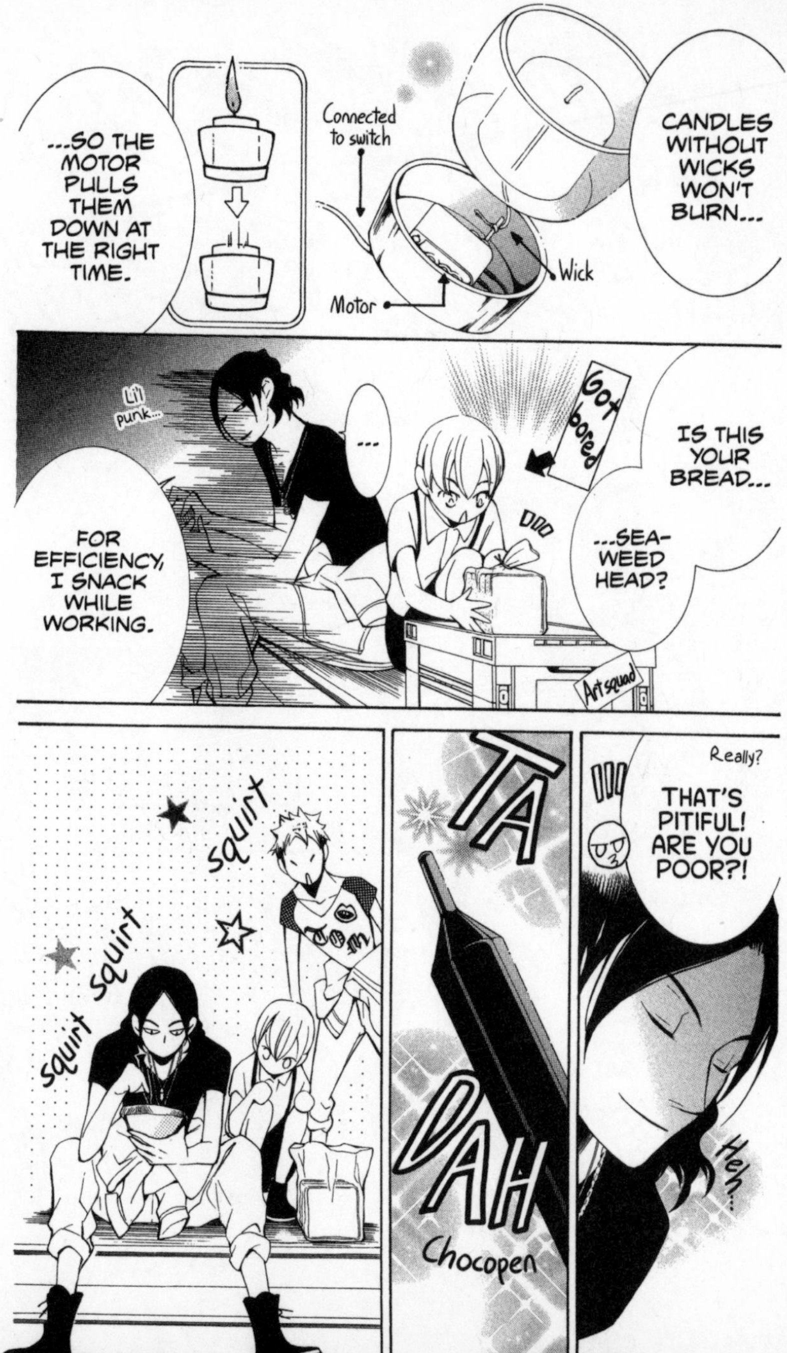
CANDLES WITHOUT WICKS WON'T BURN...
Connected to switch
Wick
Motor
...SO THE MOTOR PULLS THEM DOWN AT THE RIGHT TIME.
IS THIS YOUR BREAD...
...SEA-WEED HEAD?
Got bored
...
Li'l punk...
FOR EFFICIENCY, I SNACK WHILE WORKING.
Art squad
Really?
THAT'S PITIFUL! ARE YOU POOR?!
Heh...
TA
DAH
Chocopen
squirt
squirt
squirt
squirt

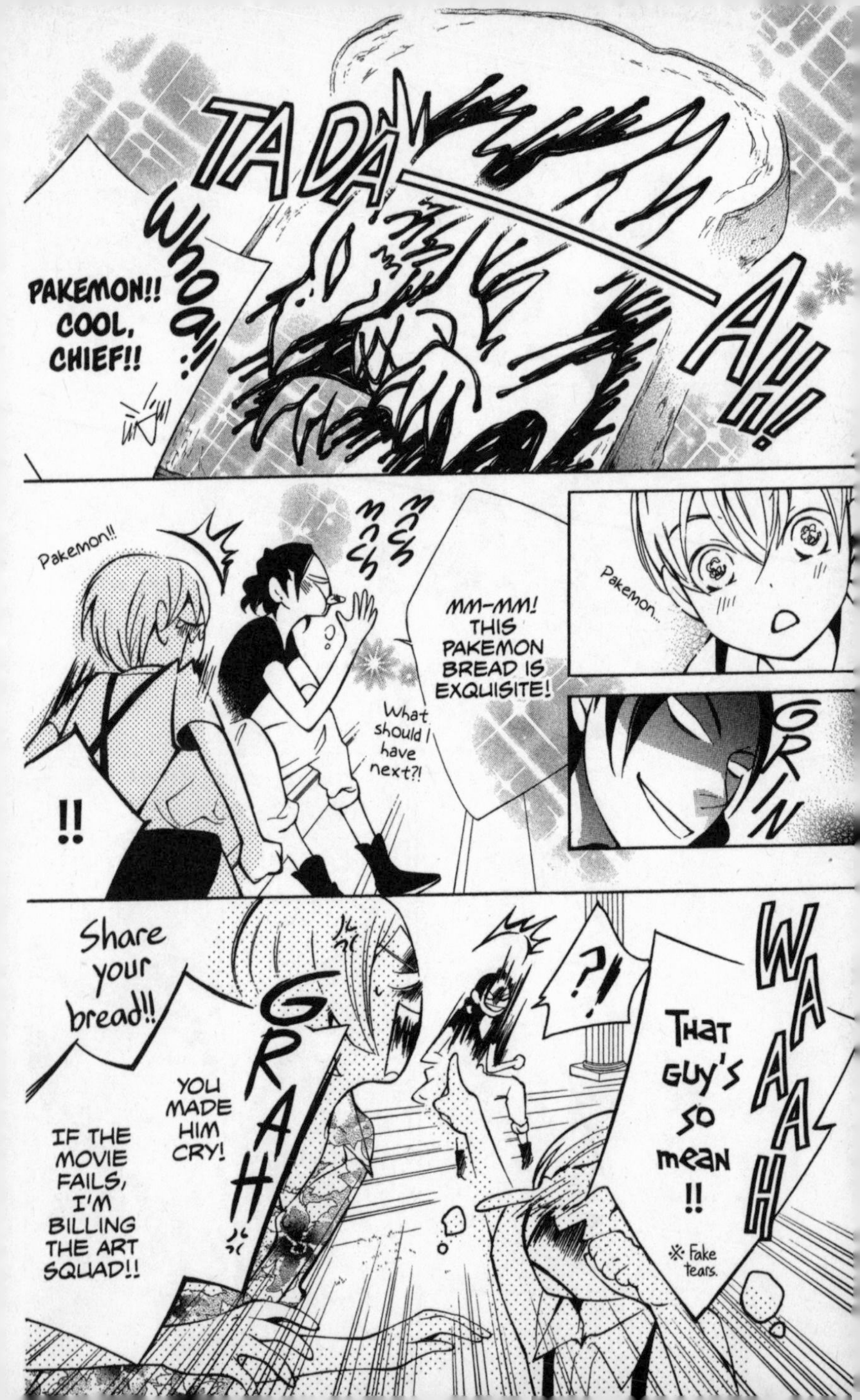
TADAAAAH!!
Whoa!!
PAKEMON!! COOL, CHIEF!!
Pakemon...
GRIN
MM-MM! THIS PAKEMON BREAD IS EXQUISITE!
What should I have next?!
Pakemon!!
!!
WAAAAH
That guy's so mean!!
※Fake tears.
?!
GRAAH!!
Share your bread!!
YOU MADE HIM CRY!
IF THE MOVIE FAILS, I'M BILLING THE ART SQUAD!!

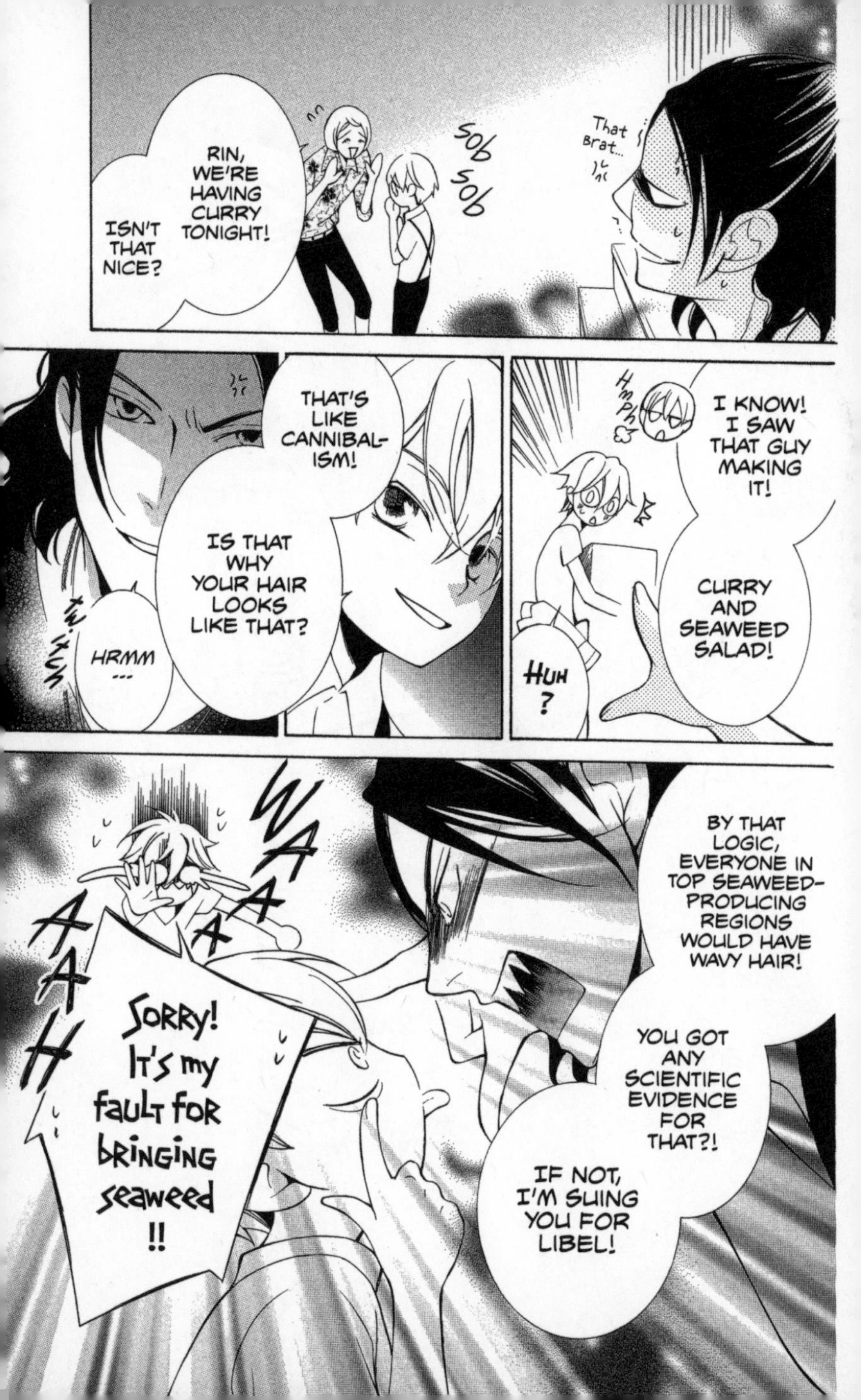
That Brat...
SOB SOB
RIN, WE'RE HAVING CURRY TONIGHT! ISN'T THAT NICE?
HMPH
I KNOW! I SAW THAT GUY MAKING IT!
CURRY AND SEAWEED SALAD!
HUH?
THAT'S LIKE CANNIBAL-ISM!
IS THAT WHY YOUR HAIR LOOKS LIKE THAT?
TWITCH
HRMM ---
BY THAT LOGIC, EVERYONE IN TOP SEAWEED-PRODUCING REGIONS WOULD HAVE WAVY HAIR!
YOU GOT ANY SCIENTIFIC EVIDENCE FOR THAT?!
IF NOT, I'M SUING YOU FOR LIBEL!
WAAAAAH
SORRY! It's my fault for bringing seaweed !!

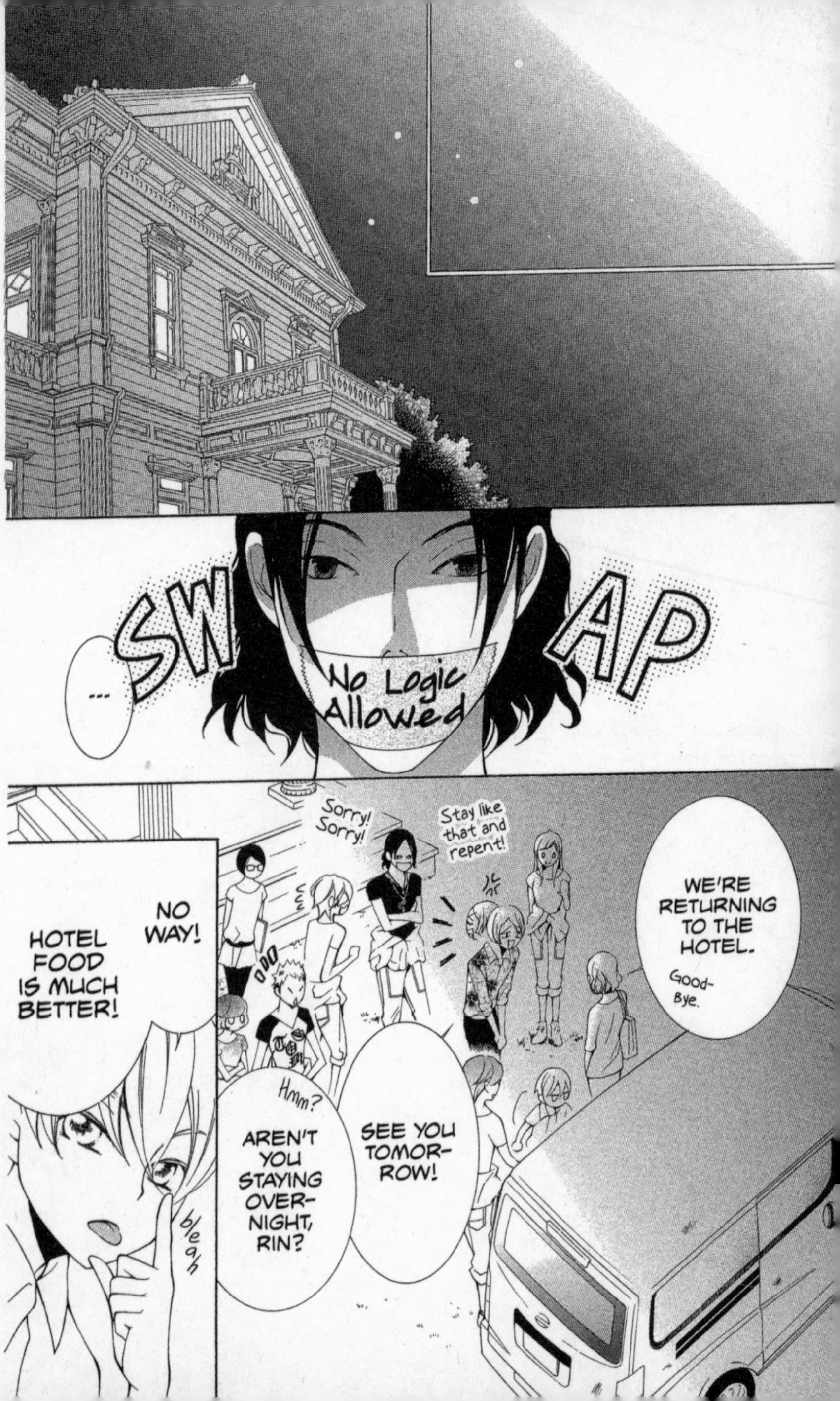
SWAP
No Logic Allowed
...
WE'RE RETURNING TO THE HOTEL.
Good-Bye.
Stay like that and repent!
Sorry! Sorry!
SEE YOU TOMORROW!
Hmm?
AREN'T YOU STAYING OVERNIGHT, RIN?
NO WAY!
HOTEL FOOD IS MUCH BETTER!
bleah

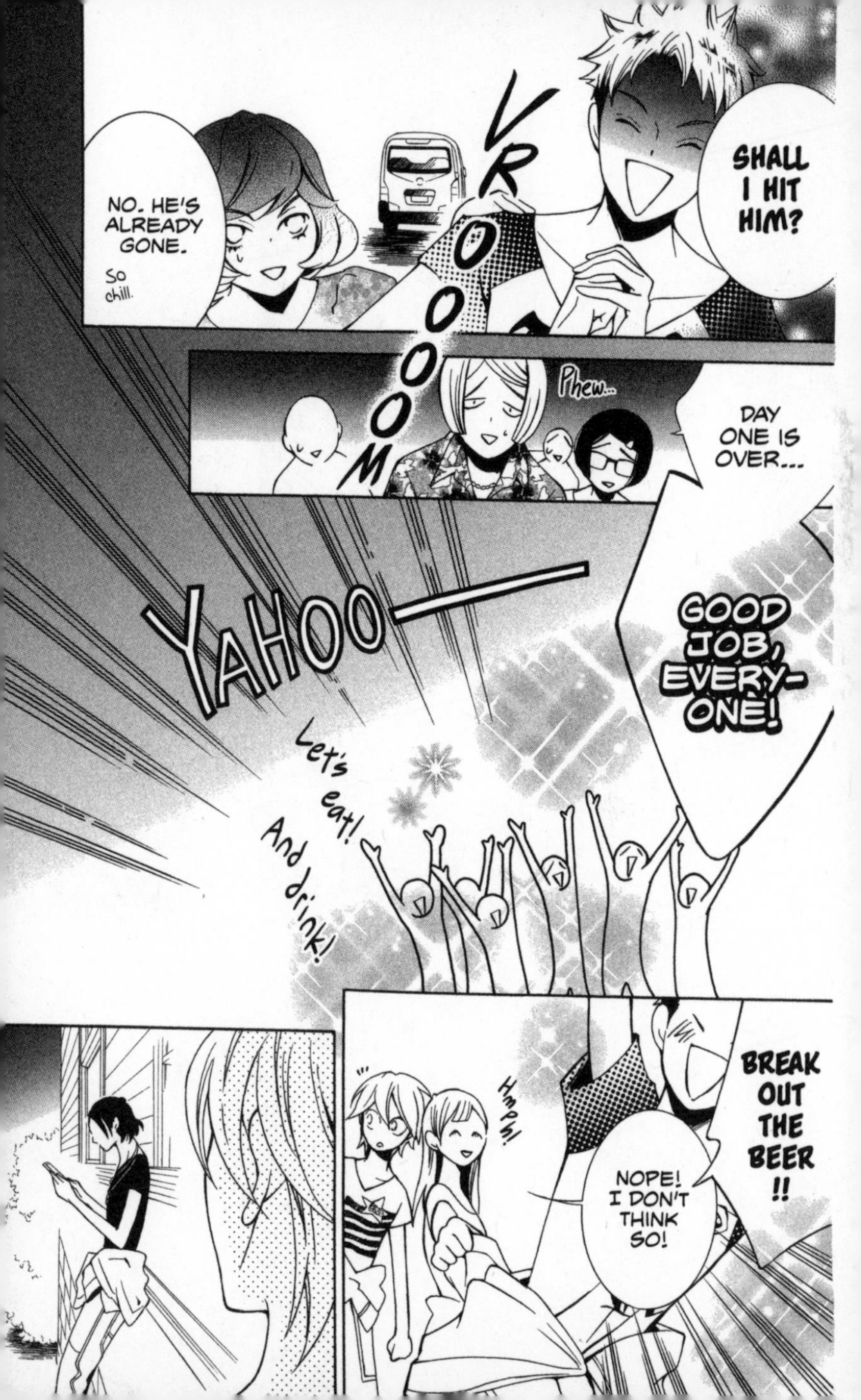
SHALL I HIT HIM?
VROOOOOOOM
NO. HE'S ALREADY GONE.
So chill.
DAY ONE IS OVER...
Phew...
GOOD JOB, EVERY-ONE!
YAHOO—
Let's eat! And drink!
BREAK OUT THE BEER!!
NOPE! I DON'T THINK SO!
Hmph!

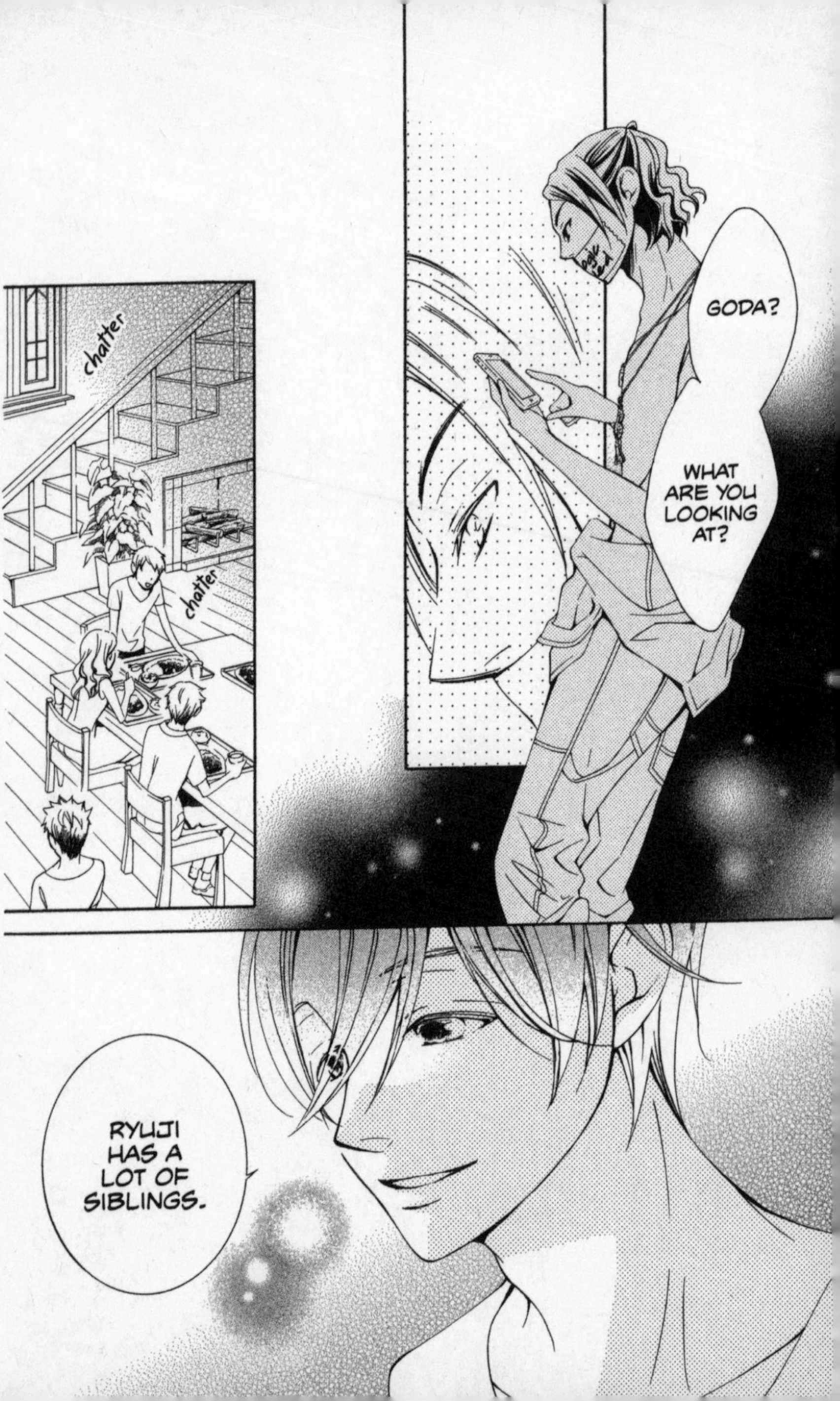
GODA?
WHAT ARE YOU LOOKING AT?
chatter
chatter
RYUJI HAS A LOT OF SIBLINGS.

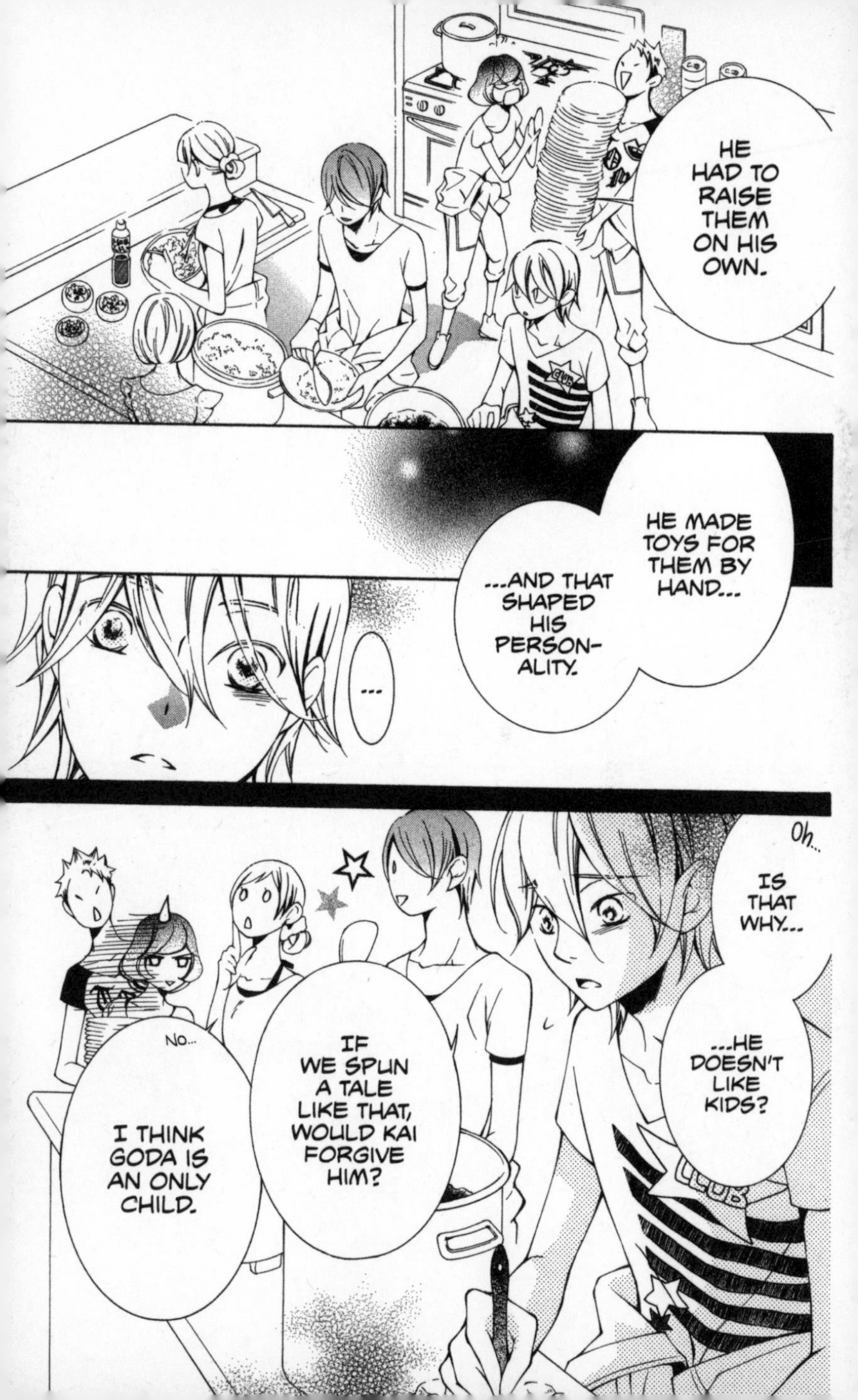
HE HAD TO RAISE THEM ON HIS OWN.
HE MADE TOYS FOR THEM BY HAND...
...AND THAT SHAPED HIS PERSON-ALITY.
...
Oh...
IS THAT WHY...
...HE DOESN'T LIKE KIDS?
IF WE SPUN A TALE LIKE THAT, WOULD KAI FORGIVE HIM?
No...
I THINK GODA IS AN ONLY CHILD.

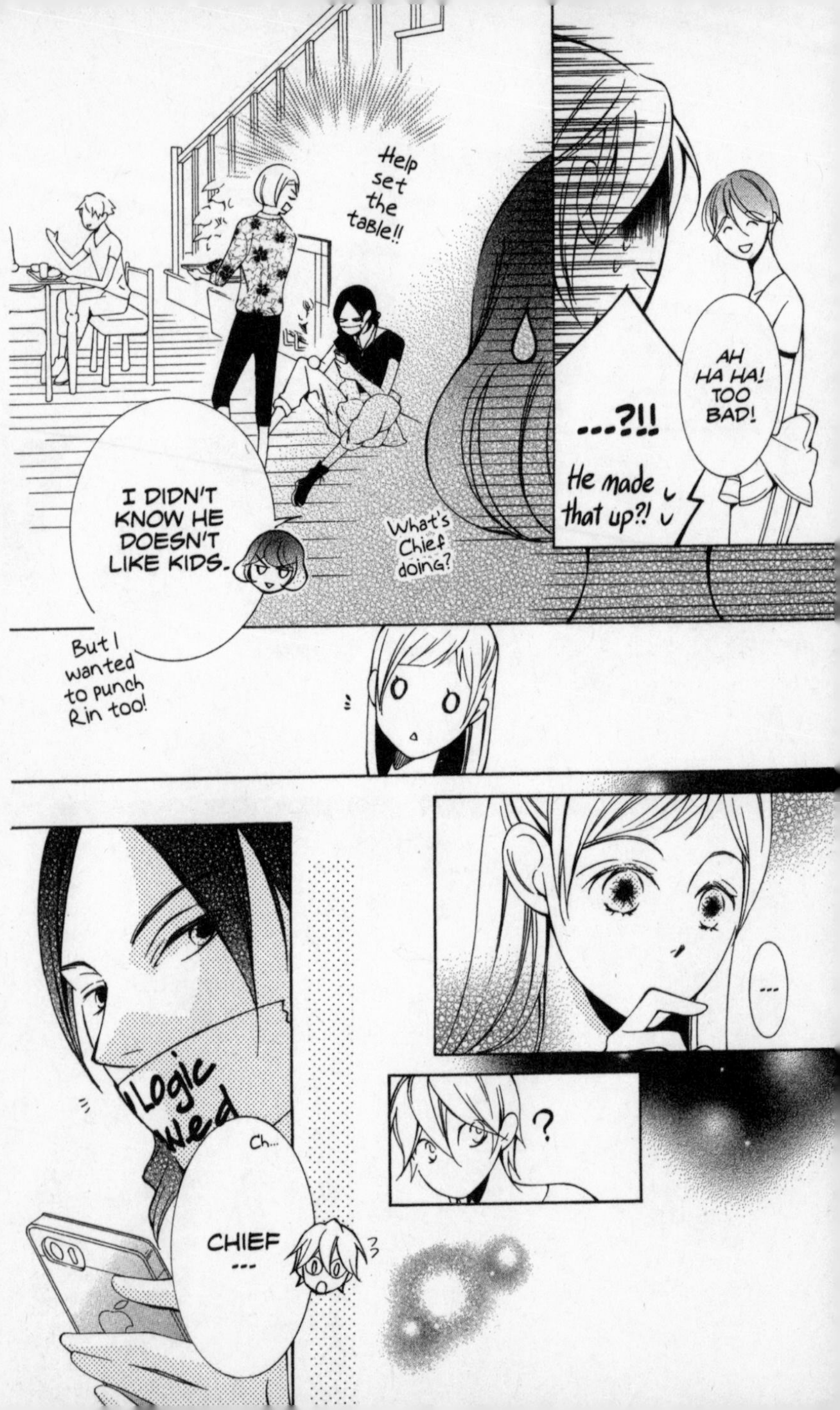
AH HA HA! TOO BAD!
...?!!
He made that up?!
Help set the table!!
What's Chief doing?
I DIDN'T KNOW HE DOESN'T LIKE KIDS.
But I wanted to punch Rin too!
...
?
Logic Wed
Ch...
CHIEF ...

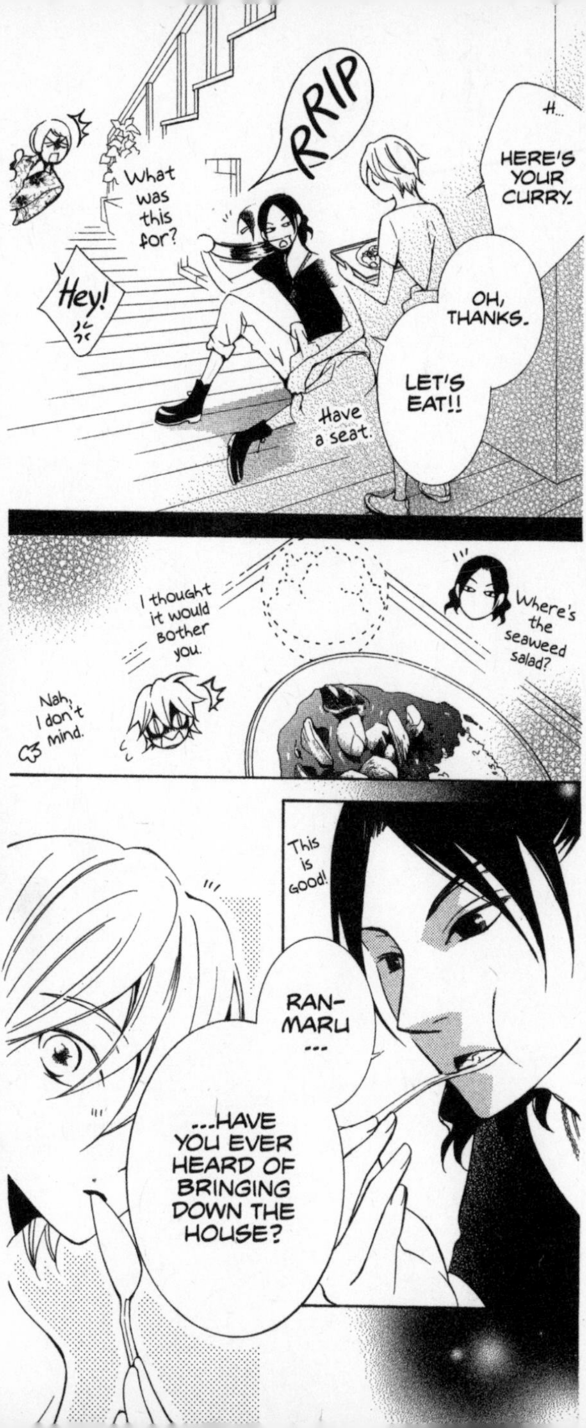
H...
HERE'S YOUR CURRY.
OH, THANKS.
LET'S EAT!!
Have a seat.
RRIP
What was this for?
Hey!
Where's the seaweed salad?
I thought it would bother you.
Nah, I don't mind.
This is good!
RAN-MARU...
...HAVE YOU EVER HEARD OF BRINGING DOWN THE HOUSE?

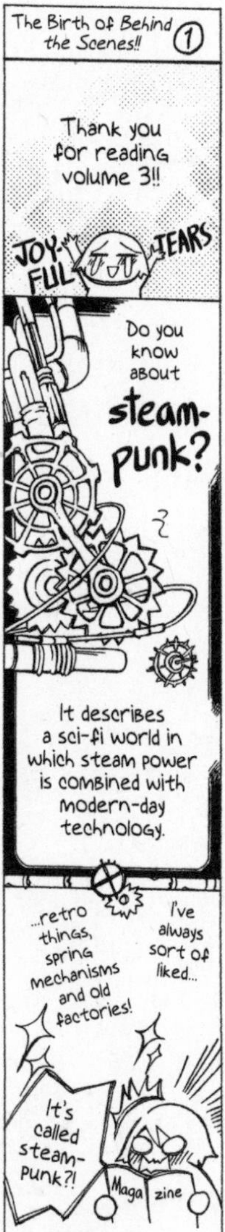
The Birth of Behind the Scenes!! 1
Thank you for reading volume 3!!
JOYFUL TEARS
Do you know about steam-punk?
It describes a sci-fi world in which steam power is combined with modern-day technology.
I've always sort of liked...
...retro things, spring mechanisms and old factories!
It's called steam-punk?!
Magazine
But I didn't know until recently that there's a genre for that stuff.

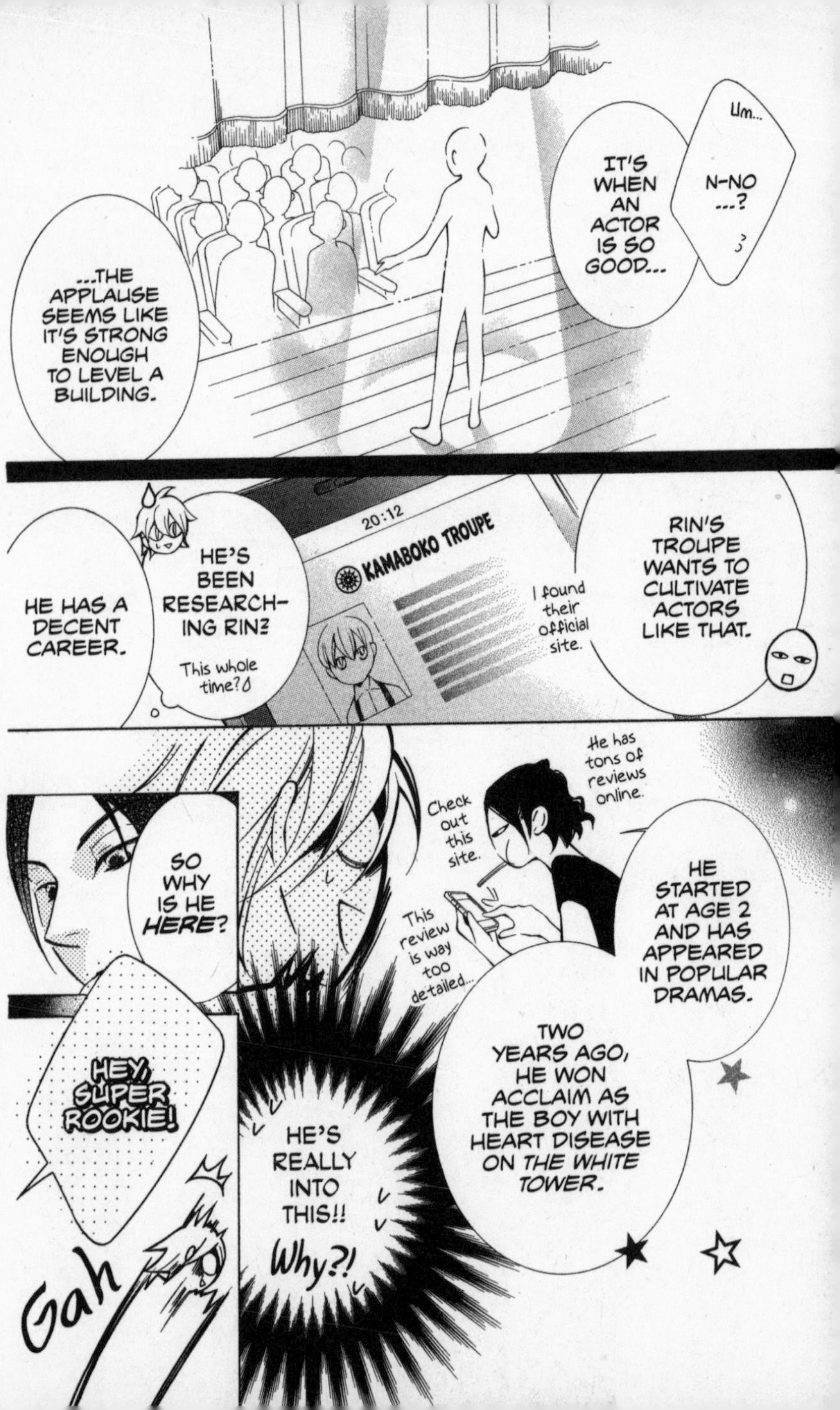

Um...
N-NO ...?
IT'S WHEN AN ACTOR IS SO GOOD...
...THE APPLAUSE SEEMS LIKE IT'S STRONG ENOUGH TO LEVEL A BUILDING.
RIN'S TROUPE WANTS TO CULTIVATE ACTORS LIKE THAT.
I found their official site.
20:12
KAMABOKO TROUPE
HE'S BEEN RESEARCHING RIN?
This whole time?
HE HAS A DECENT CAREER.
He has tons of reviews online.
HE STARTED AT AGE 2 AND HAS APPEARED IN POPULAR DRAMAS.
Check out this site.
TWO YEARS AGO, HE WON ACCLAIM AS THE BOY WITH HEART DISEASE ON *THE WHITE TOWER*.
This review is way too detailed...
SO WHY IS HE *HERE*?
HE'S REALLY INTO THIS!!
Why?!
HEY, SUPER ROOKIE!
Gah

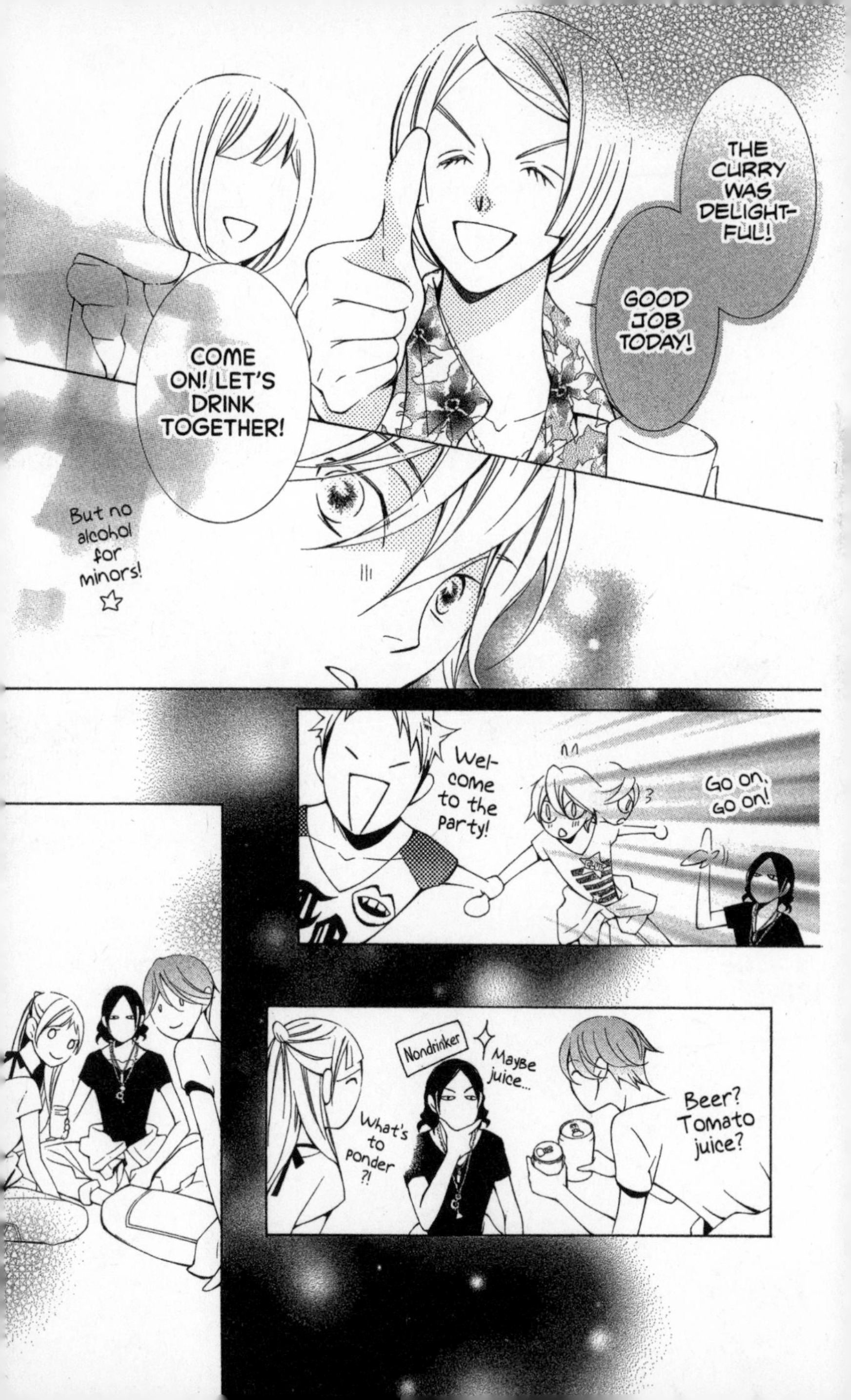
THE CURRY WAS DELIGHT-FUL!
GOOD JOB TODAY!
COME ON! LET'S DRINK TOGETHER!
But no alcohol for minors! ☆
Go on, go on!
Wel-come to the party!
Beer? Tomato juice?
Nondrinker
Maybe juice...
What's to ponder?!

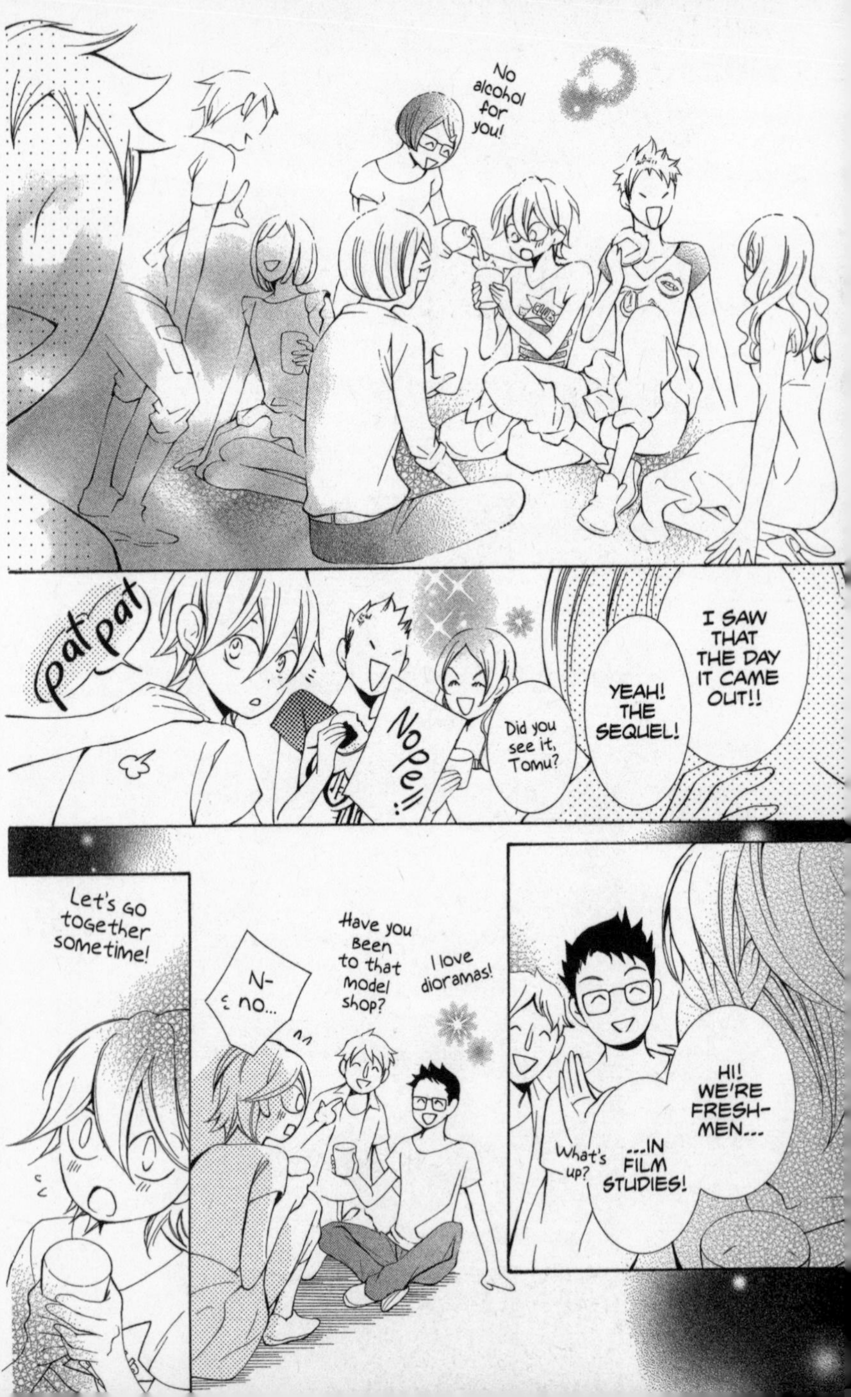
No alcohol for you!
I SAW THAT THE DAY IT CAME OUT!!
YEAH! THE SEQUEL!
Did you see it, Tomu?
NOPE!!
pat pat
HI! WE'RE FRESH-MEN...
...IN FILM STUDIES!
What's up?
I love dioramas!
Have you been to that model shop?
N-no...
Let's go together sometime!

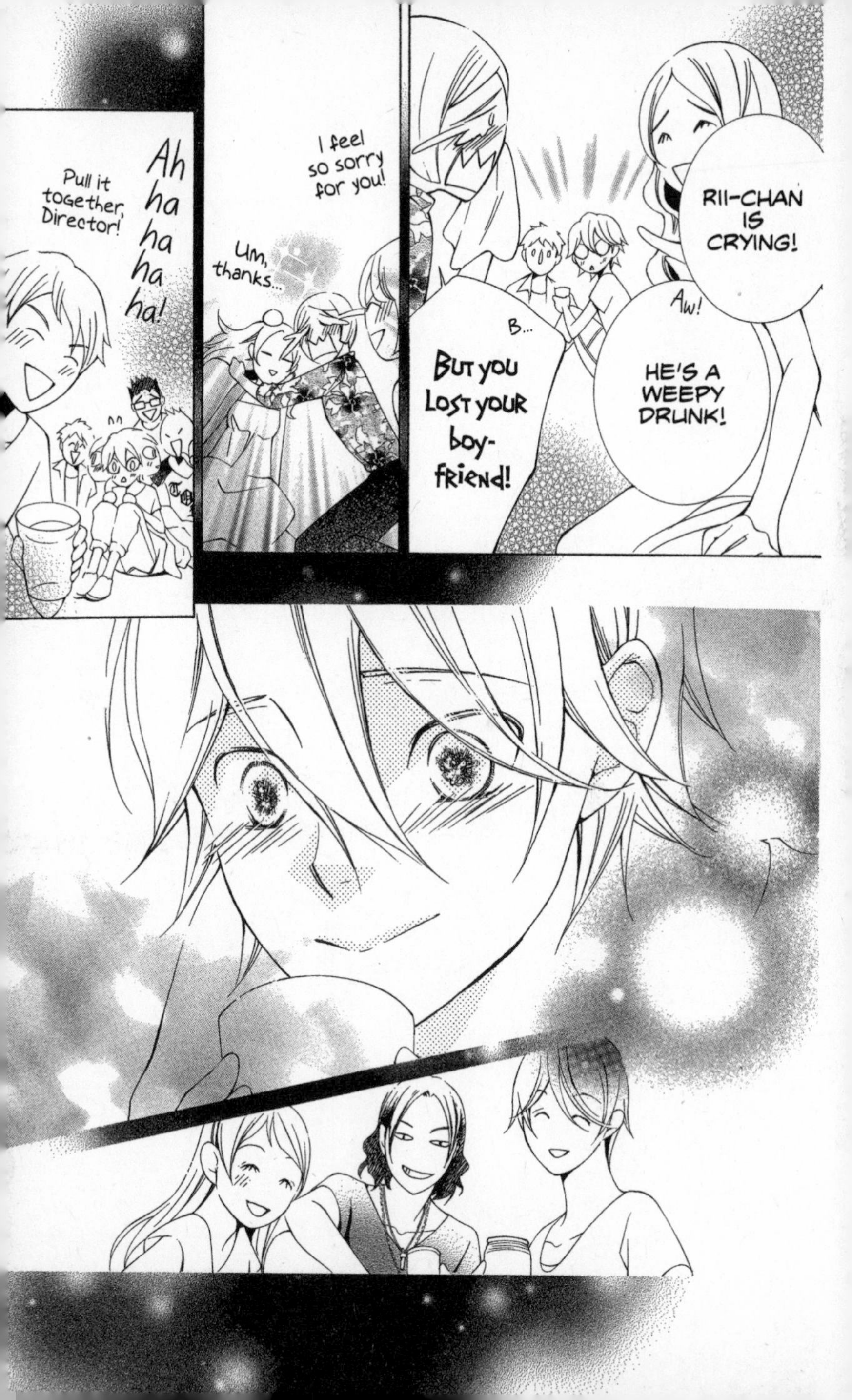

RII-CHAN IS CRYING!
Aw!
HE'S A WEEPY DRUNK!
B...
BUT YOU LOST YOUR boy-friend!
I feel so sorry for you!
Um, thanks...
Ah ha ha ha ha!
Pull it together, Director!

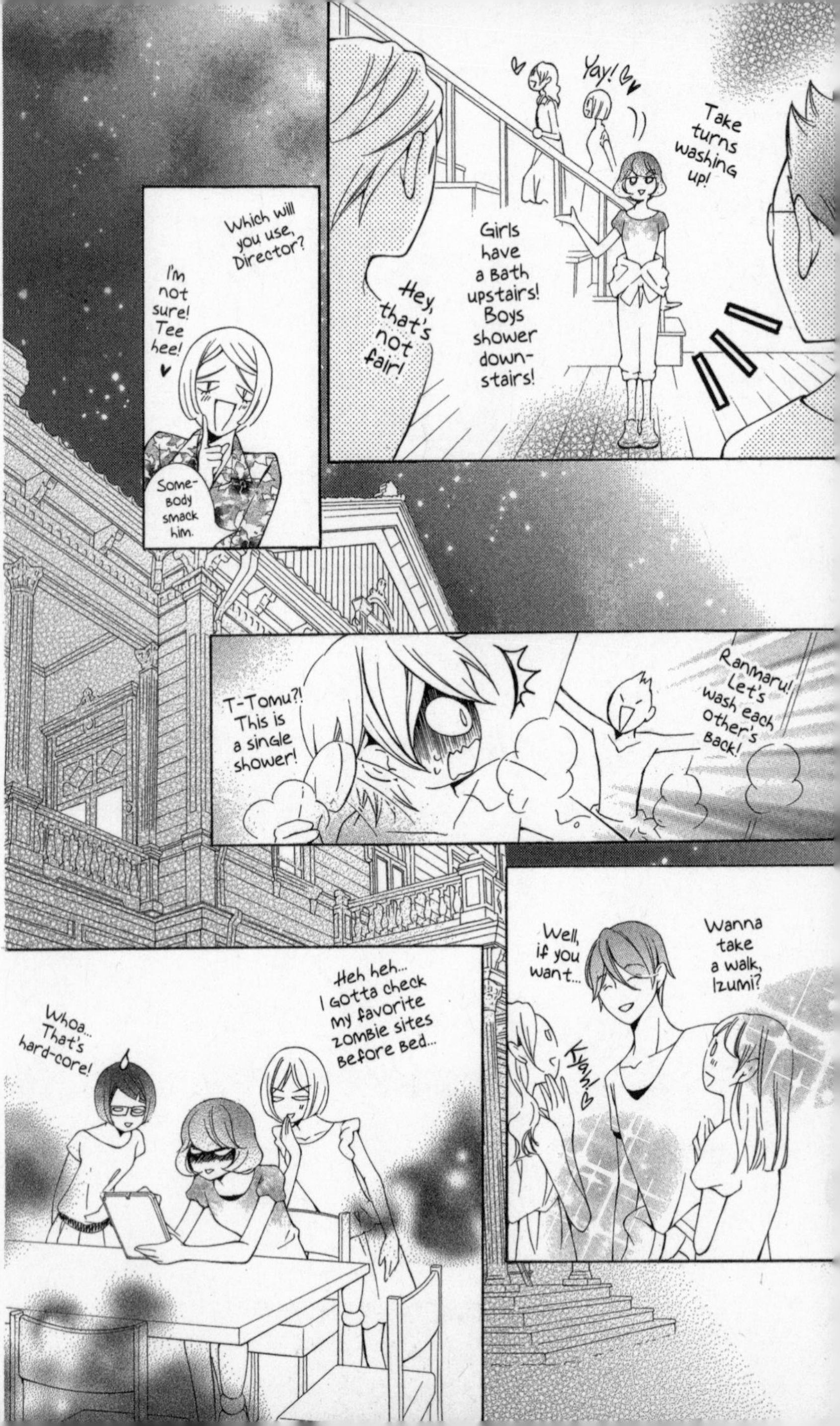
Take turns washing up!
Yay!
Girls have a Bath upstairs! Boys shower down-stairs!
Hey, that's not fair!
Which will you use, Director?
I'm not sure! Tee hee!
Some-body smack him.
Ranmaru! Let's wash each other's Back!
T-Tomu?! This is a single shower!
Wanna take a walk, Izumi?
Well, if you want...
Kyah!
Heh heh... I gotta check my favorite zombie sites Before bed...
Whoa... That's hard-core!

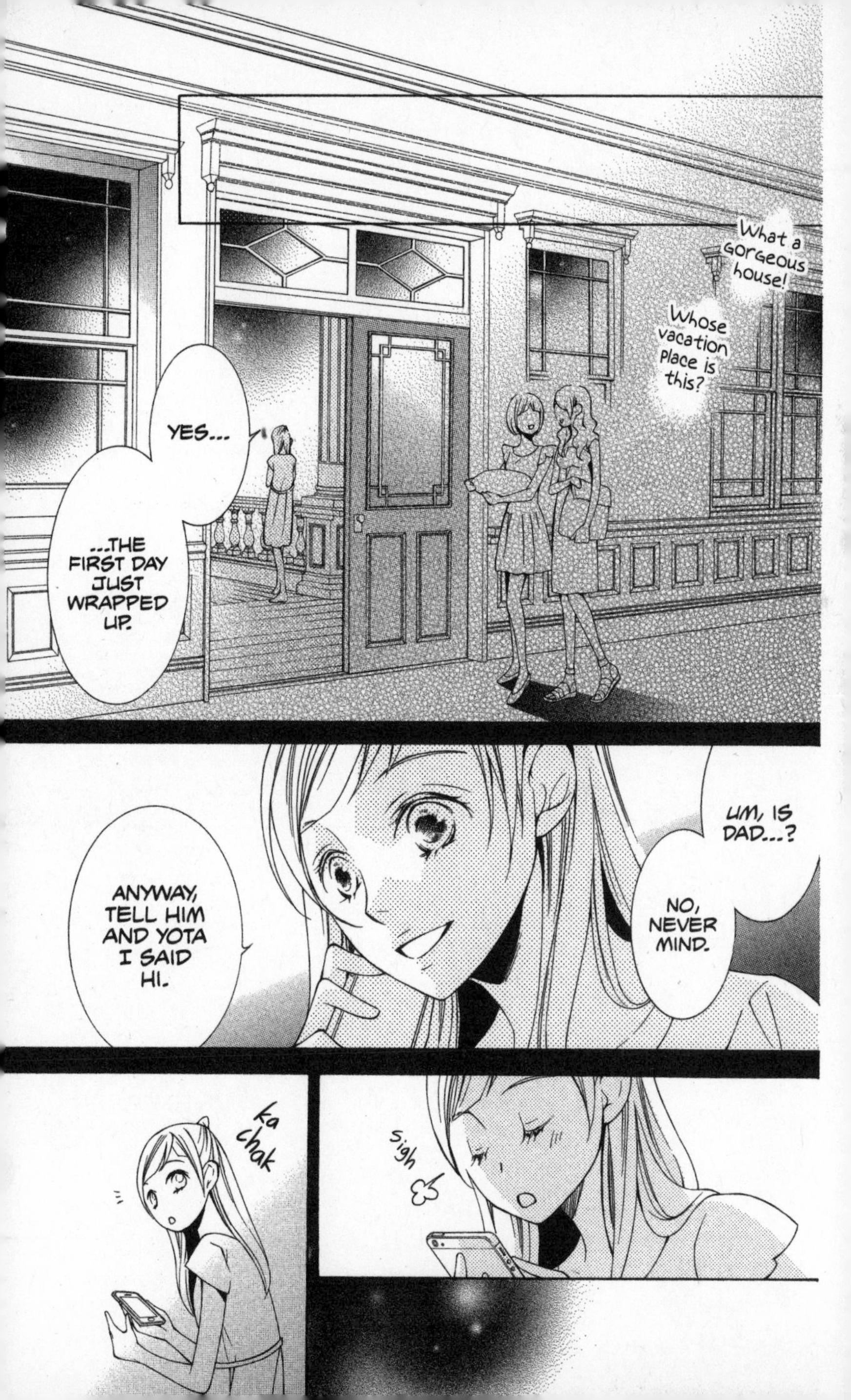
What a gorgeous house!
Whose vacation place is this?
YES...
...THE FIRST DAY JUST WRAPPED UP.
UM, IS DAD...?
NO, NEVER MIND.
ANYWAY, TELL HIM AND YOTA I SAID HI.
sigh
ka chak

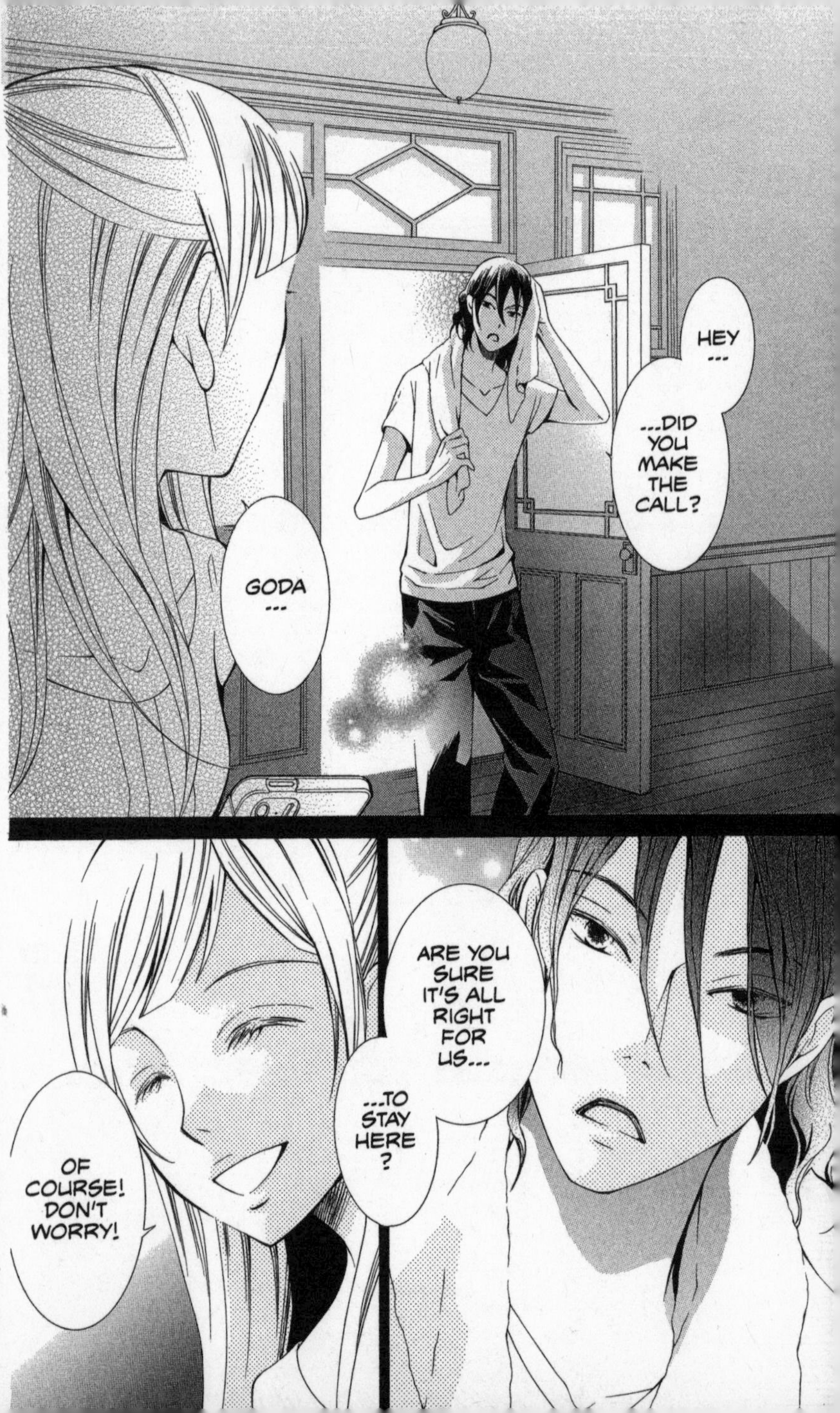
HEY ---
...DID YOU MAKE THE CALL?
GODA ---
ARE YOU SURE IT'S ALL RIGHT FOR US...
...TO STAY HERE?
OF COURSE! DON'T WORRY!

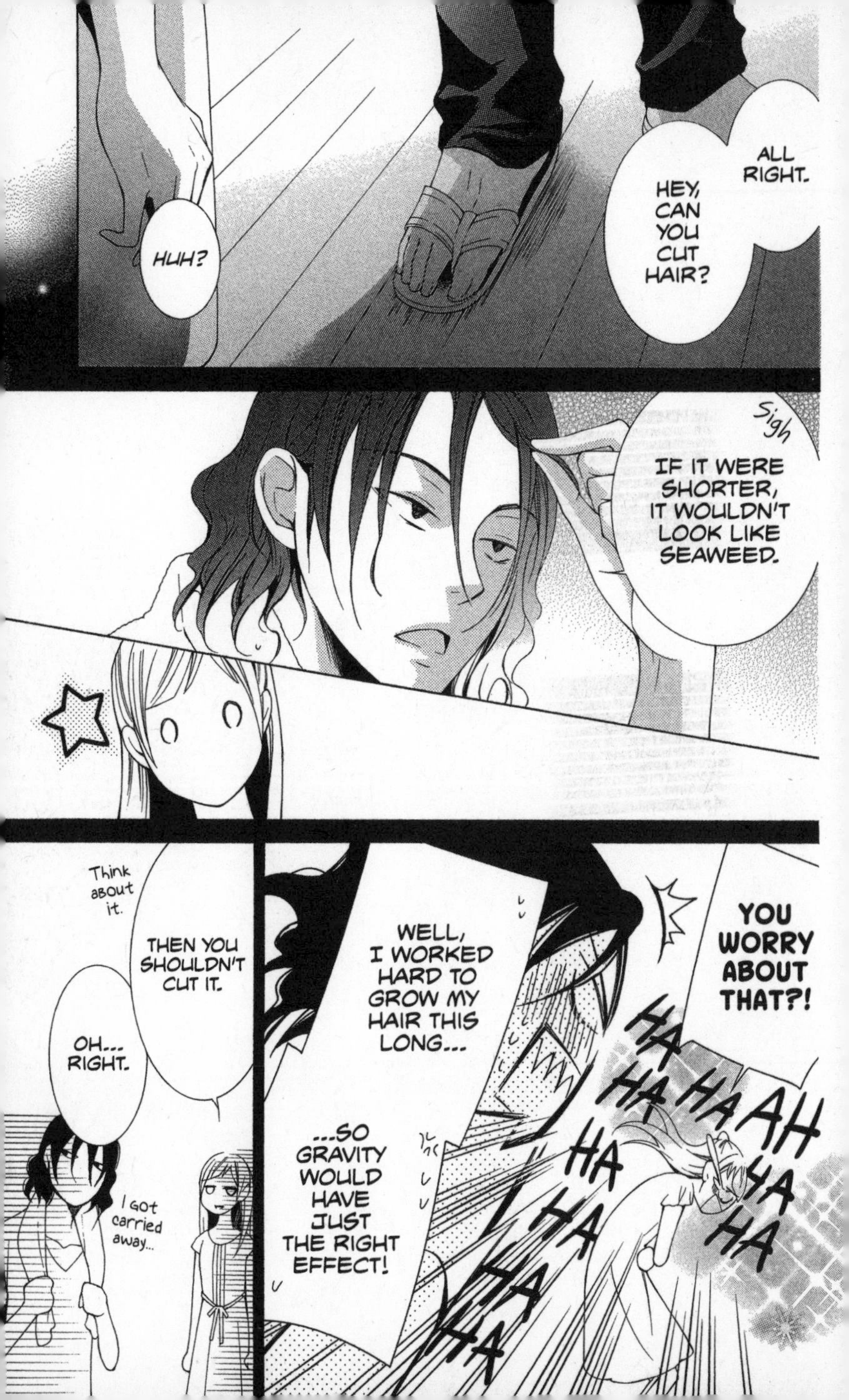
ALL RIGHT.
HEY, CAN YOU CUT HAIR?
HUH?
Sigh
IF IT WERE SHORTER, IT WOULDN'T LOOK LIKE SEAWEED.
YOU WORRY ABOUT THAT?!
AH HA HA HA HA HA HA HA HA HA HA
WELL, I WORKED HARD TO GROW MY HAIR THIS LONG...
...SO GRAVITY WOULD HAVE JUST THE RIGHT EFFECT!
Think about it.
THEN YOU SHOULDN'T CUT IT.
OH... RIGHT.
I got carried away...

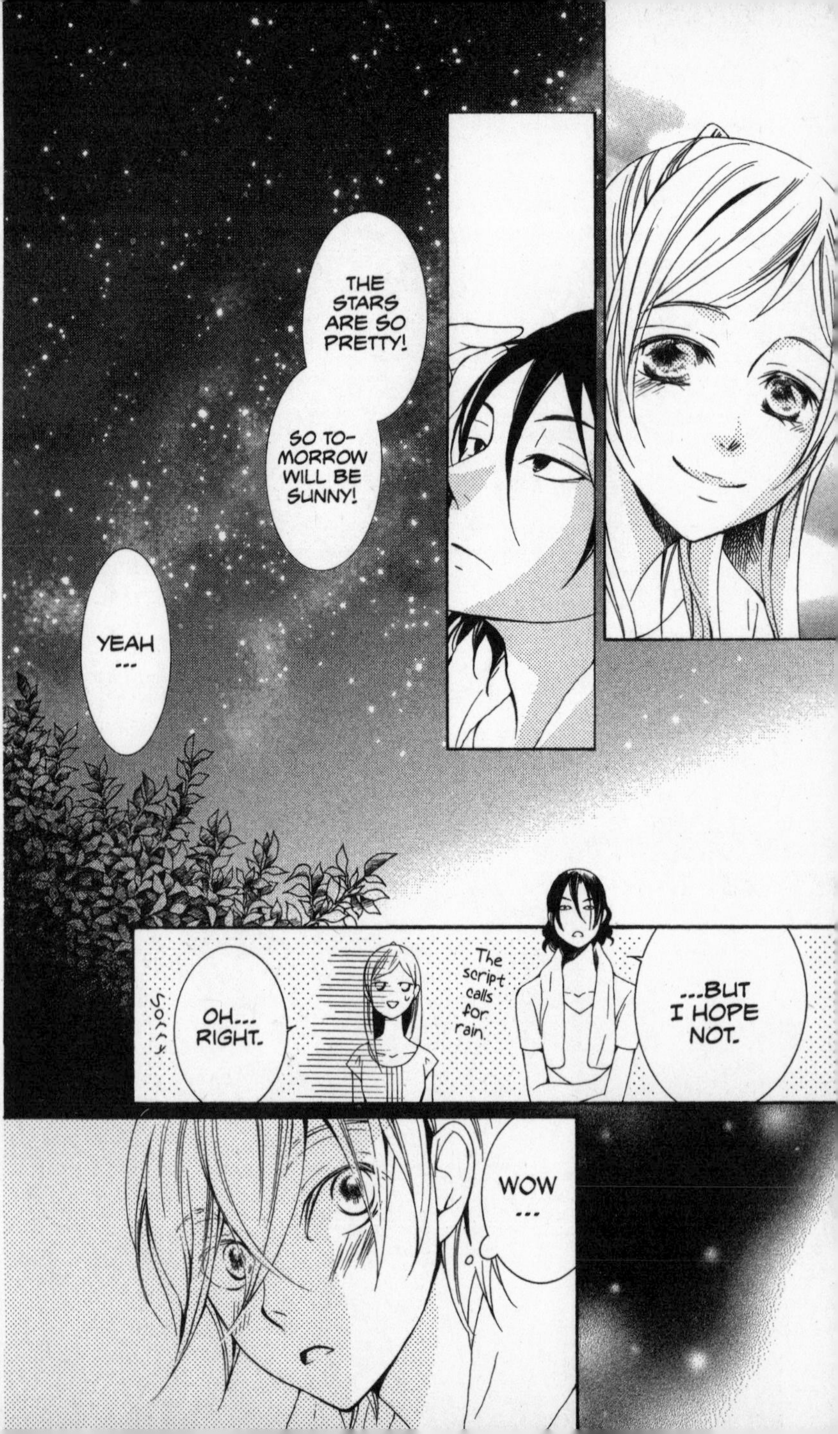
THE STARS ARE SO PRETTY!
SO TO-MORROW WILL BE SUNNY!
YEAH ...
...BUT I HOPE NOT.
The script calls for rain.
OH... RIGHT.
Sorry
WOW ...

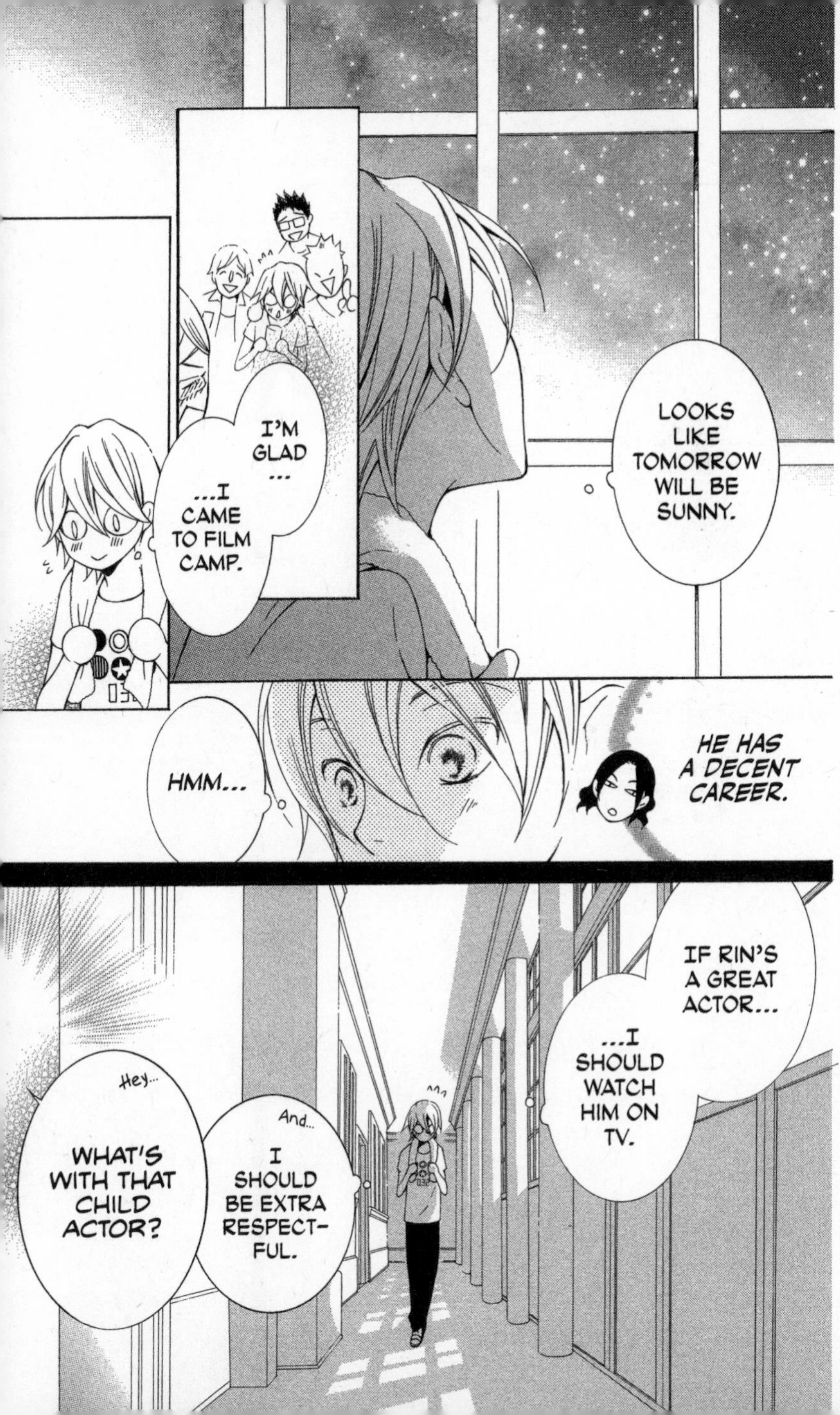
LOOKS LIKE TOMORROW WILL BE SUNNY.
I'M GLAD...
...I CAME TO FILM CAMP.
HE HAS A DECENT CAREER.
HMM...
IF RIN'S A GREAT ACTOR...
...I SHOULD WATCH HIM ON TV.
And...
I SHOULD BE EXTRA RESPECT-FUL.
Hey...
WHAT'S WITH THAT CHILD ACTOR?

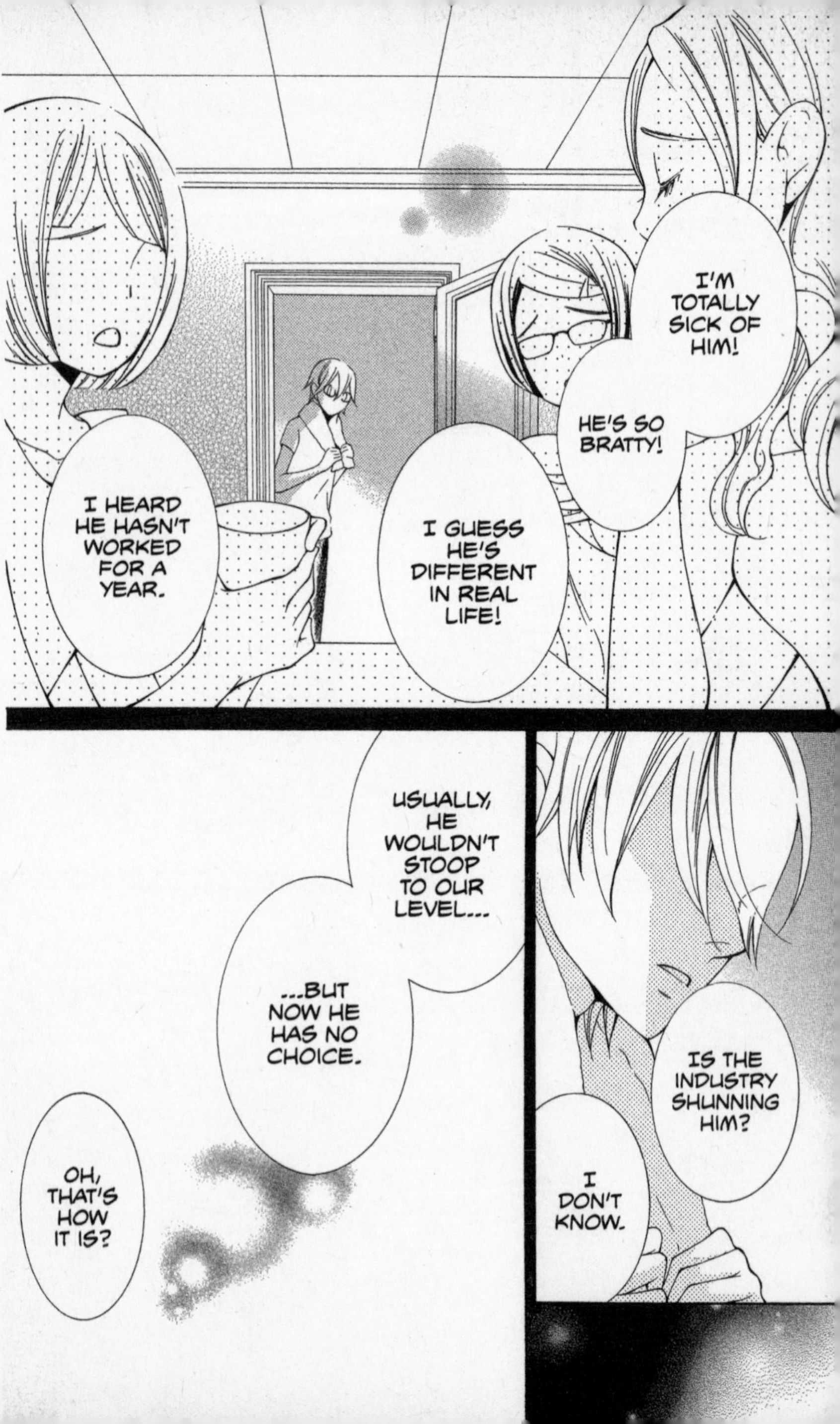
I'M TOTALLY SICK OF HIM!
HE'S SO BRATTY!
I GUESS HE'S DIFFERENT IN REAL LIFE!
I HEARD HE HASN'T WORKED FOR A YEAR.
IS THE INDUSTRY SHUNNING HIM?
I DON'T KNOW.
USUALLY, HE WOULDN'T STOOP TO OUR LEVEL...
...BUT NOW HE HAS NO CHOICE.
OH, THAT'S HOW IT IS?

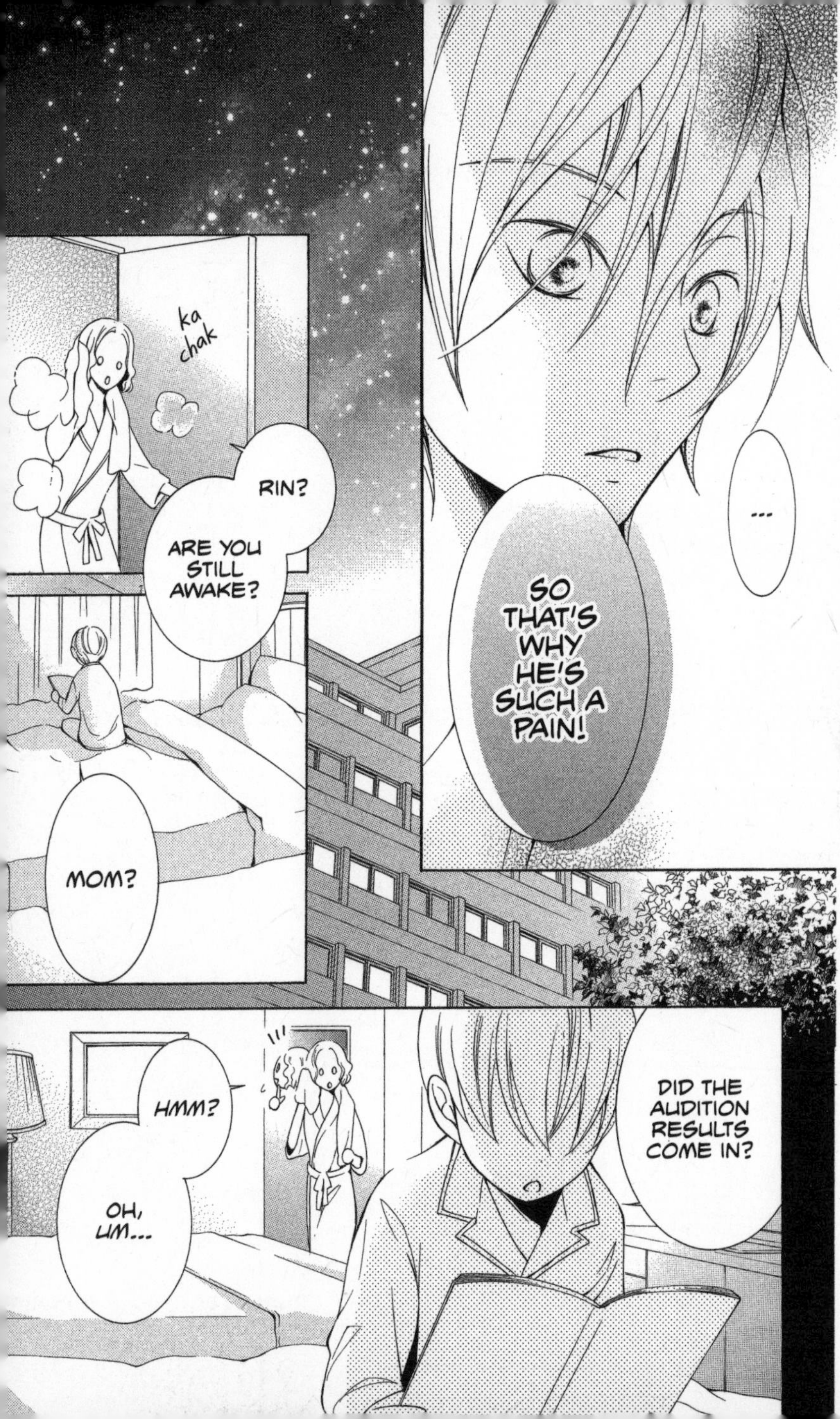
...
SO THAT'S WHY HE'S SUCH A PAIN!
ka chak
RIN?
ARE YOU STILL AWAKE?
MOM?
DID THE AUDITION RESULTS COME IN?
HMM?
OH, UM...

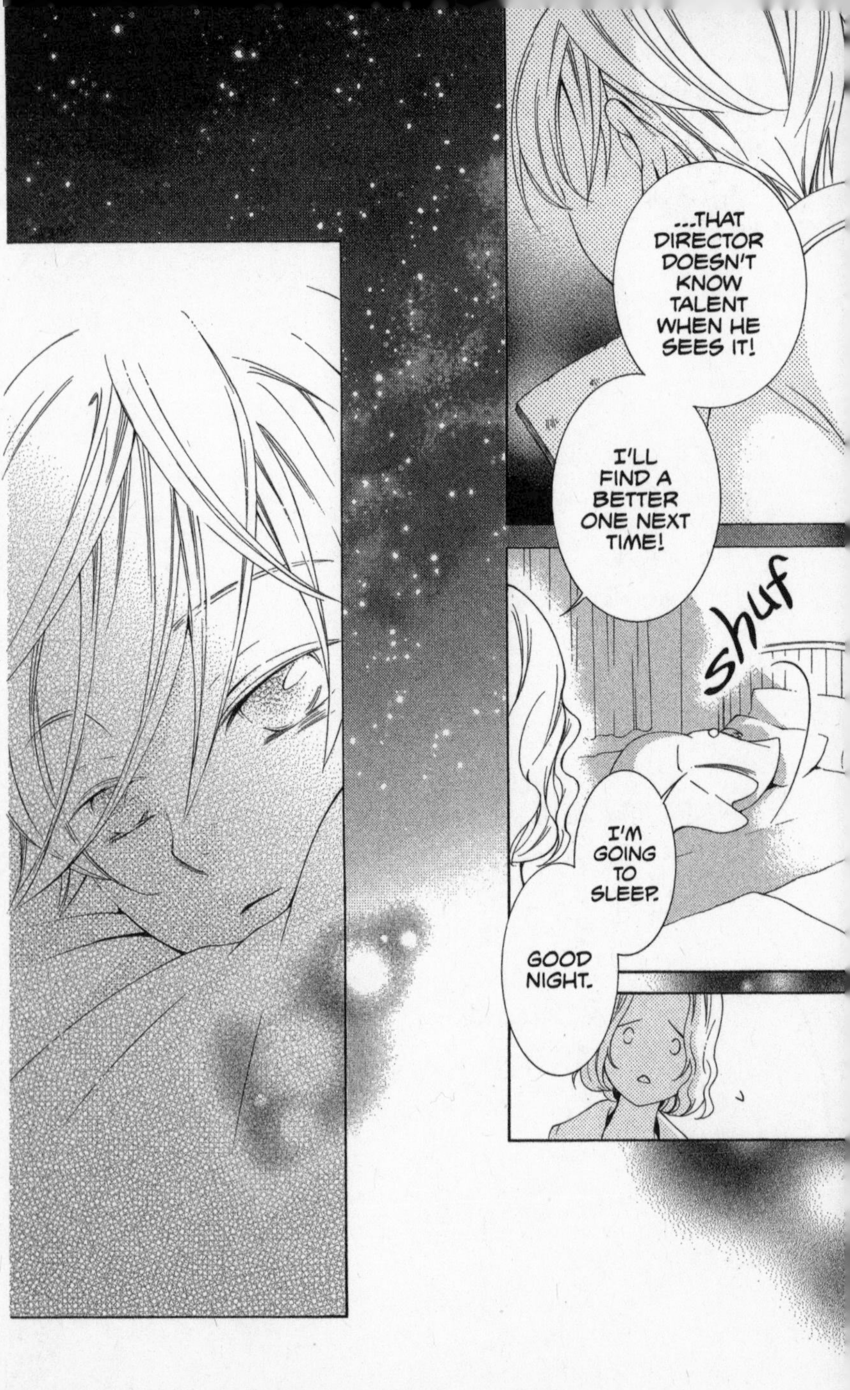
...THAT DIRECTOR DOESN'T KNOW TALENT WHEN HE SEES IT!
I'LL FIND A BETTER ONE NEXT TIME!
shuf
I'M GOING TO SLEEP.
GOOD NIGHT.

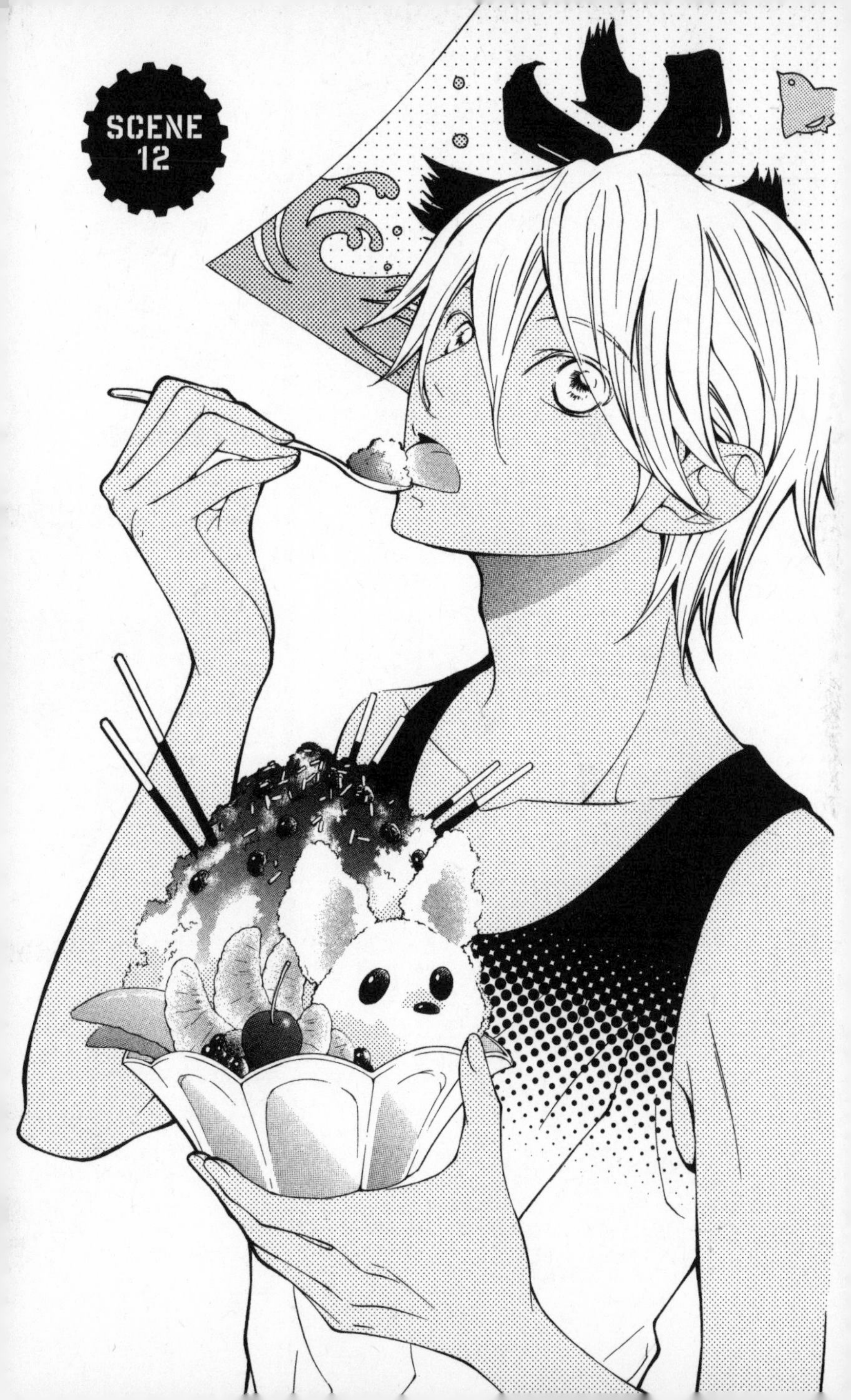
SCENE
12

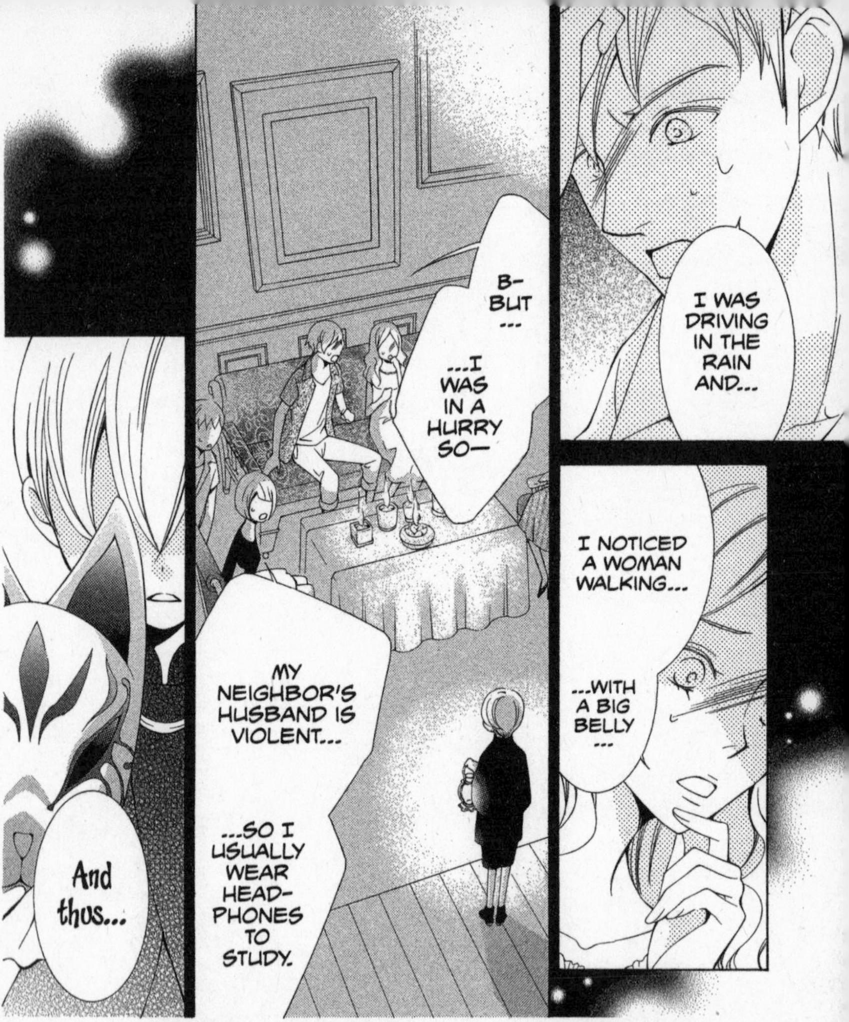
I WAS DRIVING IN THE RAIN AND...
I NOTICED A WOMAN WALKING...
...WITH A BIG BELLY...
B-BUT...
...I WAS IN A HURRY SO—
MY NEIGHBOR'S HUSBAND IS VIOLENT...
...SO I USUALLY WEAR HEAD-PHONES TO STUDY.
And thus...

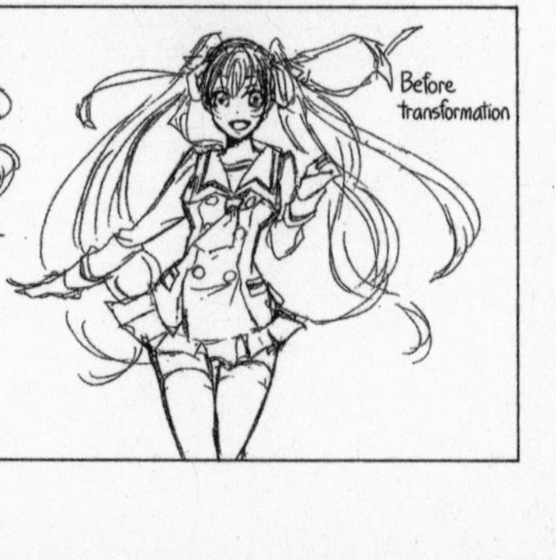
Before transformation

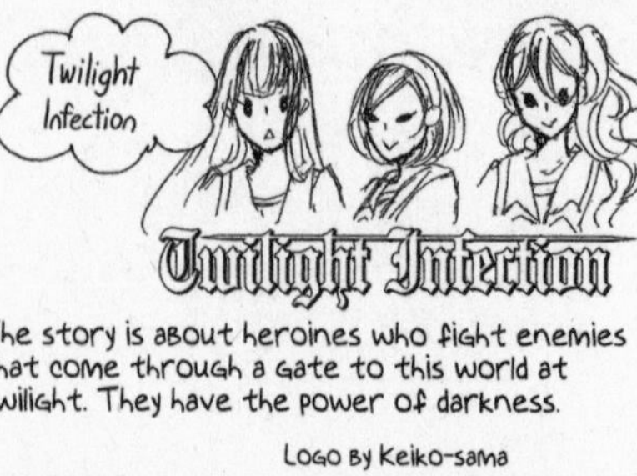
Twilight Infection
Twilight Infection

The story is about heroines who fight enemies that come through a gate to this world at twilight. They have the power of darkness.

LOGO BY Keiko-sama

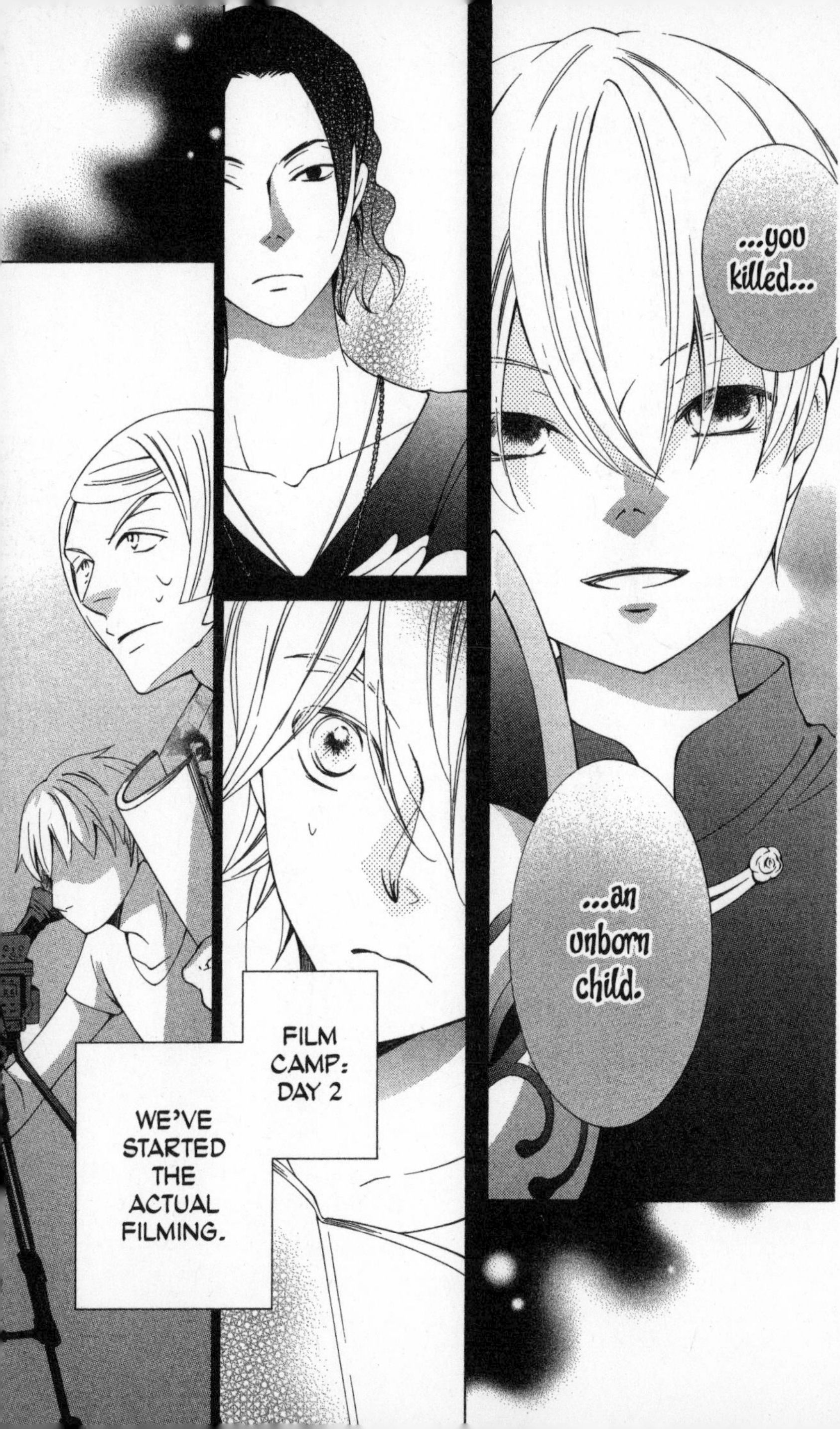
...you killed...
...an unborn child.
FILM CAMP: DAY 2
WE'VE STARTED THE ACTUAL FILMING.

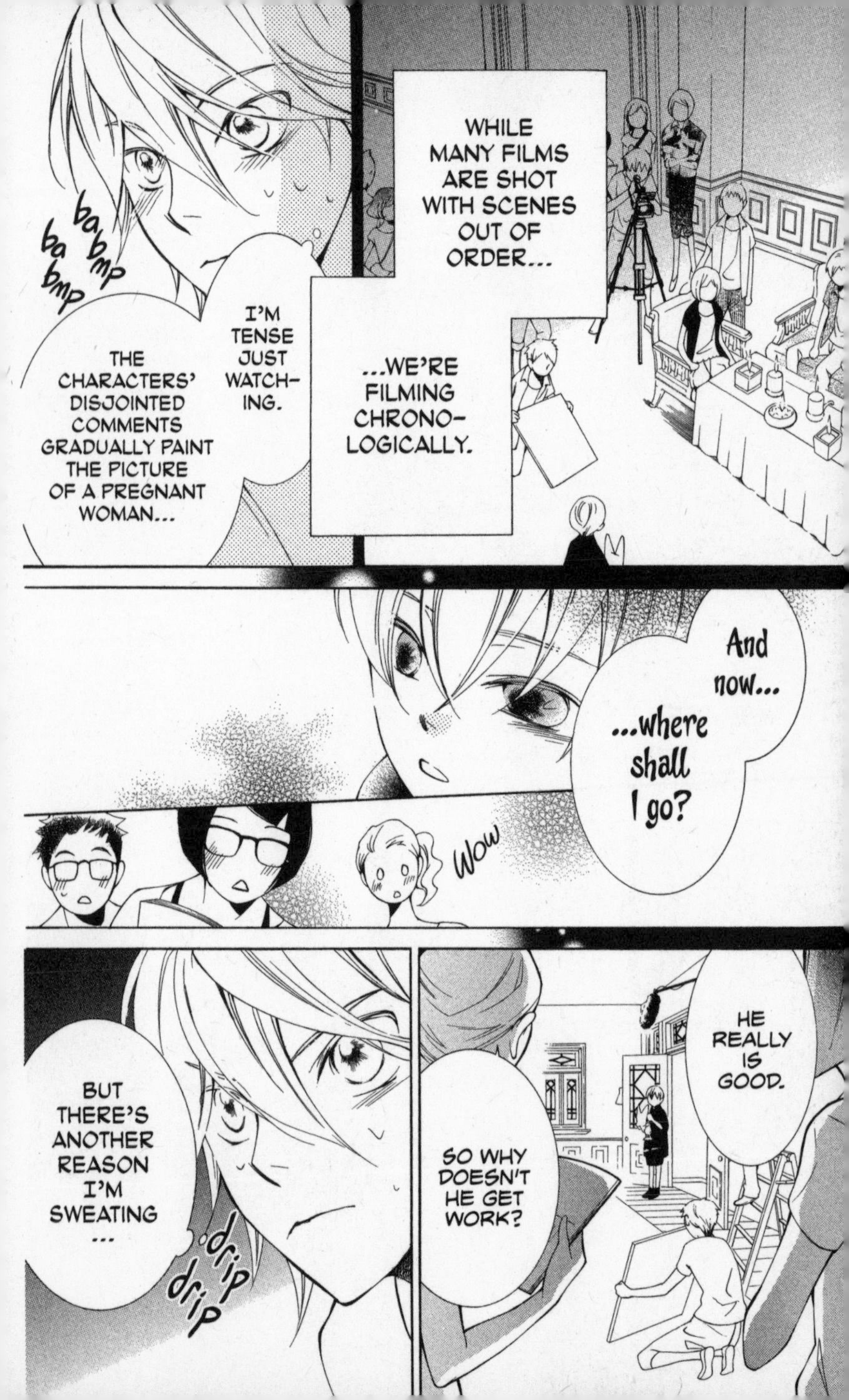
WHILE MANY FILMS ARE SHOT WITH SCENES OUT OF ORDER...
...WE'RE FILMING CHRONO-LOGICALLY.
I'M TENSE JUST WATCH-ING.
ba bmp ba bmp
THE CHARACTERS' DISJOINTED COMMENTS GRADUALLY PAINT THE PICTURE OF A PREGNANT WOMAN...
And now... ...where shall I go?
Wow
HE REALLY IS GOOD.
SO WHY DOESN'T HE GET WORK?
BUT THERE'S ANOTHER REASON I'M SWEATING...
drip drip

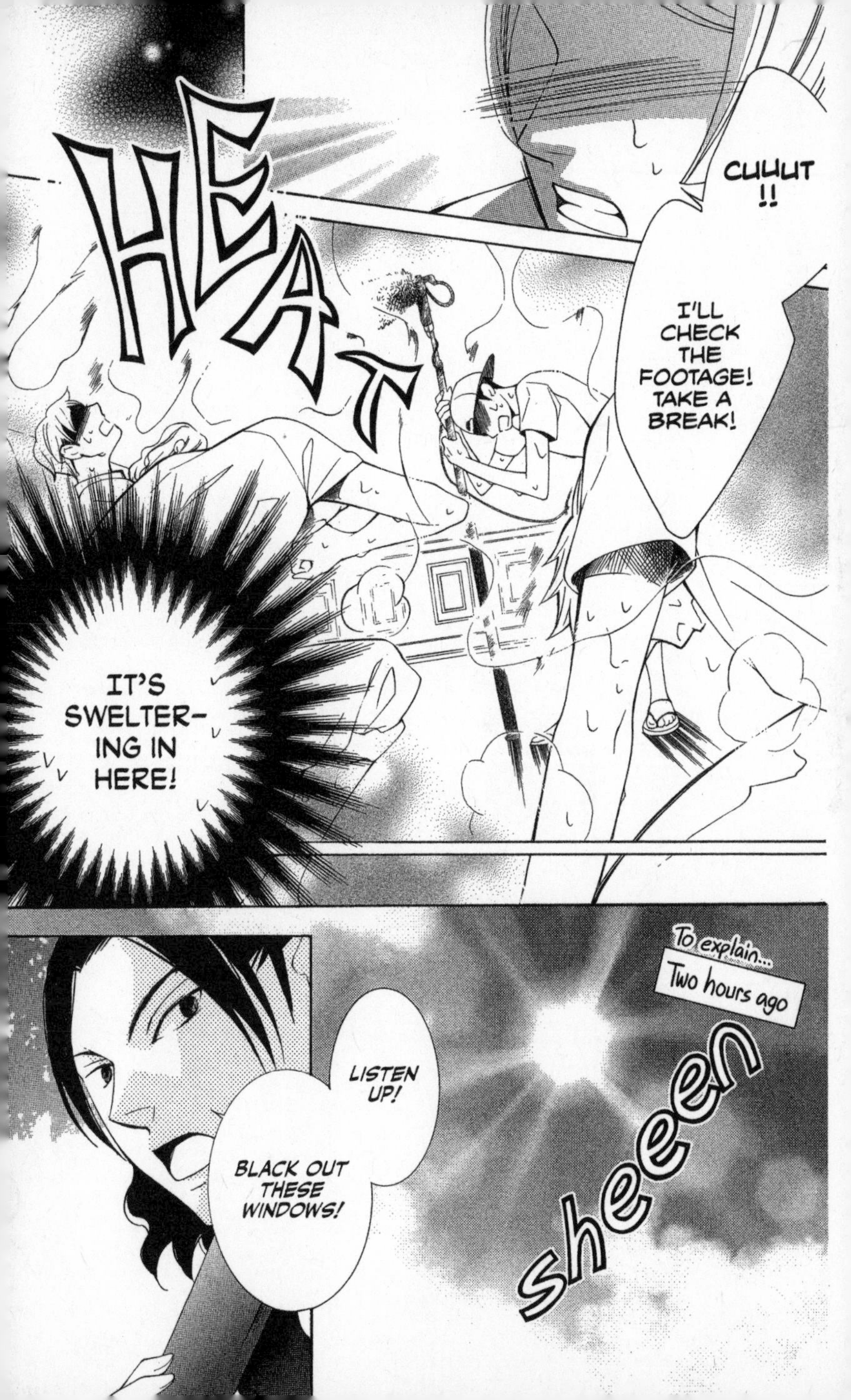
CUUUT !!
I'LL CHECK THE FOOTAGE! TAKE A BREAK!
HEAT
IT'S SWELTER-ING IN HERE!
To explain...
Two hours ago
sheeen
LISTEN UP!
BLACK OUT THESE WINDOWS!

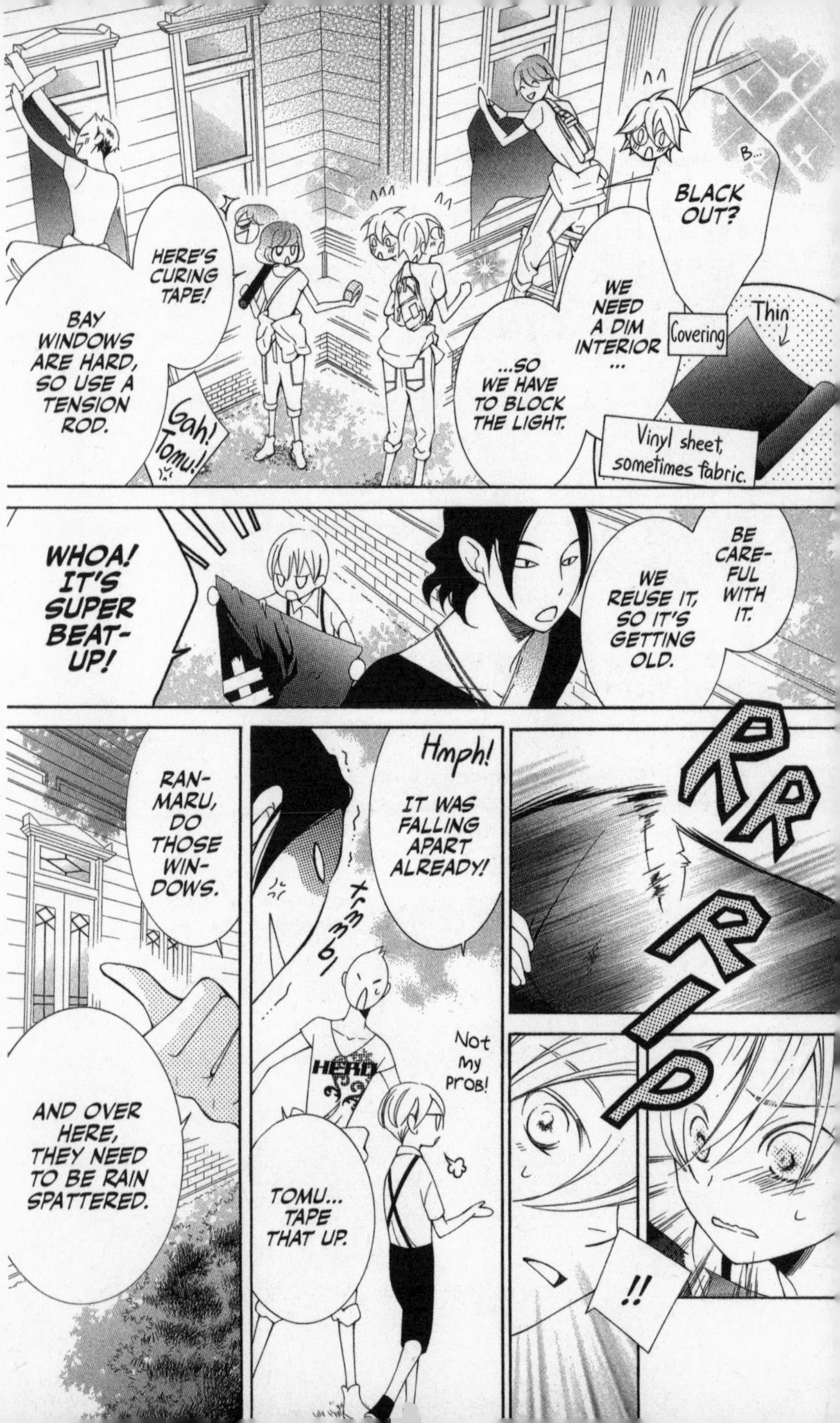
B...
BLACK OUT?
WE NEED A DIM INTERIOR ...
...SO WE HAVE TO BLOCK THE LIGHT.
Thin
Covering
Vinyl sheet, sometimes fabric.
HERE'S CURING TAPE!
BAY WINDOWS ARE HARD, SO USE A TENSION ROD.
Gah! Tomu!
BE CARE-FUL WITH IT.
WE REUSE IT, SO IT'S GETTING OLD.
WHOA! IT'S SUPER BEAT-UP!
RRRIP
!!
Hmph!
IT WAS FALLING APART ALREADY!
Not my PROB!
HERO
TOMU... TAPE THAT UP.
RAN-MARU, DO THOSE WIN-DOWS.
AND OVER HERE, THEY NEED TO BE RAIN SPATTERED.

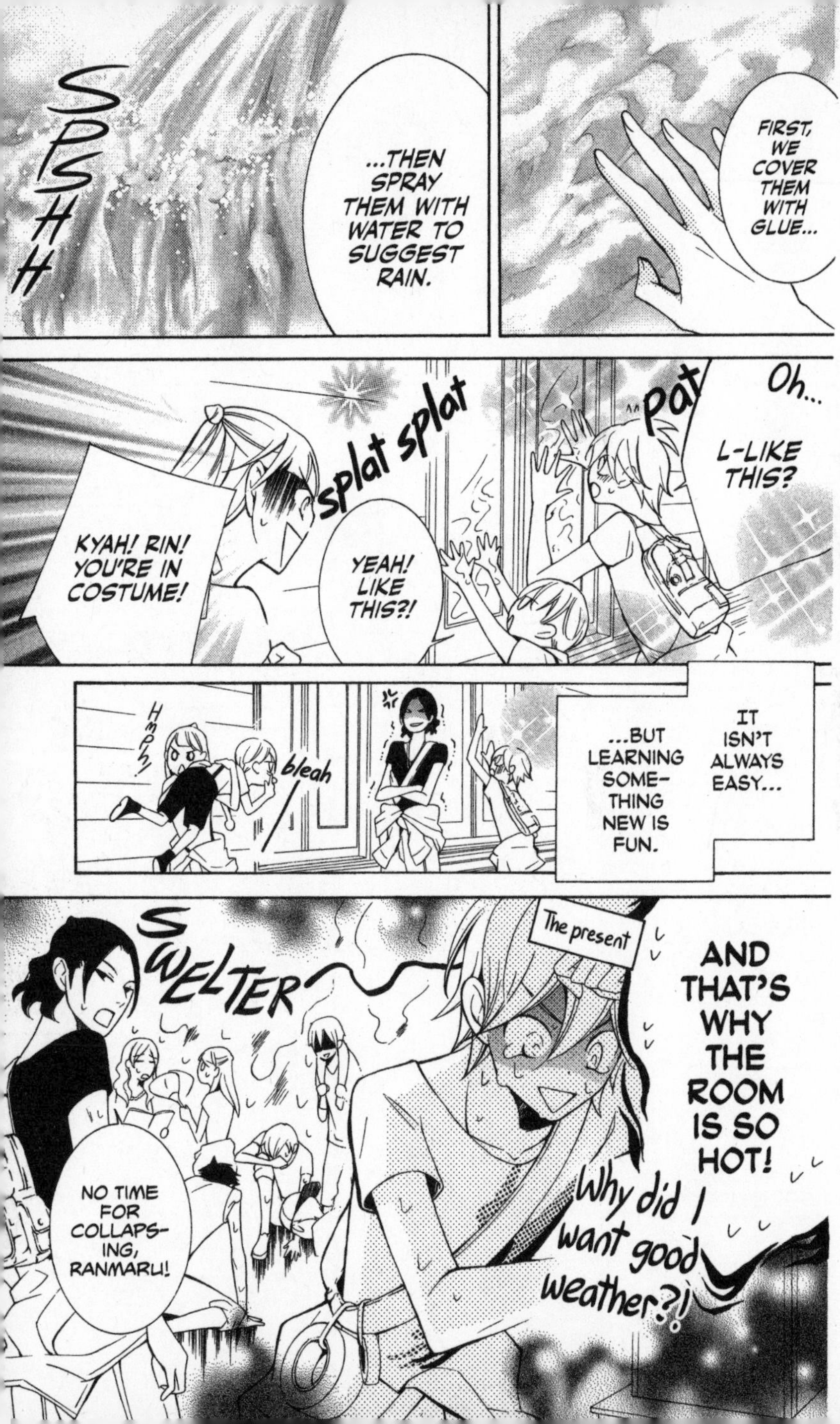
FIRST, WE COVER THEM WITH GLUE...
...THEN SPRAY THEM WITH WATER TO SUGGEST RAIN.
SPSHH
Oh...
L-LIKE THIS?
Pat
YEAH! LIKE THIS?!
splat splat
KYAH! RIN! YOU'RE IN COSTUME!
IT ISN'T ALWAYS EASY...
...BUT LEARNING SOME-THING NEW IS FUN.
bleah
Hmph!
The present
AND THAT'S WHY THE ROOM IS SO HOT!
Why did I want good weather?!
SWELTER
NO TIME FOR COLLAPS-ING, RANMARU!

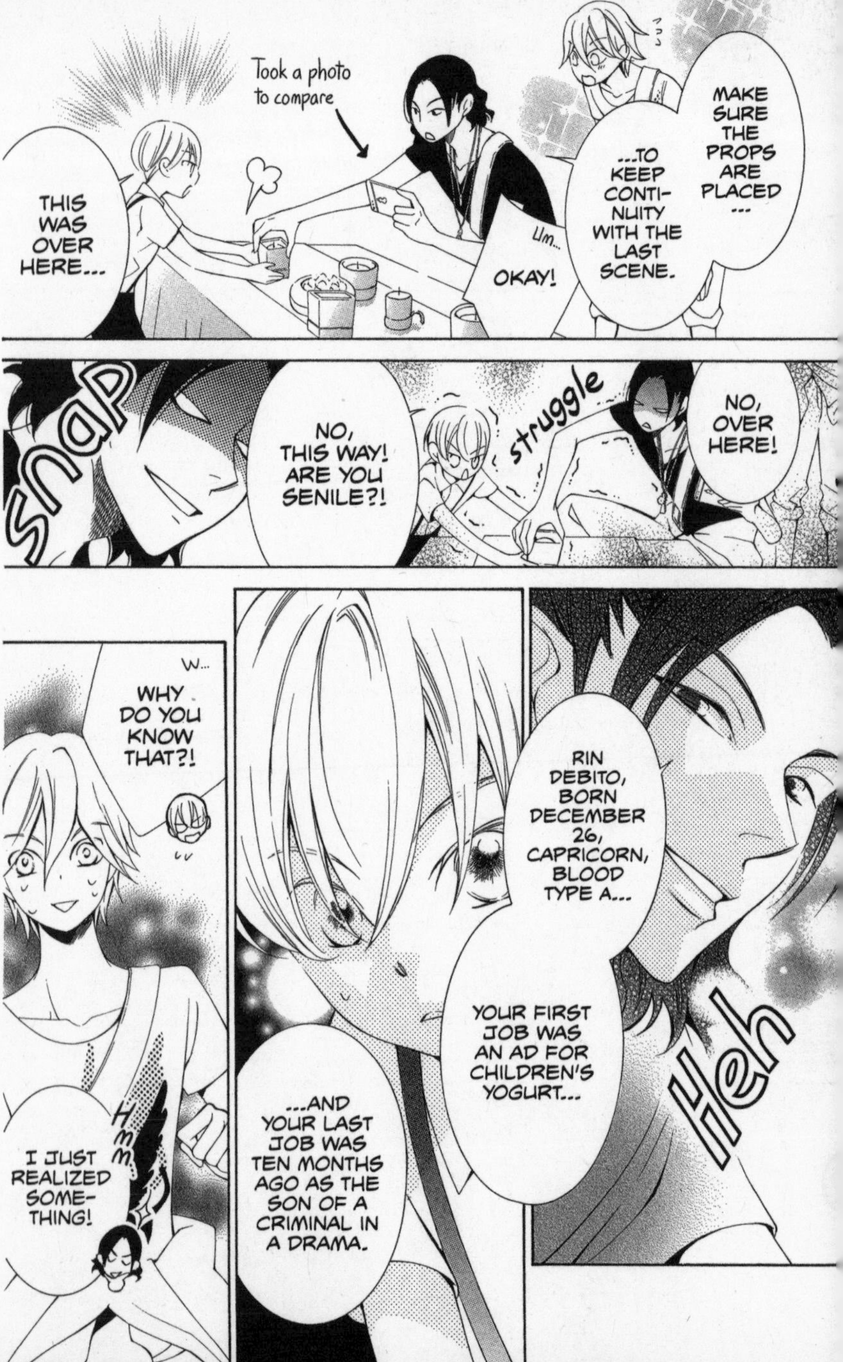
MAKE SURE THE PROPS ARE PLACED...
...TO KEEP CONTINUITY WITH THE LAST SCENE.
Um...
OKAY!
Took a photo to compare
THIS WAS OVER HERE...
NO, OVER HERE!
struggle
NO, THIS WAY! ARE YOU SENILE?!
snap
Heh
RIN DEBITO, BORN DECEMBER 26, CAPRICORN, BLOOD TYPE A...
YOUR FIRST JOB WAS AN AD FOR CHILDREN'S YOGURT...
...AND YOUR LAST JOB WAS TEN MONTHS AGO AS THE SON OF A CRIMINAL IN A DRAMA.
W...
WHY DO YOU KNOW THAT?!
Hmm
I JUST REALIZED SOMETHING!

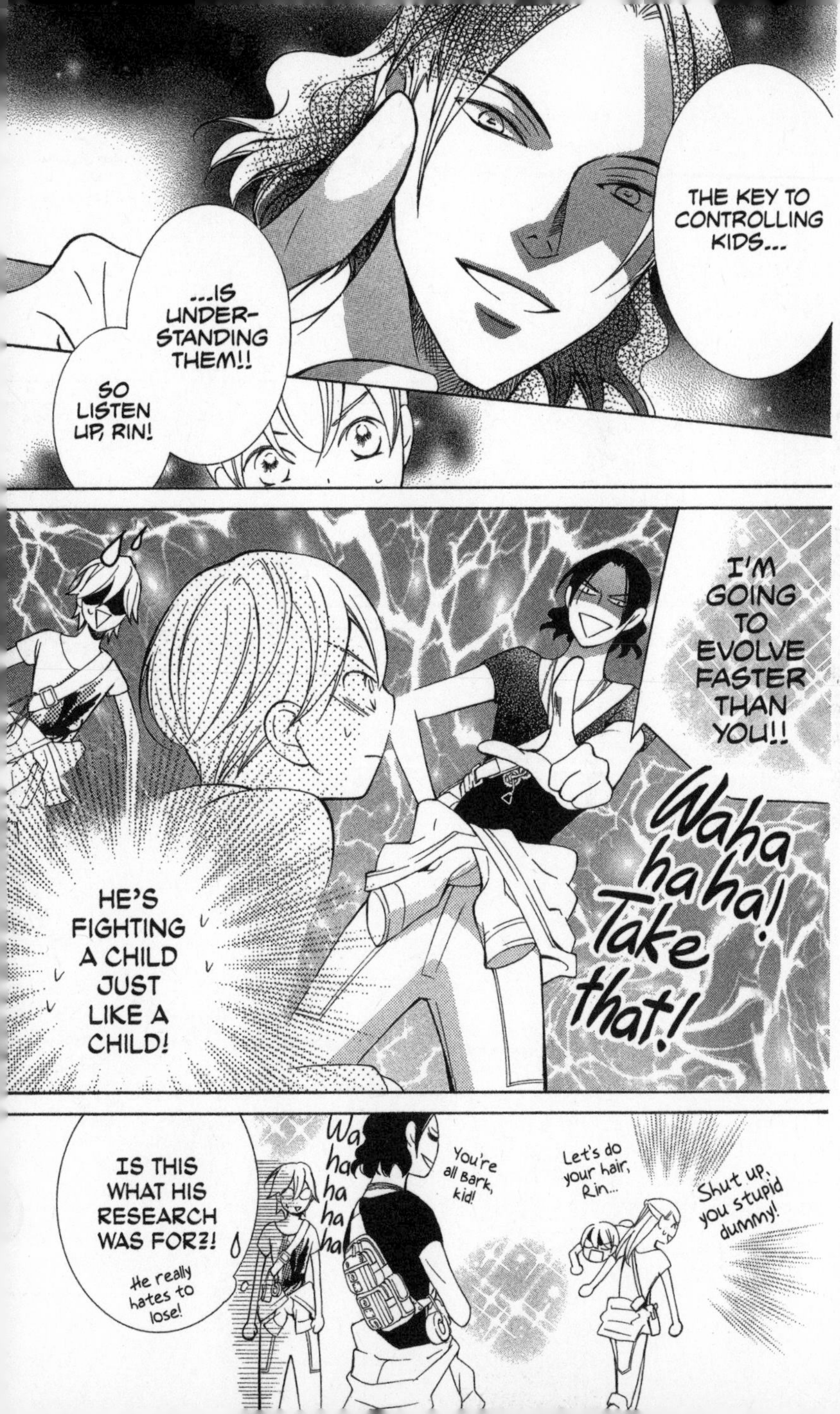
THE KEY TO CONTROLLING KIDS...
...IS UNDER-STANDING THEM!!
SO LISTEN UP, RIN!
I'M GOING TO EVOLVE FASTER THAN YOU!!
Waha ha ha! Take that!
HE'S FIGHTING A CHILD JUST LIKE A CHILD!
Shut up, you stupid dummy!
Let's do your hair, Rin...
You're all Bark, kid!
Wa ha ha ha ha ha
IS THIS WHAT HIS RESEARCH WAS FOR?!
He really hates to lose!

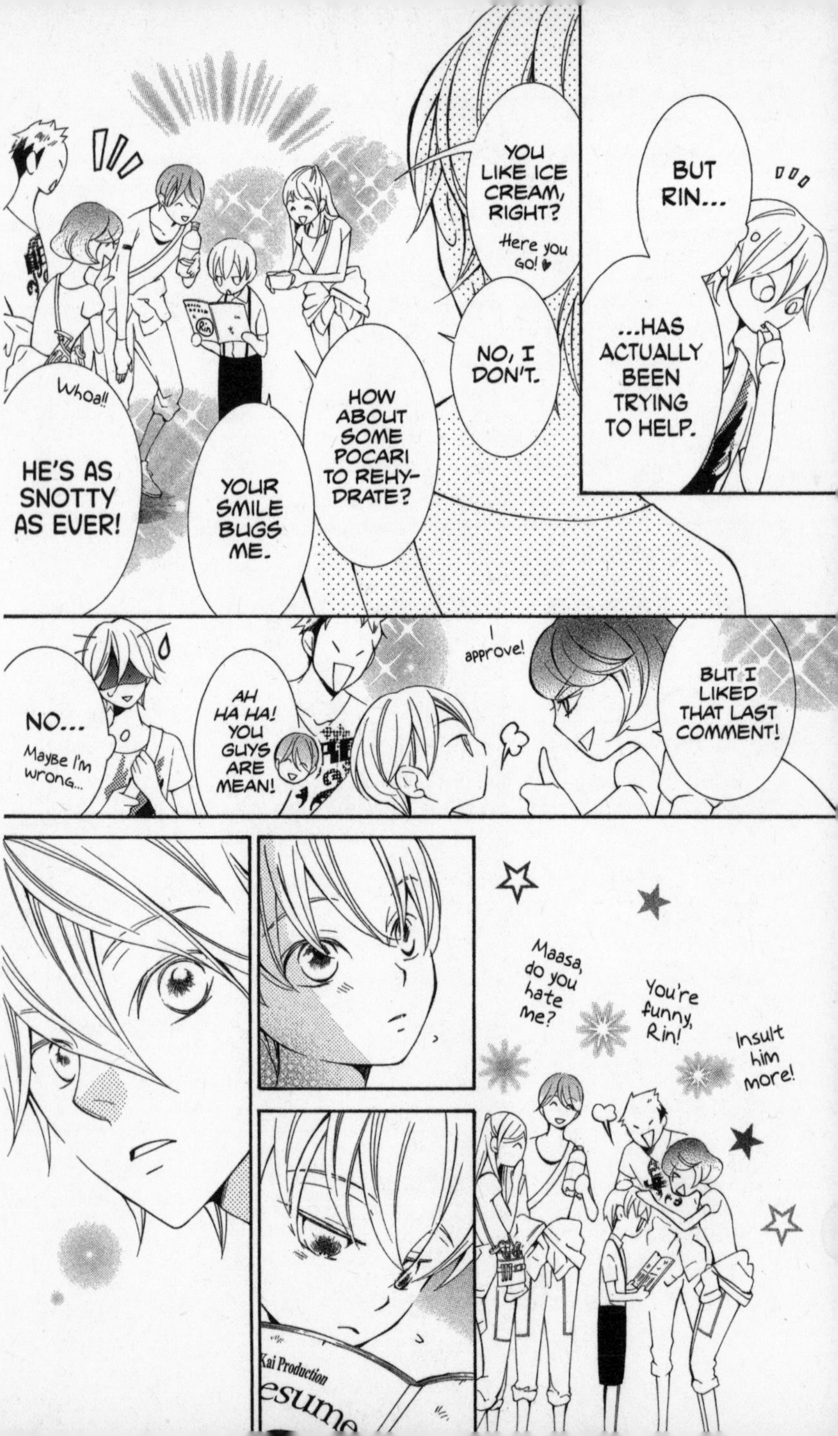
BUT RIN...
...HAS ACTUALLY BEEN TRYING TO HELP.
YOU LIKE ICE CREAM, RIGHT?
Here you go! ♥
NO, I DON'T.
HOW ABOUT SOME POCARI TO REHY-DRATE?
YOUR SMILE BUGS ME.
Whoa!!
HE'S AS SNOTTY AS EVER!
BUT I LIKED THAT LAST COMMENT!
I approve!
AH HA HA! YOU GUYS ARE MEAN!
NO...
Maybe I'm wrong...
Insult him more!
You're funny, Rin!
Maasa, do you hate me?
Kai Production

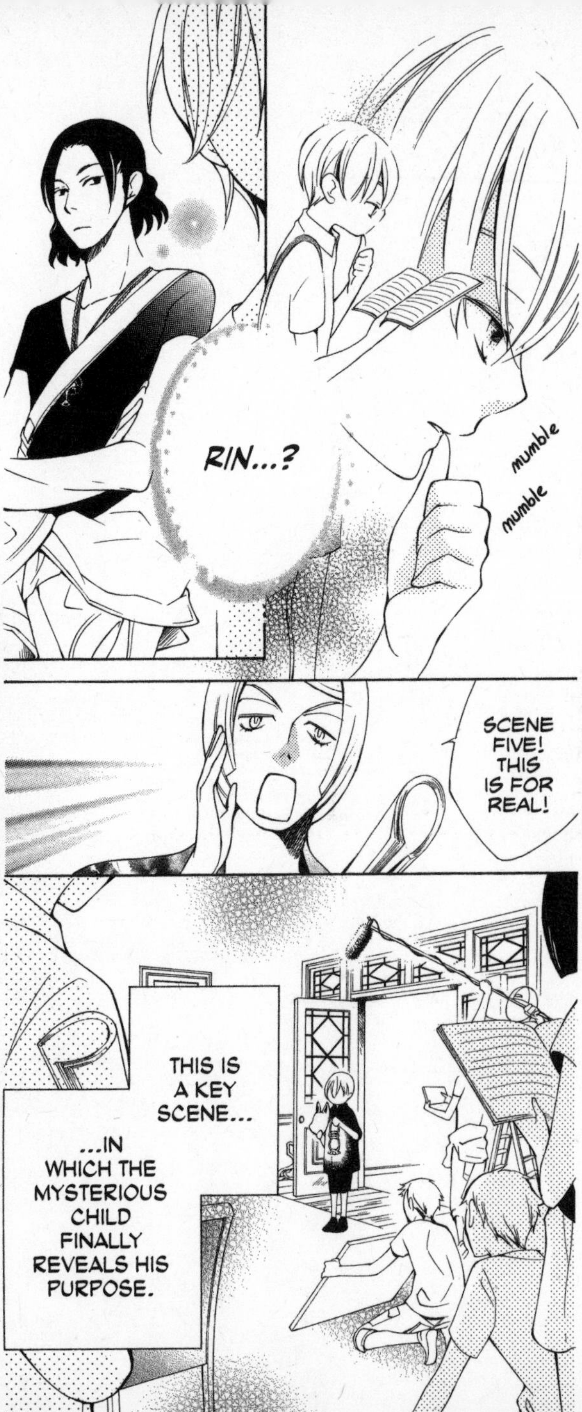
mumble mumble
RIN...?
SCENE FIVE! THIS IS FOR REAL!
THIS IS A KEY SCENE...
...IN WHICH THE MYSTERIOUS CHILD FINALLY REVEALS HIS PURPOSE.

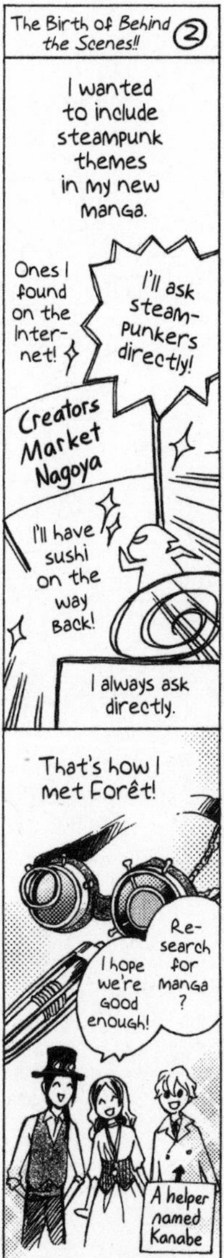
The Birth of Behind the Scenes!! 2
I wanted to include steampunk themes in my new manga.
I'll ask steam-punkers directly!
Ones I found on the Inter-net!
Creators Market Nagoya
I'll have sushi on the way back!
I always ask directly.
That's how I met Forêt!
Re-search for manga?
I hope we're good enough!
A helper named Kanabe
Later, I learned they're famous in the steampunk world...

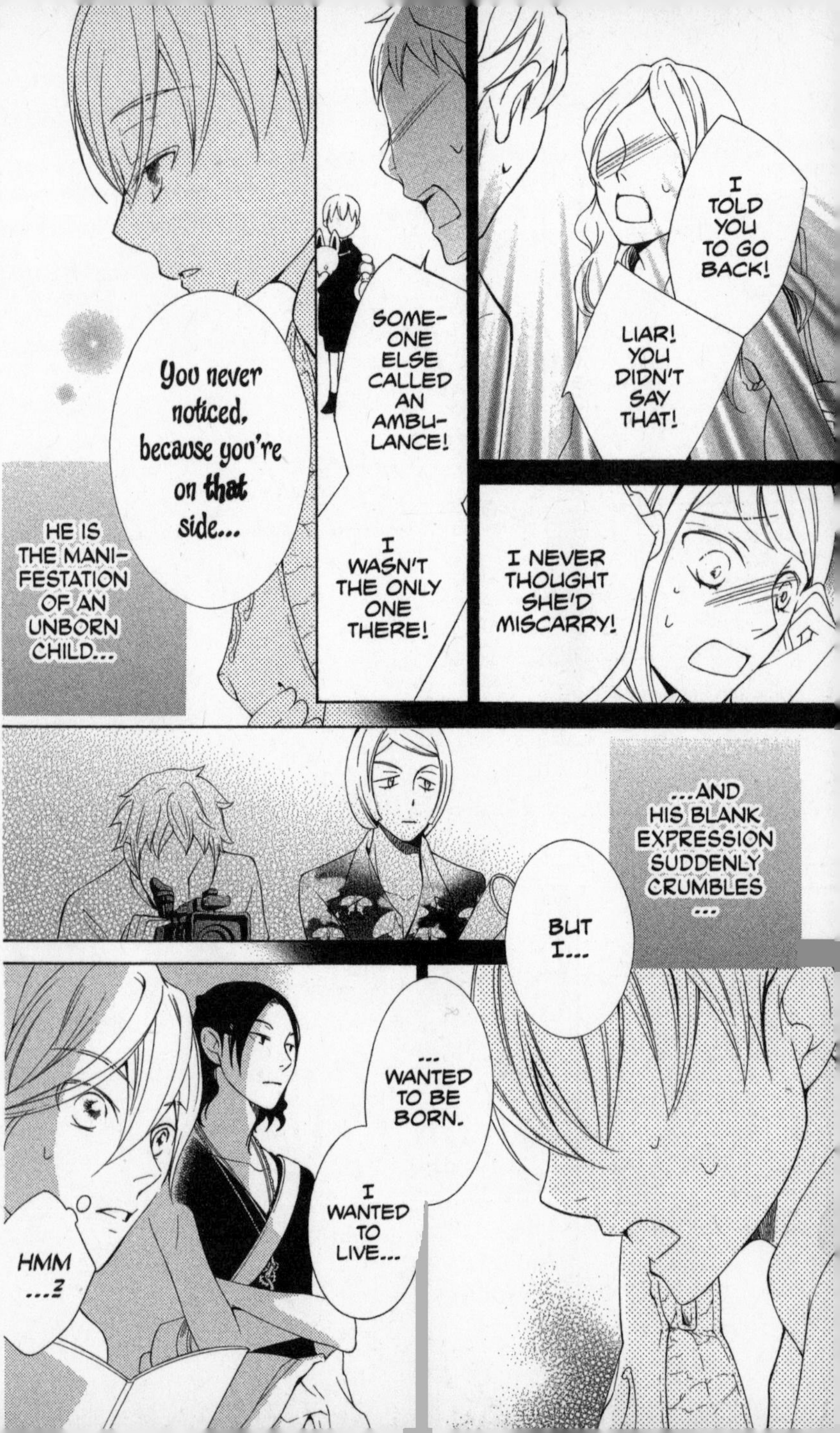
I TOLD YOU TO GO BACK!
LIAR! YOU DIDN'T SAY THAT!
I NEVER THOUGHT SHE'D MISCARRY!
SOME-ONE ELSE CALLED AN AMBU-LANCE!
I WASN'T THE ONLY ONE THERE!
You never noticed, because you're on that side...
HE IS THE MANI-FESTATION OF AN UNBORN CHILD...
...AND HIS BLANK EXPRESSION SUDDENLY CRUMBLES...
BUT I...
...WANTED TO BE BORN.
I WANTED TO LIVE...
HMM...?

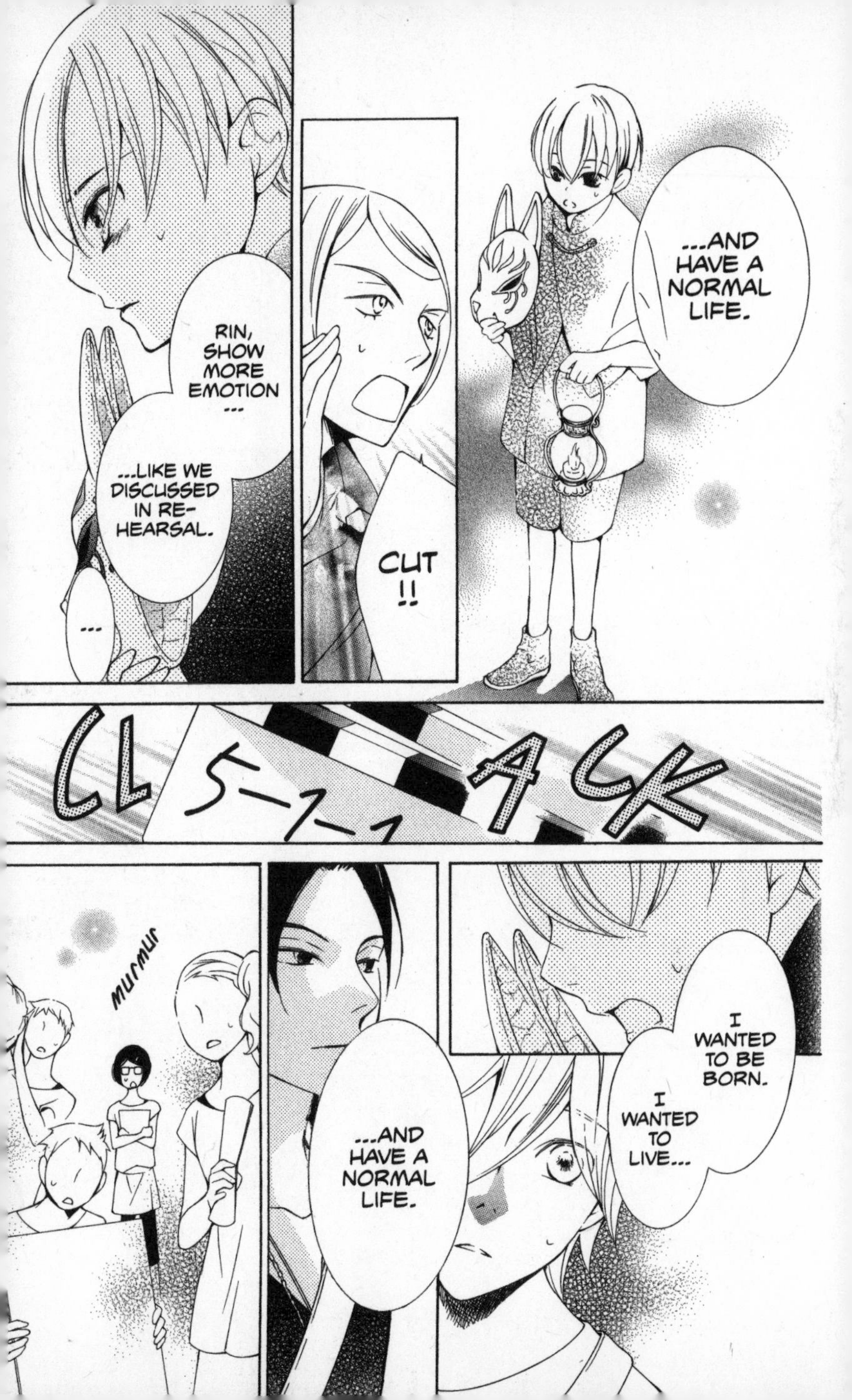
...AND HAVE A NORMAL LIFE.
CUT!!
RIN, SHOW MORE EMOTION...
...LIKE WE DISCUSSED IN RE-HEARSAL.
...
CLACK
5-1-1
I WANTED TO BE BORN.
I WANTED TO LIVE...
...AND HAVE A NORMAL LIFE.
MURMUR

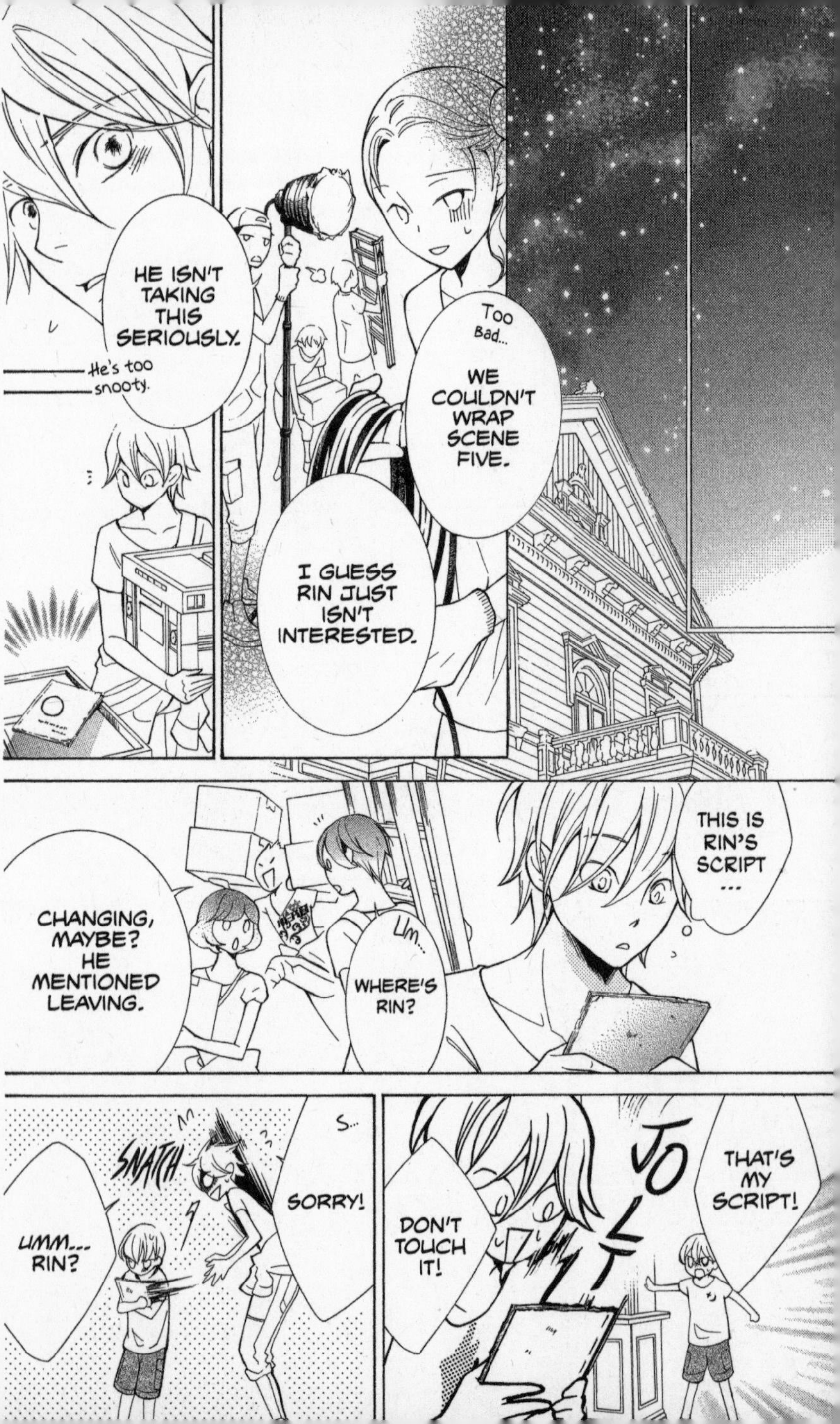
Too Bad...
WE COULDN'T WRAP SCENE FIVE.
I GUESS RIN JUST ISN'T INTERESTED.
HE ISN'T TAKING THIS SERIOUSLY.
He's too snooty.
THIS IS RIN'S SCRIPT ...
Um...
WHERE'S RIN?
CHANGING, MAYBE? HE MENTIONED LEAVING.
THAT'S MY SCRIPT!
JOLT
DON'T TOUCH IT!
S...
SORRY!
SNATCH
UMM... RIN?

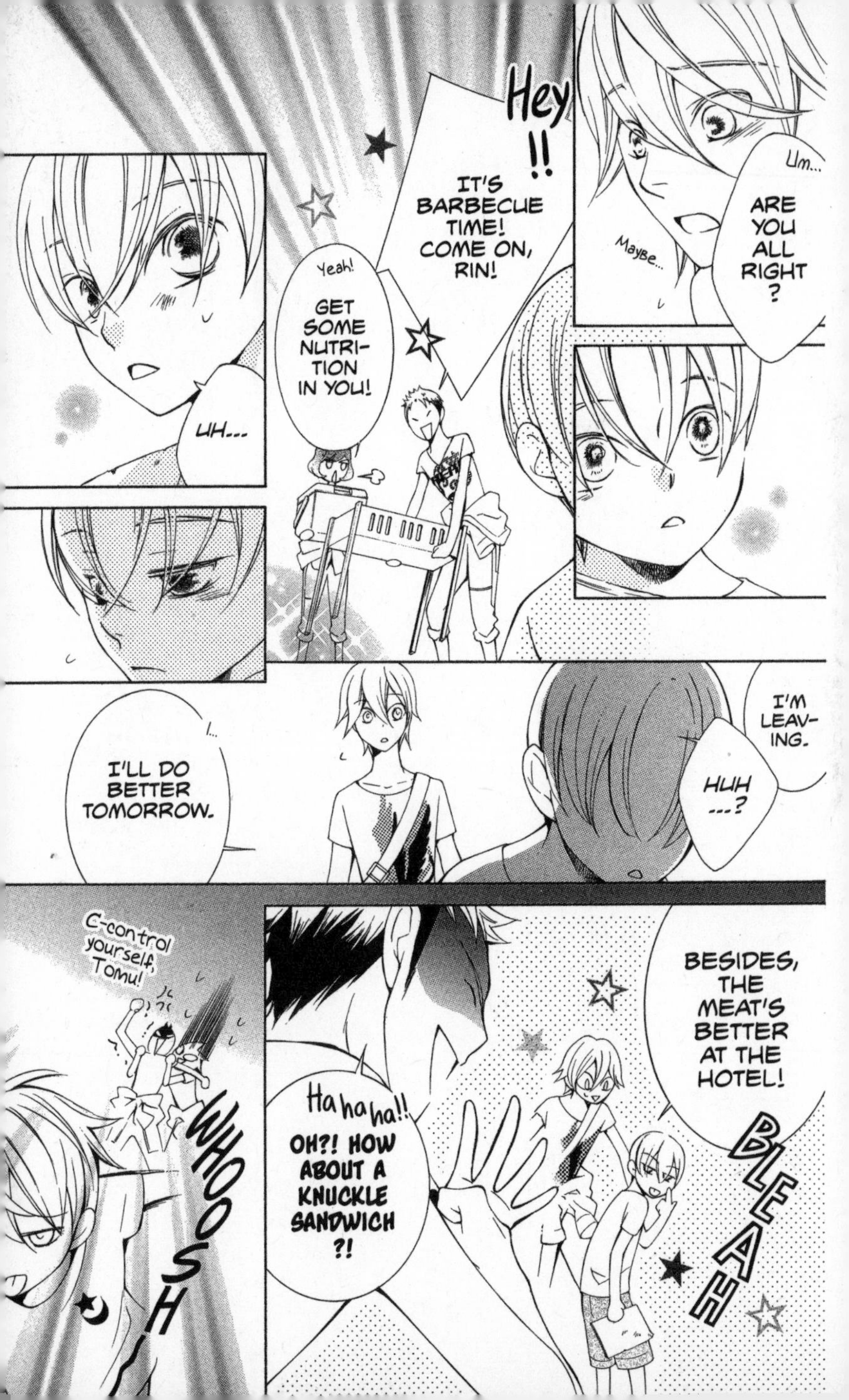
Um...
ARE YOU ALL RIGHT?
Maybe...
Hey!!
IT'S BARBECUE TIME! COME ON, RIN!
Yeah!
GET SOME NUTRITION IN YOU!
UH...
I'M LEAVING.
HUH...?
I...
I'LL DO BETTER TOMORROW.
BESIDES, THE MEAT'S BETTER AT THE HOTEL!
BLEAH
Ha ha ha!!
OH?! HOW ABOUT A KNUCKLE SANDWICH?!
C-control yourself, Tomu!
WHOOSH

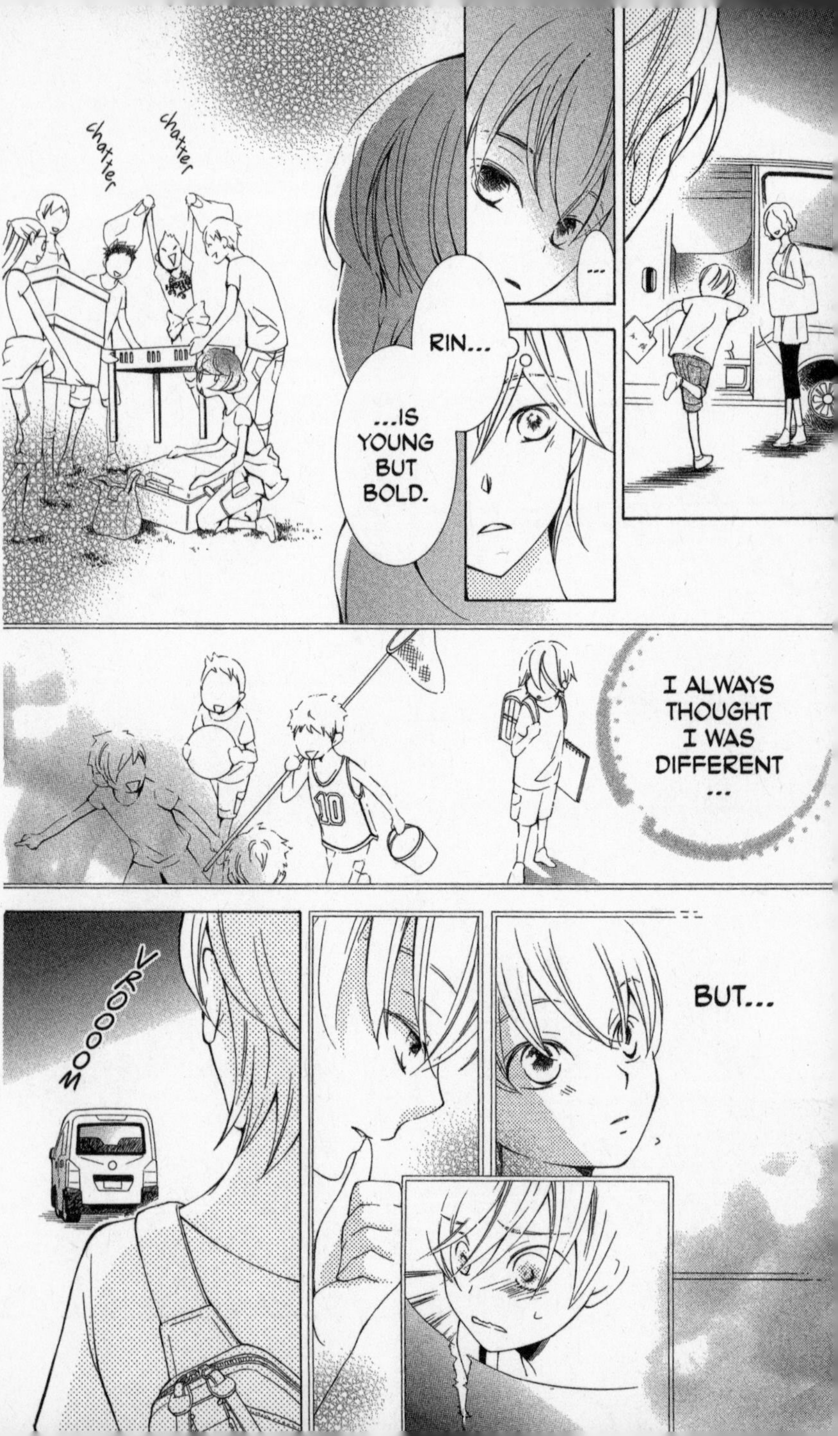
...
RIN...
...IS YOUNG BUT BOLD.
chatter
chatter
I ALWAYS THOUGHT I WAS DIFFERENT...
BUT...
VROOOOOM

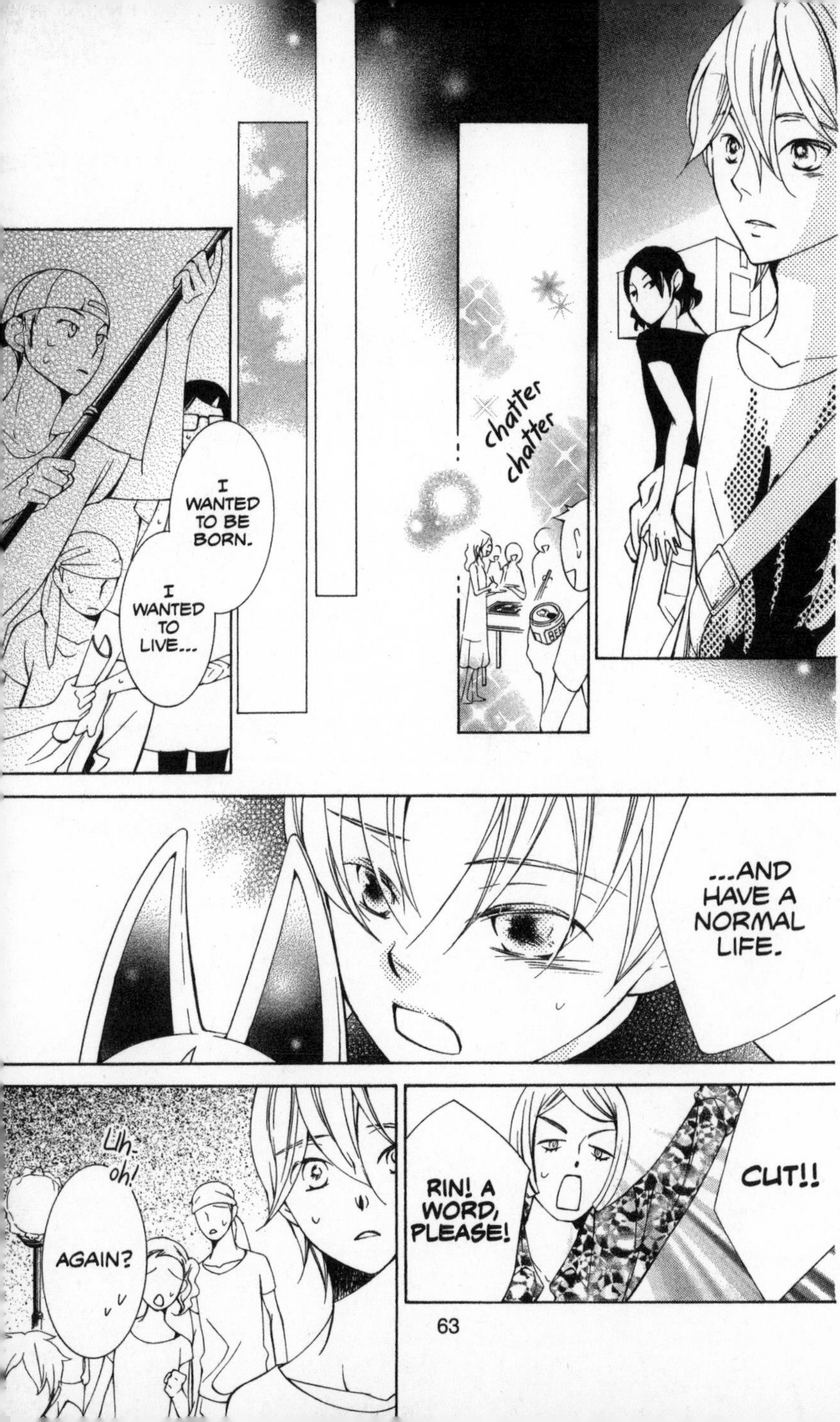
chatter chatter
I WANTED TO BE BORN.
I WANTED TO LIVE...
...AND HAVE A NORMAL LIFE.
CUT!!
RIN! A WORD, PLEASE!
Uh-oh!
AGAIN?

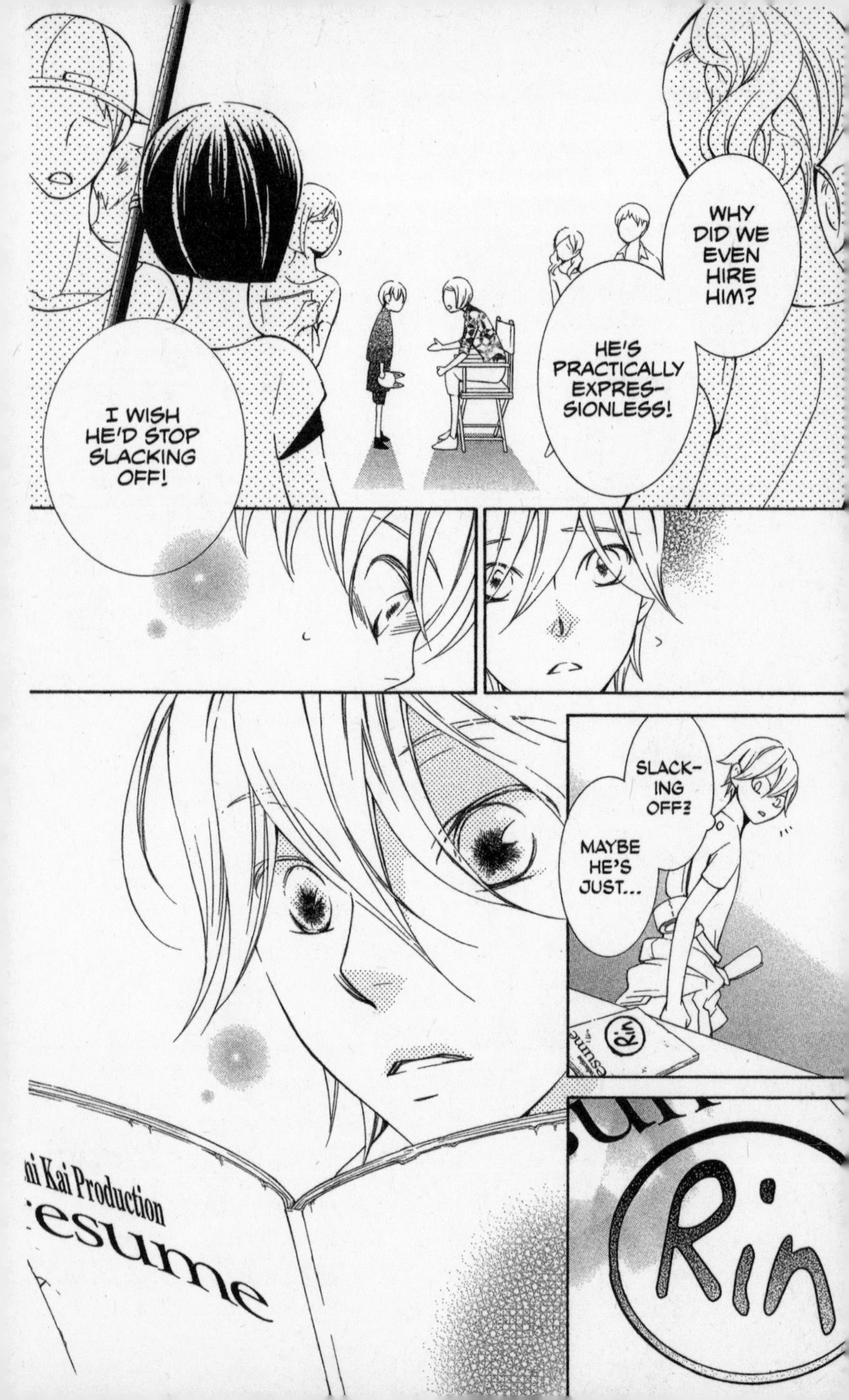
WHY DID WE EVEN HIRE HIM?
HE'S PRACTICALLY EXPRES-SIONLESS!
I WISH HE'D STOP SLACKING OFF!
SLACK-ING OFF?
MAYBE HE'S JUST...
Rin
ni Kai Production
esume
Rin

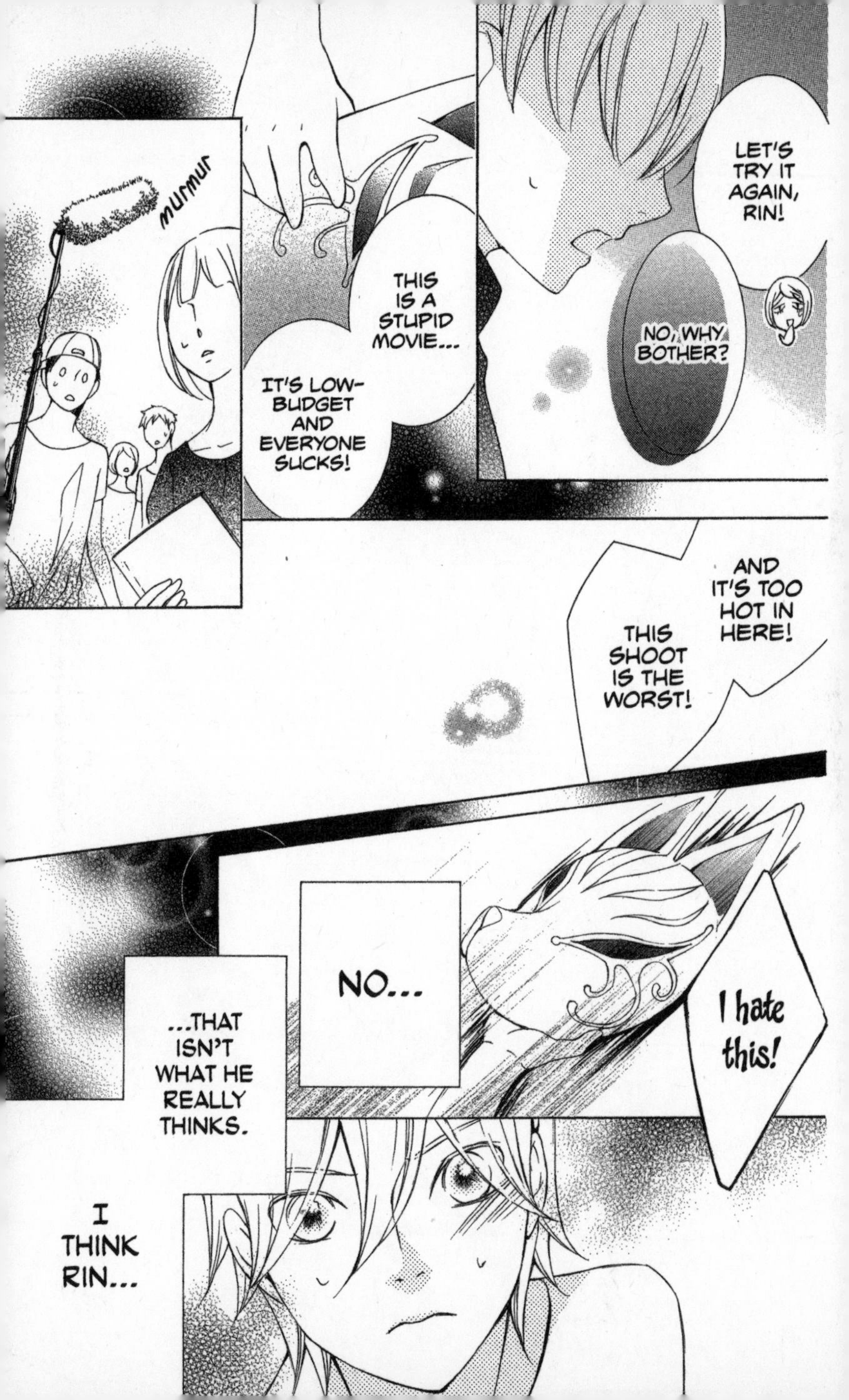
LET'S TRY IT AGAIN, RIN!
NO, WHY BOTHER?
THIS IS A STUPID MOVIE...
IT'S LOW-BUDGET AND EVERYONE SUCKS!
murmur
AND IT'S TOO HOT IN HERE!
THIS SHOOT IS THE WORST!
I hate this!
NO...
...THAT ISN'T WHAT HE REALLY THINKS.
I THINK RIN...

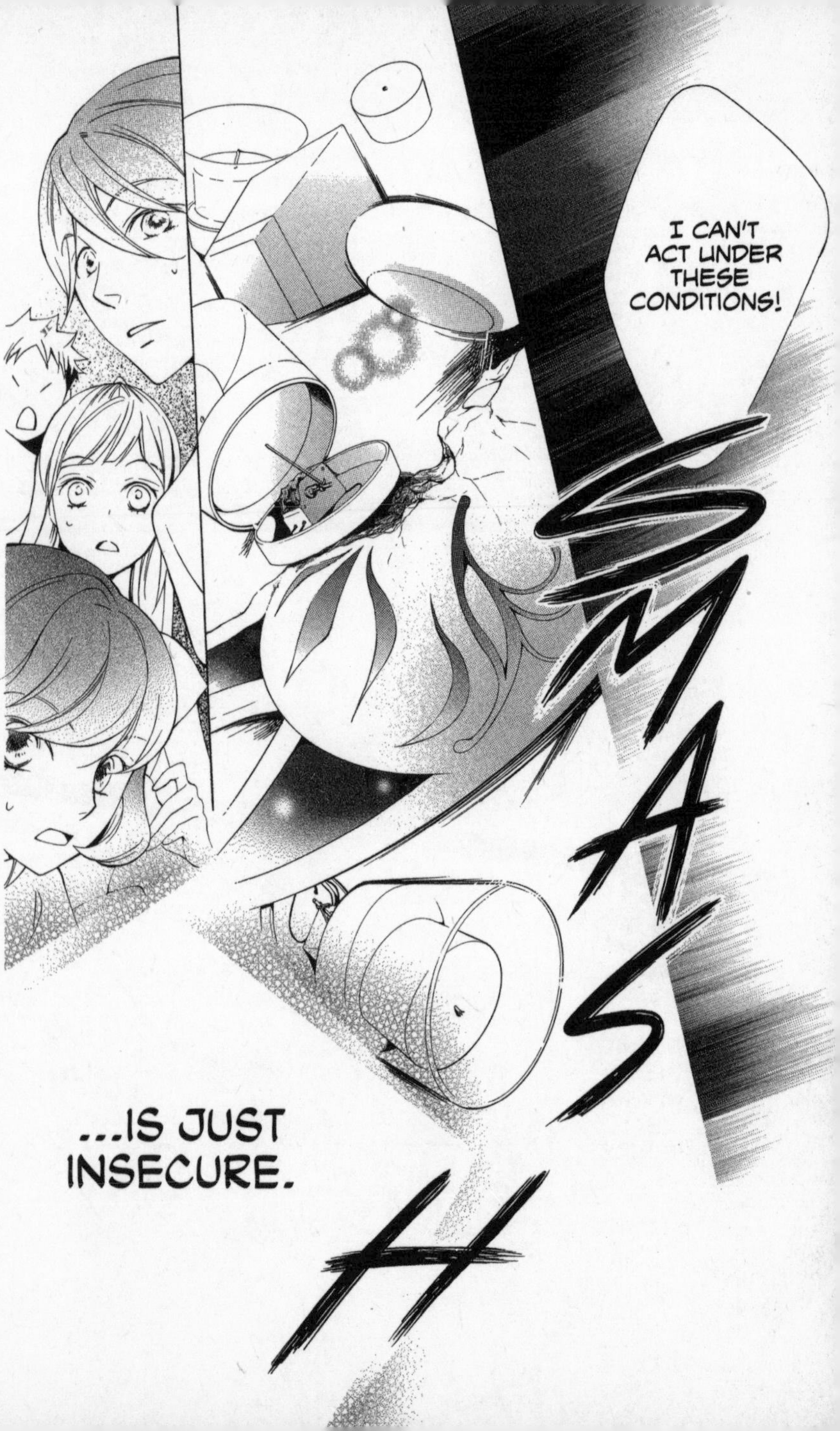
I CAN'T ACT UNDER THESE CONDITIONS!
SMASH
...IS JUST INSECURE.

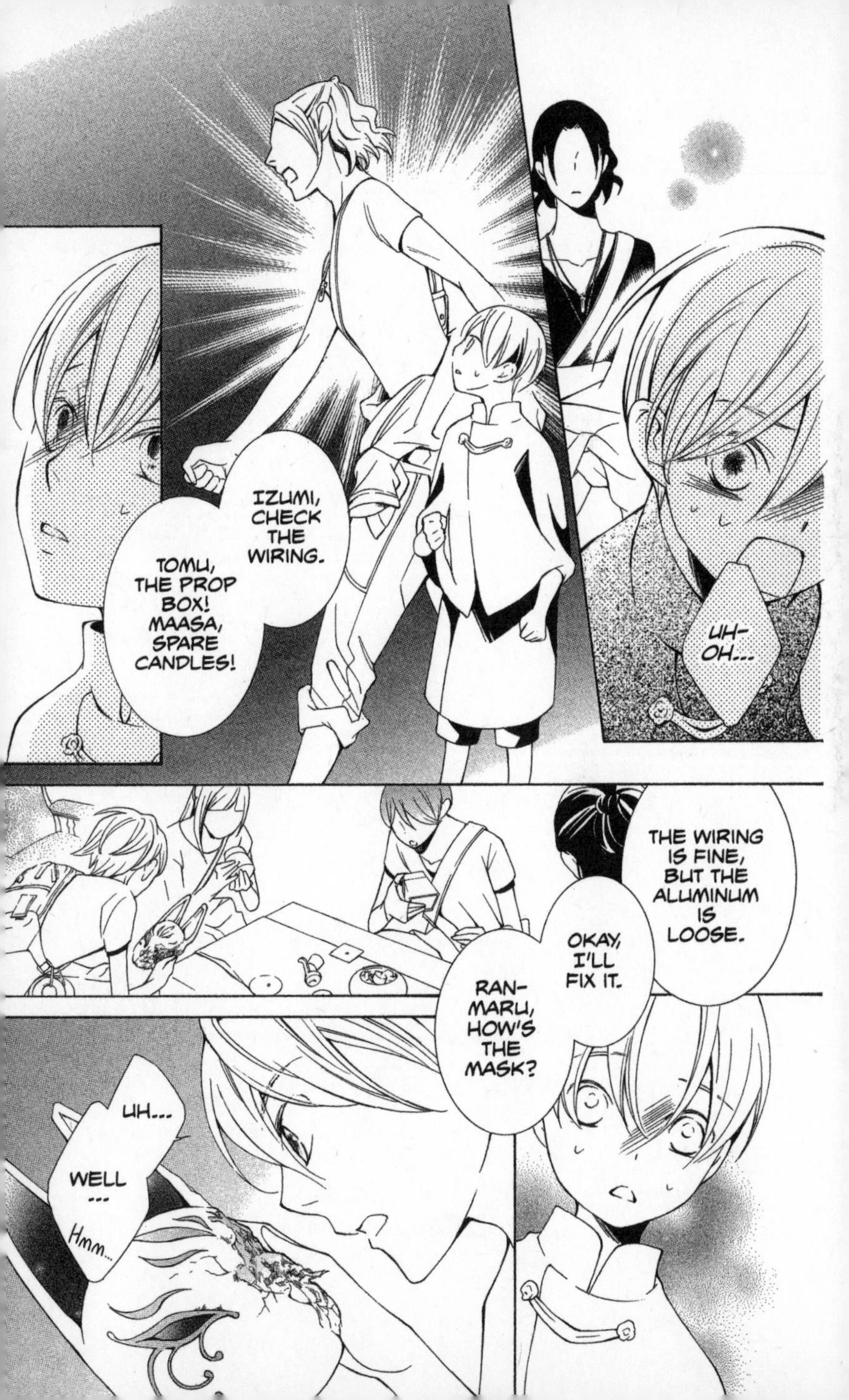
UH-OH...
IZUMI, CHECK THE WIRING.
TOMU, THE PROP BOX! MAASA, SPARE CANDLES!
THE WIRING IS FINE, BUT THE ALUMINUM IS LOOSE.
OKAY, I'LL FIX IT.
RAN-MARU, HOW'S THE MASK?
UH...
WELL...
Hmm...

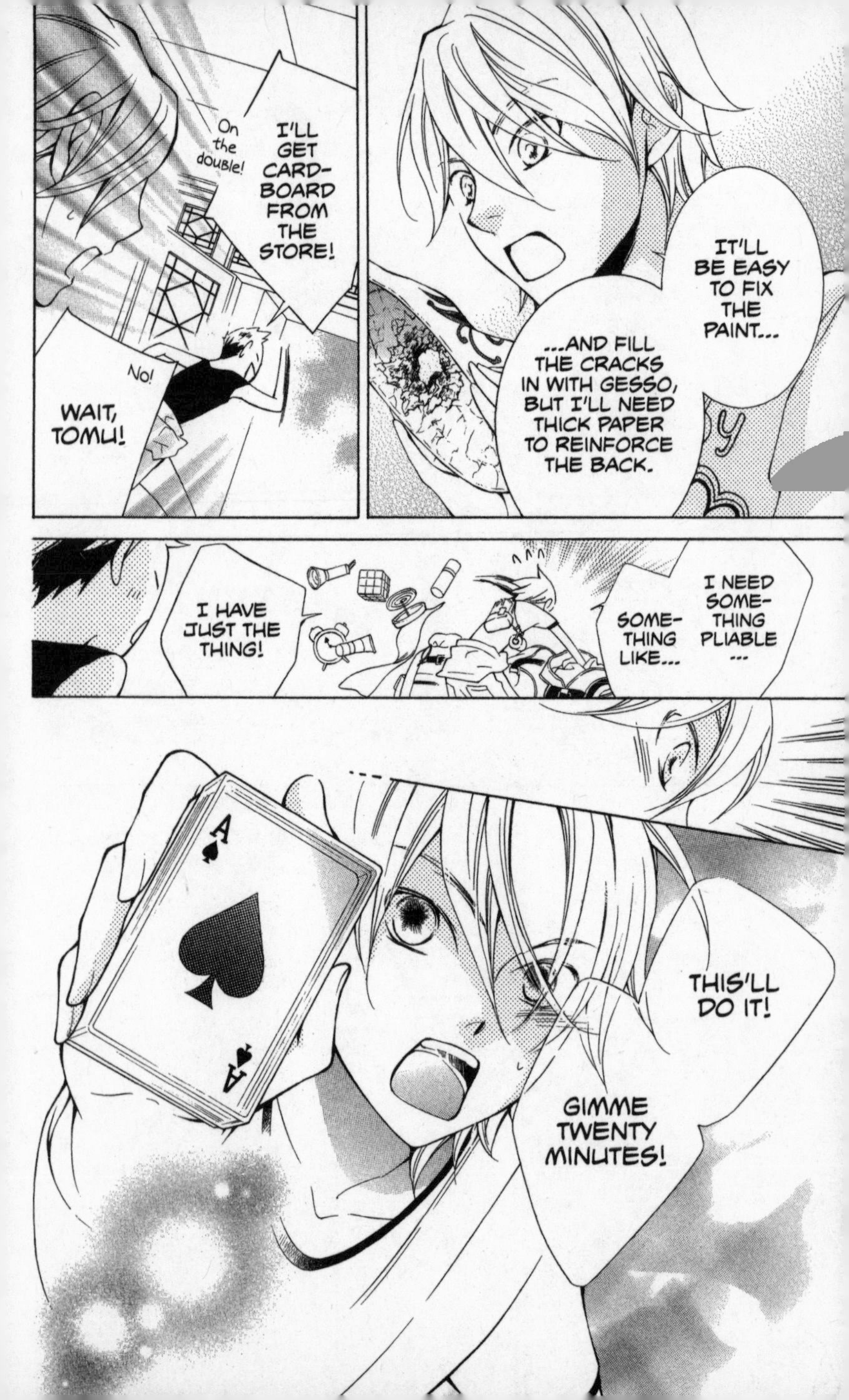
IT'LL BE EASY TO FIX THE PAINT...
...AND FILL THE CRACKS IN WITH GESSO, BUT I'LL NEED THICK PAPER TO REINFORCE THE BACK.
I'LL GET CARDBOARD FROM THE STORE!
On the double!
No!
WAIT, TOMU!
I NEED SOMETHING PLIABLE...
SOMETHING LIKE...
I HAVE JUST THE THING!
...
THIS'LL DO IT!
GIMME TWENTY MINUTES!

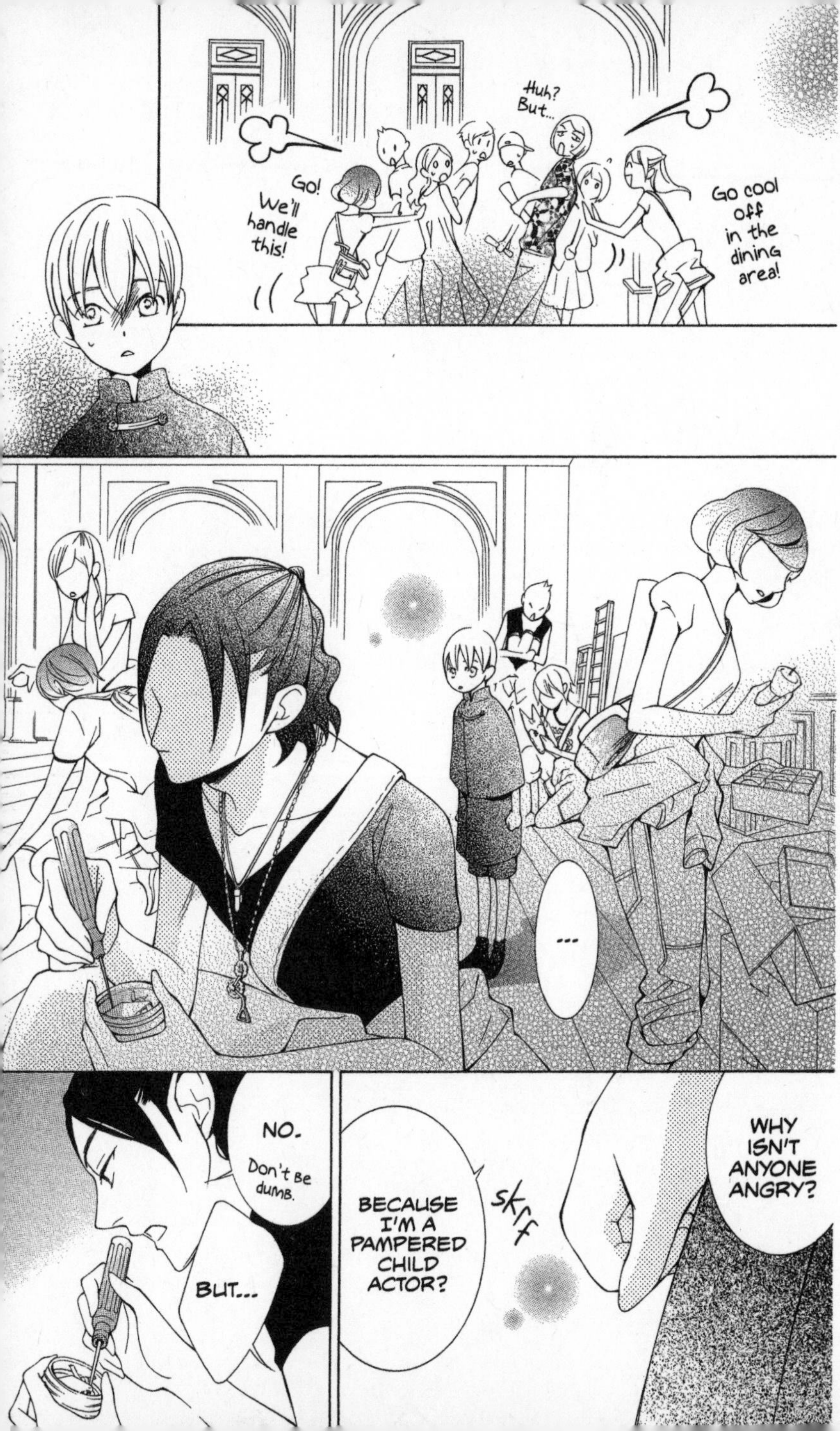
Go cool off in the dining area!
Huh? But...
Go! We'll handle this!
...
WHY ISN'T ANYONE ANGRY?
skff
BECAUSE I'M A PAMPERED CHILD ACTOR?
NO.
Don't be dumb.
BUT...

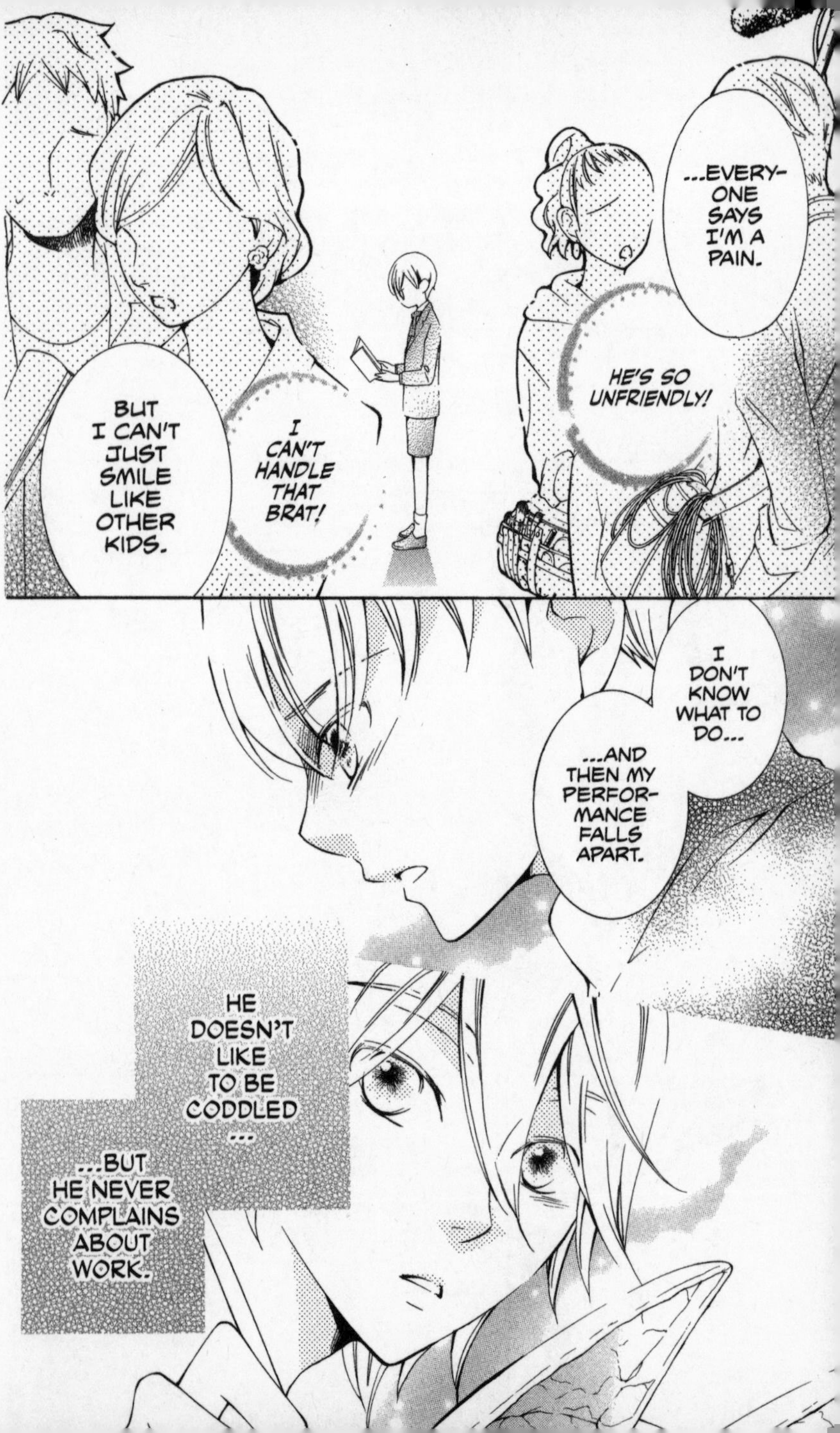
...EVERYONE SAYS I'M A PAIN.
HE'S SO UNFRIENDLY!
I CAN'T HANDLE THAT BRAT!
BUT I CAN'T JUST SMILE LIKE OTHER KIDS.
I DON'T KNOW WHAT TO DO...
...AND THEN MY PERFORMANCE FALLS APART.
HE DOESN'T LIKE TO BE CODDLED...
...BUT HE NEVER COMPLAINS ABOUT WORK.

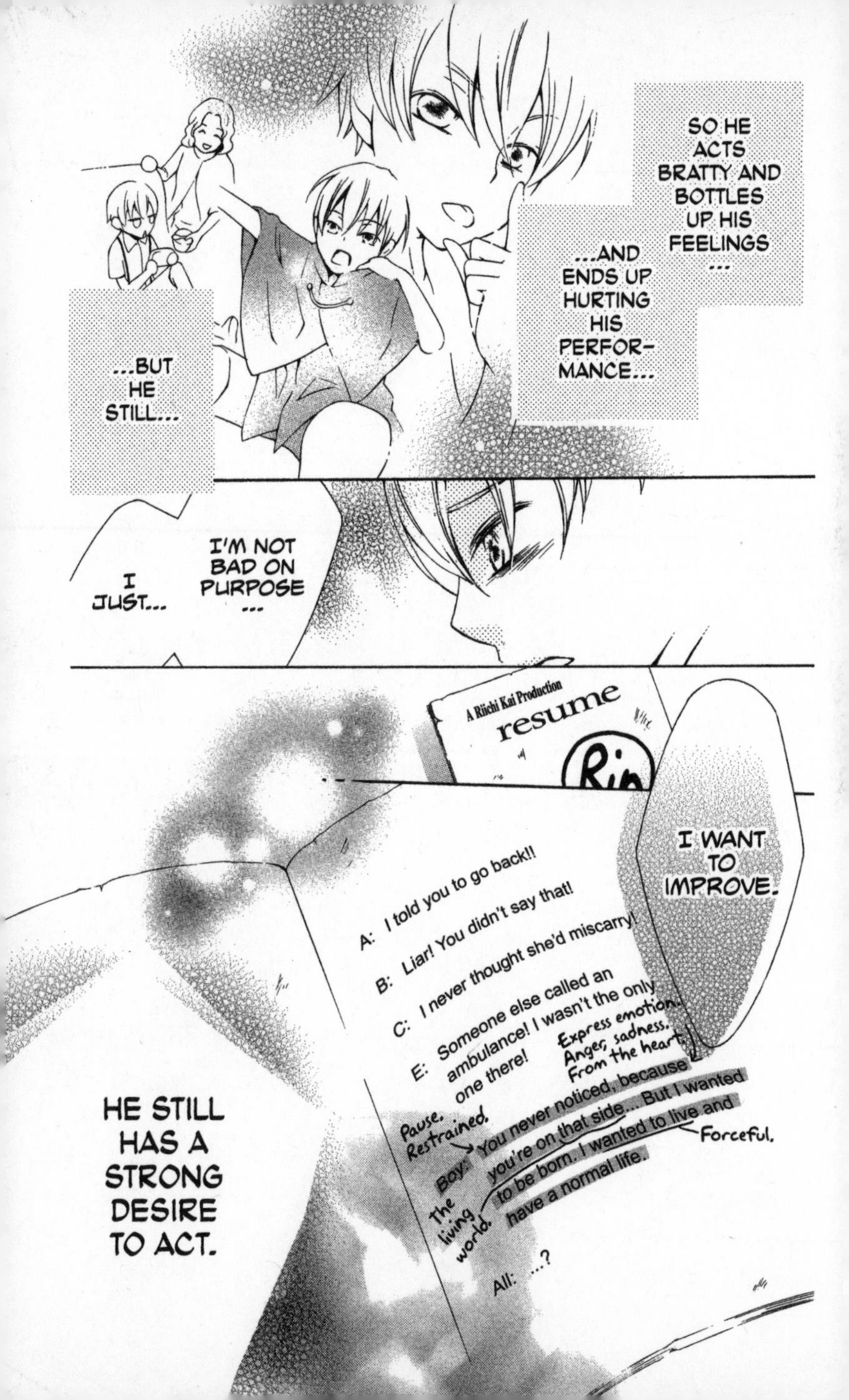
SO HE ACTS BRATTY AND BOTTLES UP HIS FEELINGS...
...AND ENDS UP HURTING HIS PERFORMANCE...
...BUT HE STILL...
I'M NOT BAD ON PURPOSE...
I JUST...
A Riichi Kai Production
resume
I WANT TO IMPROVE.
A: I told you to go back!!
B: Liar! You didn't say that!
C: I never thought she'd miscarry!
E: Someone else called an ambulance! I wasn't the only one there!
Express emotion. Anger, sadness. From the heart.
Pause. Restrained.
Boy: You never noticed, because you're on that side... But I wanted to be born. I wanted to live and have a normal life.
Forceful.
The living world.
All: ...?
HE STILL HAS A STRONG DESIRE TO ACT.

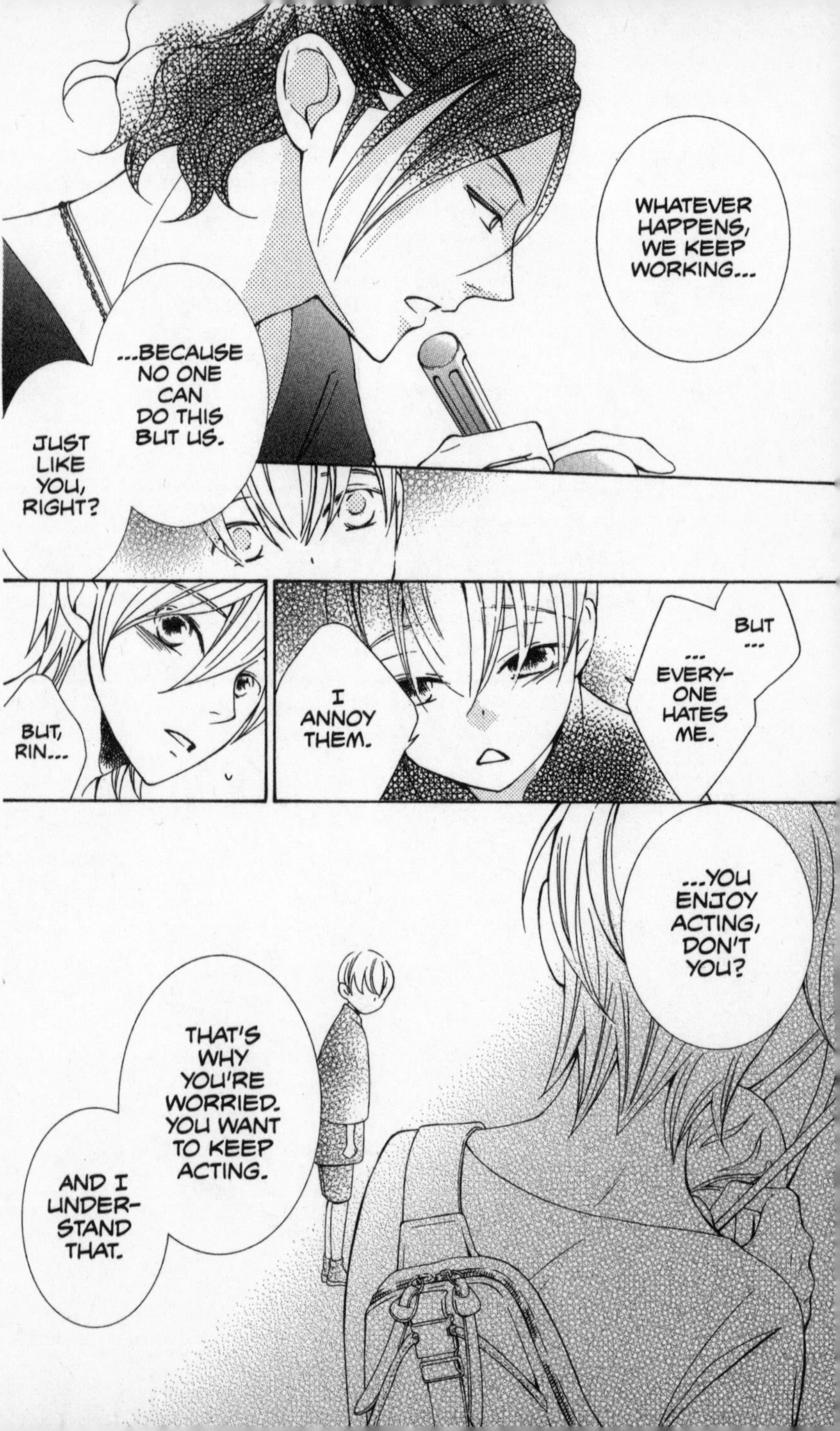
WHATEVER HAPPENS, WE KEEP WORKING...
...BECAUSE NO ONE CAN DO THIS BUT US.
JUST LIKE YOU, RIGHT?
BUT... ...EVERY-ONE HATES ME.
I ANNOY THEM.
BUT, RIN...
...YOU ENJOY ACTING, DON'T YOU?
THAT'S WHY YOU'RE WORRIED. YOU WANT TO KEEP ACTING.
AND I UNDER-STAND THAT.

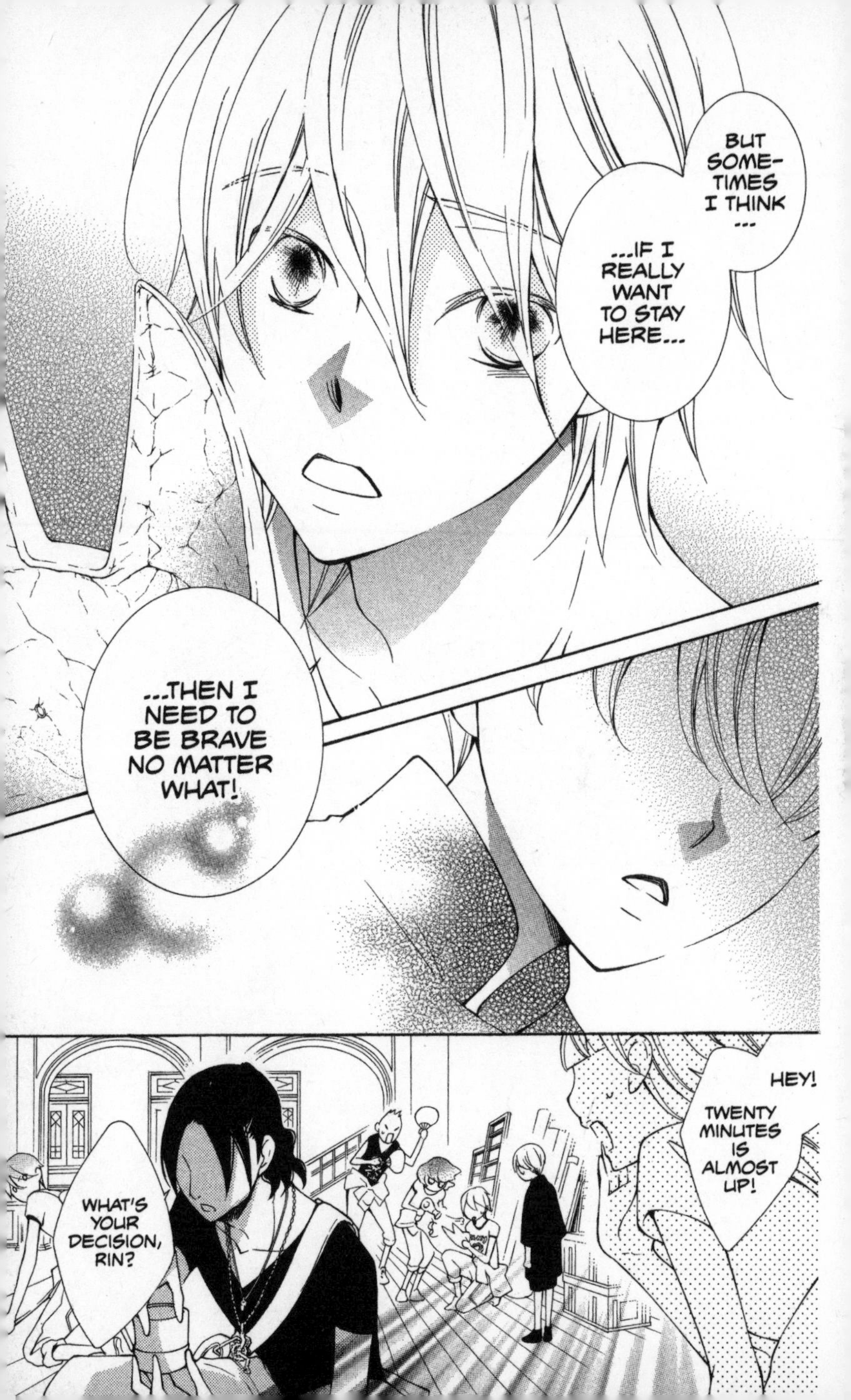
BUT SOMETIMES I THINK...
...IF I REALLY WANT TO STAY HERE...
...THEN I NEED TO BE BRAVE NO MATTER WHAT!
HEY!
TWENTY MINUTES IS ALMOST UP!
WHAT'S YOUR DECISION, RIN?

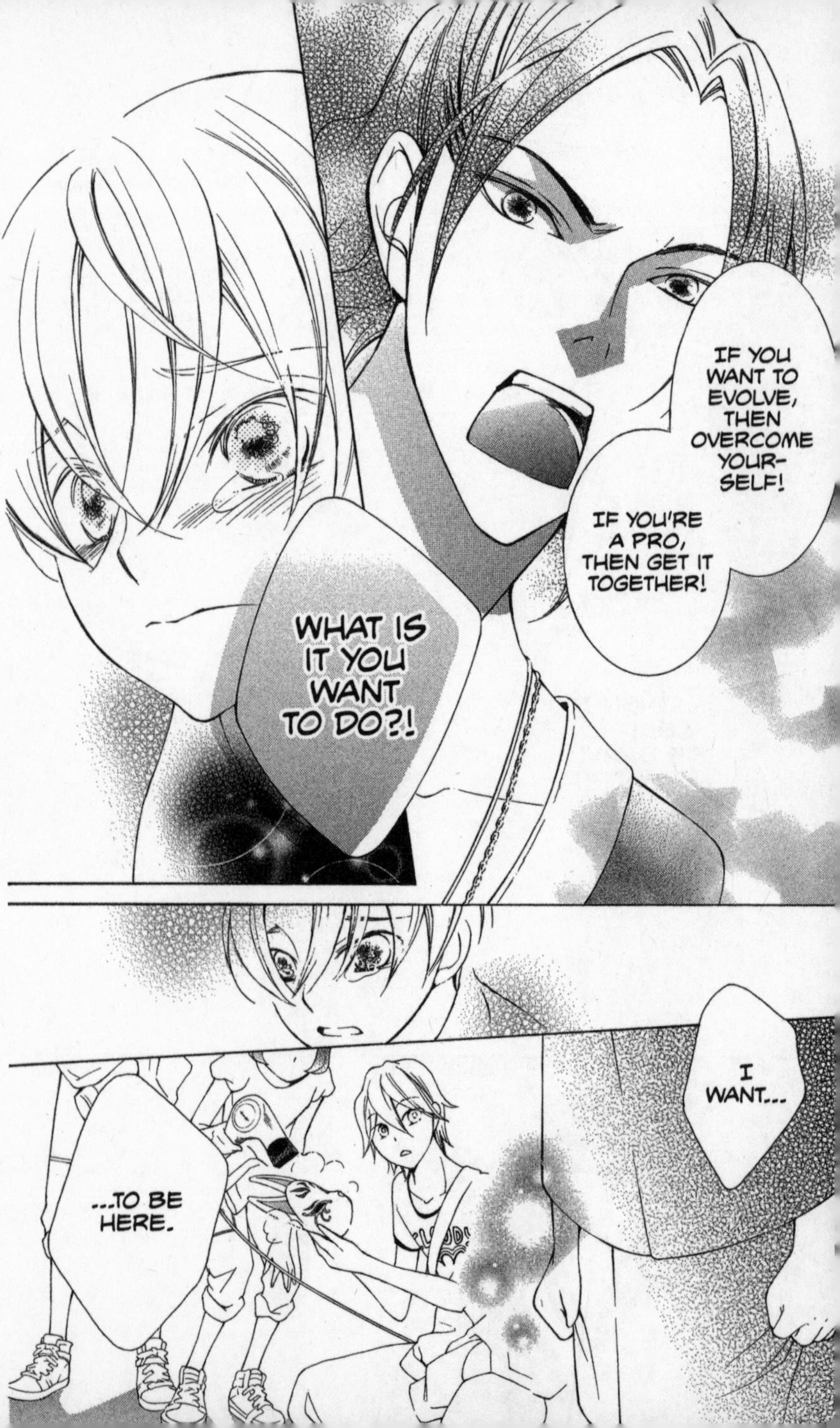
IF YOU WANT TO EVOLVE, THEN OVERCOME YOUR-SELF!
IF YOU'RE A PRO, THEN GET IT TOGETHER!
WHAT IS IT YOU WANT TO DO?!
I WANT...
...TO BE HERE.

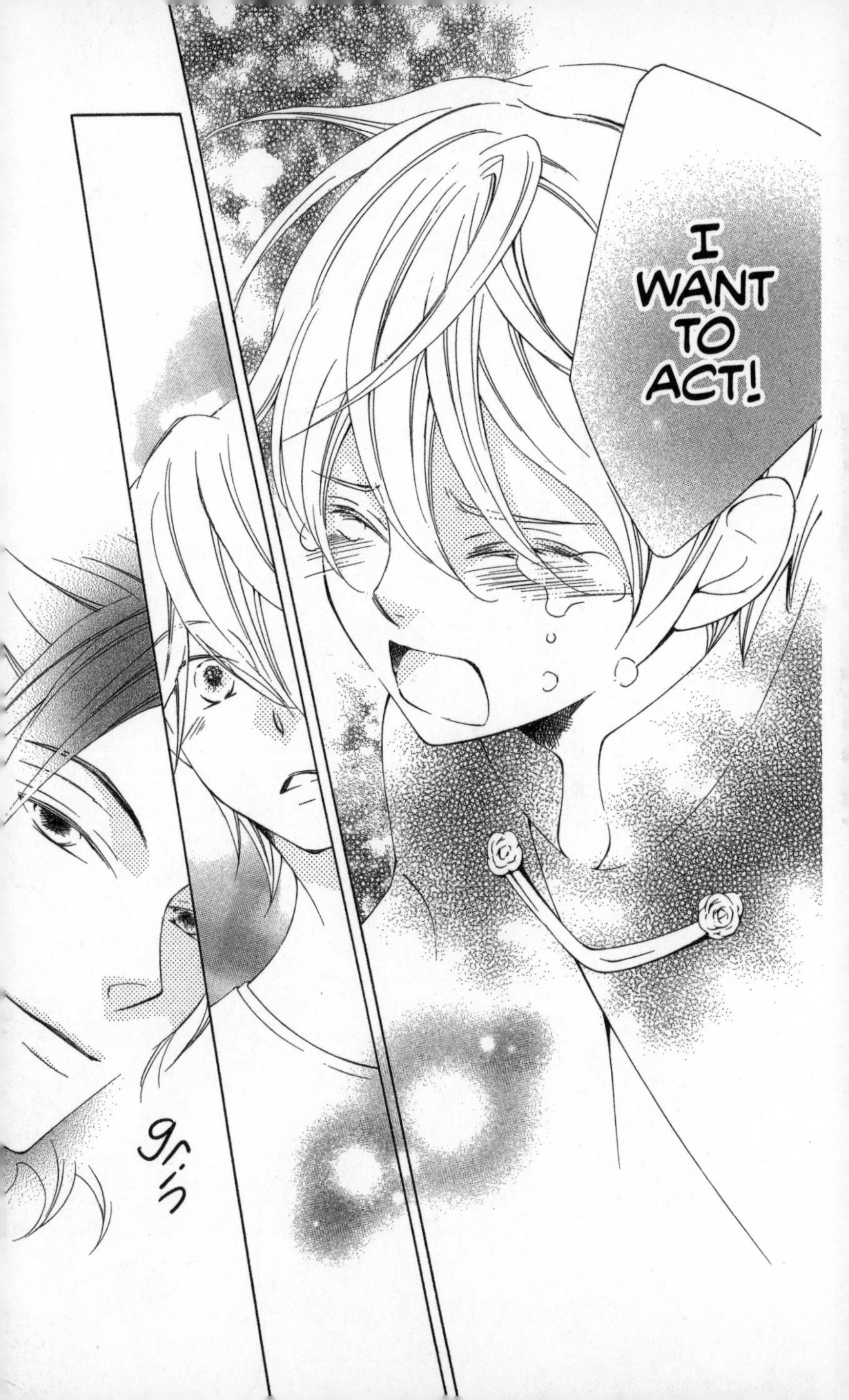
I WANT TO ACT!
grin

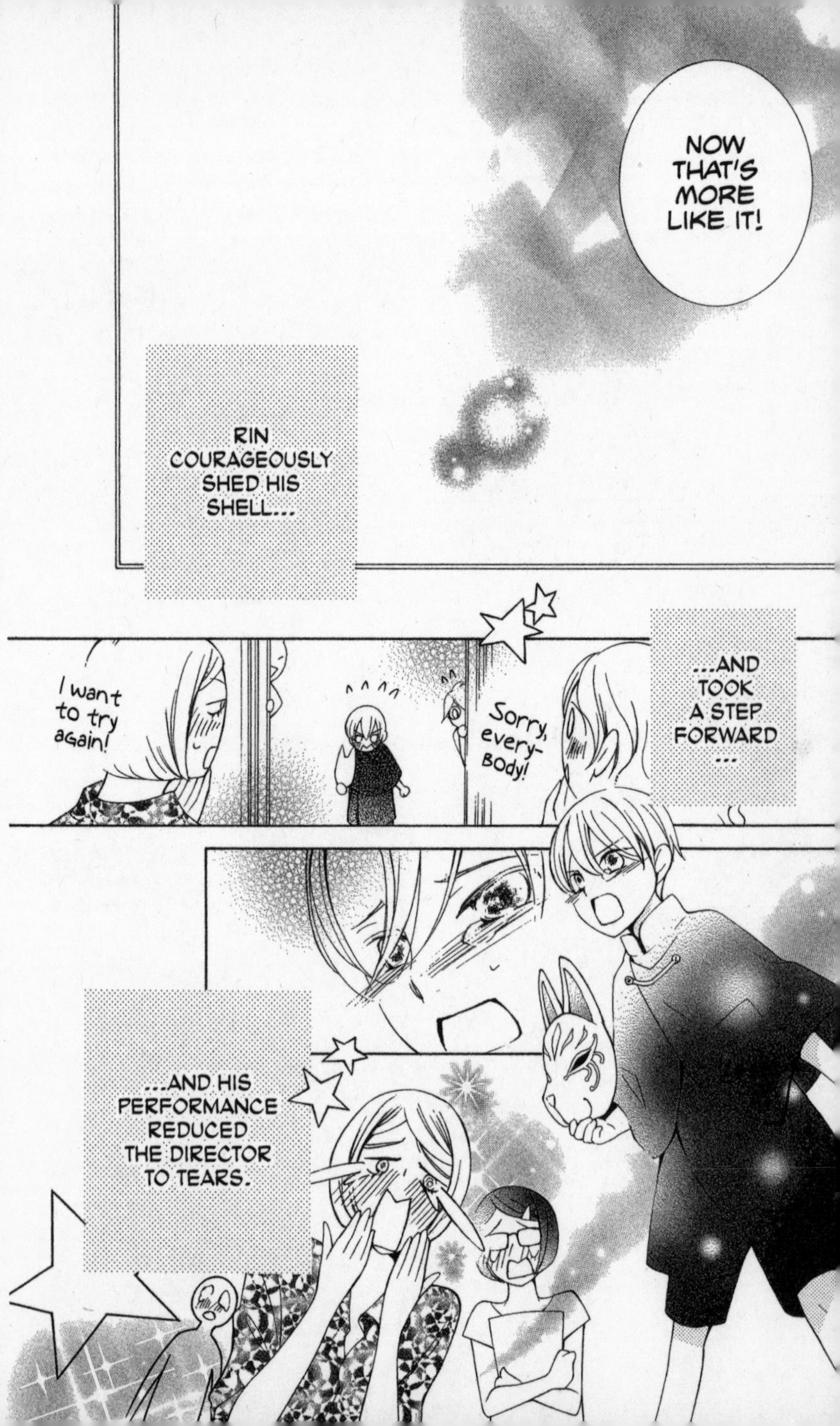
NOW THAT'S MORE LIKE IT!
RIN COURAGEOUSLY SHED HIS SHELL...
...AND TOOK A STEP FORWARD ...
Sorry, every-body!
I want to try again!
...AND HIS PERFORMANCE REDUCED THE DIRECTOR TO TEARS.

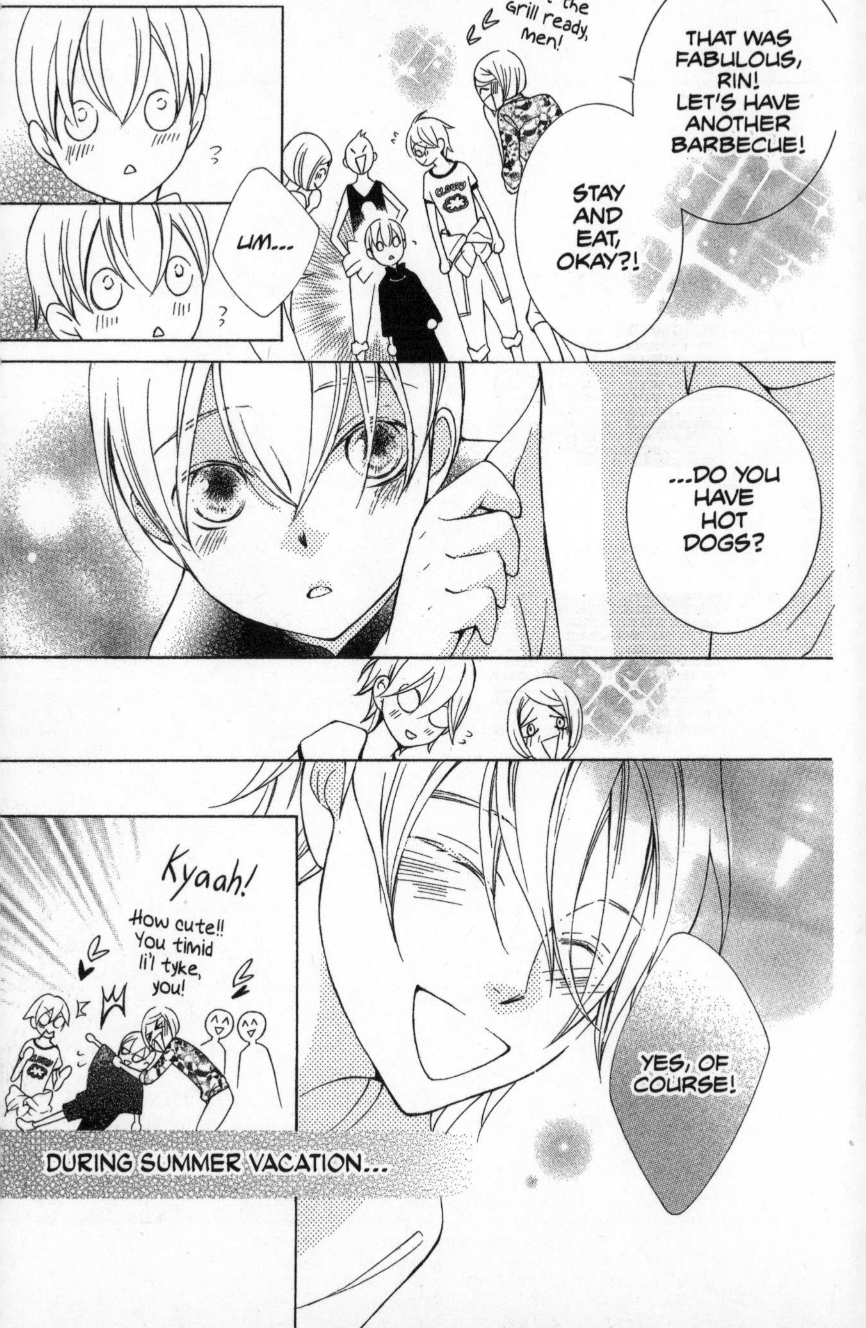
THAT WAS FABULOUS, RIN! LET'S HAVE ANOTHER BARBECUE!
Get the grill ready, men!
STAY AND EAT, OKAY?!
UM...
...DO YOU HAVE HOT DOGS?
YES, OF COURSE!
Kyaah!
How cute!! You timid li'l tyke, you!
DURING SUMMER VACATION...

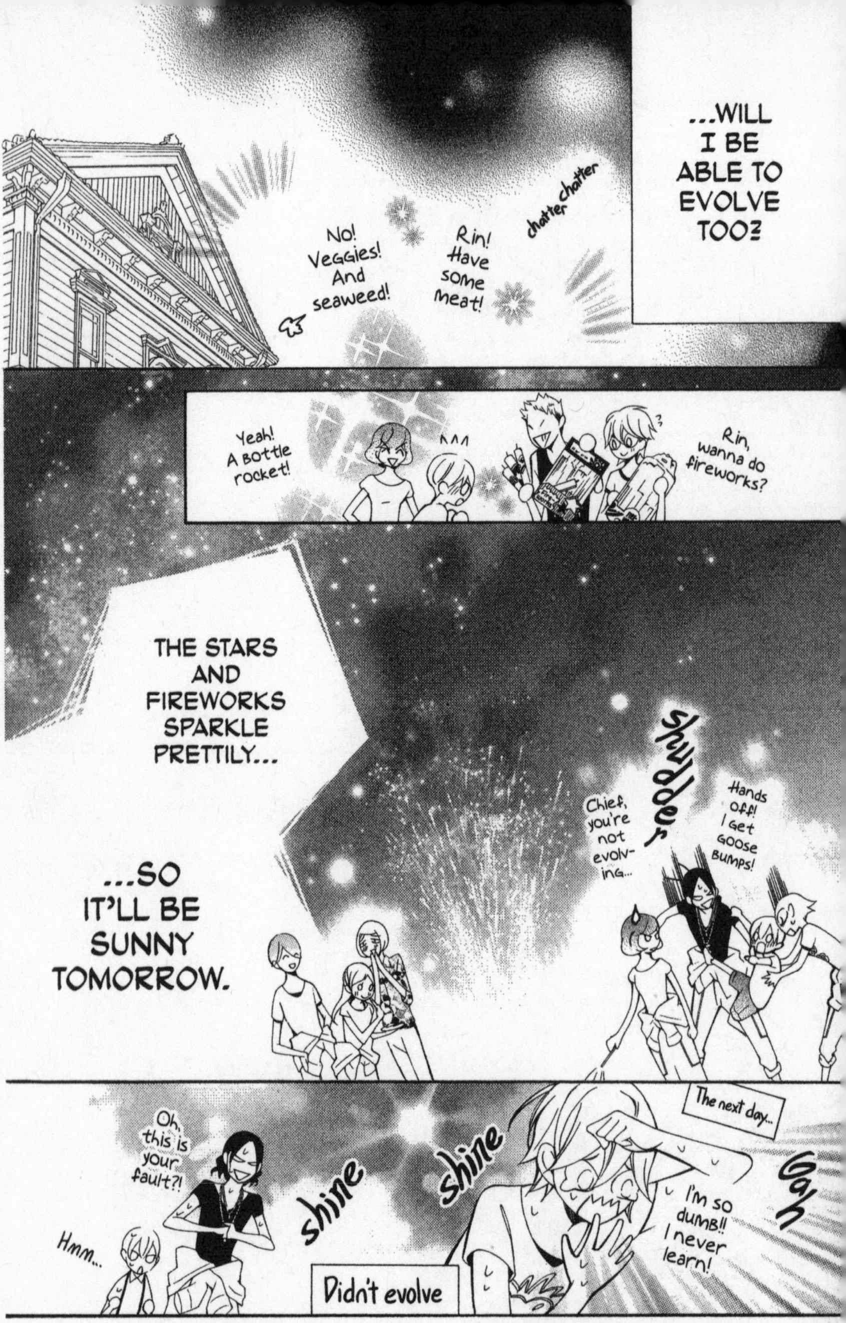
...WILL I BE ABLE TO EVOLVE TOO?
chatter chatter
Rin! Have some meat!
No! Veggies! And seaweed!
Rin, wanna do fireworks?
Yeah! A bottle rocket!
Hands off! I get goose bumps!
shudder
Chief, you're not evolv-ing...
THE STARS AND FIREWORKS SPARKLE PRETTILY...
...SO IT'LL BE SUNNY TOMORROW.
The next day...
Gah
I'm so dumb!! I never learn!
shine
shine
Oh, this is your fault?!
Hmm...
Didn't evolve

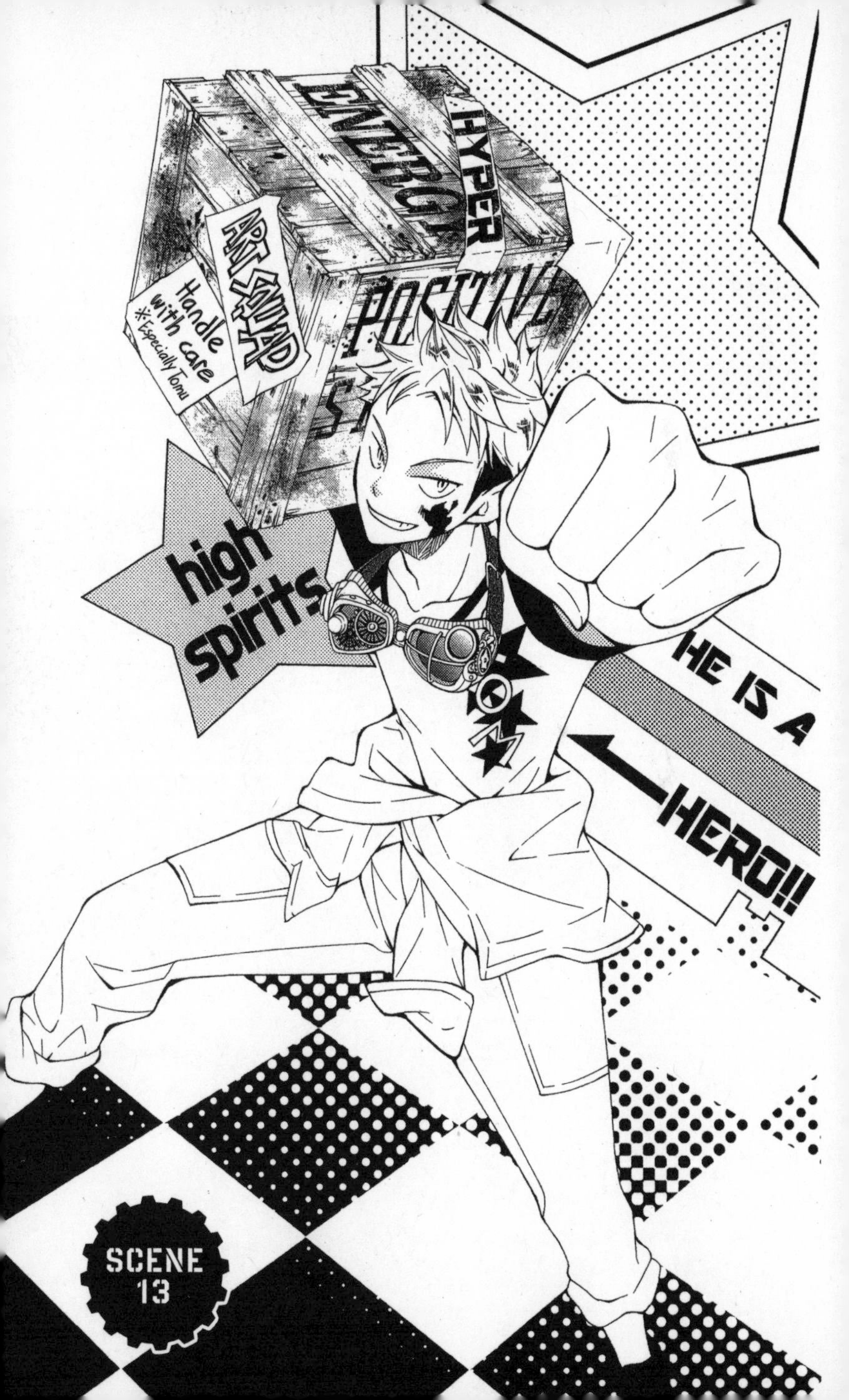
HYPER
ENERGY
POSITIVE
ART SQUAD
Handle with care
※Especially Tomu
high spirits
HE IS A
HERO!!
SCENE 13

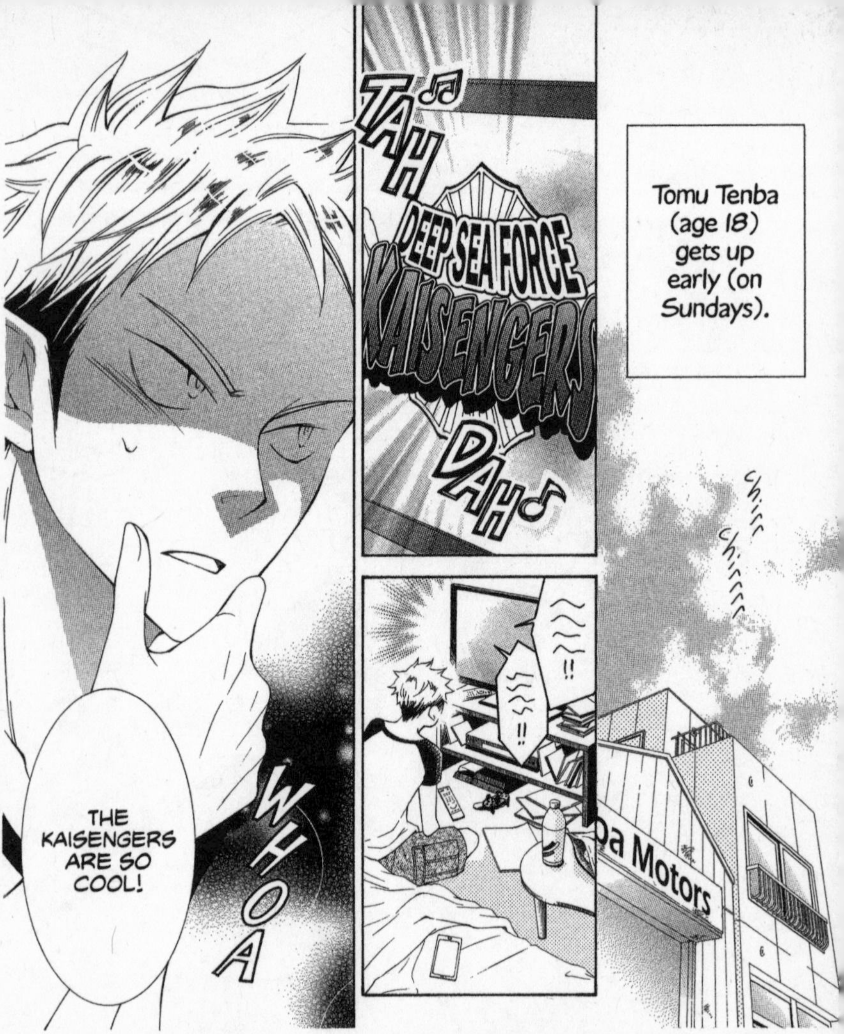
Tomu Tenba (age 18) gets up early (on Sundays).
chirrr chirrrr
TAH♪ DEEP SEA FORCE KAISENGERS DAH♪
~~~ !!
~~~ !!
WHOA
THE KAISENGERS ARE SO COOL!
pa Motors

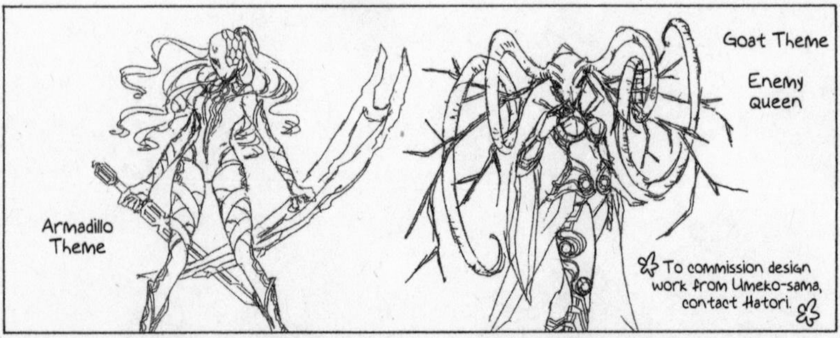
Goat Theme
Enemy Queen
Armadillo Theme
To commission design work from Umeko-sama, contact Hatori.

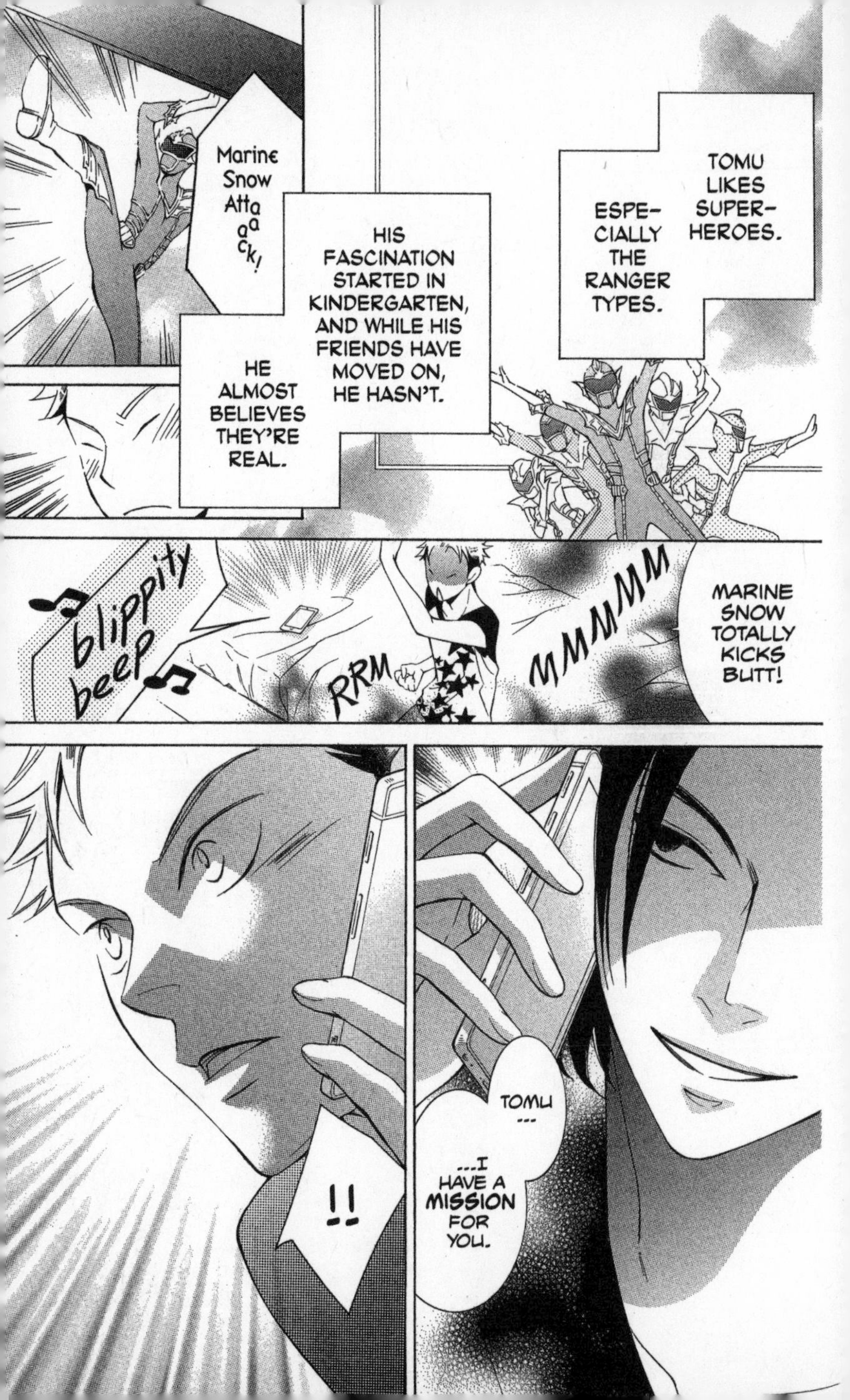
TOMU LIKES SUPER-HEROES.
ESPE-CIALLY THE RANGER TYPES.
HIS FASCINATION STARTED IN KINDERGARTEN, AND WHILE HIS FRIENDS HAVE MOVED ON, HE HASN'T.
HE ALMOST BELIEVES THEY'RE REAL.
Marine Snow Attaaack!
MARINE SNOW TOTALLY KICKS BUTT!
MMMMMM
RRM
blippity beep
TOMU...
...I HAVE A MISSION FOR YOU.
!!

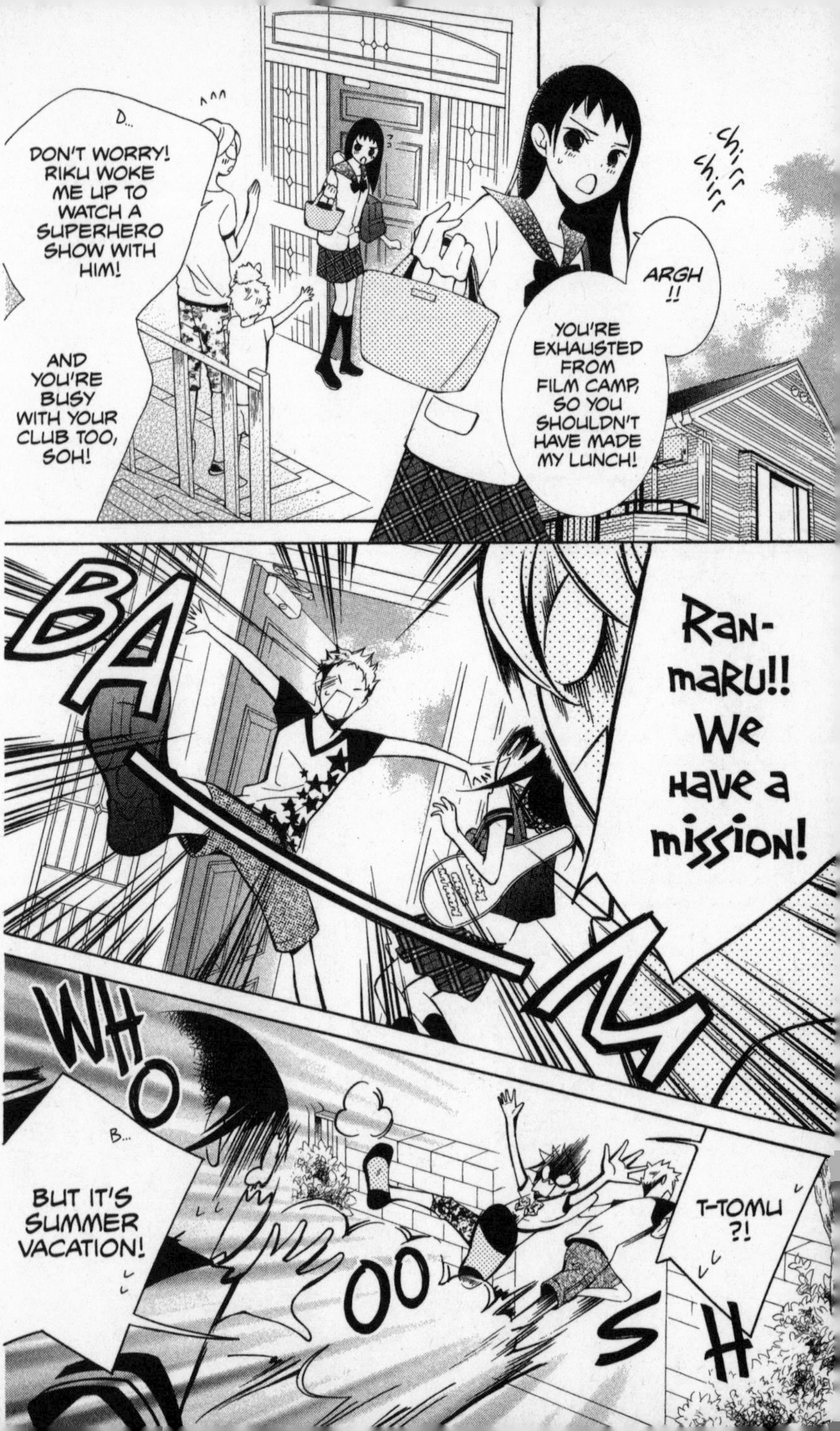
chirr chirr
ARGH!!
YOU'RE EXHAUSTED FROM FILM CAMP, SO YOU SHOULDN'T HAVE MADE MY LUNCH!
D... DON'T WORRY! RIKU WOKE ME UP TO WATCH A SUPERHERO SHOW WITH HIM!
AND YOU'RE BUSY WITH YOUR CLUB TOO, SOH!
Ran-maru!! We have a mission!
BAM
T-TOMU?!
B... BUT IT'S SUMMER VACATION!
WHOOSH

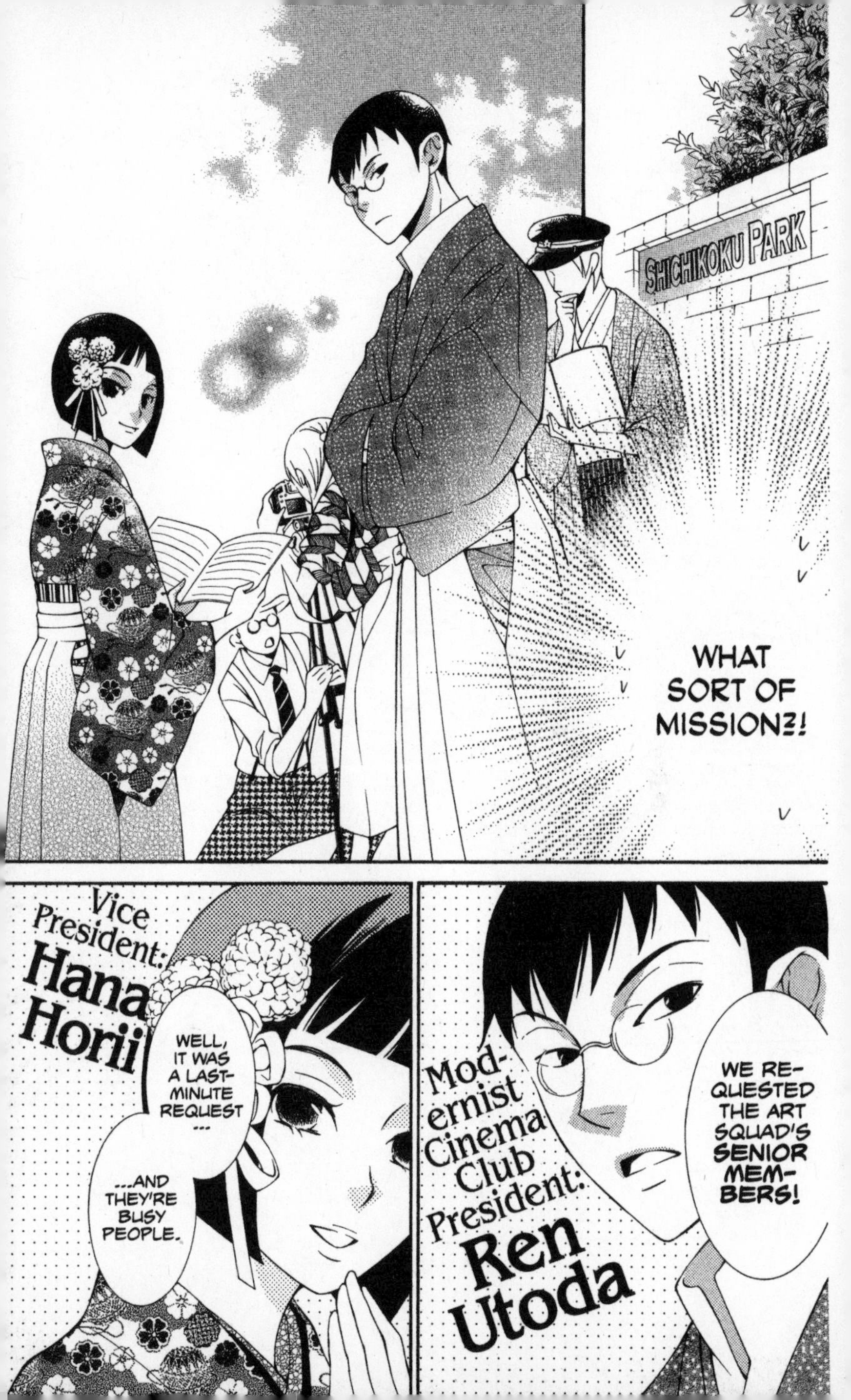
SHICHIKOKU PARK
WHAT SORT OF MISSION?!
Modernist Cinema Club President: Ren Utoda
WE REQUESTED THE ART SQUAD'S SENIOR MEMBERS!
Vice President: Hana Horii
WELL, IT WAS A LAST-MINUTE REQUEST...
...AND THEY'RE BUSY PEOPLE.

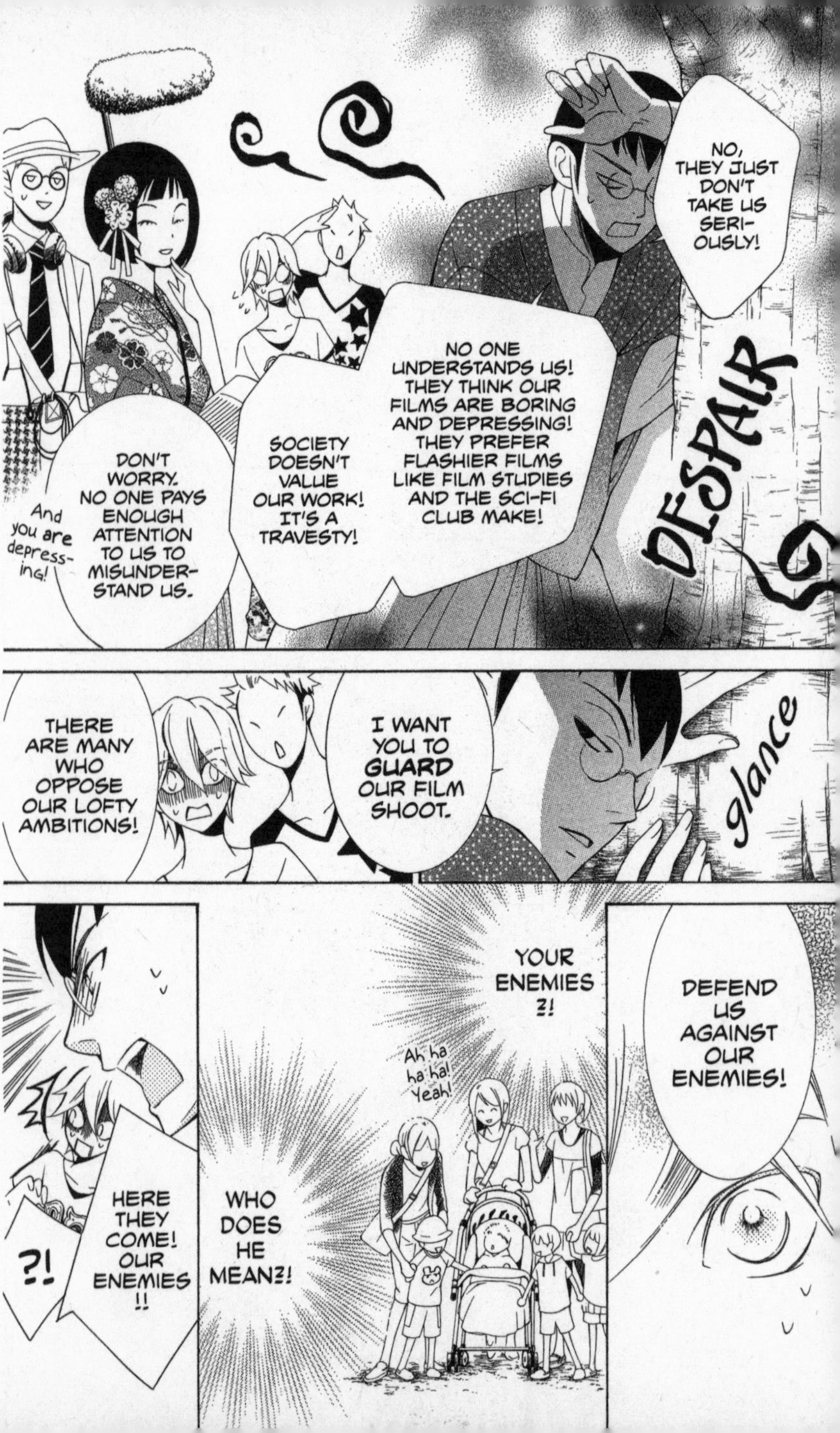
NO, THEY JUST DON'T TAKE US SERI-OUSLY!
DESPAIR
NO ONE UNDERSTANDS US! THEY THINK OUR FILMS ARE BORING AND DEPRESSING! THEY PREFER FLASHIER FILMS LIKE FILM STUDIES AND THE SCI-FI CLUB MAKE!
SOCIETY DOESN'T VALUE OUR WORK! IT'S A TRAVESTY!
DON'T WORRY. NO ONE PAYS ENOUGH ATTENTION TO US TO MISUNDER-STAND US.
And you are depress-ing!
glance
I WANT YOU TO GUARD OUR FILM SHOOT.
THERE ARE MANY WHO OPPOSE OUR LOFTY AMBITIONS!
DEFEND US AGAINST OUR ENEMIES!
YOUR ENEMIES ?!
Ah ha ha ha! Yeah!
WHO DOES HE MEAN?!
HERE THEY COME! OUR ENEMIES !!
?!

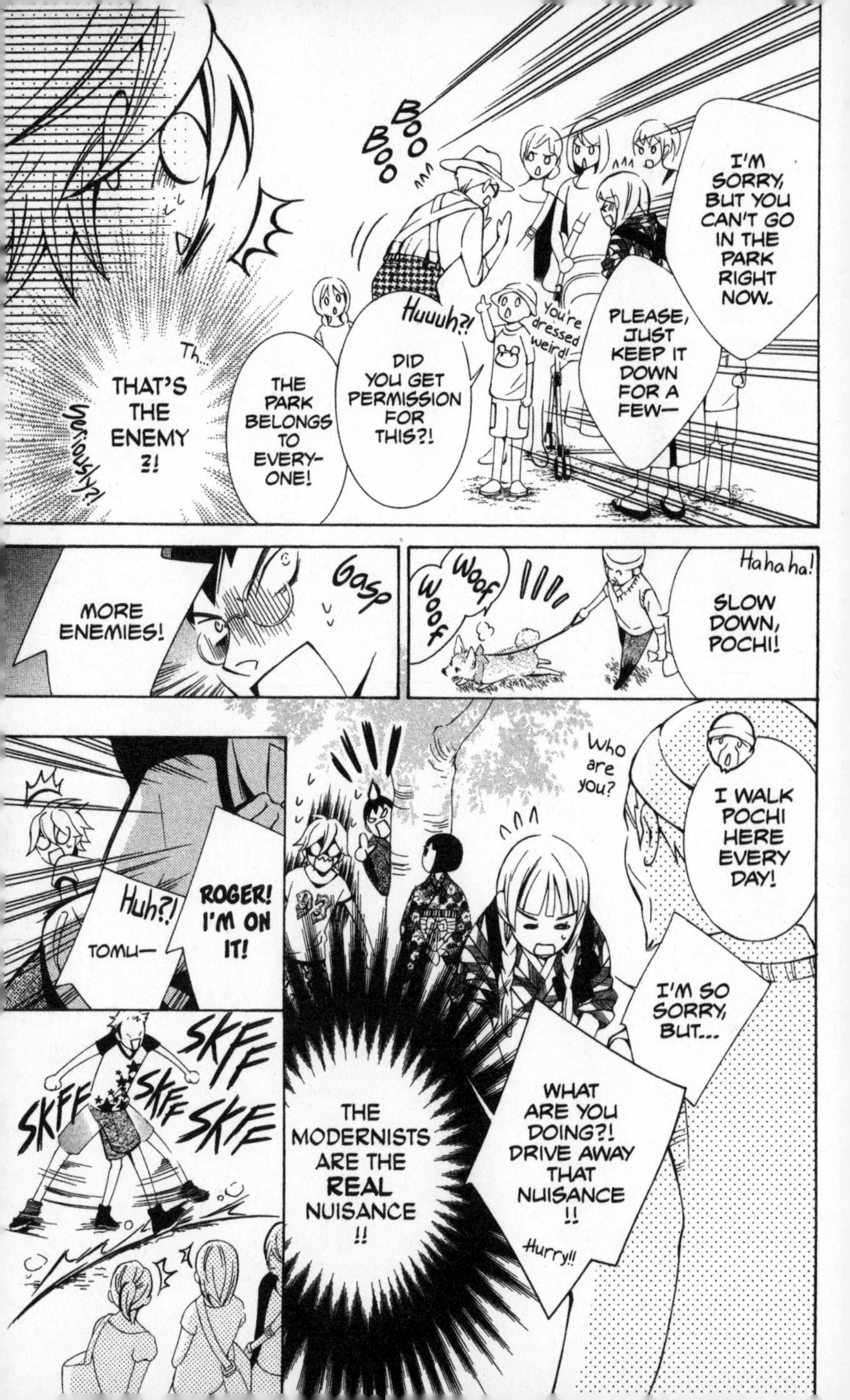
BOO BOO
I'M SORRY, BUT YOU CAN'T GO IN THE PARK RIGHT NOW.
PLEASE, JUST KEEP IT DOWN FOR A FEW—
You're dressed weird!
Huuuh?!
DID YOU GET PERMISSION FOR THIS?!
THE PARK BELONGS TO EVERY-ONE!
Th...
THAT'S THE ENEMY ?!
Seriously?!
Hahaha!
SLOW DOWN, POCHI!
Woof Woof
Gasp
MORE ENEMIES!
Who are you?
I WALK POCHI HERE EVERY DAY!
I'M SO SORRY, BUT...
WHAT ARE YOU DOING?! DRIVE AWAY THAT NUISANCE !!
Hurry!!
THE MODERNISTS ARE THE REAL NUISANCE !!
ROGER! I'M ON IT!
Huh?!
TOMU—
SKFF SKFF SKFF SKFF

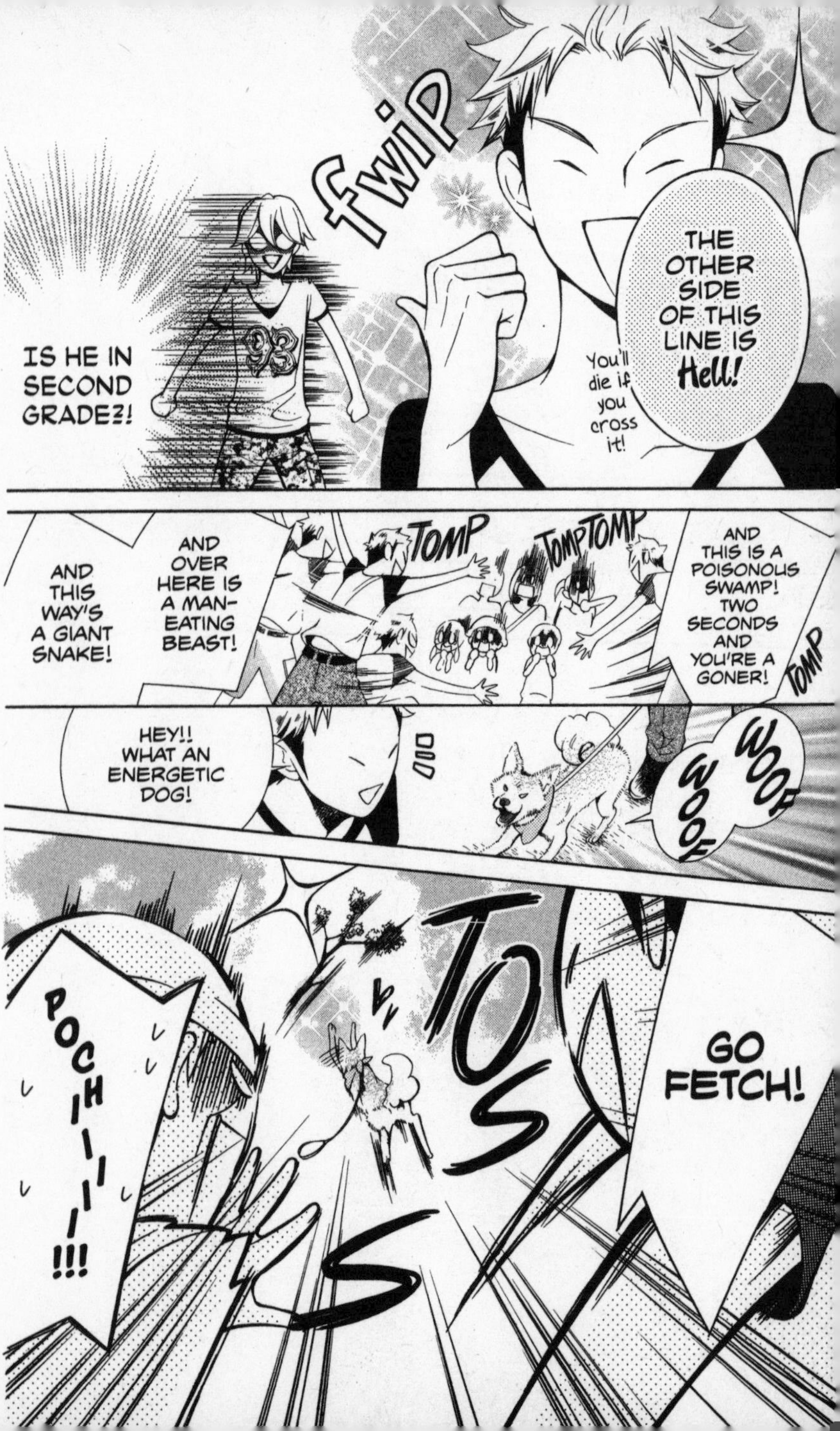
fwip
THE OTHER SIDE OF THIS LINE IS Hell!
You'll die if you cross it!
IS HE IN SECOND GRADE?!
AND THIS IS A POISONOUS SWAMP! TWO SECONDS AND YOU'RE A GONER!
TOMP
TOMPTOMP
TOMP
AND OVER HERE IS A MAN-EATING BEAST!
AND THIS WAY'S A GIANT SNAKE!
WOOF WOOF
HEY!! WHAT AN ENERGETIC DOG!
GO FETCH!
TOSS
POCHI-I-I-I!!!

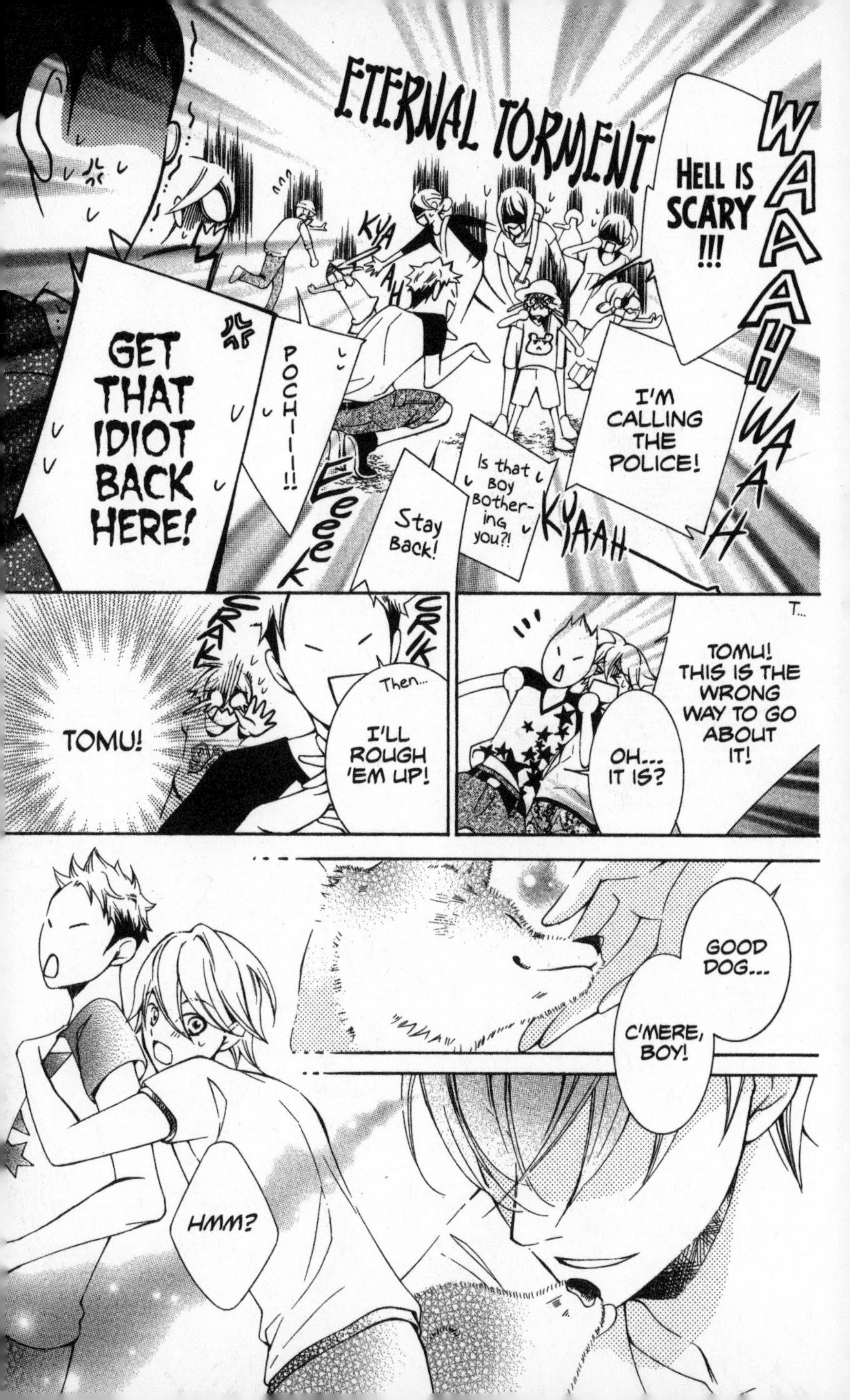
WAAAAHWAAH
HELL IS SCARY !!!
ETERNAL TORMENT
I'M CALLING THE POLICE!
KYAAH
KYAAH
Is that boy bothering you?!
Stay back!
POCHI---!!
Eeeek
GET THAT IDIOT BACK HERE!
T...
TOMU! THIS IS THE WRONG WAY TO GO ABOUT IT!
OH... IT IS?
CRIK
Then...
I'LL ROUGH 'EM UP!
CRAK
TOMU!
GOOD DOG...
C'MERE, BOY!
HMM?

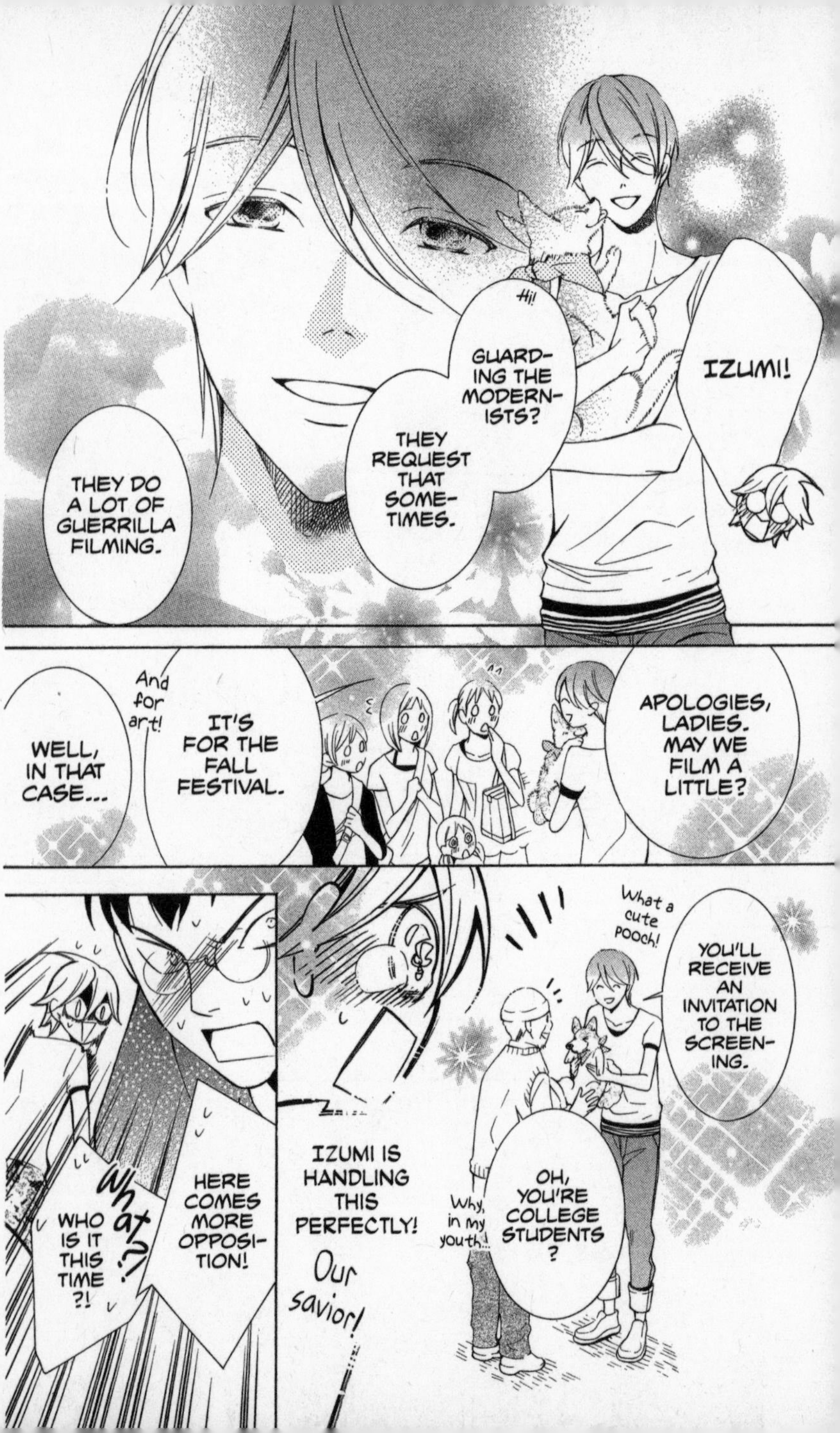
IZUMI!
Hi!
GUARDING THE MODERNISTS?
THEY REQUEST THAT SOMETIMES.
THEY DO A LOT OF GUERRILLA FILMING.
APOLOGIES, LADIES. MAY WE FILM A LITTLE?
IT'S FOR THE FALL FESTIVAL.
And for art!
WELL, IN THAT CASE...
What a cute pooch!
YOU'LL RECEIVE AN INVITATION TO THE SCREENING.
OH, YOU'RE COLLEGE STUDENTS?
Why, in my youth...
IZUMI IS HANDLING THIS PERFECTLY!
Our savior!
HERE COMES MORE OPPOSITION!
What?!
WHO IS IT THIS TIME?!

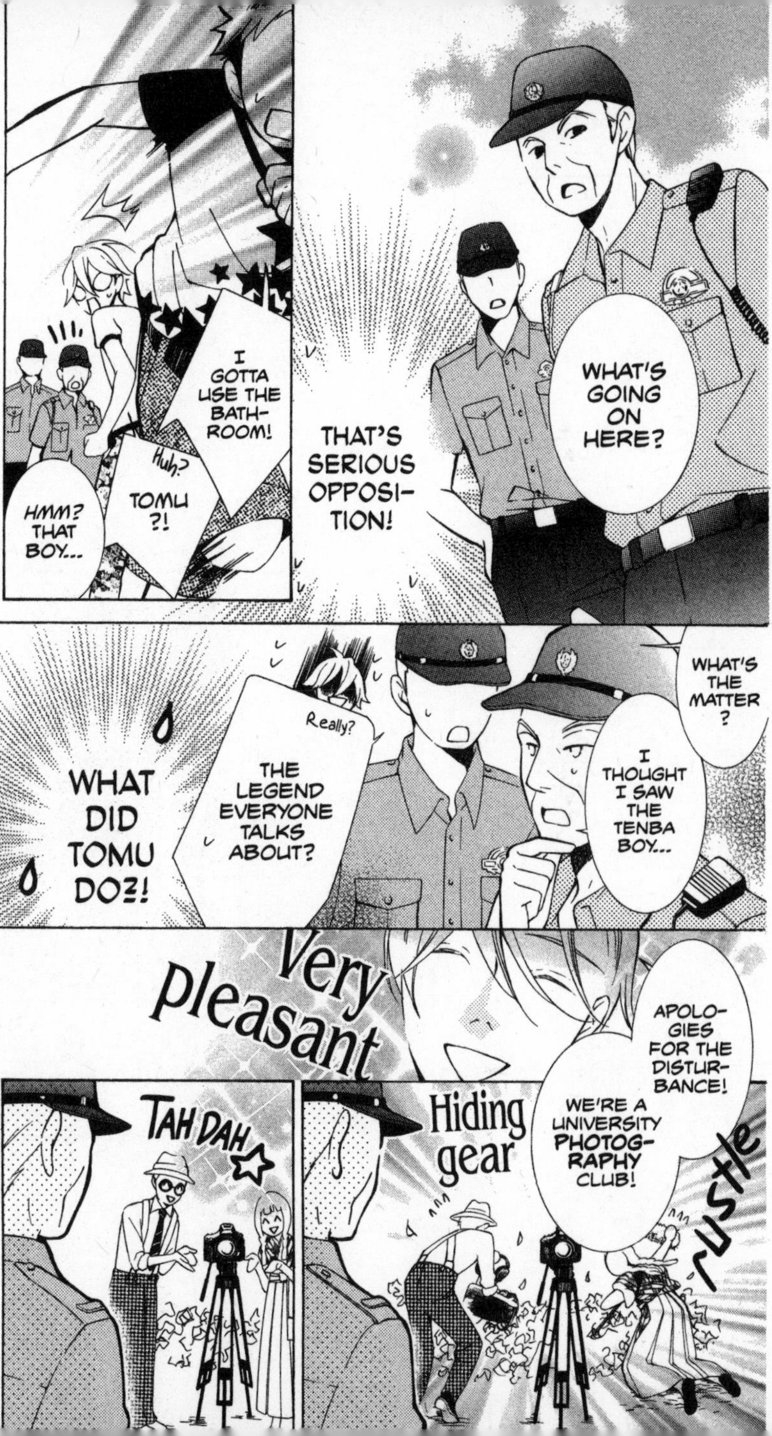
WHAT'S GOING ON HERE?
THAT'S SERIOUS OPPOSITION!
I GOTTA USE THE BATHROOM!
Huh?
TOMU?!
HMM? THAT BOY...
WHAT'S THE MATTER?
I THOUGHT I SAW THE TENBA BOY...
Really?
THE LEGEND EVERYONE TALKS ABOUT?
WHAT DID TOMU DO?!
APOLOGIES FOR THE DISTURBANCE!
Very pleasant
WE'RE A UNIVERSITY PHOTOGRAPHY CLUB!
rustle
Hiding gear
TAH DAH

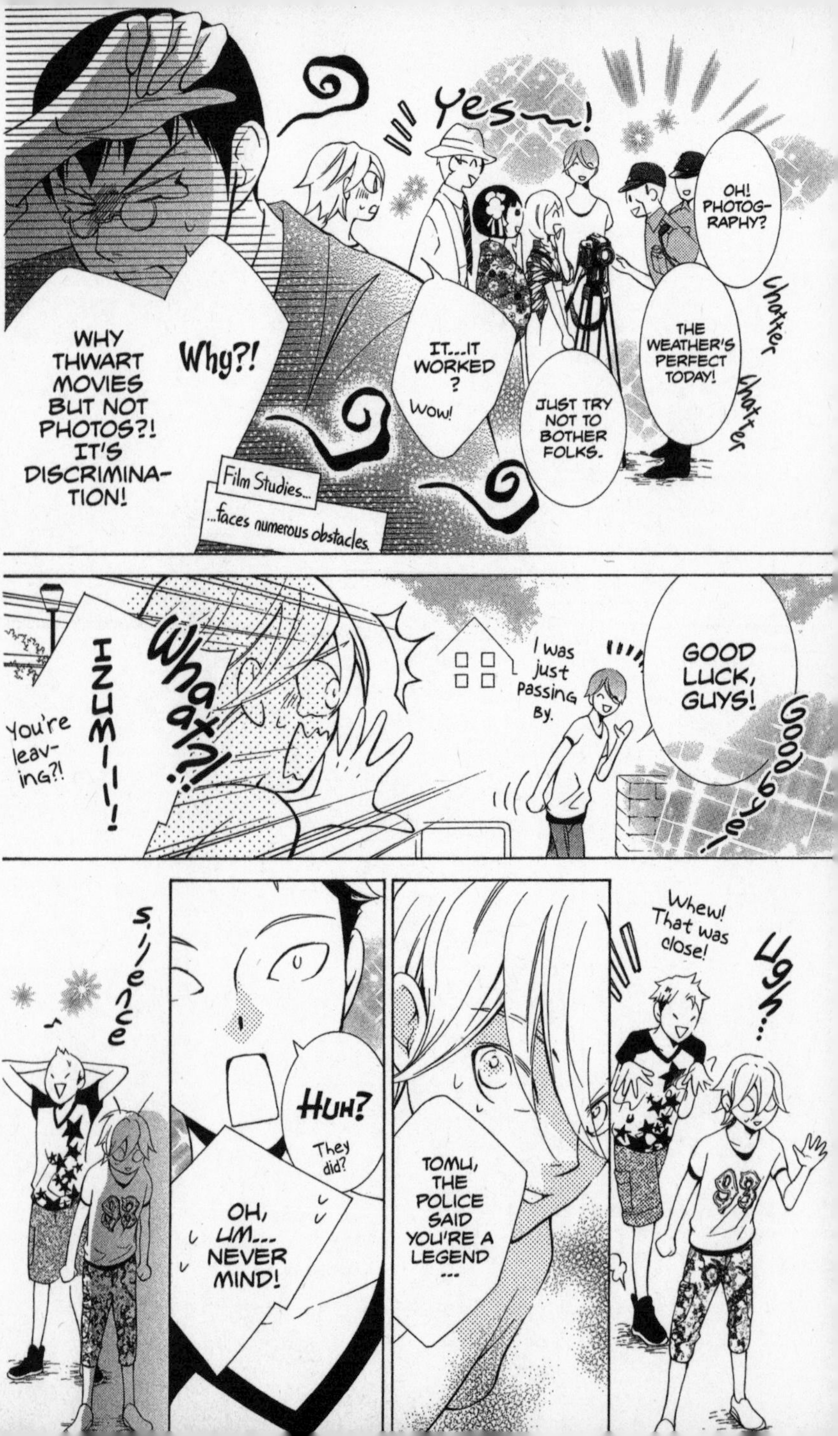
OH! PHOTOGRAPHY?
THE WEATHER'S PERFECT TODAY!
Chatter chatter
JUST TRY NOT TO BOTHER FOLKS.
Yes~~!
IT...IT WORKED?
Wow!
Why?!
WHY THWART MOVIES BUT NOT PHOTOS?! IT'S DISCRIMINATION!
Film Studies...
...faces numerous obstacles.
GOOD LUCK, GUYS!
Good-bye!
I was just passing by.
What?!
IZUMI--!
You're leaving?!
Whew! That was close!
Ugh...
TOMU, THE POLICE SAID YOU'RE A LEGEND...
HUH?
They did?
OH, UM... NEVER MIND!
silence

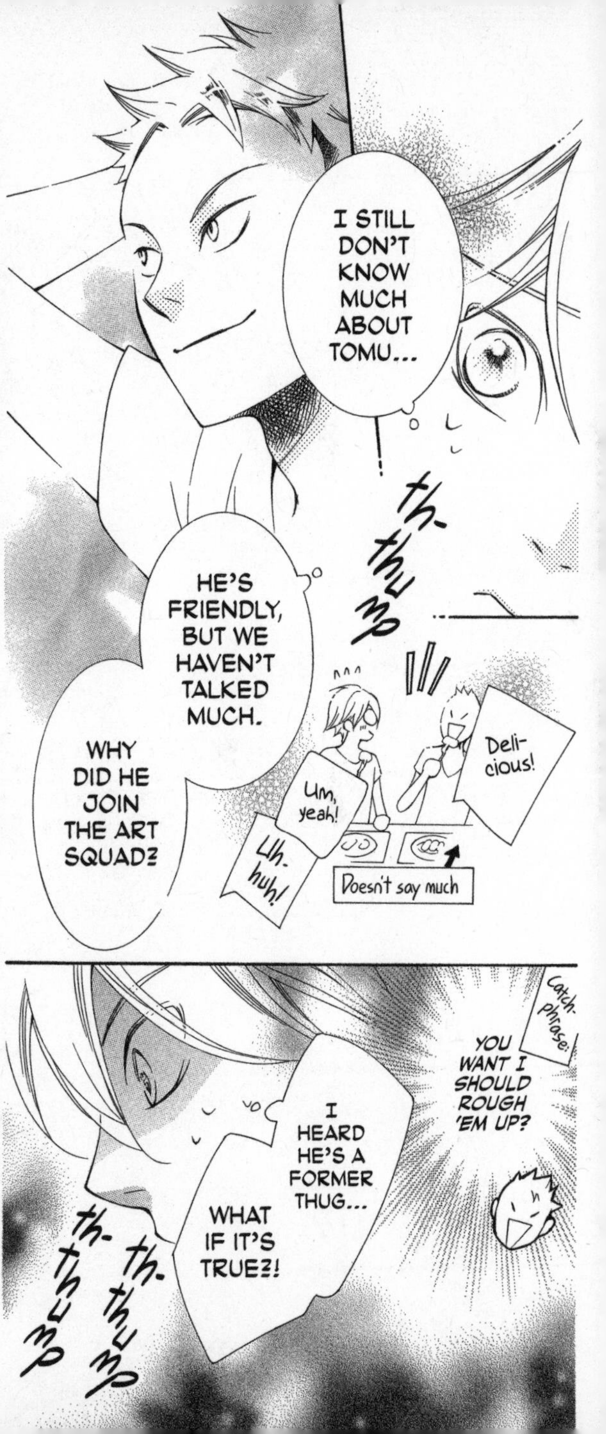
I STILL DON'T KNOW MUCH ABOUT TOMU...
th-thump
HE'S FRIENDLY, BUT WE HAVEN'T TALKED MUCH.
WHY DID HE JOIN THE ART SQUAD?
Deli-cious!
Um, yeah!
Uh-huh!
Doesn't say much
Catch-phrase:
YOU WANT I SHOULD ROUGH 'EM UP?
I HEARD HE'S A FORMER THUG...
WHAT IF IT'S TRUE?!
th-thump
th-thump

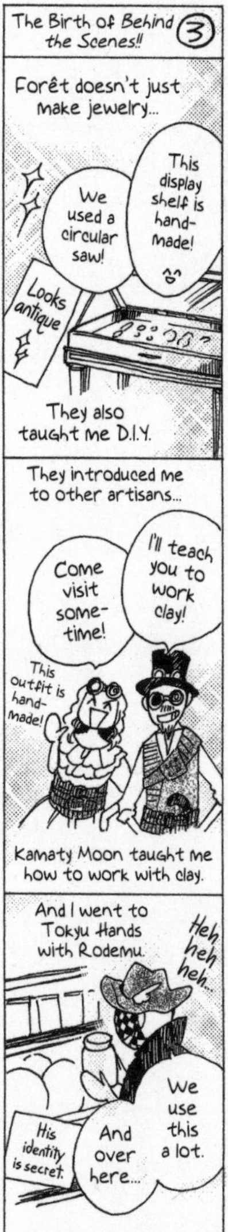
The Birth of Behind the Scenes!! 3
Forêt doesn't just make jewelry...
This display shelf is hand-made!
We used a circular saw!
Looks antique
They also taught me D.I.Y.
They introduced me to other artisans...
I'll teach you to work clay!
Come visit some-time!
This outfit is hand-made!
Kamaty Moon taught me how to work with clay.
And I went to Tokyu Hands with Rodemu.
Heh heh heh...
We use this a lot.
And over here...
His identity is secret.
They helped me with a lot besides steampunk. Thank you!

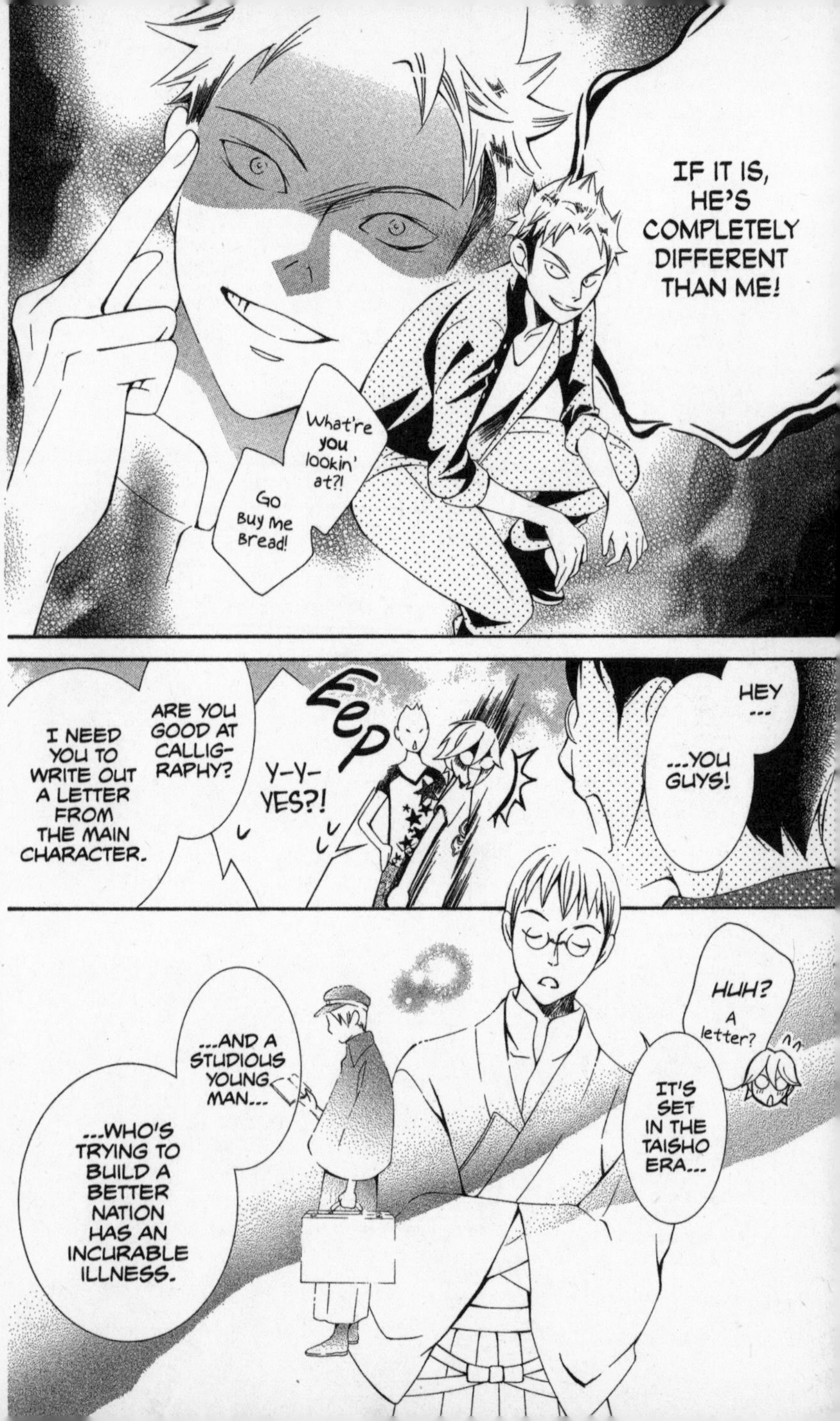
IF IT IS, HE'S COMPLETELY DIFFERENT THAN ME!
What're you lookin' at?!
Go Buy me Bread!
HEY... ...YOU GUYS!
Eep
Y-Y-YES?!
ARE YOU GOOD AT CALLIG-RAPHY?
I NEED YOU TO WRITE OUT A LETTER FROM THE MAIN CHARACTER.
HUH? A letter?
IT'S SET IN THE TAISHO ERA...
...AND A STUDIOUS YOUNG MAN...
...WHO'S TRYING TO BUILD A BETTER NATION HAS AN INCURABLE ILLNESS.

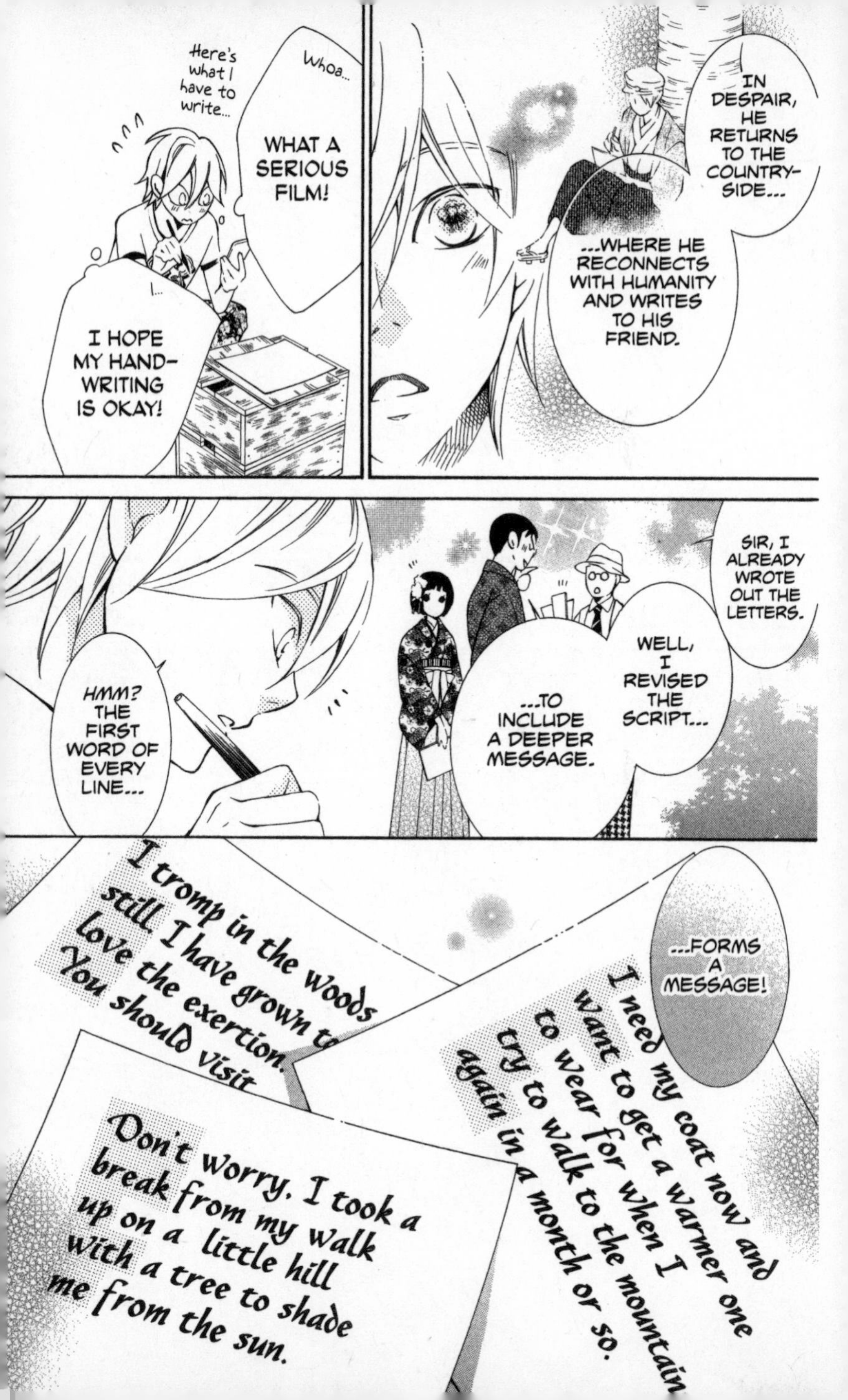
IN DESPAIR, HE RETURNS TO THE COUNTRYSIDE...
...WHERE HE RECONNECTS WITH HUMANITY AND WRITES TO HIS FRIEND.
Whoa...
WHAT A SERIOUS FILM!
Here's what I have to write...
I...
I HOPE MY HANDWRITING IS OKAY!
SIR, I ALREADY WROTE OUT THE LETTERS.
WELL, I REVISED THE SCRIPT...
...TO INCLUDE A DEEPER MESSAGE.
HMM? THE FIRST WORD OF EVERY LINE...
...FORMS A MESSAGE!
I need my coat now and
want to get a warmer one
to wear for when I
try to walk to the mountain
again in a month or so.
I tromp in the woods
still. I have grown to
love the exertion.
You should visit
Don't worry. I took a
break from my walk
up on a little hill
with a tree to shade
me from the sun.

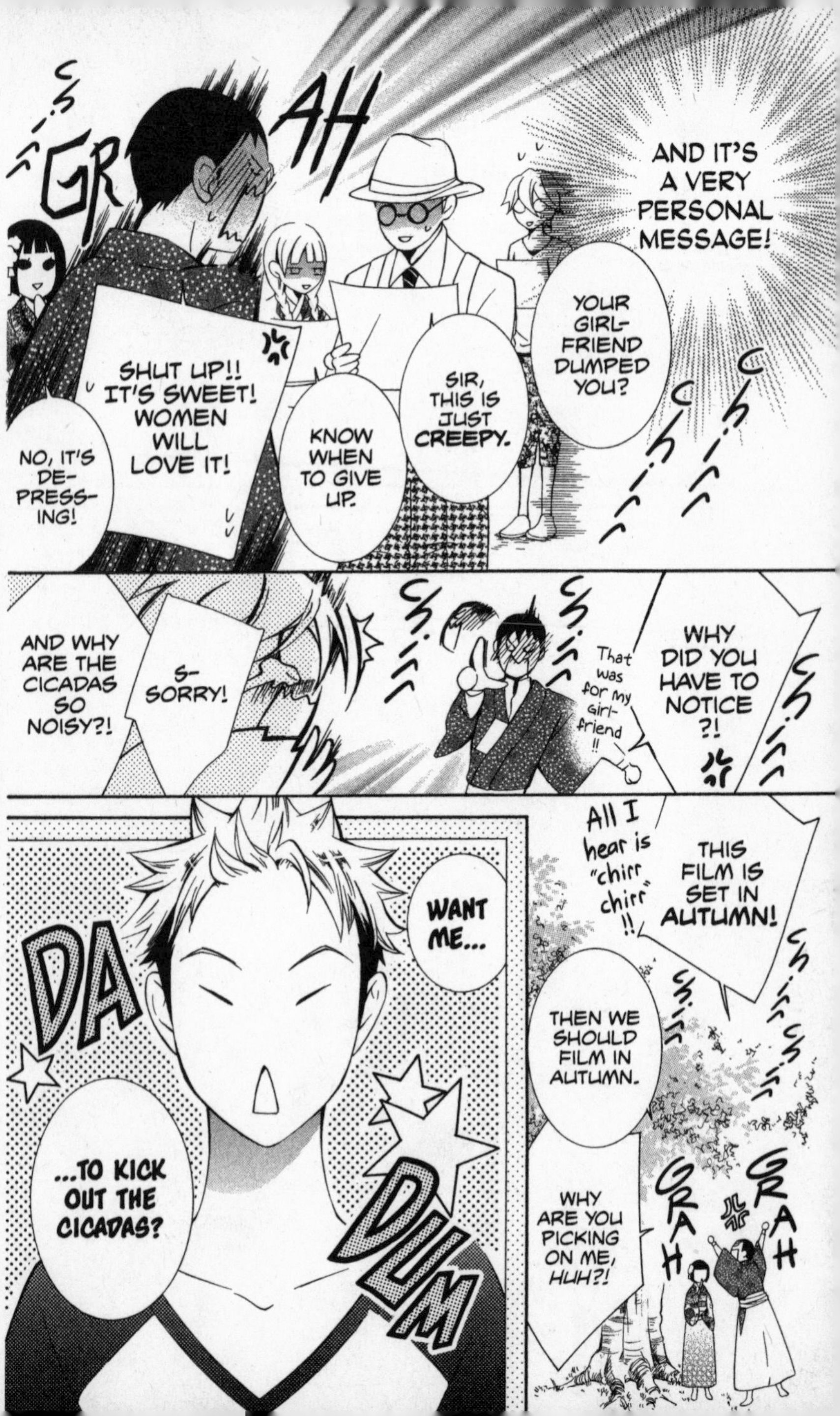
AND IT'S A VERY PERSONAL MESSAGE!
YOUR GIRL-FRIEND DUMPED YOU?
SIR, THIS IS JUST CREEPY.
KNOW WHEN TO GIVE UP.
GRAH
SHUT UP!! IT'S SWEET! WOMEN WILL LOVE IT!
NO, IT'S DE-PRESS-ING!
WHY DID YOU HAVE TO NOTICE?!
That was for my girl-friend!!
S-SORRY!
AND WHY ARE THE CICADAS SO NOISY?!
THIS FILM IS SET IN AUTUMN!
All I hear is "chirr chirr"!!
THEN WE SHOULD FILM IN AUTUMN.
GRAH GRAH
WHY ARE YOU PICKING ON ME, HUH?!
WANT ME...
DA DUM
...TO KICK OUT THE CICADAS?

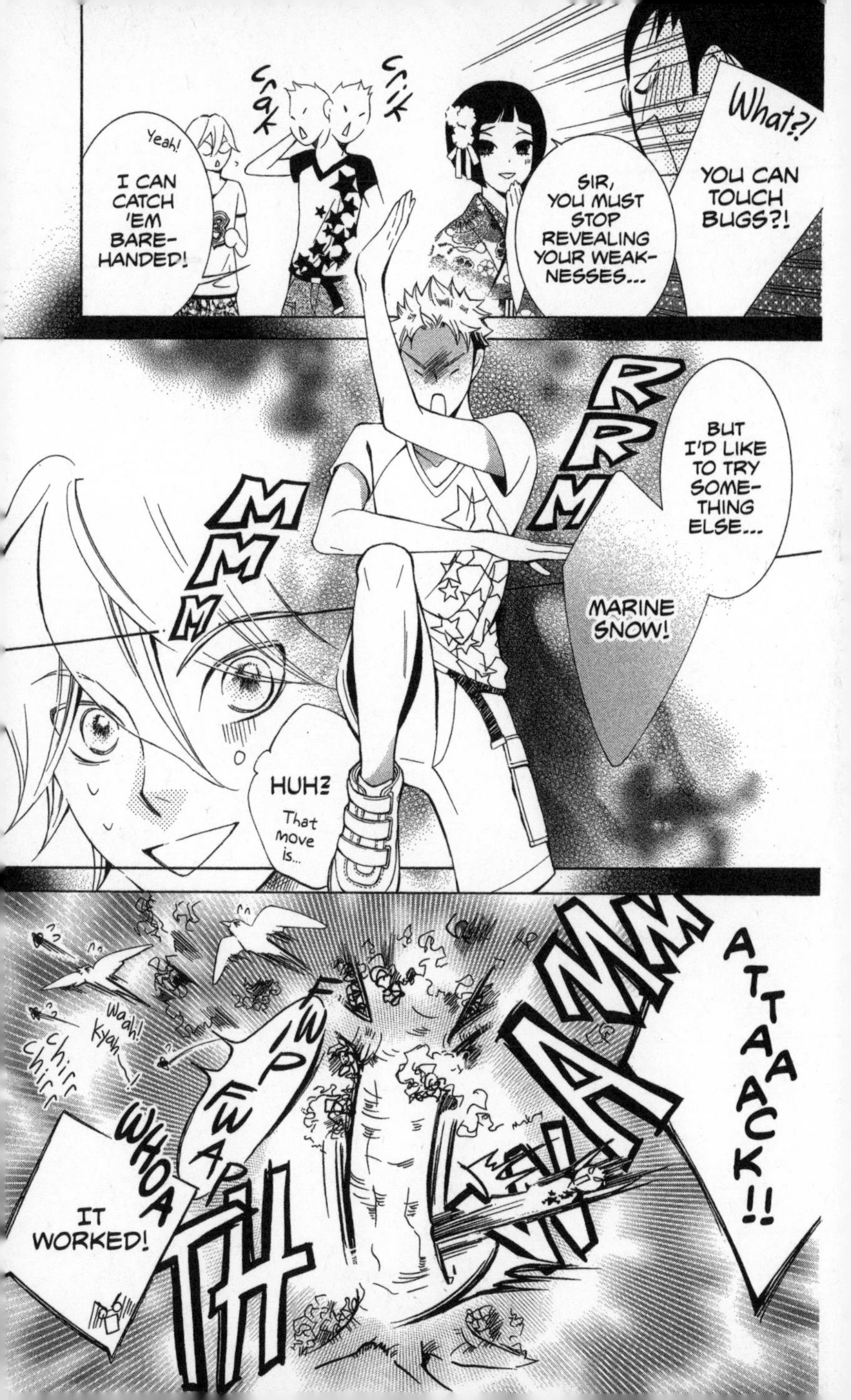
What?!
YOU CAN TOUCH BUGS?!
SIR, YOU MUST STOP REVEALING YOUR WEAKNESSES...
crik
crak
Yeah!
I CAN CATCH 'EM BARE-HANDED!
RRM
BUT I'D LIKE TO TRY SOMETHING ELSE...
MARINE SNOW!
MMMM
HUH?
That move is...
ATTAAACK!!
THWAMM
FWAP FWAP
Waah! Kyah!
chirr chirr
WHOA
IT WORKED!

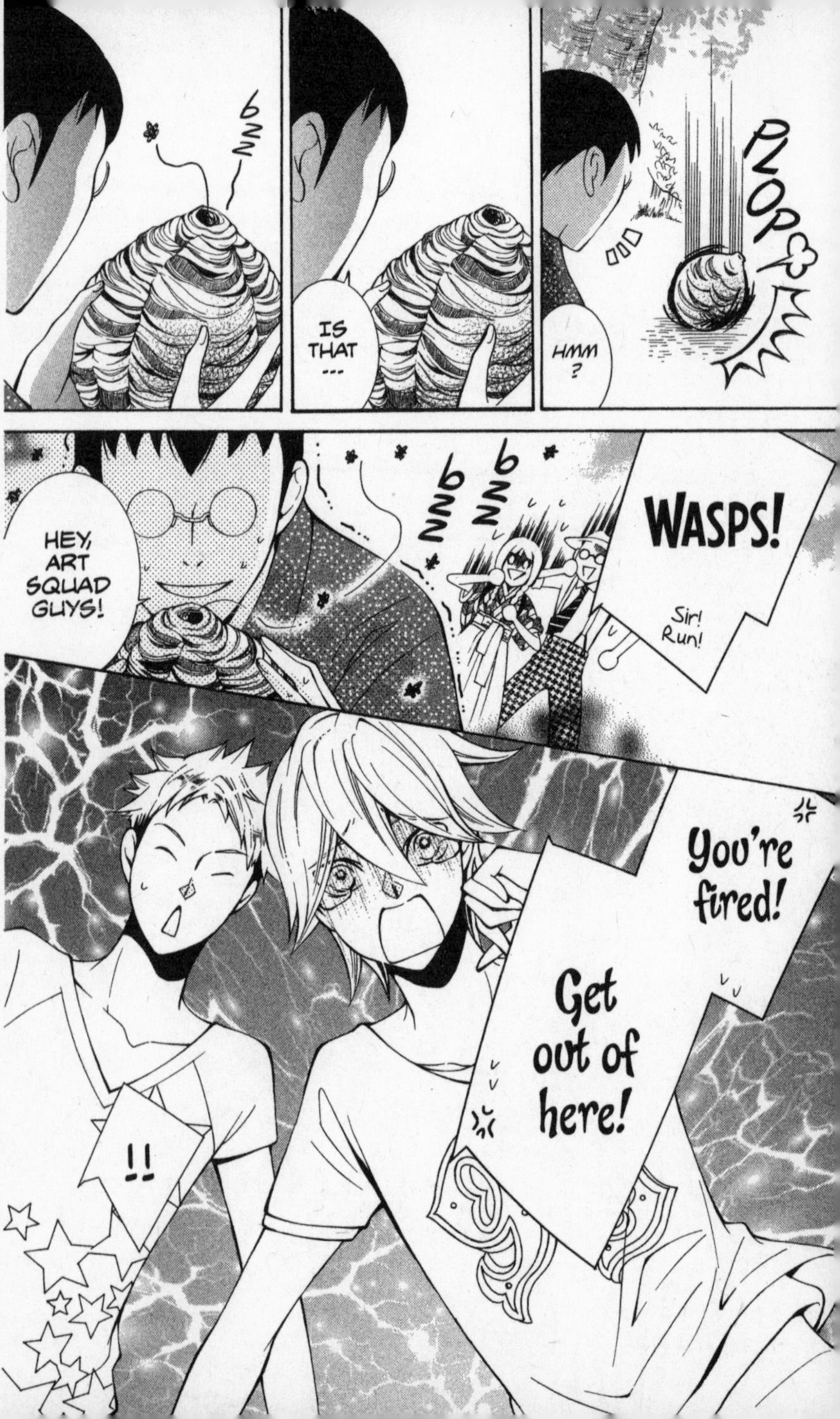
PLOP
HMM?
IS THAT ---
bzz
WASPS!
Sir! Run!
bzz
bzz
HEY, ART SQUAD GUYS!
You're fired!
Get out of here!
!!

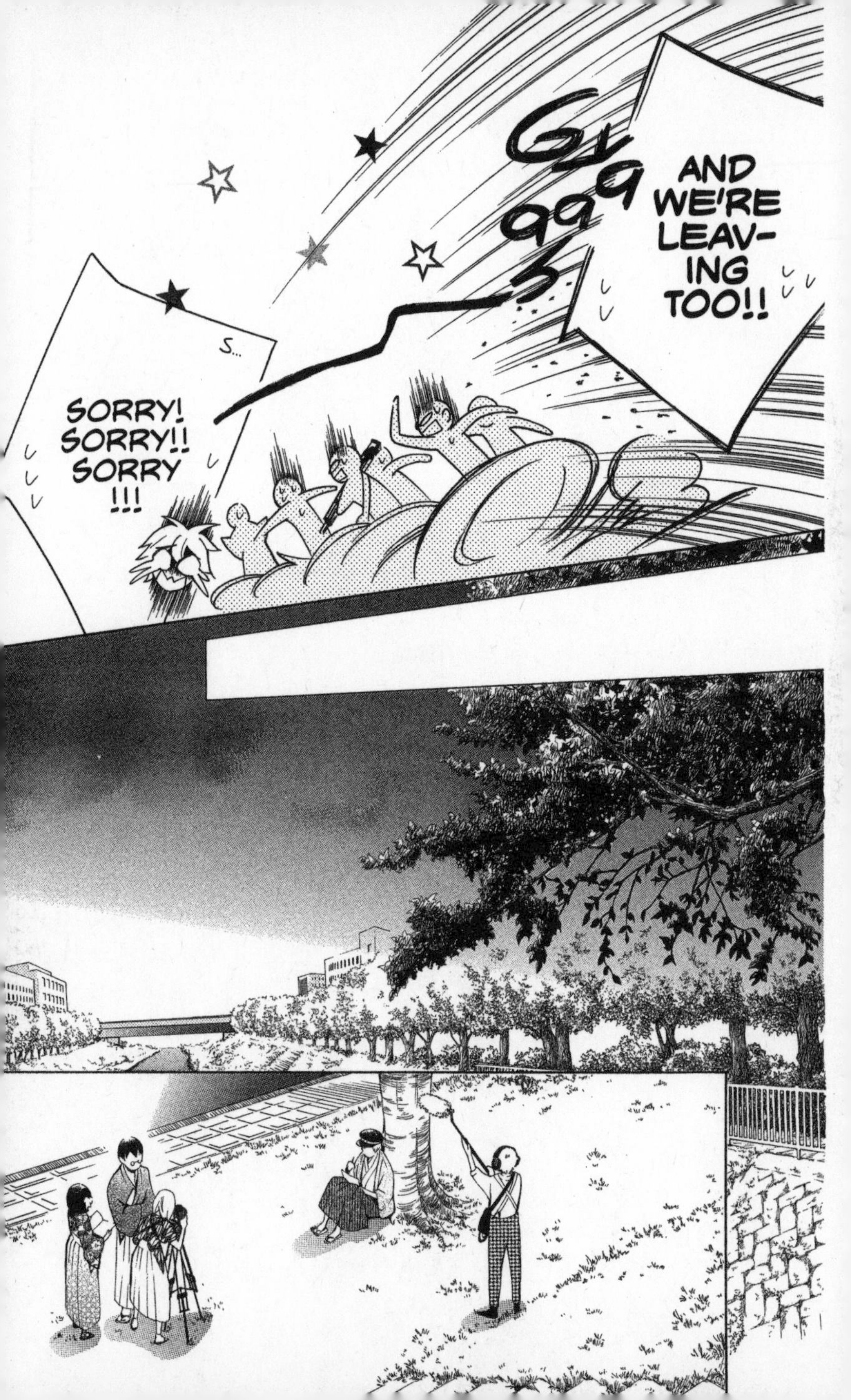
AND WE'RE LEAV-ING TOO!!
S...
SORRY! SORRY!! SORRY !!!

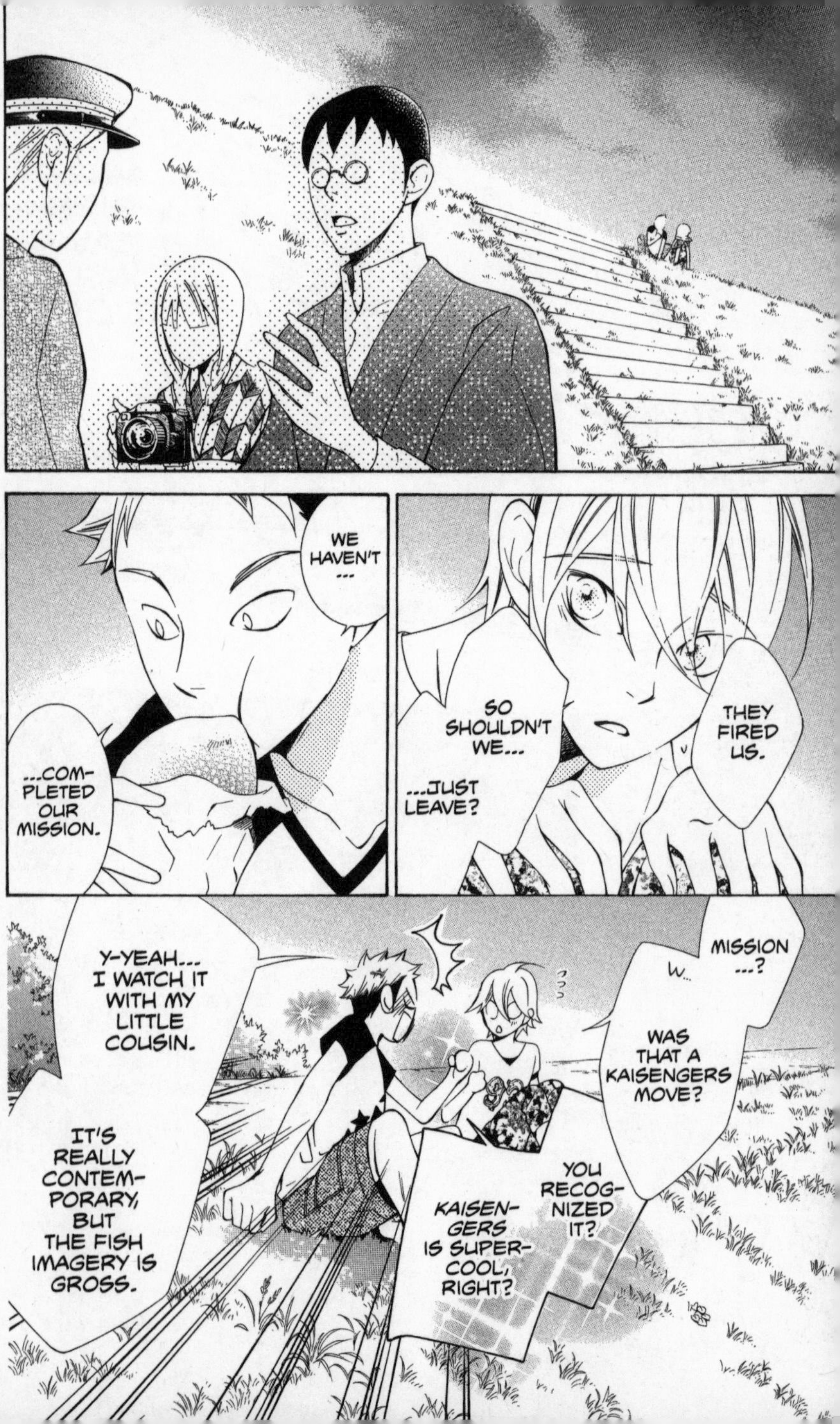
THEY FIRED US.
SO SHOULDN'T WE...
...JUST LEAVE?
WE HAVEN'T...
...COMPLETED OUR MISSION.
W...
MISSION...?
WAS THAT A KAISENGERS MOVE?
YOU RECOGNIZED IT?
KAISENGERS IS SUPER-COOL, RIGHT?
Y-YEAH... I WATCH IT WITH MY LITTLE COUSIN.
IT'S REALLY CONTEMPORARY, BUT THE FISH IMAGERY IS GROSS.

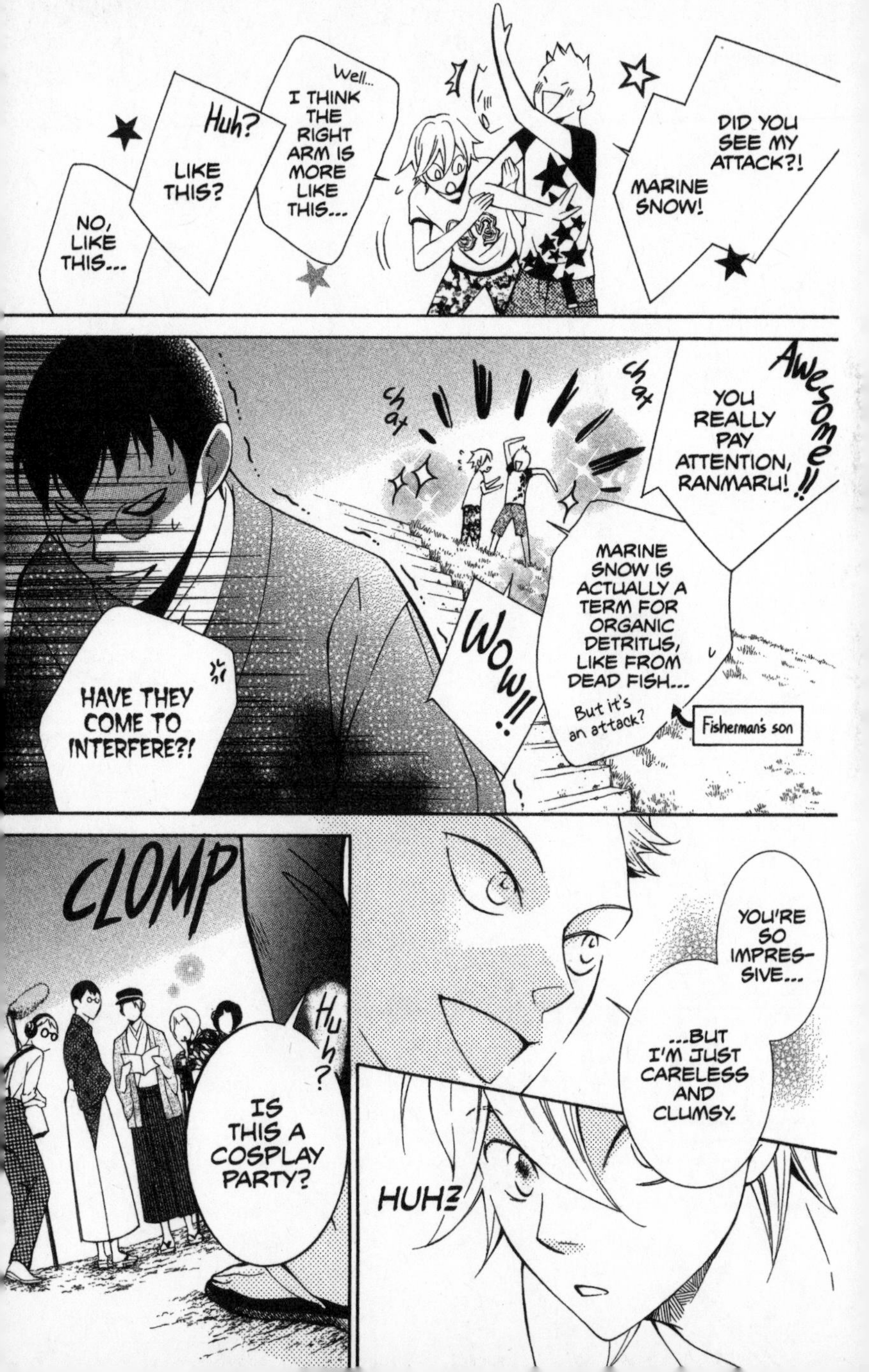
DID YOU SEE MY ATTACK?!
MARINE SNOW!
Well... I THINK THE RIGHT ARM IS MORE LIKE THIS...
Huh? LIKE THIS?
NO, LIKE THIS...
Awesome!!
YOU REALLY PAY ATTENTION, RANMARU!
chat
chat
MARINE SNOW IS ACTUALLY A TERM FOR ORGANIC DETRITUS, LIKE FROM DEAD FISH...
But it's an attack?
Fisherman's son
WOW!!
HAVE THEY COME TO INTERFERE?!
YOU'RE SO IMPRES-SIVE...
...BUT I'M JUST CARELESS AND CLUMSY.
HUH?
CLOMP
Huh?
IS THIS A COSPLAY PARTY?

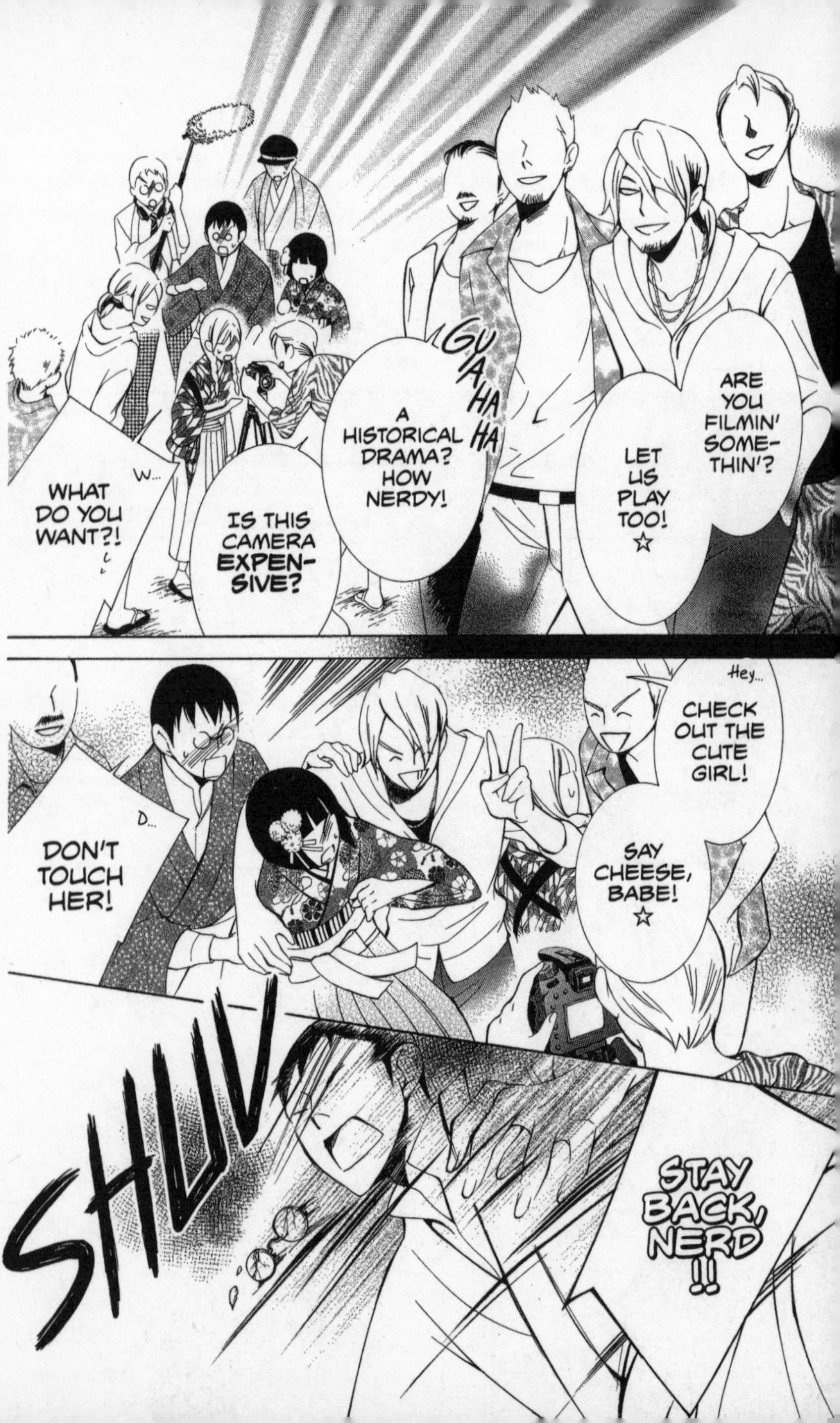
ARE YOU FILMIN' SOME-THIN'?
LET US PLAY TOO! ☆
GUAHAHAHA
A HISTORICAL DRAMA? HOW NERDY!
IS THIS CAMERA EXPEN-SIVE?
W... WHAT DO YOU WANT?!
Hey... CHECK OUT THE CUTE GIRL!
SAY CHEESE, BABE! ☆
D... DON'T TOUCH HER!
STAY BACK, NERD!!
SHUV

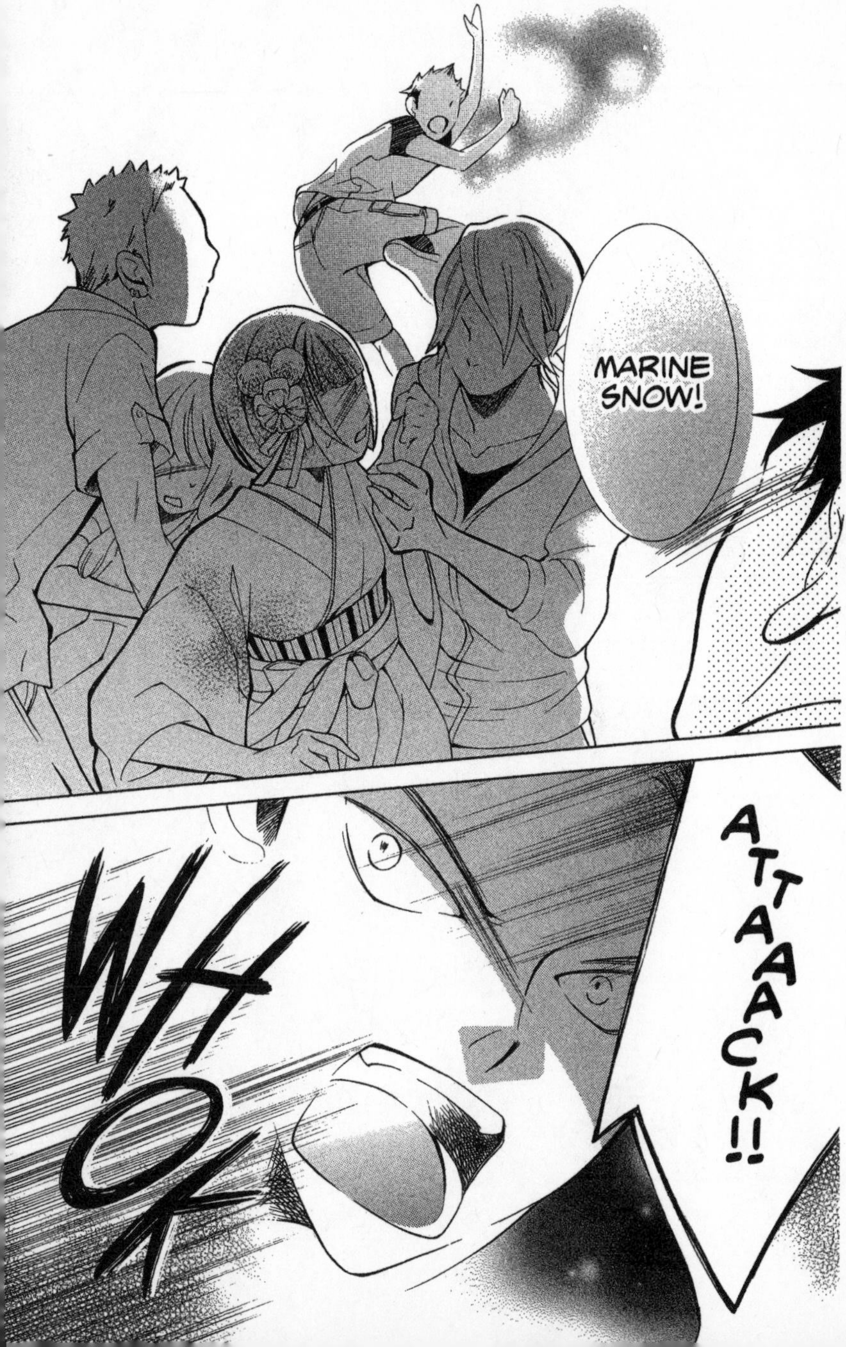
MARINE SNOW!
ATTAAACK!!
WHOOK

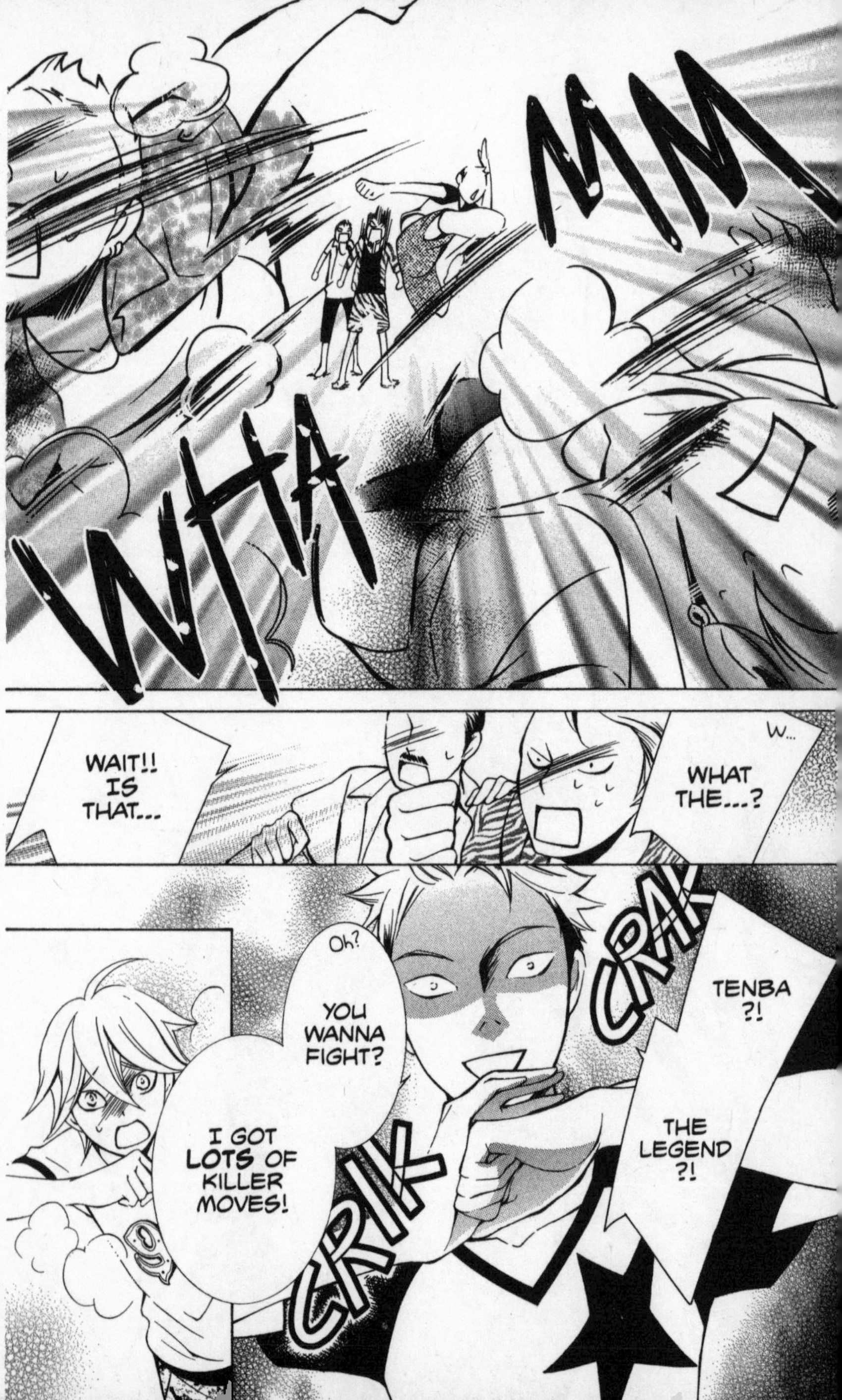
WHA
MM
W...
WHAT THE...?
WAIT!! IS THAT...
TENBA ?!
THE LEGEND ?!
CRAK
Oh?
YOU WANNA FIGHT?
I GOT LOTS OF KILLER MOVES!
CRIK

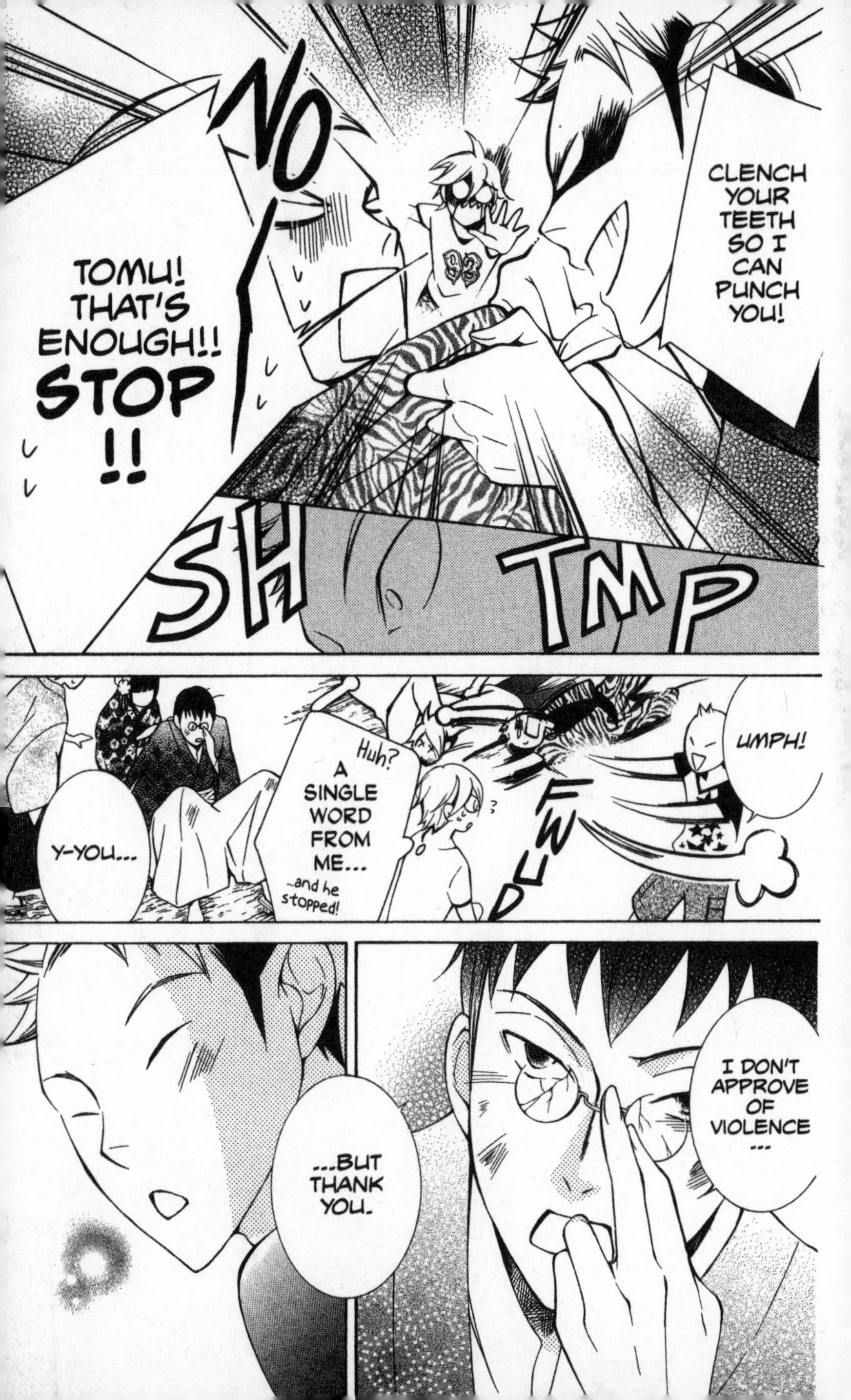
CLENCH YOUR TEETH SO I CAN PUNCH YOU!
NO
TOMU! THAT'S ENOUGH!! STOP!!
SH TMP
UMPH!
FWUD
Huh?
A SINGLE WORD FROM ME...
...and he stopped!
Y-YOU...
I DON'T APPROVE OF VIOLENCE...
...BUT THANK YOU.

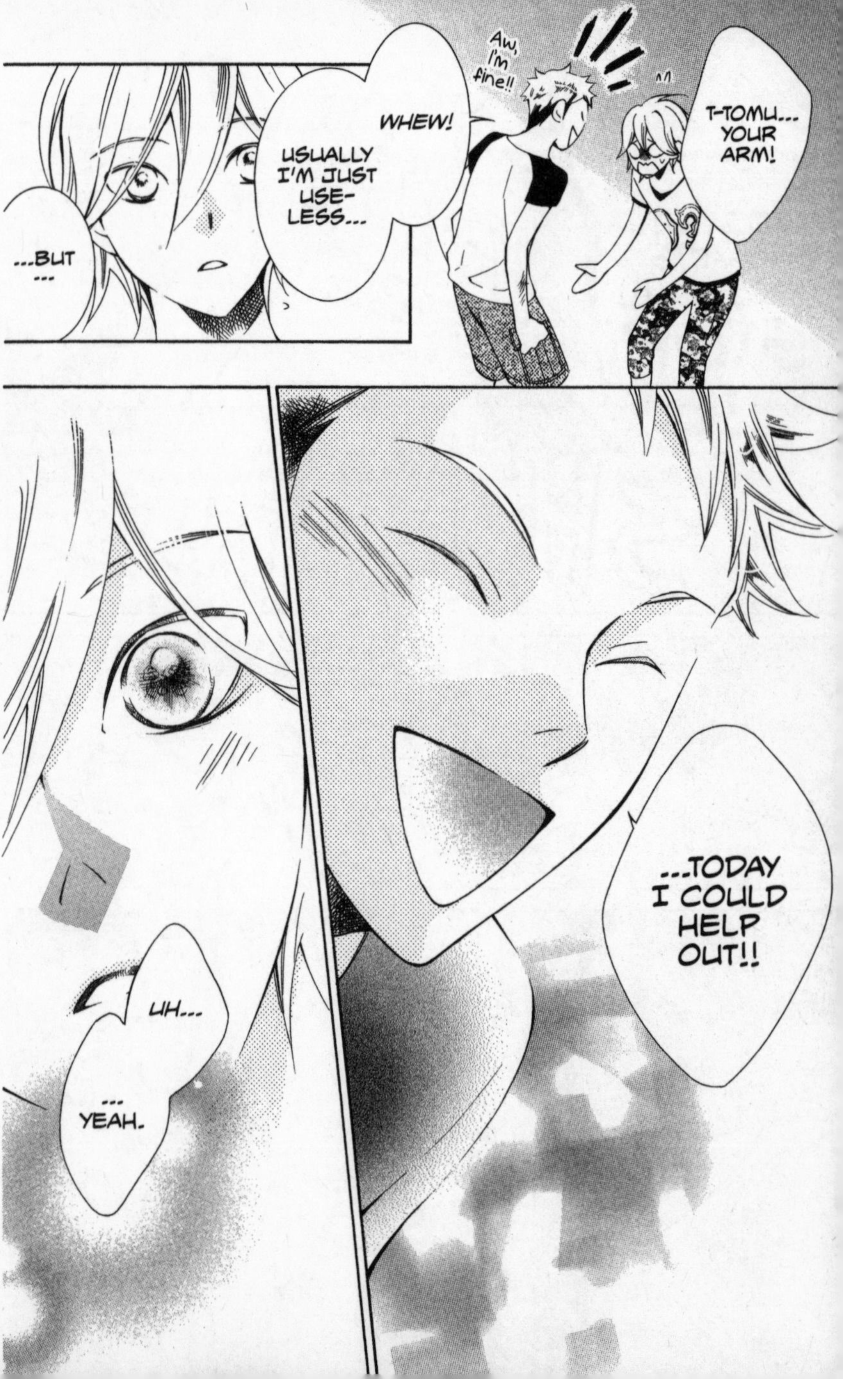
T-TOMU... YOUR ARM!
Aw, I'm fine!!
WHEW!
USUALLY I'M JUST USE-LESS...
...BUT ...
...TODAY I COULD HELP OUT!!
UH...
... YEAH.

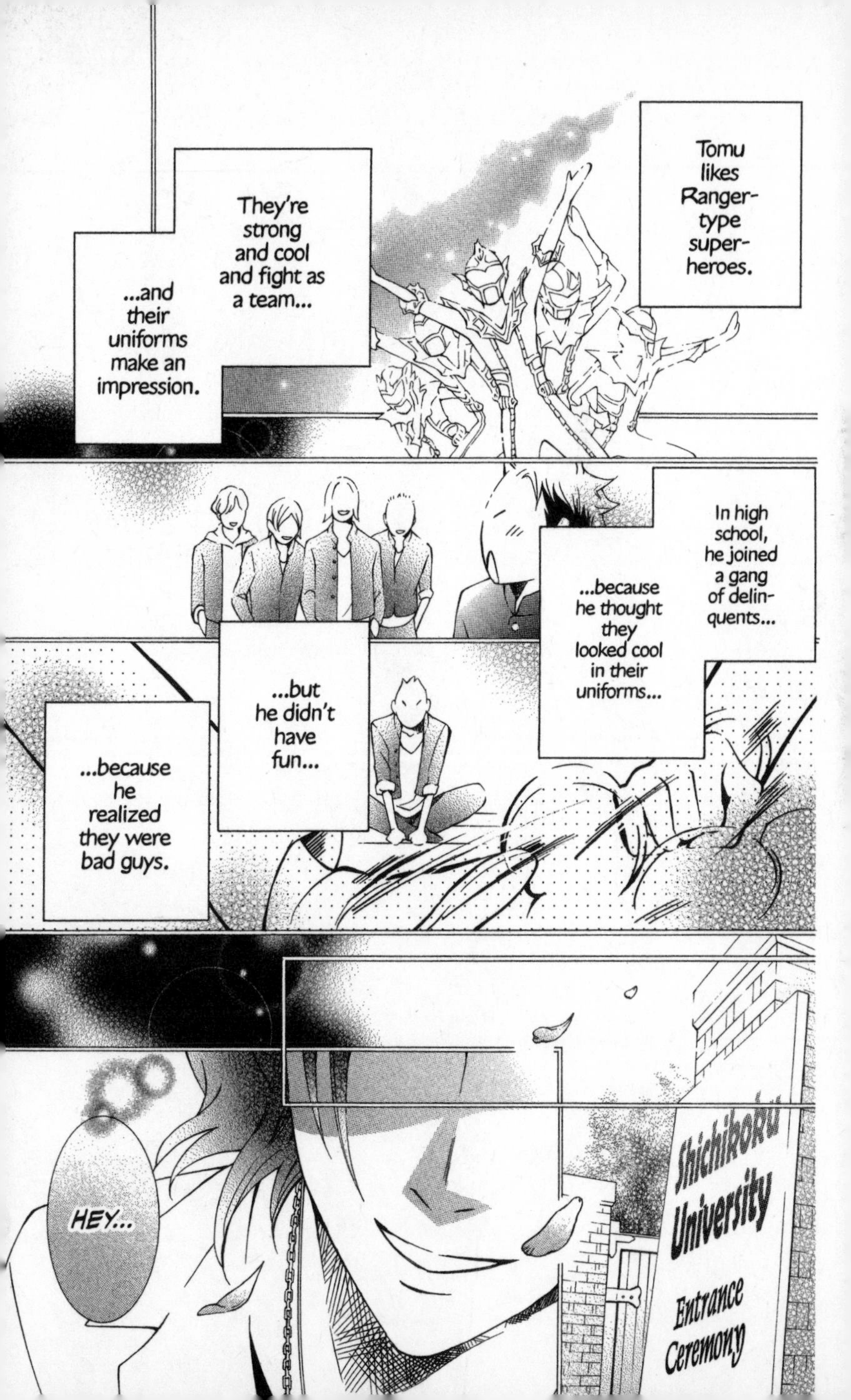
Tomu likes Ranger-type super-heroes.
They're strong and cool and fight as a team...
...and their uniforms make an impression.
In high school, he joined a gang of delin-quents...
...because he thought they looked cool in their uniforms...
...but he didn't have fun...
...because he realized they were bad guys.
Shichihoku University Entrance Ceremony
HEY...

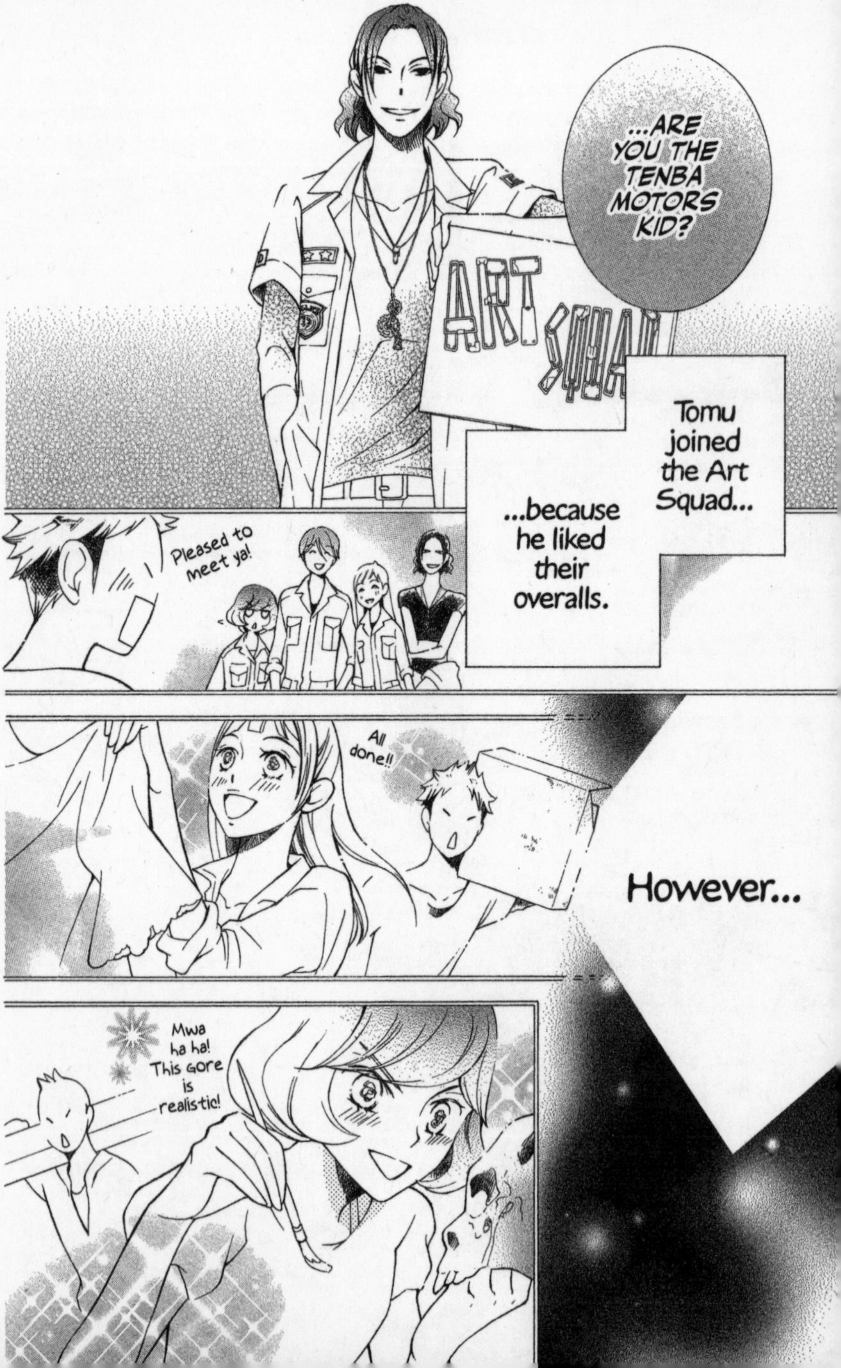
...ARE YOU THE TENBA MOTORS KID?
ART
Tomu joined the Art Squad...
...because he liked their overalls.
Pleased to meet ya!
All done!!
However...
Mwa ha ha! This gore is realistic!

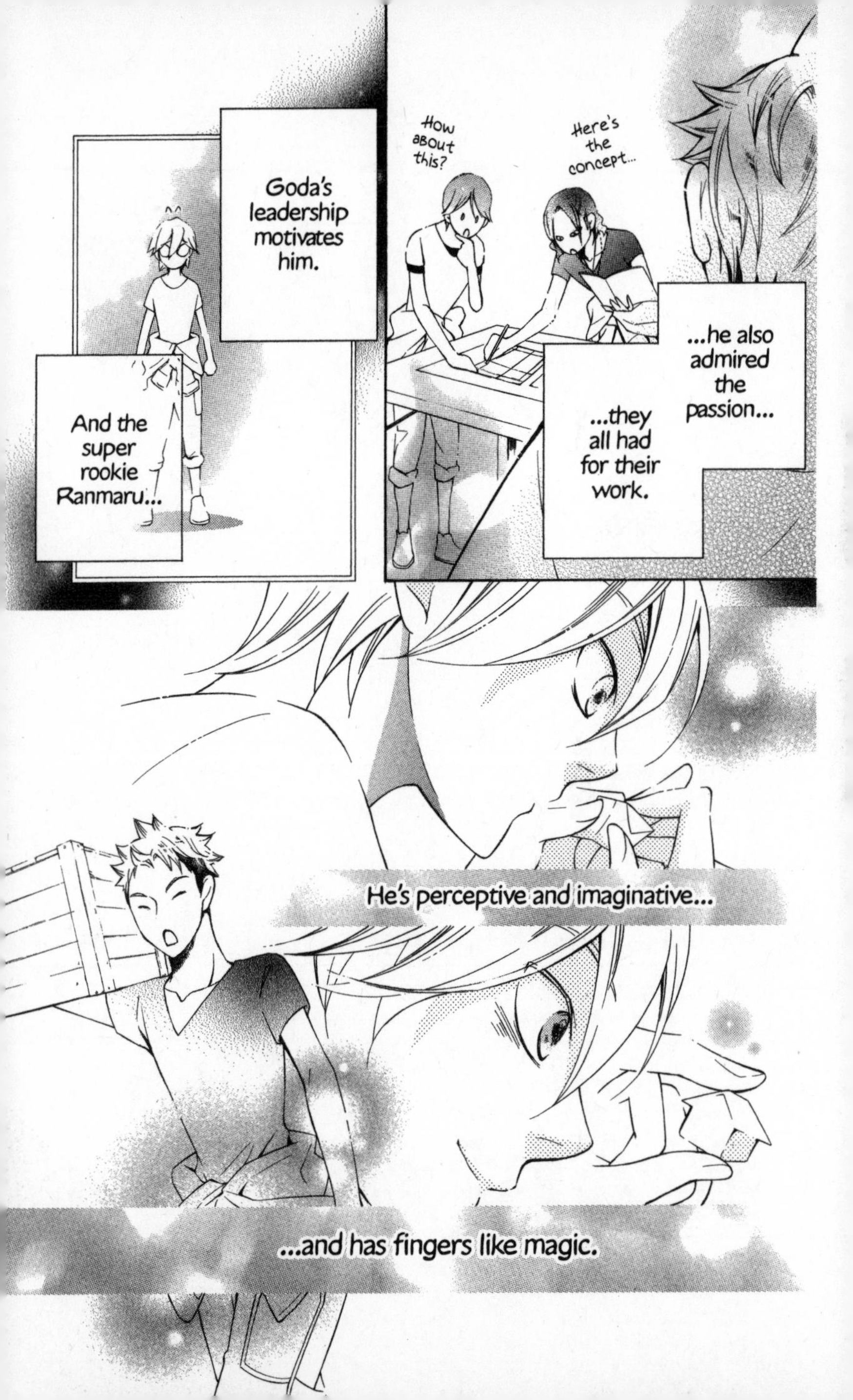
Here's the concept...
How about this?
...he also admired the passion...
...they all had for their work.
Goda's leadership motivates him.
And the super rookie Ranmaru...
He's perceptive and imaginative...
...and has fingers like magic.

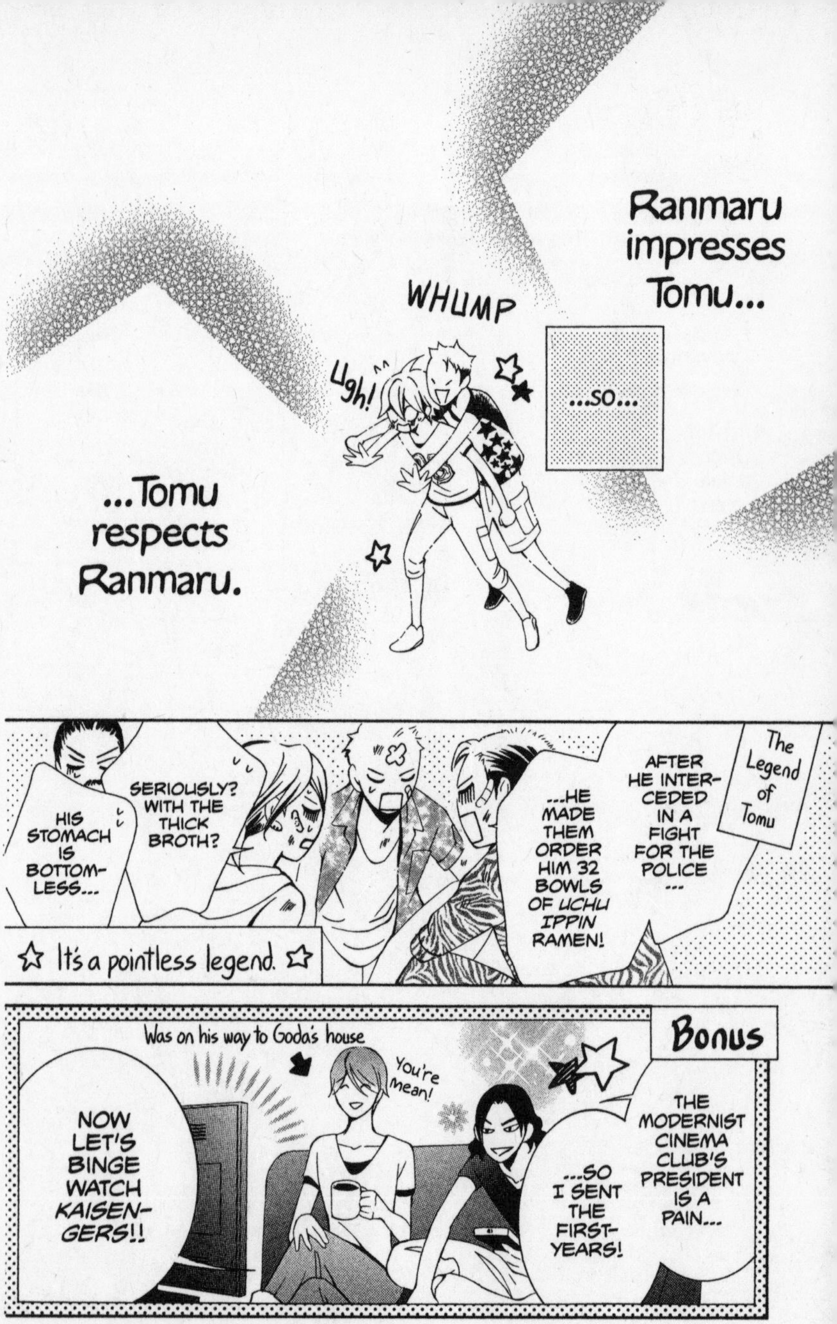
Ranmaru impresses Tomu...
WHUMP
...so...
Ugh!
...Tomu respects Ranmaru.
The Legend of Tomu
AFTER HE INTER-CEDED IN A FIGHT FOR THE POLICE...
...HE MADE THEM ORDER HIM 32 BOWLS OF UCHU IPPIN RAMEN!
SERIOUSLY? WITH THE THICK BROTH?
HIS STOMACH IS BOTTOM-LESS...
☆ It's a pointless legend. ☆
Bonus
THE MODERNIST CINEMA CLUB'S PRESIDENT IS A PAIN...
...SO I SENT THE FIRST-YEARS!
You're mean!
Was on his way to Goda's house
NOW LET'S BINGE WATCH KAISEN-GERS!!

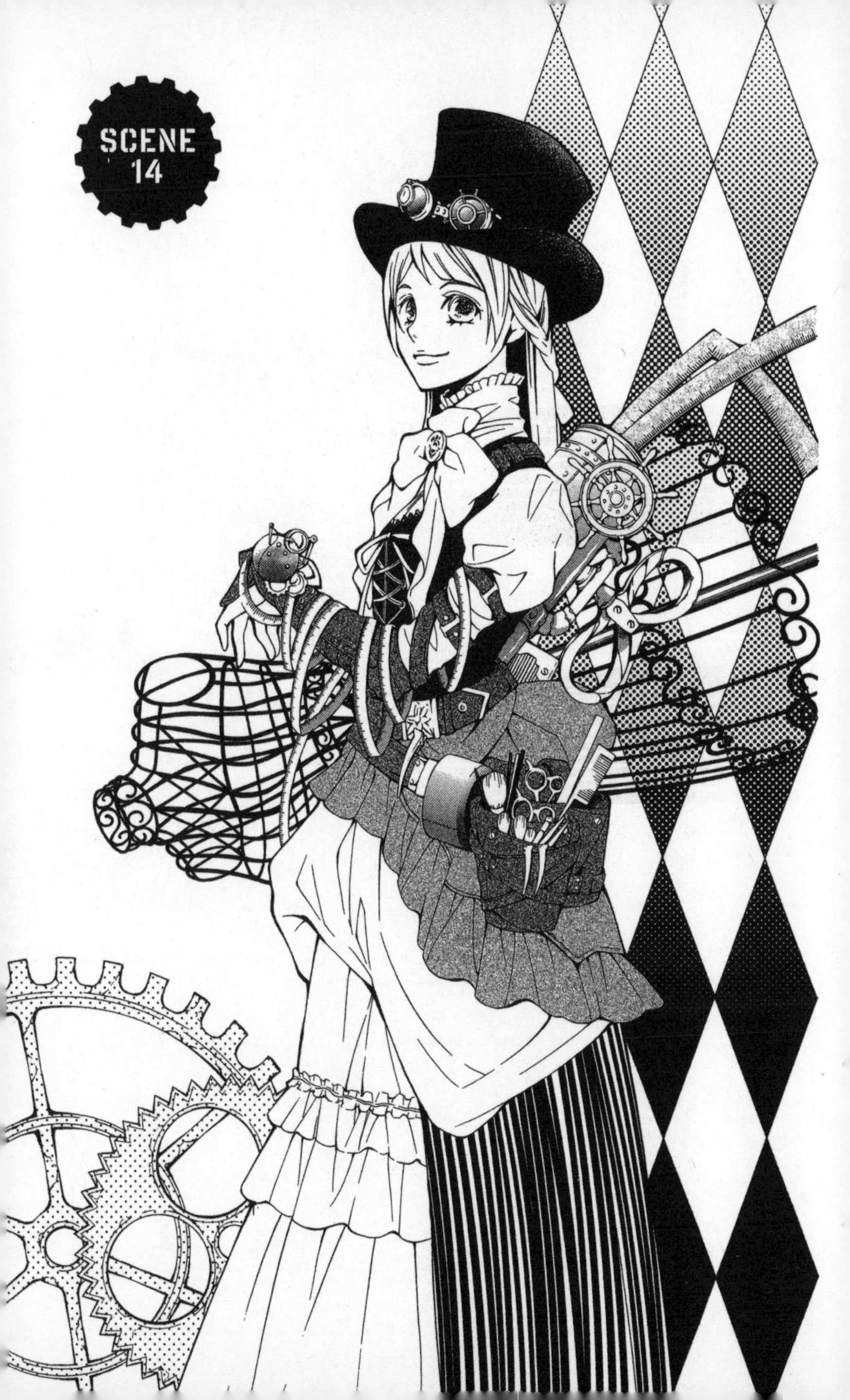
SCENE
14

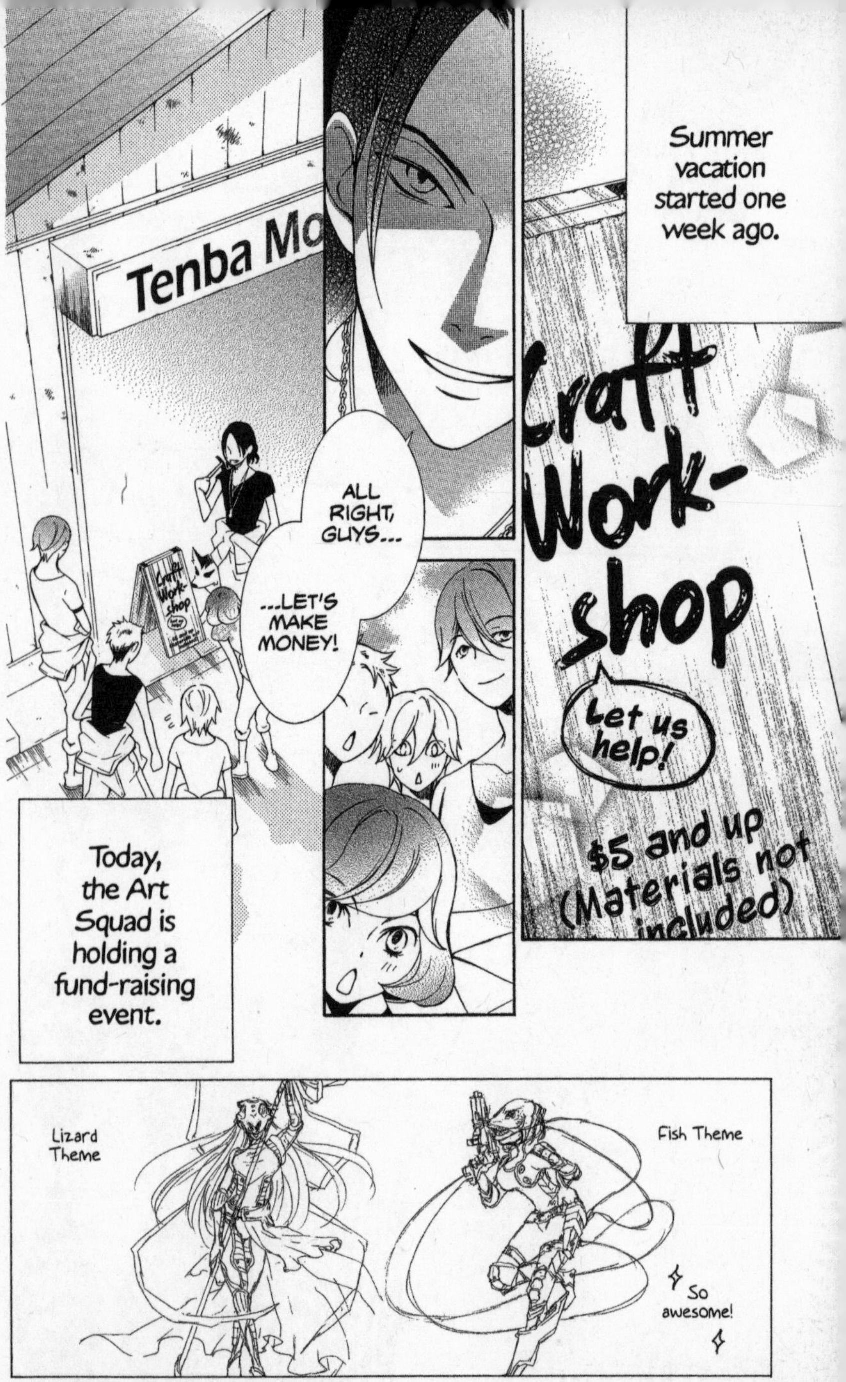
Summer vacation started one week ago.
Craft Work-shop
Let us help!
$5 and up
(Materials not included)
ALL RIGHT, GUYS...
...LET'S MAKE MONEY!
Tenba Mo
Today, the Art Squad is holding a fund-raising event.
Fish Theme
So awesome!
Lizard Theme

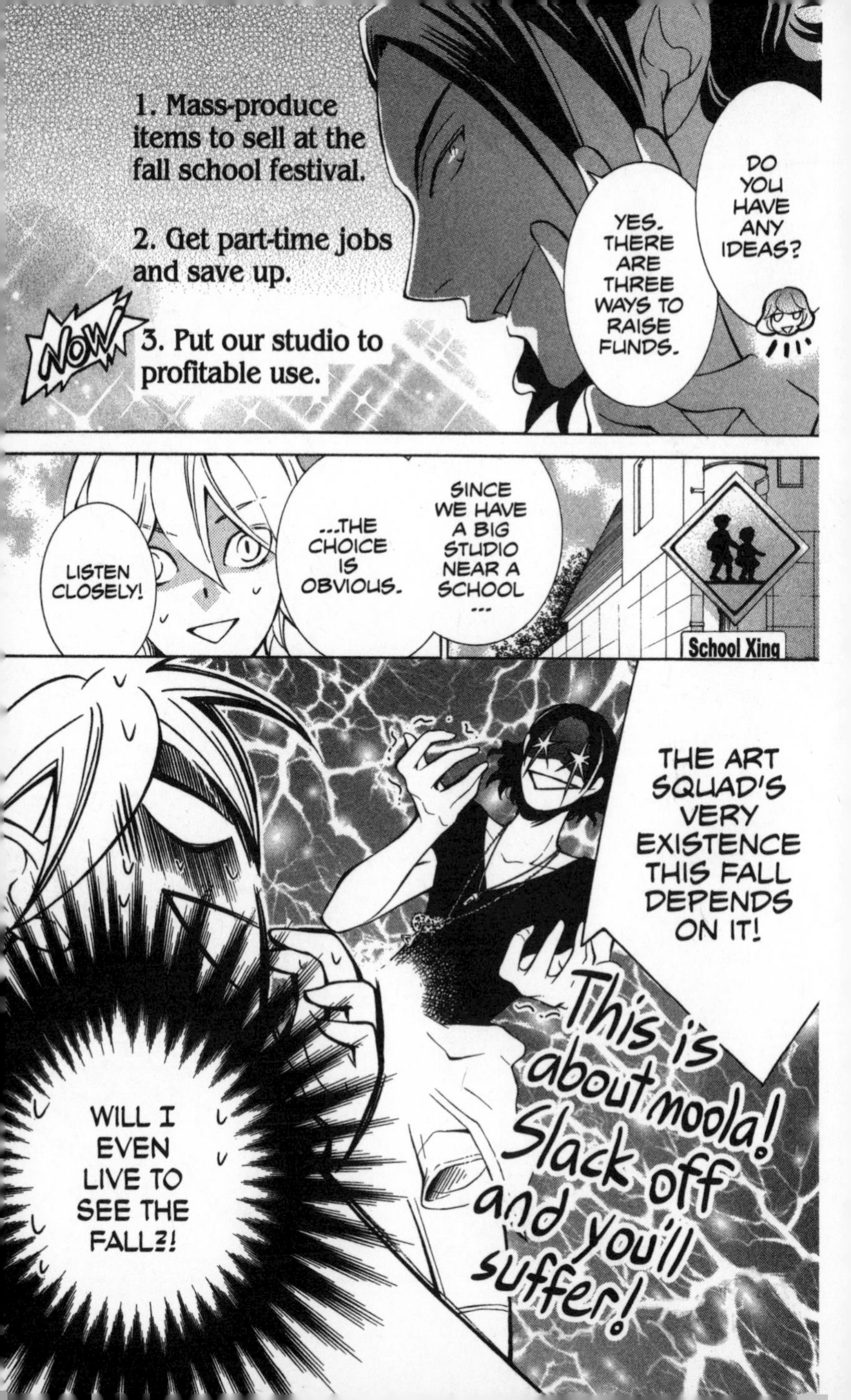
DO YOU HAVE ANY IDEAS?
YES. THERE ARE THREE WAYS TO RAISE FUNDS.
1. Mass-produce items to sell at the fall school festival.
2. Get part-time jobs and save up.
NOW!
3. Put our studio to profitable use.
School Xing
SINCE WE HAVE A BIG STUDIO NEAR A SCHOOL ...
...THE CHOICE IS OBVIOUS.
LISTEN CLOSELY!
THE ART SQUAD'S VERY EXISTENCE THIS FALL DEPENDS ON IT!
This is about moola! Slack off and you'll suffer!
WILL I EVEN LIVE TO SEE THE FALL?!

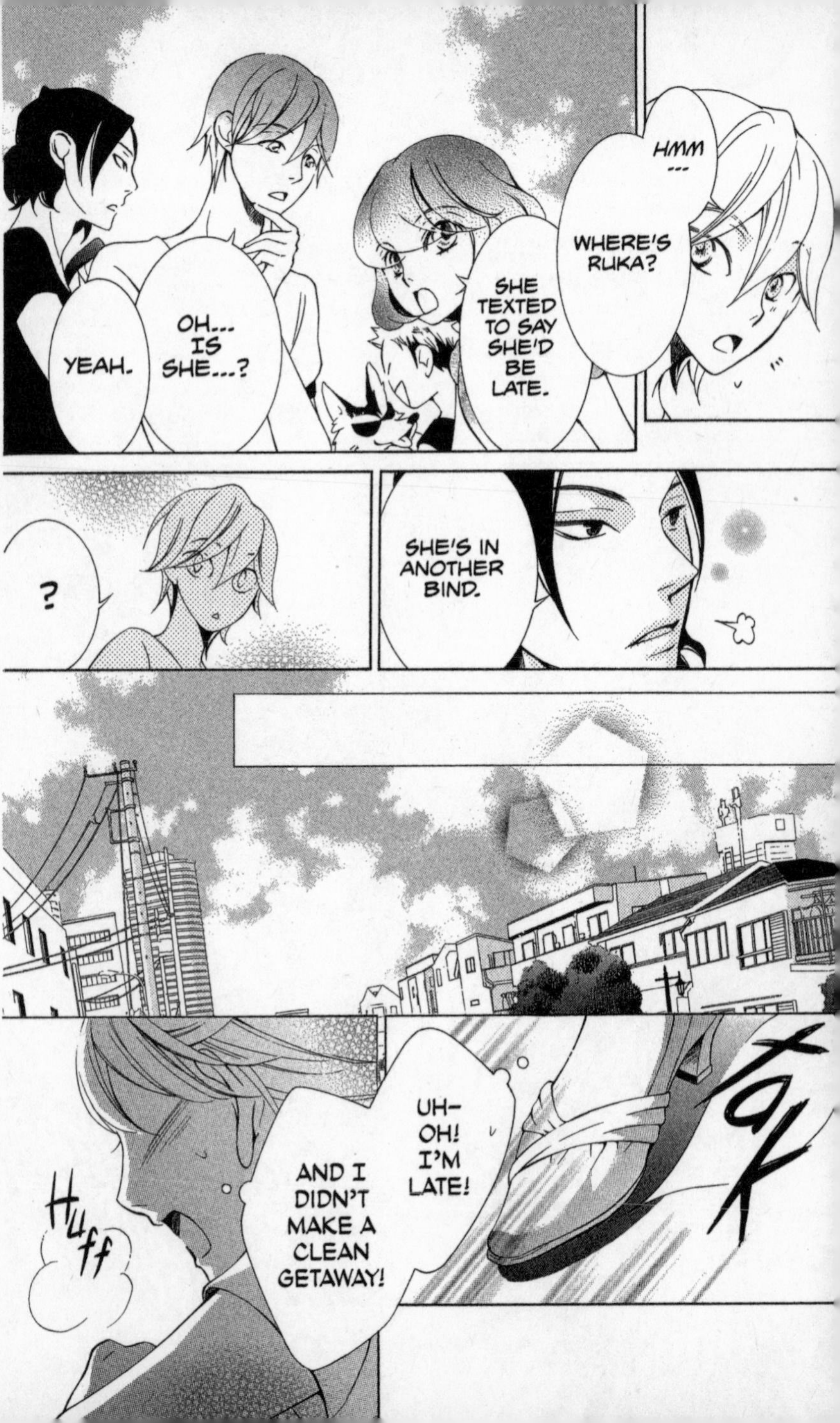
HMM...
WHERE'S RUKA?
SHE TEXTED TO SAY SHE'D BE LATE.
OH... IS SHE...?
YEAH.
SHE'S IN ANOTHER BIND.
?
TAK
UH-OH! I'M LATE!
AND I DIDN'T MAKE A CLEAN GETAWAY!
HUFF

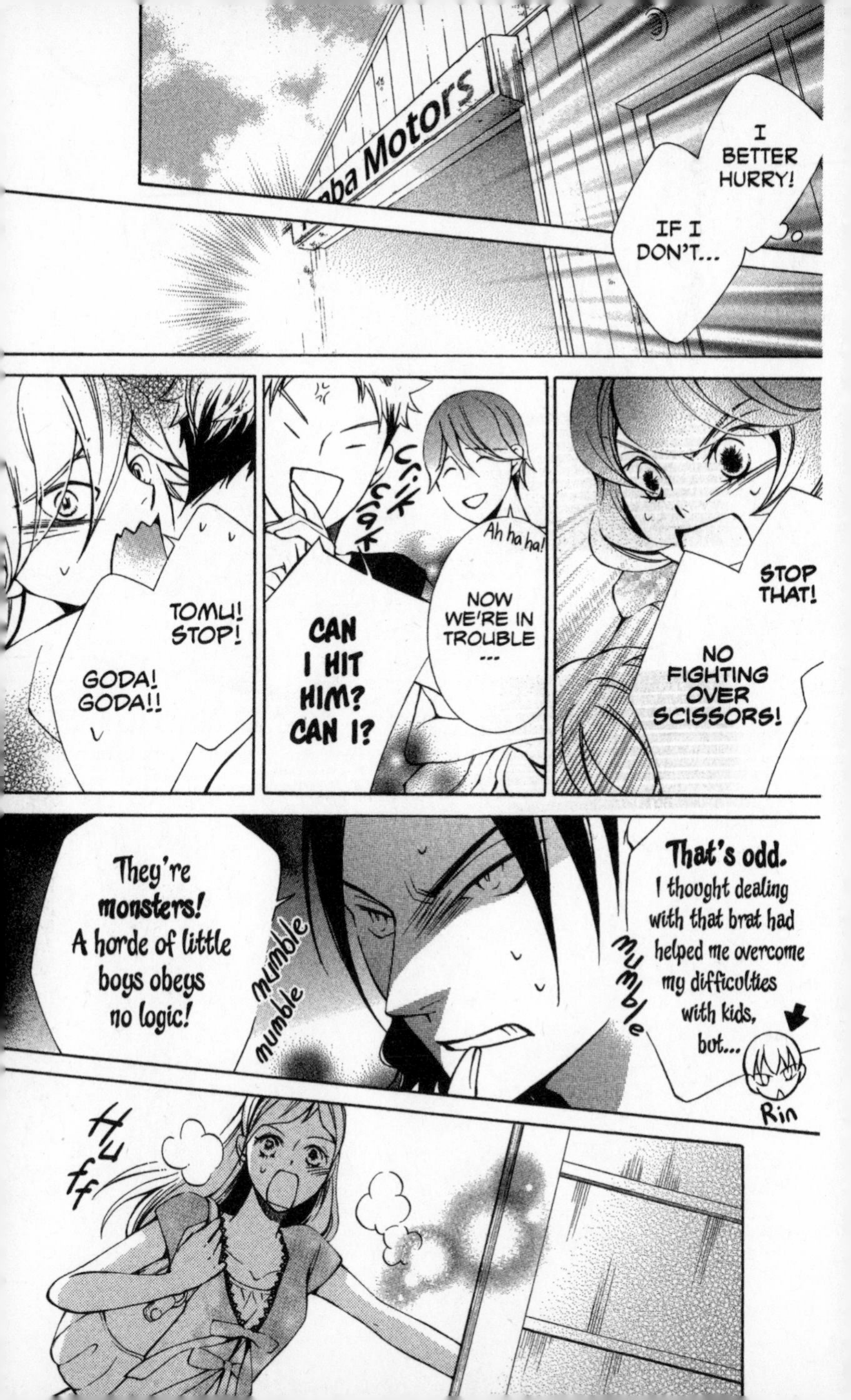

Motors
I BETTER HURRY!
IF I DON'T...
STOP THAT!
NO FIGHTING OVER SCISSORS!
Ah ha ha!
NOW WE'RE IN TROUBLE...
CAN I HIT HIM? CAN I?
TOMU! STOP!
GODA! GODA!!
That's odd. I thought dealing with that brat had helped me overcome my difficulties with kids, but...
Rin
mumble
They're monsters! A horde of little boys obeys no logic!
mumble mumble
Huff

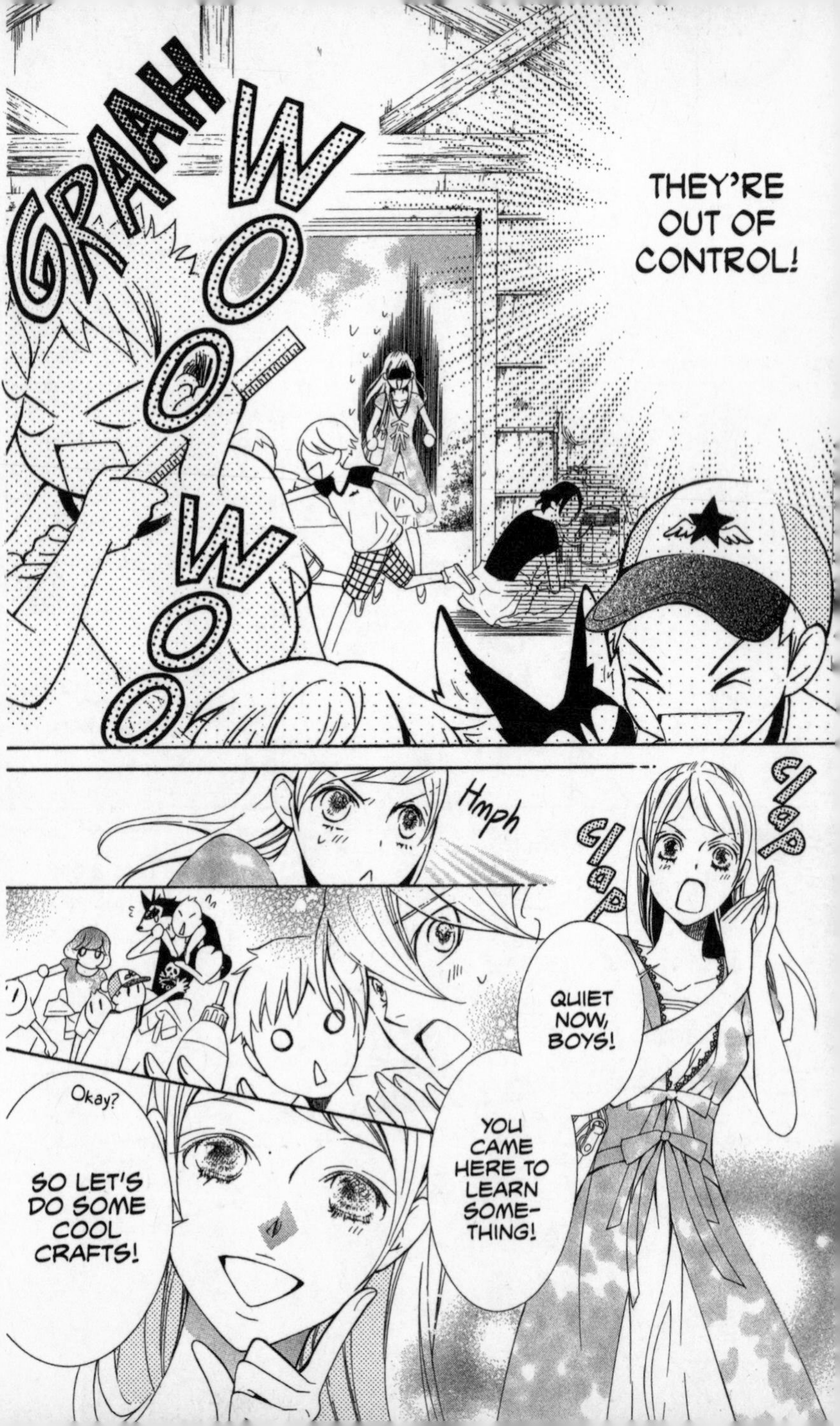
THEY'RE OUT OF CONTROL!
GRAAHWOOOWOOO
Clap Clap
Hmph
QUIET NOW, BOYS!
YOU CAME HERE TO LEARN SOME-THING!
Okay?
SO LET'S DO SOME COOL CRAFTS!

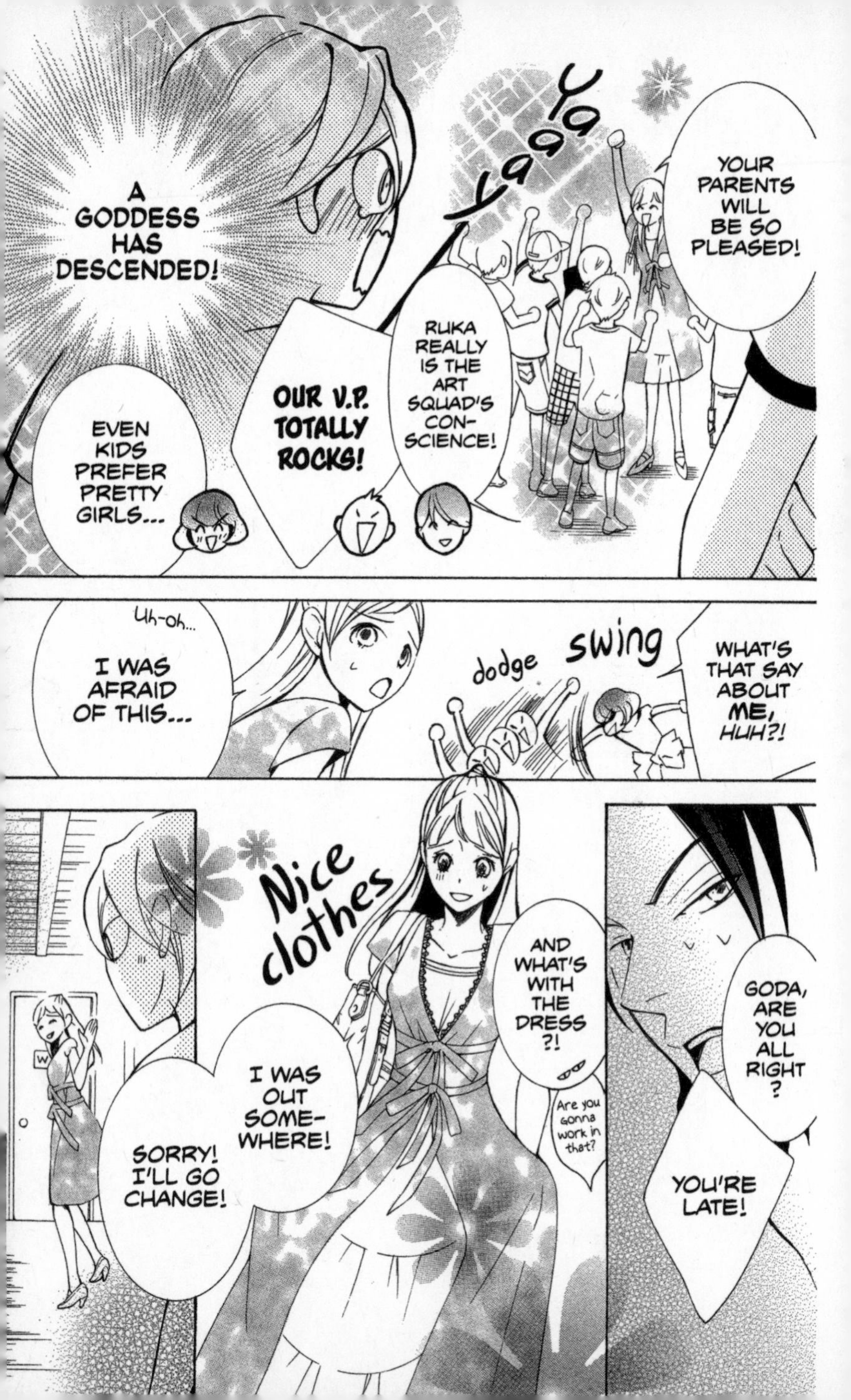
YOUR PARENTS WILL BE SO PLEASED!
Yaaay
RUKA REALLY IS THE ART SQUAD'S CON-SCIENCE!
OUR V.P. TOTALLY ROCKS!
A GODDESS HAS DESCENDED!
EVEN KIDS PREFER PRETTY GIRLS...
WHAT'S THAT SAY ABOUT ME, HUH?!
swing
dodge
Uh-oh...
I WAS AFRAID OF THIS...
GODA, ARE YOU ALL RIGHT?
YOU'RE LATE!
AND WHAT'S WITH THE DRESS?!
Are you gonna work in that?
Nice clothes
I WAS OUT SOMEWHERE!
SORRY! I'LL GO CHANGE!

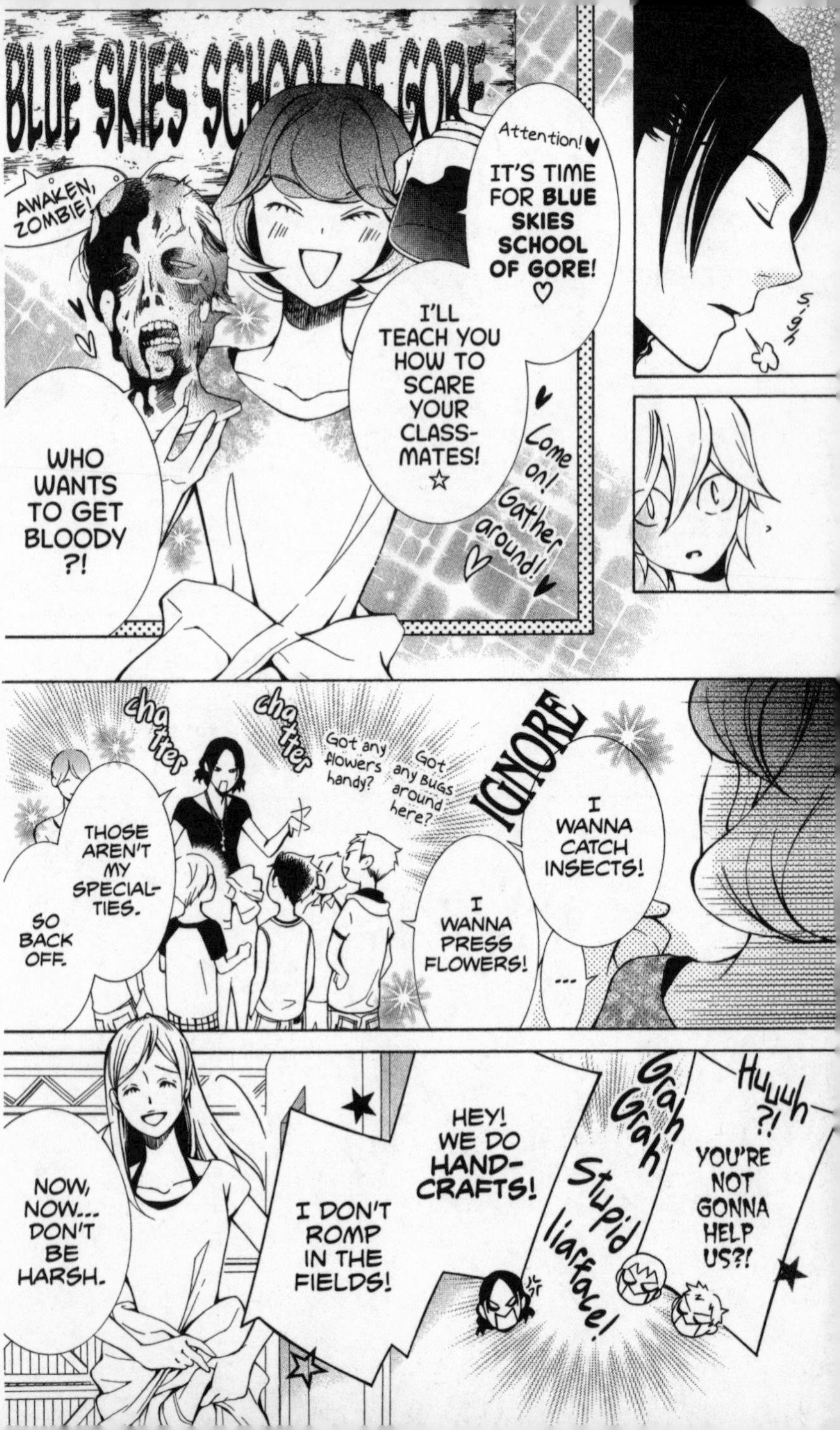
sigh
BLUE SKIES SCHOOL OF GORE
Attention! IT'S TIME FOR BLUE SKIES SCHOOL OF GORE!
I'LL TEACH YOU HOW TO SCARE YOUR CLASSMATES!
Come on! Gather around!
AWAKEN, ZOMBIE!
WHO WANTS TO GET BLOODY?!
IGNORE
I WANNA CATCH INSECTS!
I WANNA PRESS FLOWERS!
...
Got any bugs around here?
Got any flowers handy?
chatter chatter
THOSE AREN'T MY SPECIALTIES.
SO BACK OFF.
Huuuh?!
YOU'RE NOT GONNA HELP US?!
Grah Grah
Stupid liarface!
HEY! WE DO HANDCRAFTS!
I DON'T ROMP IN THE FIELDS!
NOW, NOW... DON'T BE HARSH.

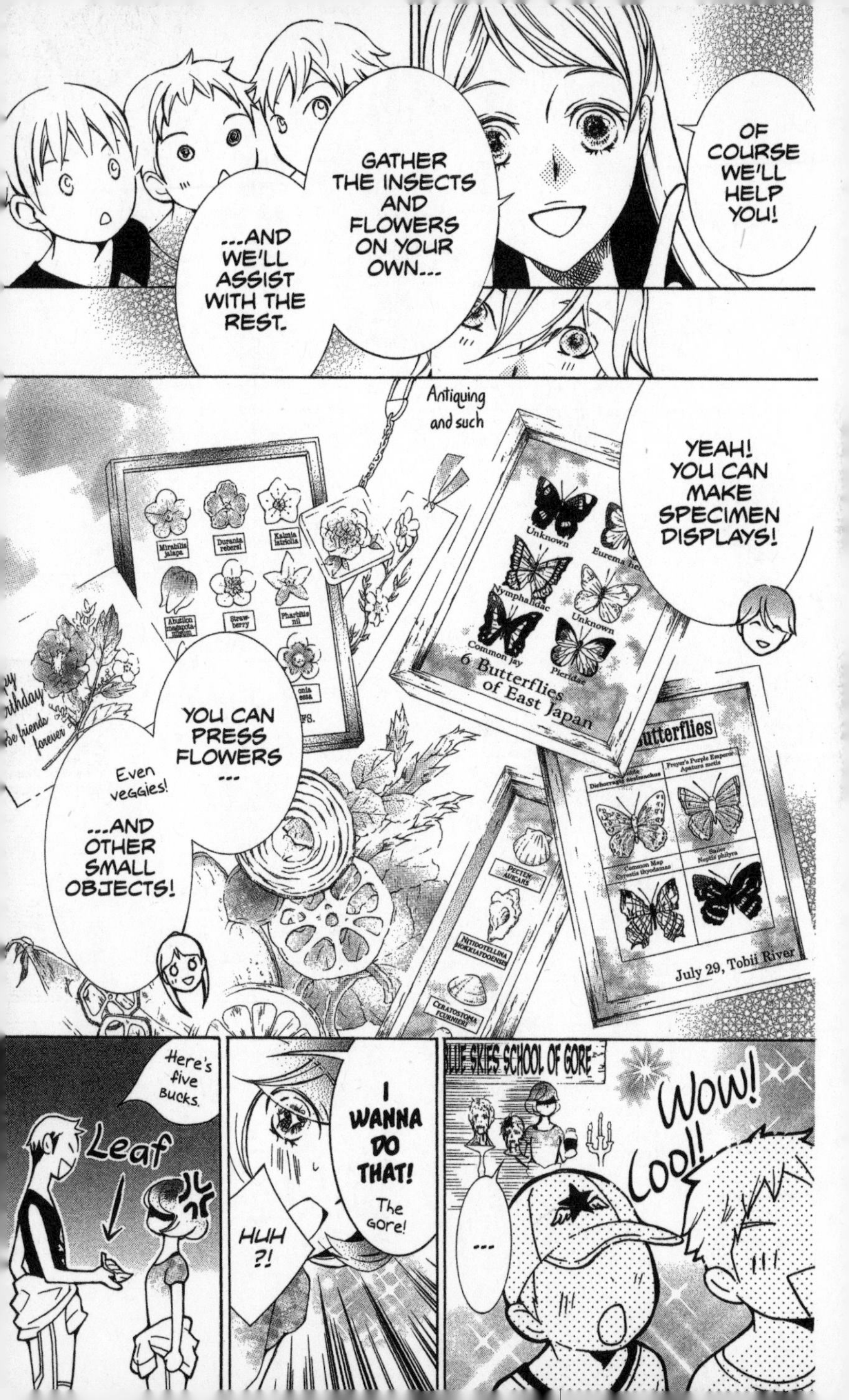
OF COURSE WE'LL HELP YOU!
GATHER THE INSECTS AND FLOWERS ON YOUR OWN...
...AND WE'LL ASSIST WITH THE REST.
YEAH! YOU CAN MAKE SPECIMEN DISPLAYS!
Antiquing and such
6 Butterflies of East Japan
Butterflies
July 29, Tobii River
YOU CAN PRESS FLOWERS ---
Even veggies!
...AND OTHER SMALL OBJECTS!
BLUE SKIES SCHOOL OF GORE
WOW! COOL!!
...
I WANNA DO THAT!
The gore!
HUH ?!
Here's five bucks.
Leaf

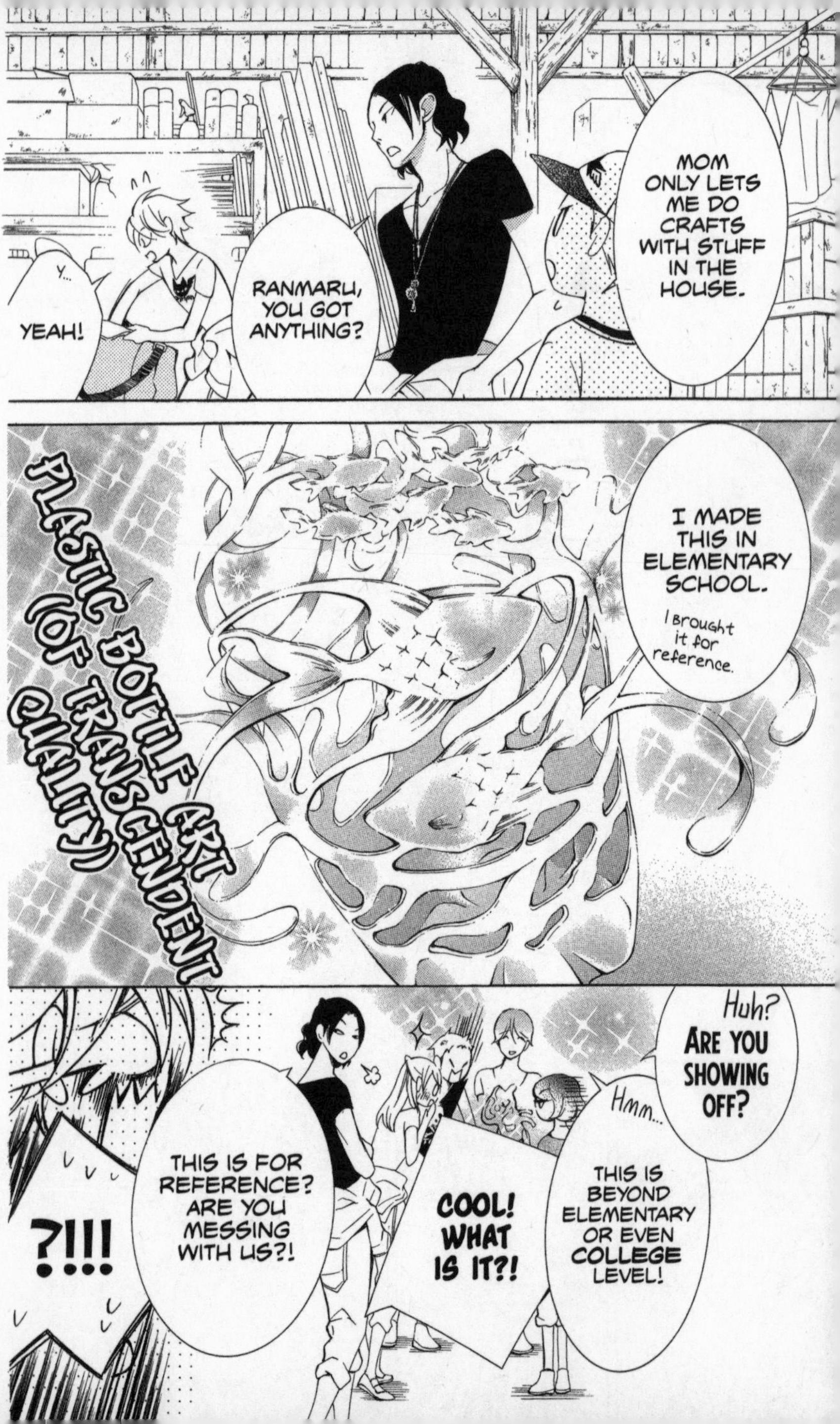
MOM ONLY LETS ME DO CRAFTS WITH STUFF IN THE HOUSE.
RANMARU, YOU GOT ANYTHING?
Y... YEAH!
I MADE THIS IN ELEMENTARY SCHOOL.
I brought it for reference.
PLASTIC BOTTLE ART (OF TRANSCENDENT QUALITY)
Huh? ARE YOU SHOWING OFF?
Hmm...
THIS IS BEYOND ELEMENTARY OR EVEN COLLEGE LEVEL!
COOL! WHAT IS IT?!
THIS IS FOR REFERENCE? ARE YOU MESSING WITH US?!
?!!!

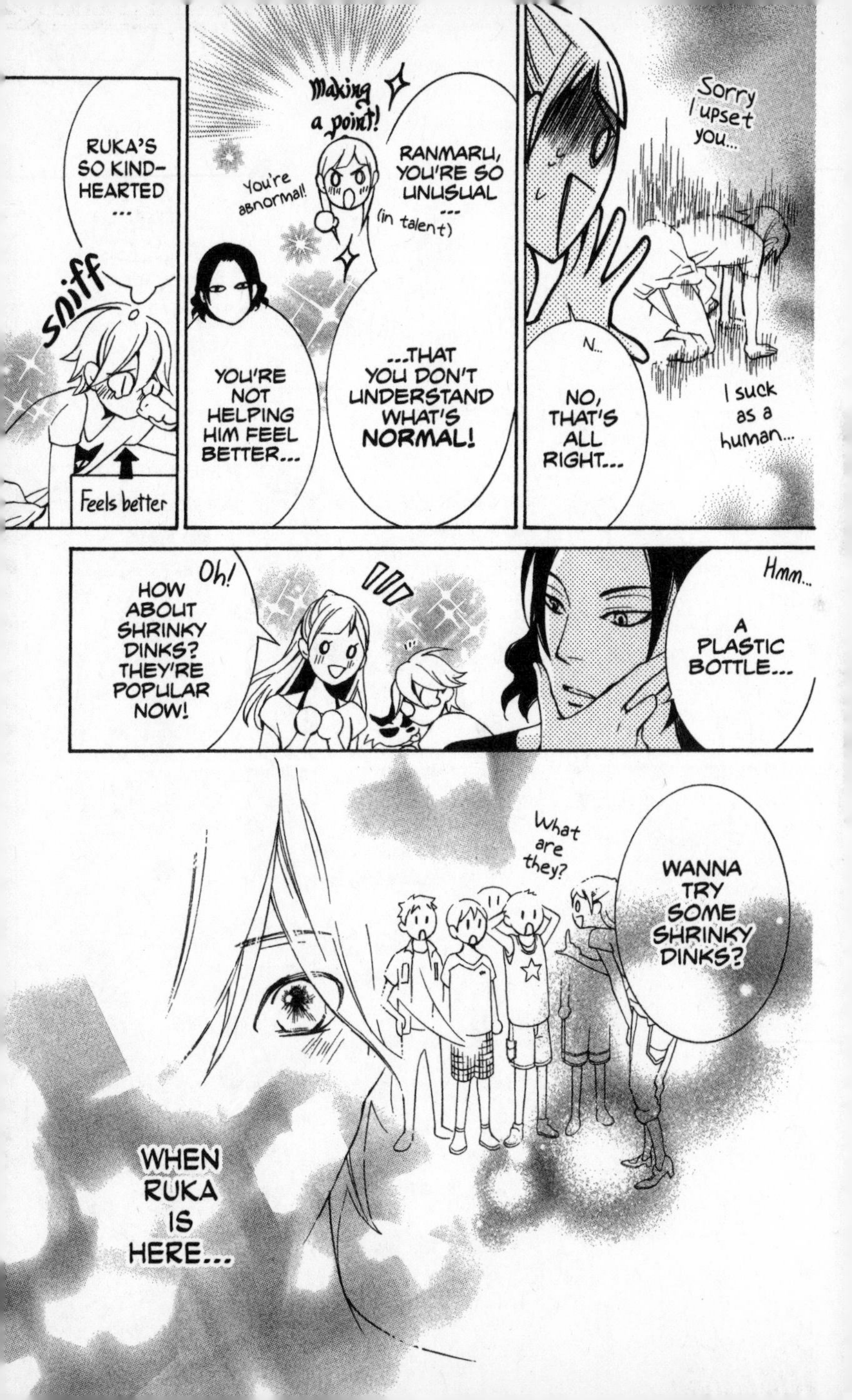
Sorry I upset you...
I suck as a human...
N...
NO, THAT'S ALL RIGHT...
Making a point!
RANMARU, YOU'RE SO UNUSUAL ...
(in talent)
You're abnormal!
...THAT YOU DON'T UNDERSTAND WHAT'S NORMAL!
YOU'RE NOT HELPING HIM FEEL BETTER...
RUKA'S SO KIND-HEARTED ...
sniff
Feels better
Hmm...
A PLASTIC BOTTLE...
Oh!
HOW ABOUT SHRINKY DINKS? THEY'RE POPULAR NOW!
WANNA TRY SOME SHRINKY DINKS?
What are they?
WHEN RUKA IS HERE...

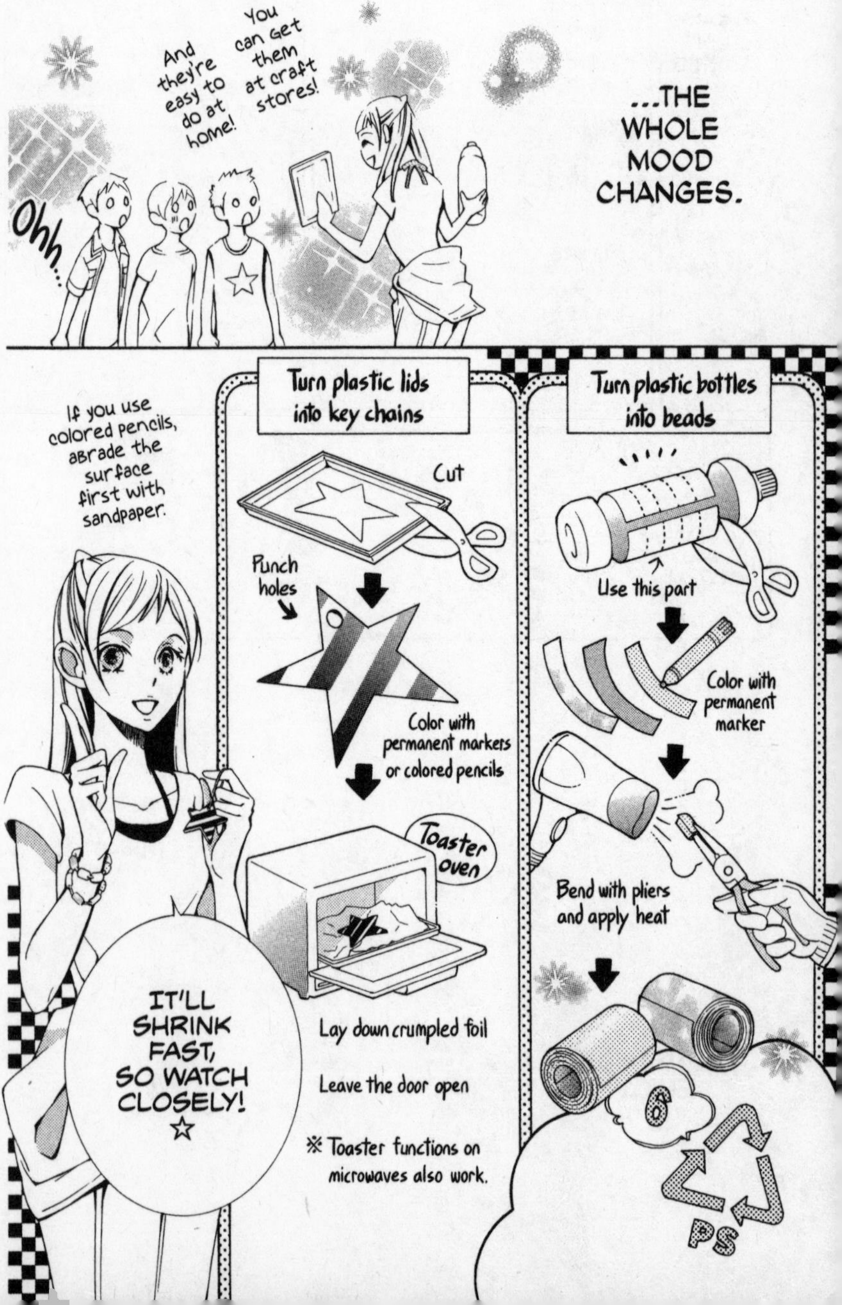
...THE WHOLE MOOD CHANGES.
You can get them at craft stores!
And they're easy to do at home!
Ohh...
Turn plastic bottles into beads
Use this part
Color with permanent marker
Bend with pliers and apply heat
Turn plastic lids into key chains
Cut
Punch holes
Color with permanent markers or colored pencils
Toaster oven
Lay down crumpled foil
Leave the door open
※ Toaster functions on microwaves also work.
If you use colored pencils, abrade the surface first with sandpaper.
IT'LL SHRINK FAST, SO WATCH CLOSELY! ☆
PS

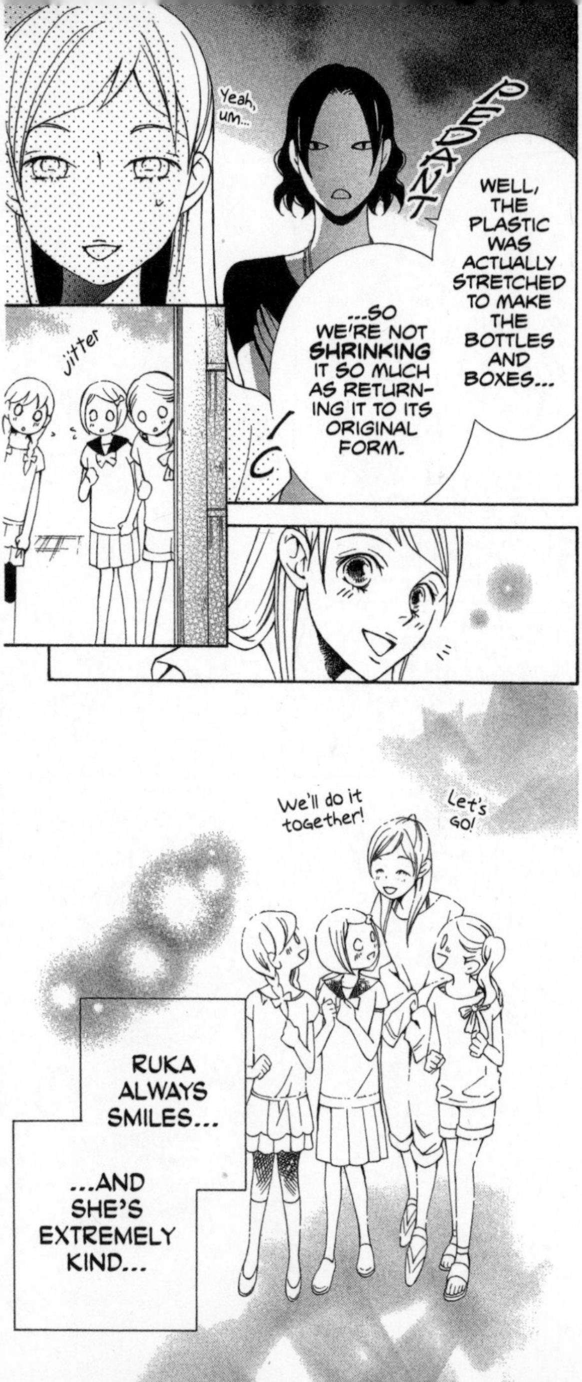
PEDANT
WELL, THE PLASTIC WAS ACTUALLY STRETCHED TO MAKE THE BOTTLES AND BOXES...
...SO WE'RE NOT SHRINKING IT SO MUCH AS RETURNING IT TO ITS ORIGINAL FORM.
Yeah, um...
jitter
Let's go!
We'll do it together!
RUKA ALWAYS SMILES...
...AND SHE'S EXTREMELY KIND...

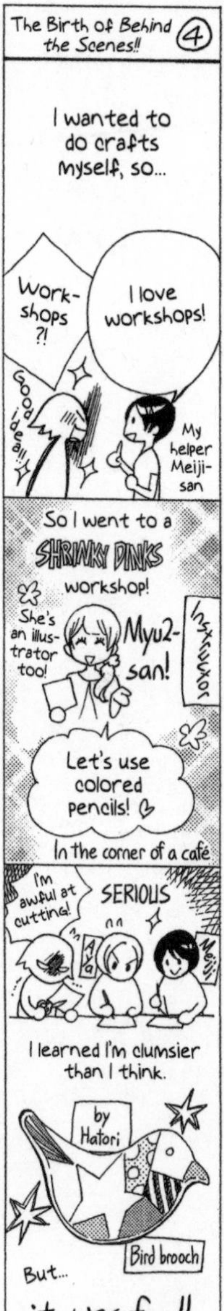
The Birth of Behind the Scenes!! 4
I wanted to do crafts myself, so...
I love workshops!
Work-shops ?!
Good idea!!
My helper Meiji-san
So I went to a
SHRINKY DINKS
workshop!
She's an illus-trator too!
Myu2-san!
Instructor
Let's use colored pencils!
In the corner of a café
I'm awful at cutting!
SERIOUS
Aya
Meiji
I learned I'm clumsier than I think.
by Hatori
Bird brooch
But...
...it was fun!!

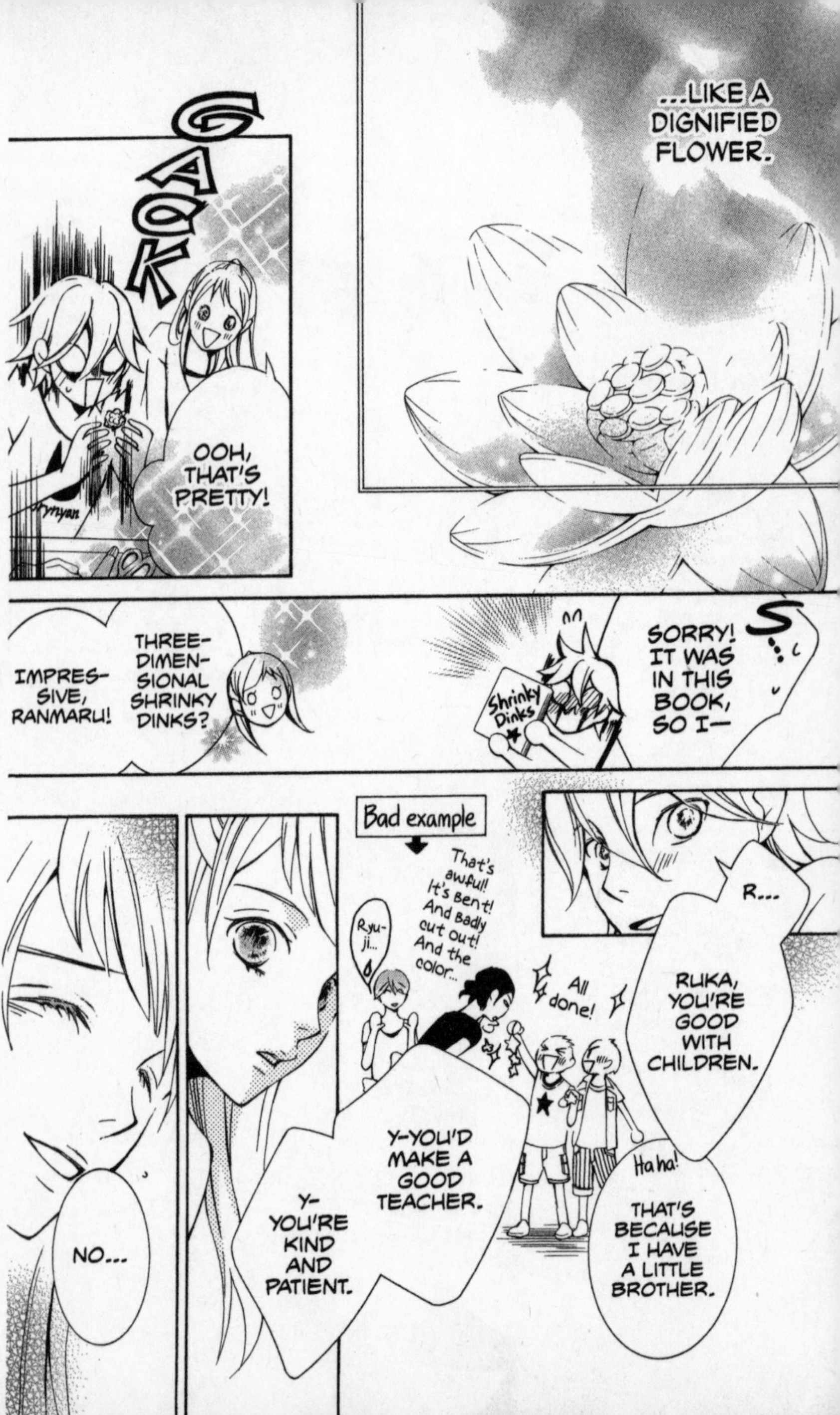
...LIKE A DIGNIFIED FLOWER.
GACK
OOH, THAT'S PRETTY!
S...
SORRY! IT WAS IN THIS BOOK, SO I—
Shrinky Dinks
THREE-DIMENSIONAL SHRINKY DINKS?
IMPRESSIVE, RANMARU!
R...
RUKA, YOU'RE GOOD WITH CHILDREN.
Ha ha!
THAT'S BECAUSE I HAVE A LITTLE BROTHER.
Bad example
That's awful! It's bent! And badly cut out! And the color...
Ryu-ji...
All done!
Y-YOU'D MAKE A GOOD TEACHER.
Y-YOU'RE KIND AND PATIENT.
NO...

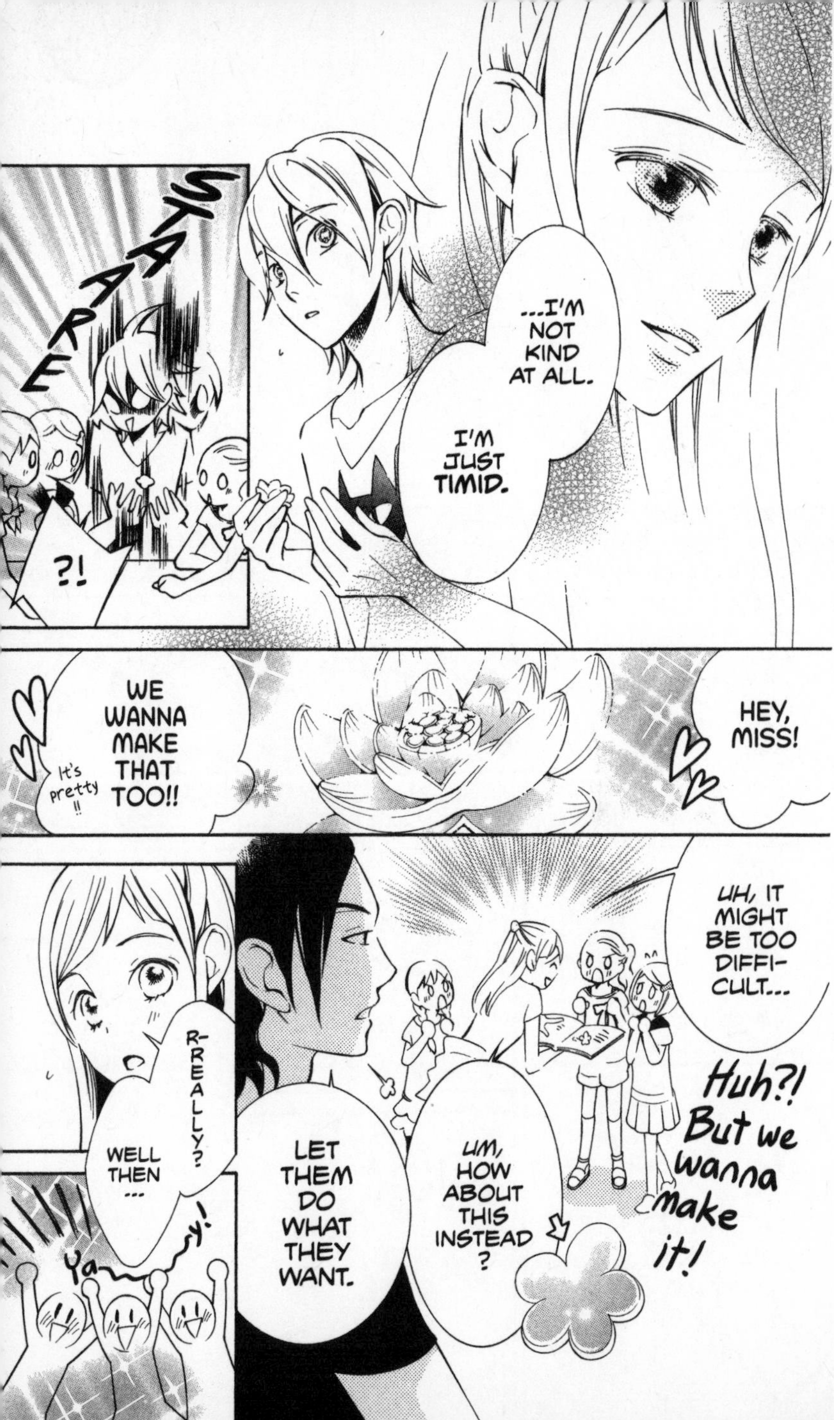
...I'M NOT KIND AT ALL.
I'M JUST TIMID.
STAARE
?!
HEY, MISS!
WE WANNA MAKE THAT TOO!!
It's pretty!!
UH, IT MIGHT BE TOO DIFFI-CULT...
Huh?! But we wanna make it!
UM, HOW ABOUT THIS INSTEAD?
LET THEM DO WHAT THEY WANT.
R-REALLY?
WELL THEN...
Ya~y!

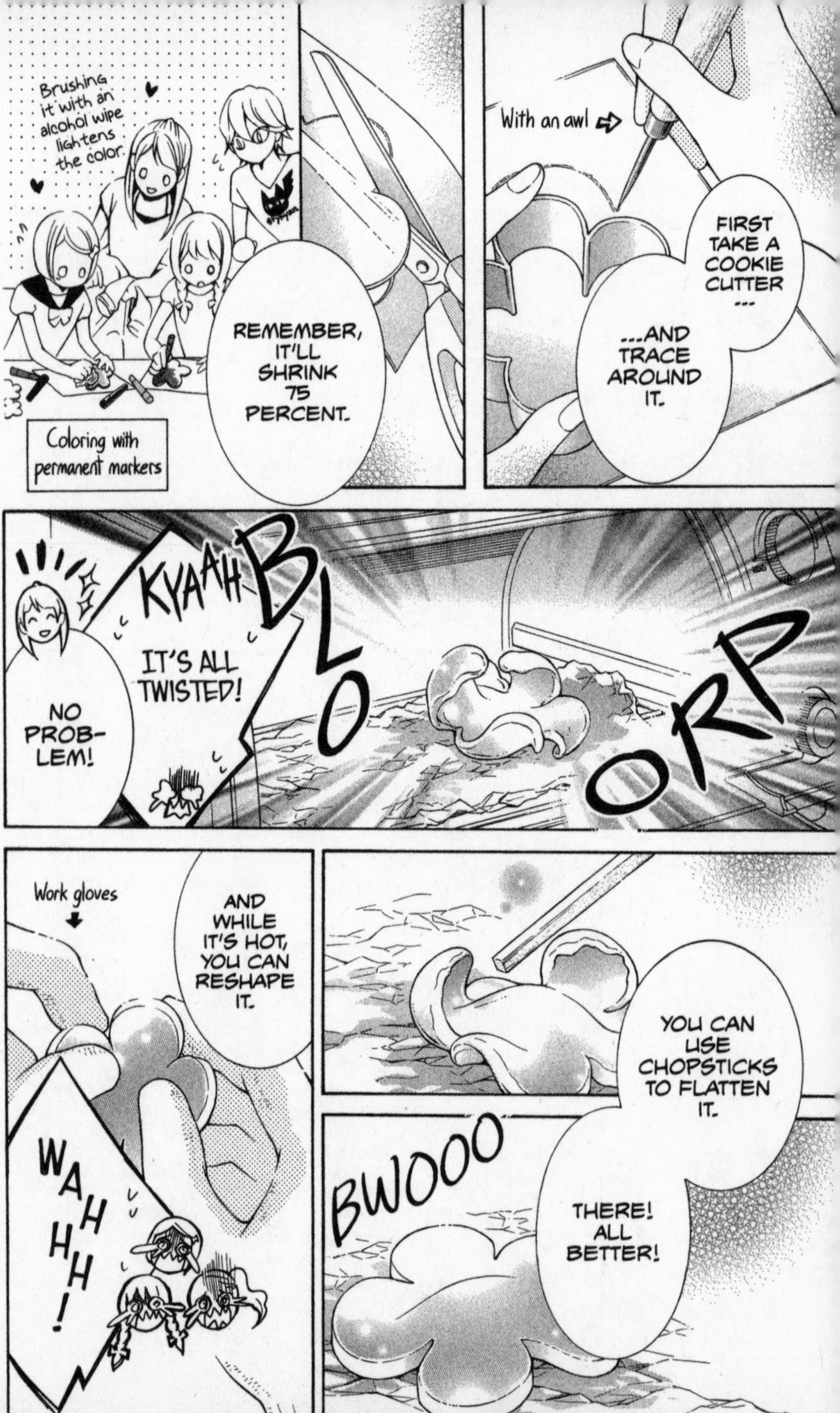
With an awl
FIRST TAKE A COOKIE CUTTER ...
...AND TRACE AROUND IT.
REMEMBER, IT'LL SHRINK 75 PERCENT.
Brushing it with an alcohol wipe lightens the color.
Coloring with permanent markers
BLOORP
KYAAH
IT'S ALL TWISTED!
NO PROB-LEM!
YOU CAN USE CHOPSTICKS TO FLATTEN IT.
THERE! ALL BETTER!
BWOOO
Work gloves
AND WHILE IT'S HOT, YOU CAN RESHAPE IT.
WAHHHH!

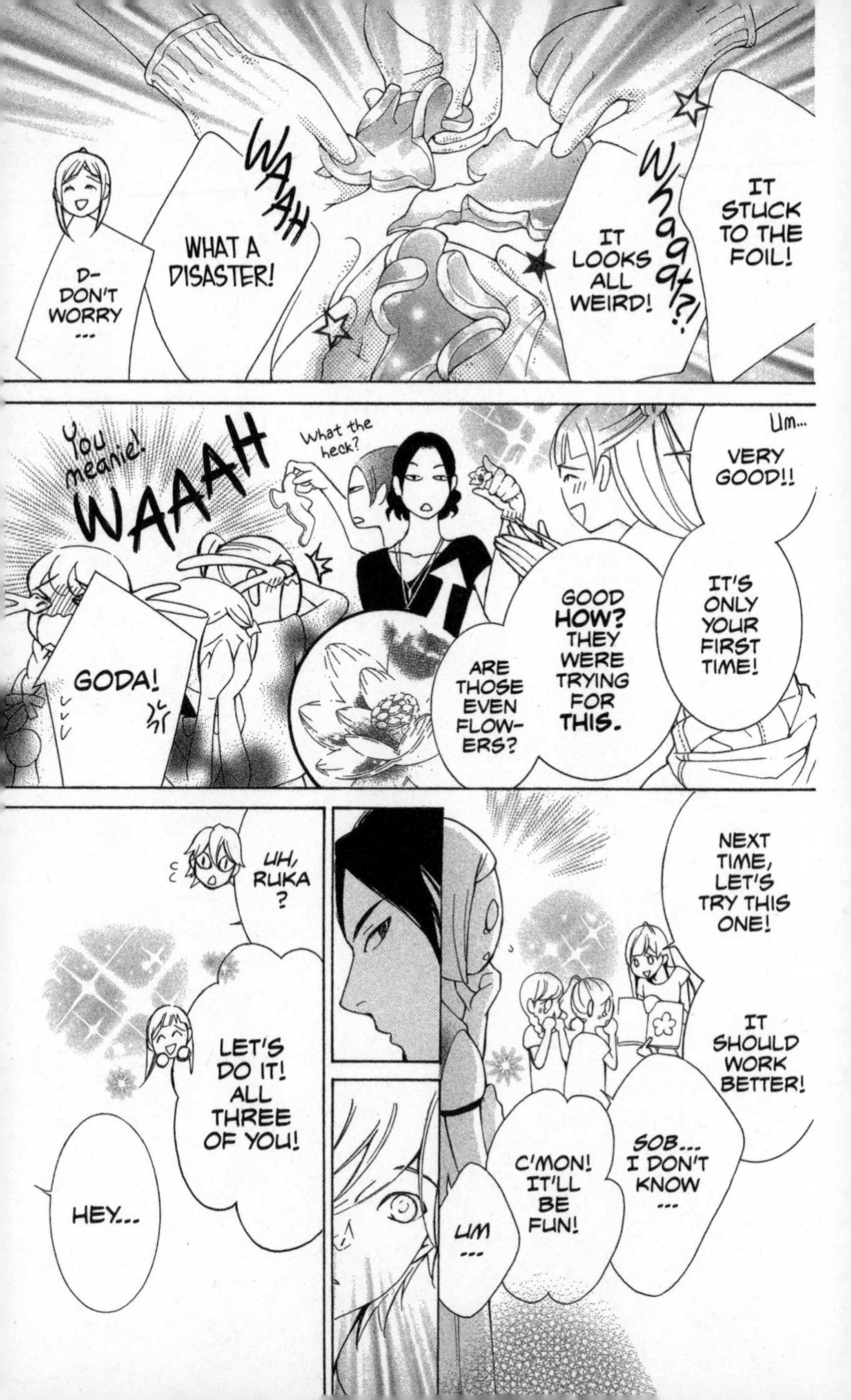
IT STUCK TO THE FOIL!
Whaaat?!
IT LOOKS ALL WEIRD!
WAAAH
WHAT A DISASTER!
D-DON'T WORRY...
Um... VERY GOOD!!
IT'S ONLY YOUR FIRST TIME!
GOOD HOW? THEY WERE TRYING FOR THIS.
ARE THOSE EVEN FLOWERS?
What the heck?
You meanie!
WAAAH
GODA!
NEXT TIME, LET'S TRY THIS ONE!
IT SHOULD WORK BETTER!
SOB... I DON'T KNOW...
C'MON! IT'LL BE FUN!
UM...
UH, RUKA?
LET'S DO IT! ALL THREE OF YOU!
HEY...

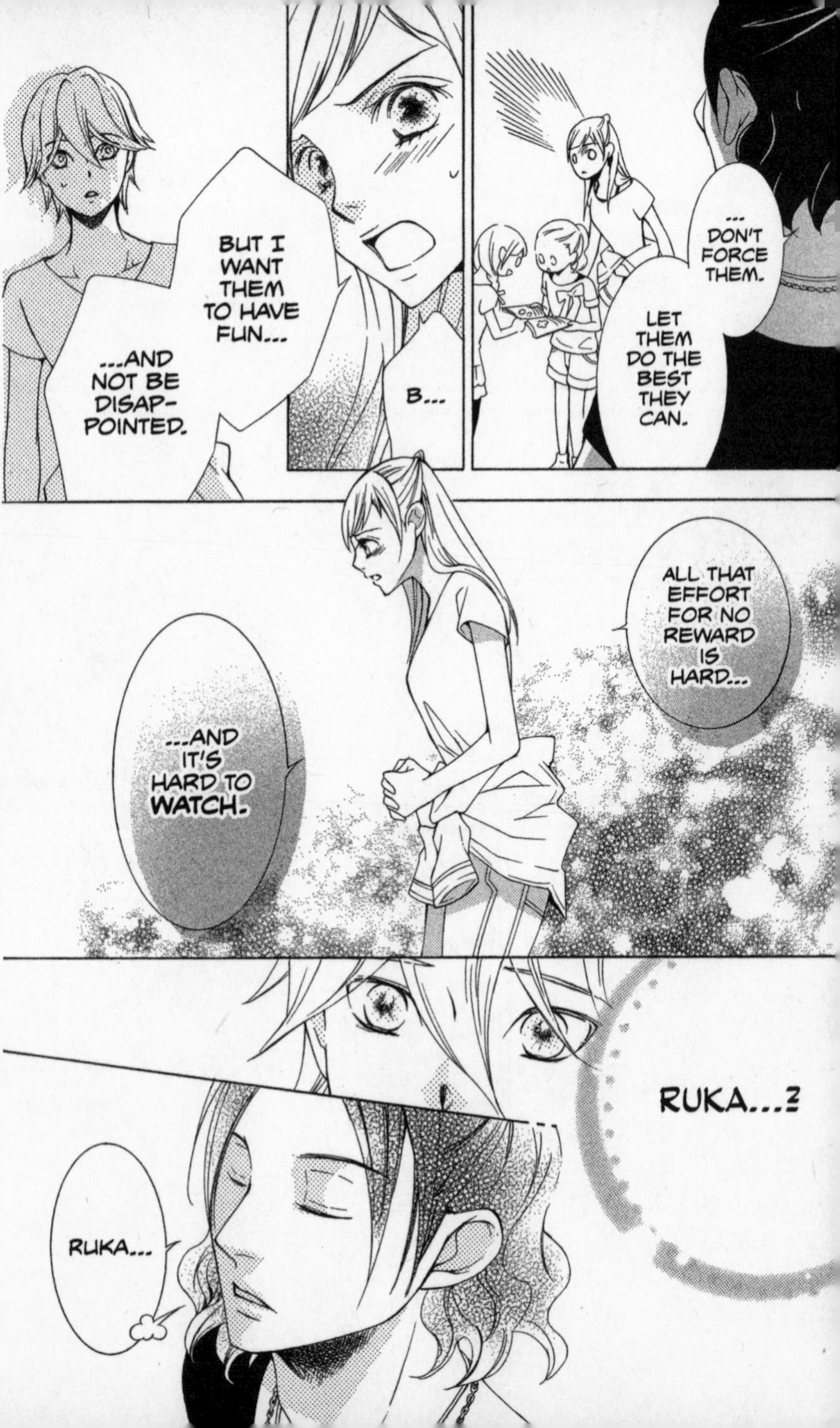
... DON'T FORCE THEM.
LET THEM DO THE BEST THEY CAN.
B...
BUT I WANT THEM TO HAVE FUN...
...AND NOT BE DISAP-POINTED.
ALL THAT EFFORT FOR NO REWARD IS HARD...
...AND IT'S HARD TO WATCH.
RUKA...?
RUKA...

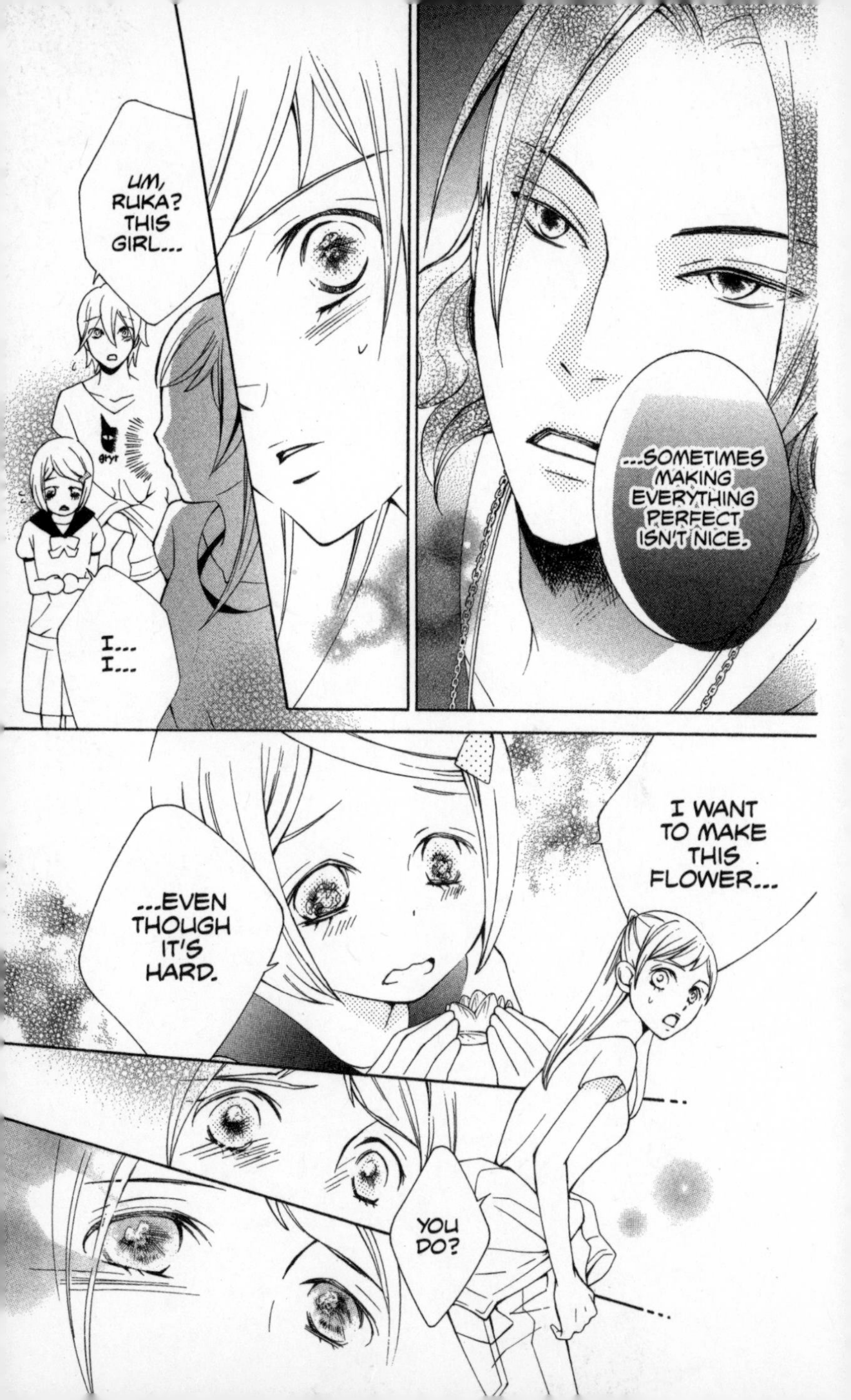
...SOMETIMES MAKING EVERYTHING PERFECT ISN'T NICE.
UM, RUKA? THIS GIRL...
I... I...
I WANT TO MAKE THIS FLOWER...
...EVEN THOUGH IT'S HARD.
YOU DO?

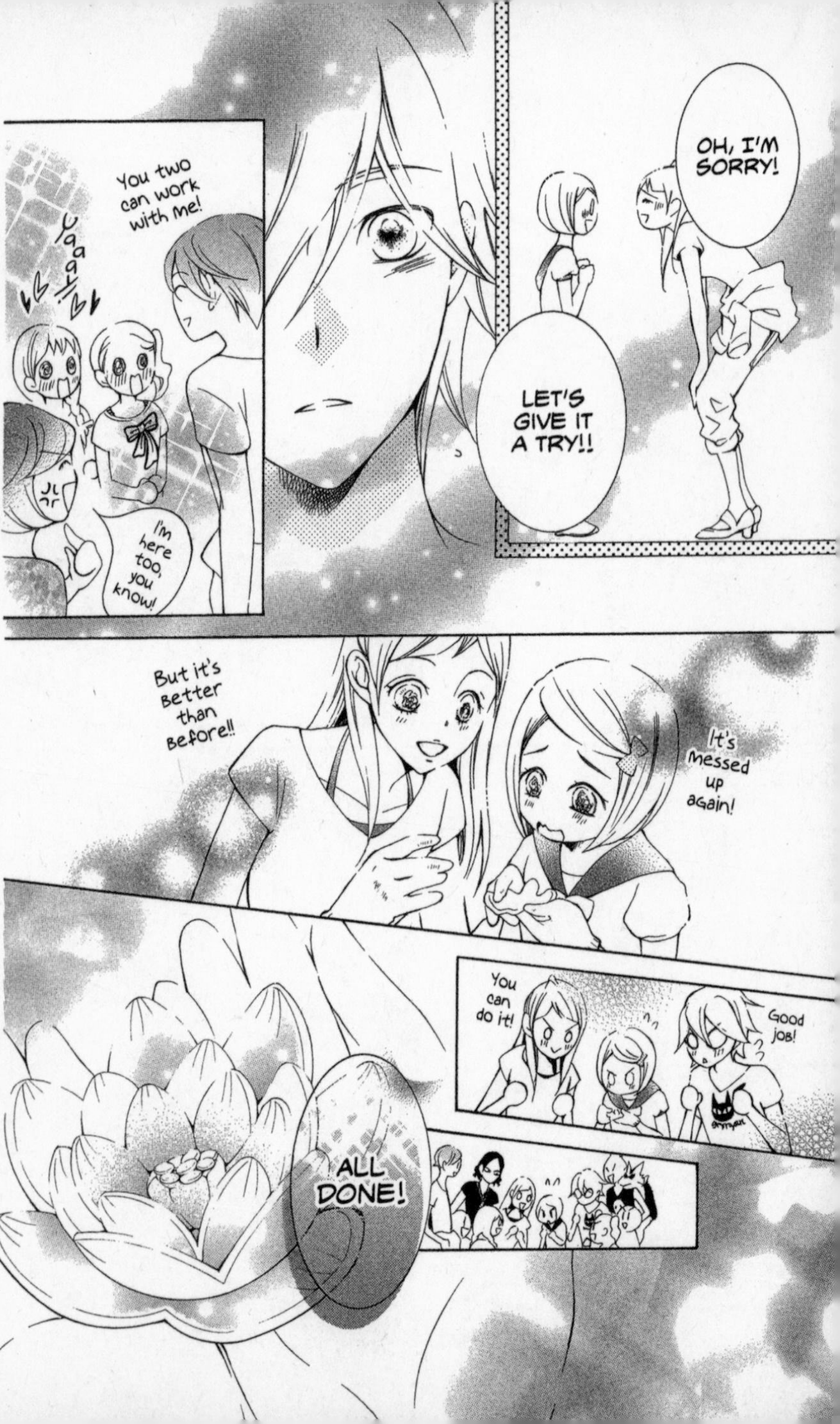
OH, I'M SORRY!
LET'S GIVE IT A TRY!!
You two can work with me!
Yaaay!!
I'm here too, you know!
It's messed up again!
But it's better than before!!
Good job!
You can do it!
ALL DONE!

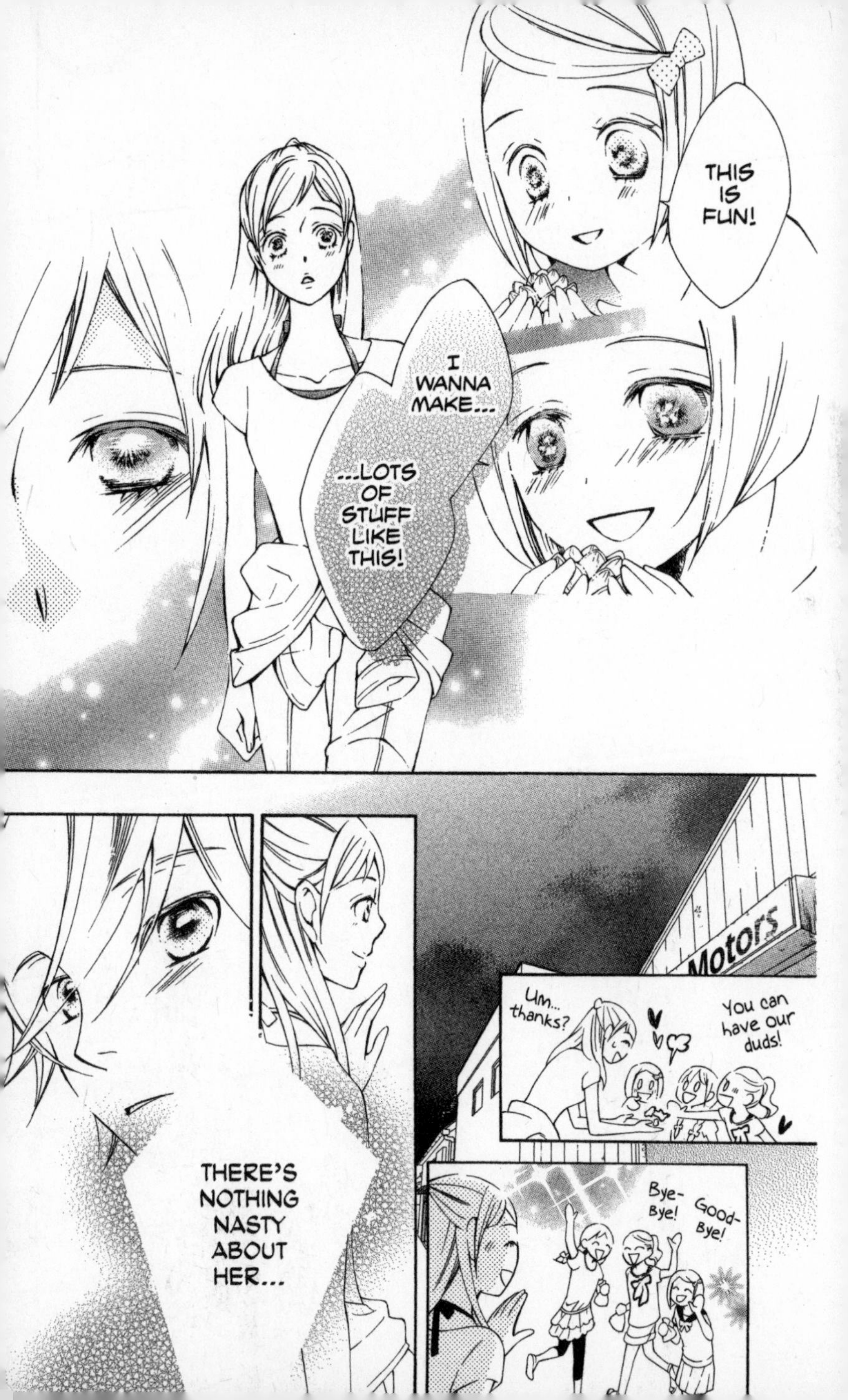
THIS IS FUN!
I WANNA MAKE...
...LOTS OF STUFF LIKE THIS!
Motors
You can have our duds!
Um... thanks?
Good-Bye!
Bye-Bye!
THERE'S NOTHING NASTY ABOUT HER...

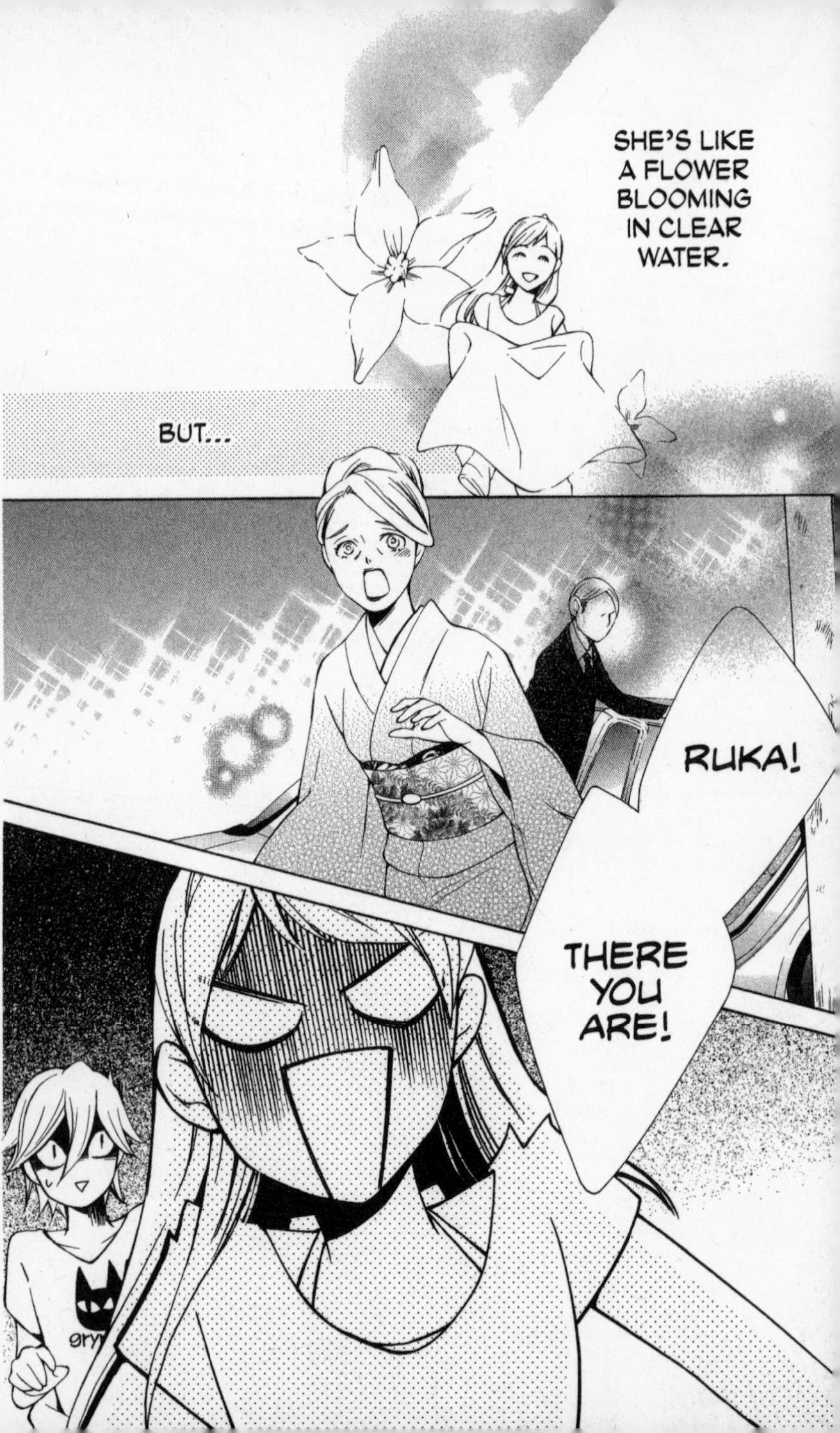
SHE'S LIKE A FLOWER BLOOMING IN CLEAR WATER.
BUT...
RUKA!
THERE YOU ARE!

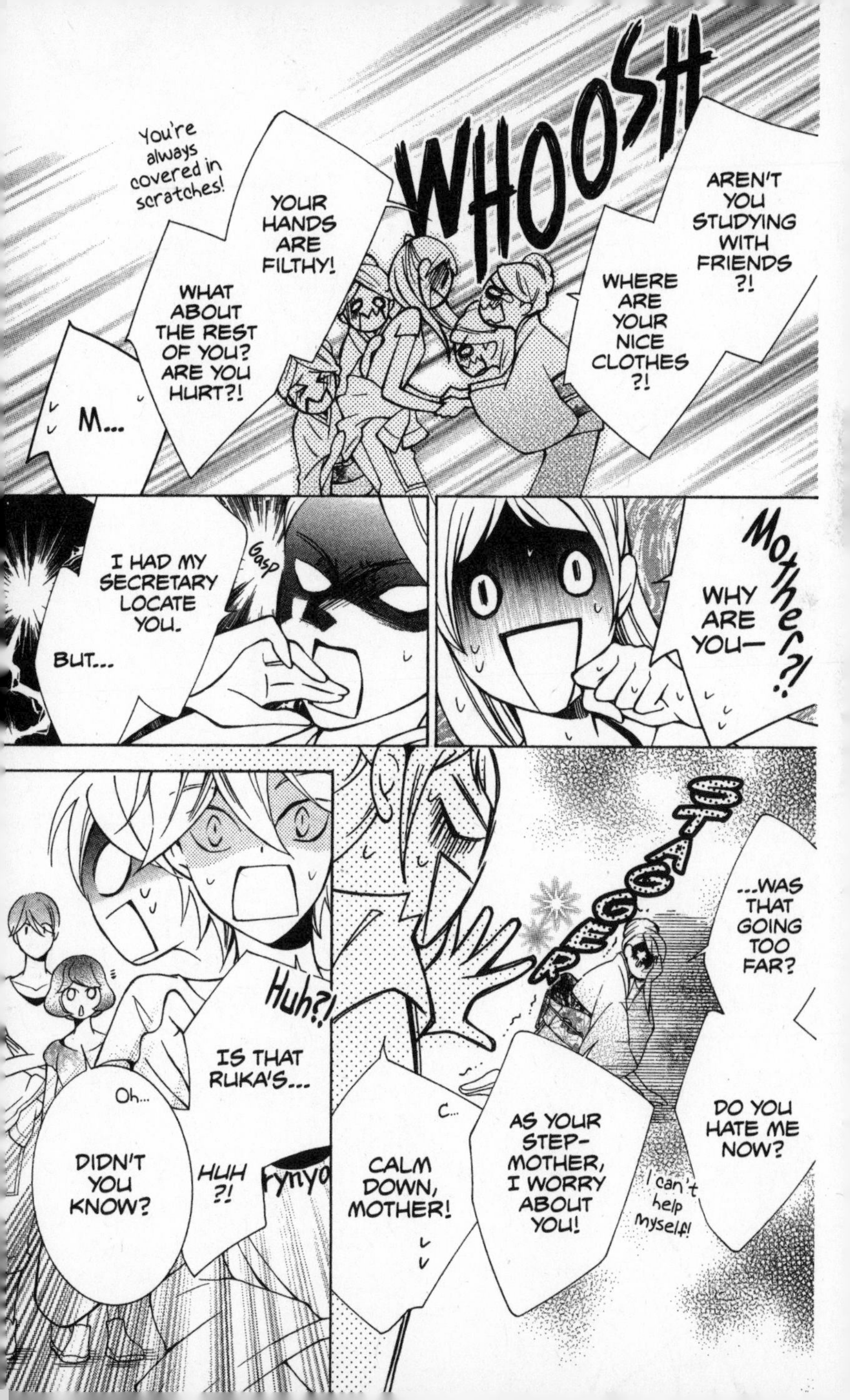
AREN'T YOU STUDYING WITH FRIENDS?!
WHERE ARE YOUR NICE CLOTHES?!
WHOOSH
YOUR HANDS ARE FILTHY!
You're always covered in scratches!
WHAT ABOUT THE REST OF YOU? ARE YOU HURT?!
M...
Mother?!
WHY ARE YOU—
Gasp
I HAD MY SECRETARY LOCATE YOU.
BUT...
...WAS THAT GOING TOO FAR?
DO YOU HATE ME NOW?
I can't help myself!
AS YOUR STEP-MOTHER, I WORRY ABOUT YOU!
C...
CALM DOWN, MOTHER!
Huh?!
IS THAT RUKA'S...
Oh...
DIDN'T YOU KNOW?
HUH?!

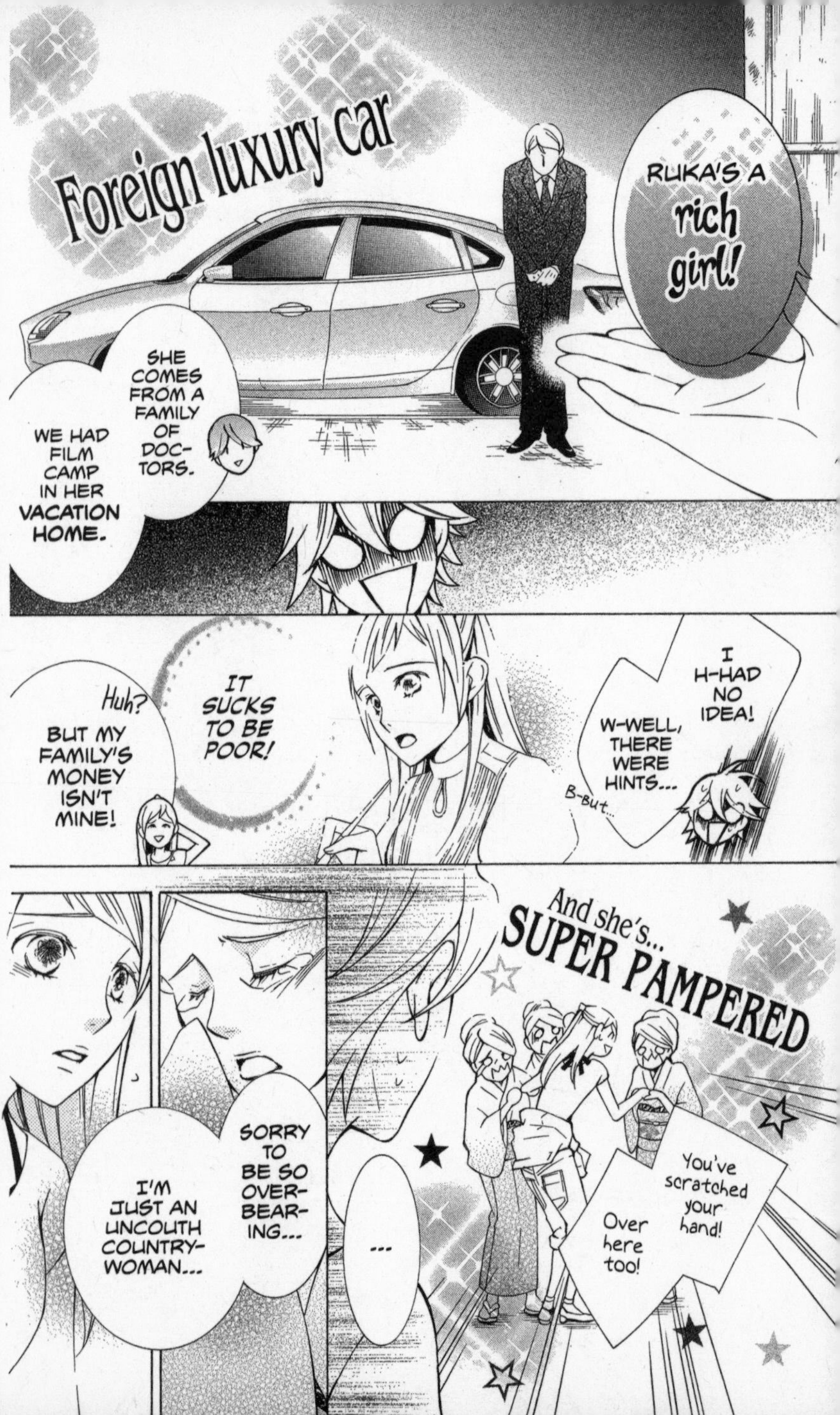
RUKA'S A rich girl!
Foreign luxury car
SHE COMES FROM A FAMILY OF DOC-TORS.
WE HAD FILM CAMP IN HER VACATION HOME.
I H-HAD NO IDEA!
W-WELL, THERE WERE HINTS...
B-but...
IT SUCKS TO BE POOR!
Huh?
BUT MY FAMILY'S MONEY ISN'T MINE!
And she's... SUPER PAMPERED
You've scratched your hand!
Over here too!
...
SORRY TO BE SO OVER-BEARING...
I'M JUST AN UNCOUTH COUNTRY-WOMAN...

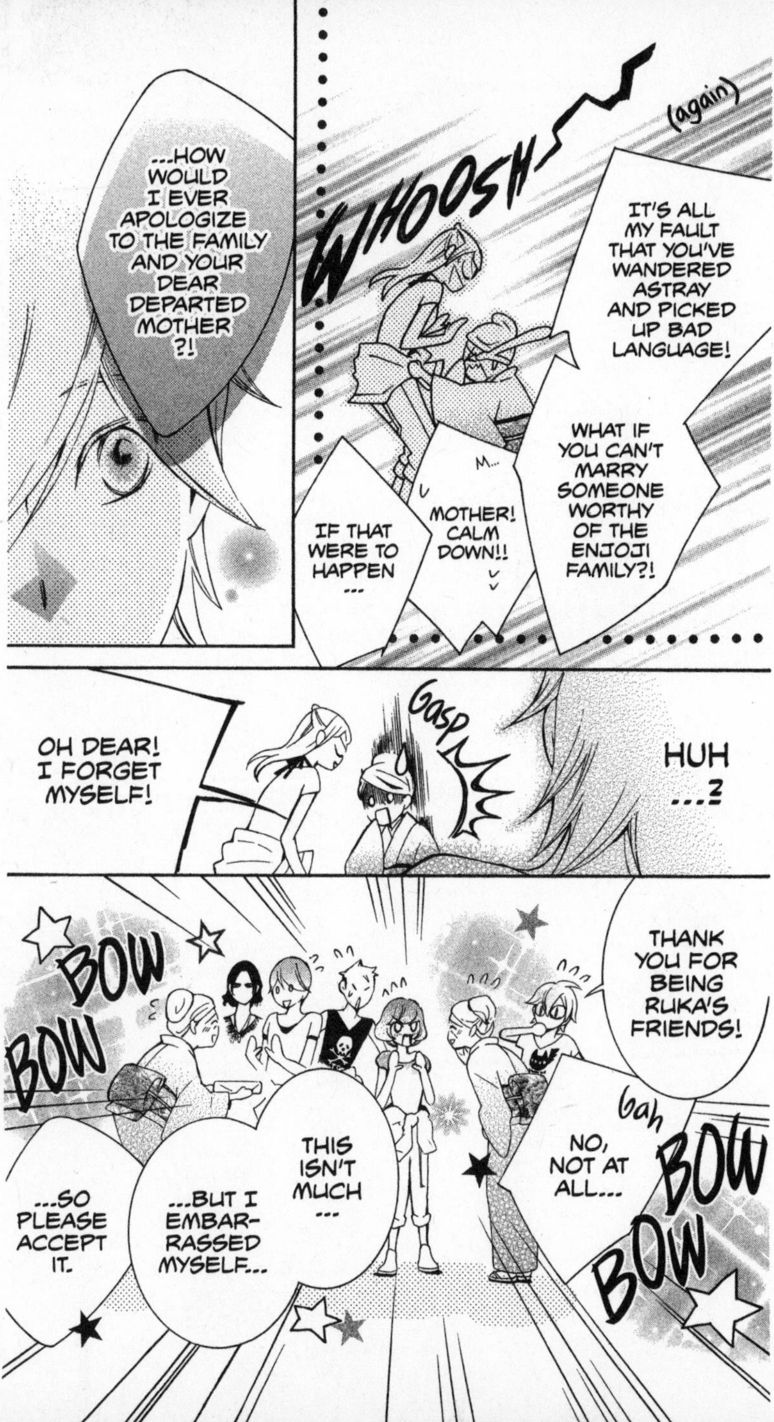
(again)
WHOOSH
IT'S ALL MY FAULT THAT YOU'VE WANDERED ASTRAY AND PICKED UP BAD LANGUAGE!
WHAT IF YOU CAN'T MARRY SOMEONE WORTHY OF THE ENJOJI FAMILY?!
M... MOTHER! CALM DOWN!!
IF THAT WERE TO HAPPEN...
...HOW WOULD I EVER APOLOGIZE TO THE FAMILY AND YOUR DEAR DEPARTED MOTHER?!
HUH...?
Gasp
OH DEAR! I FORGET MYSELF!
THANK YOU FOR BEING RUKA'S FRIENDS!
BOW BOW
Gah
NO, NOT AT ALL...
THIS ISN'T MUCH...
...BUT I EMBAR-RASSED MYSELF...
...SO PLEASE ACCEPT IT.
BOW BOW

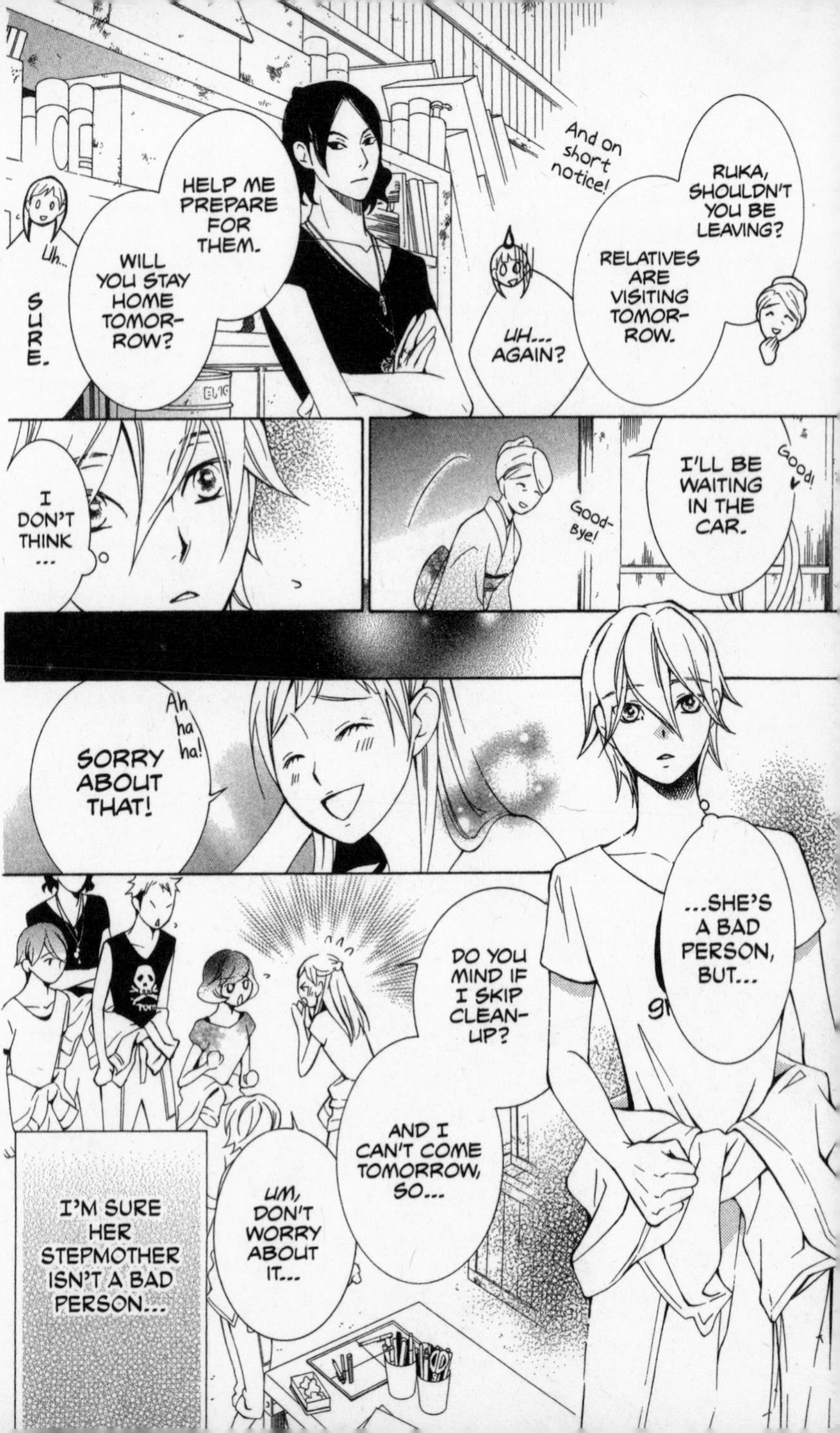
RUKA, SHOULDN'T YOU BE LEAVING?
RELATIVES ARE VISITING TOMORROW.
And on short notice!
UH... AGAIN?
HELP ME PREPARE FOR THEM.
WILL YOU STAY HOME TOMORROW?
Uh...
SURE.
I'LL BE WAITING IN THE CAR.
Good!
Good-Bye!
I DON'T THINK...
...SHE'S A BAD PERSON, BUT...
SORRY ABOUT THAT!
Ah ha ha!
DO YOU MIND IF I SKIP CLEAN-UP?
AND I CAN'T COME TOMORROW, SO...
UM, DON'T WORRY ABOUT IT...
I'M SURE HER STEPMOTHER ISN'T A BAD PERSON...

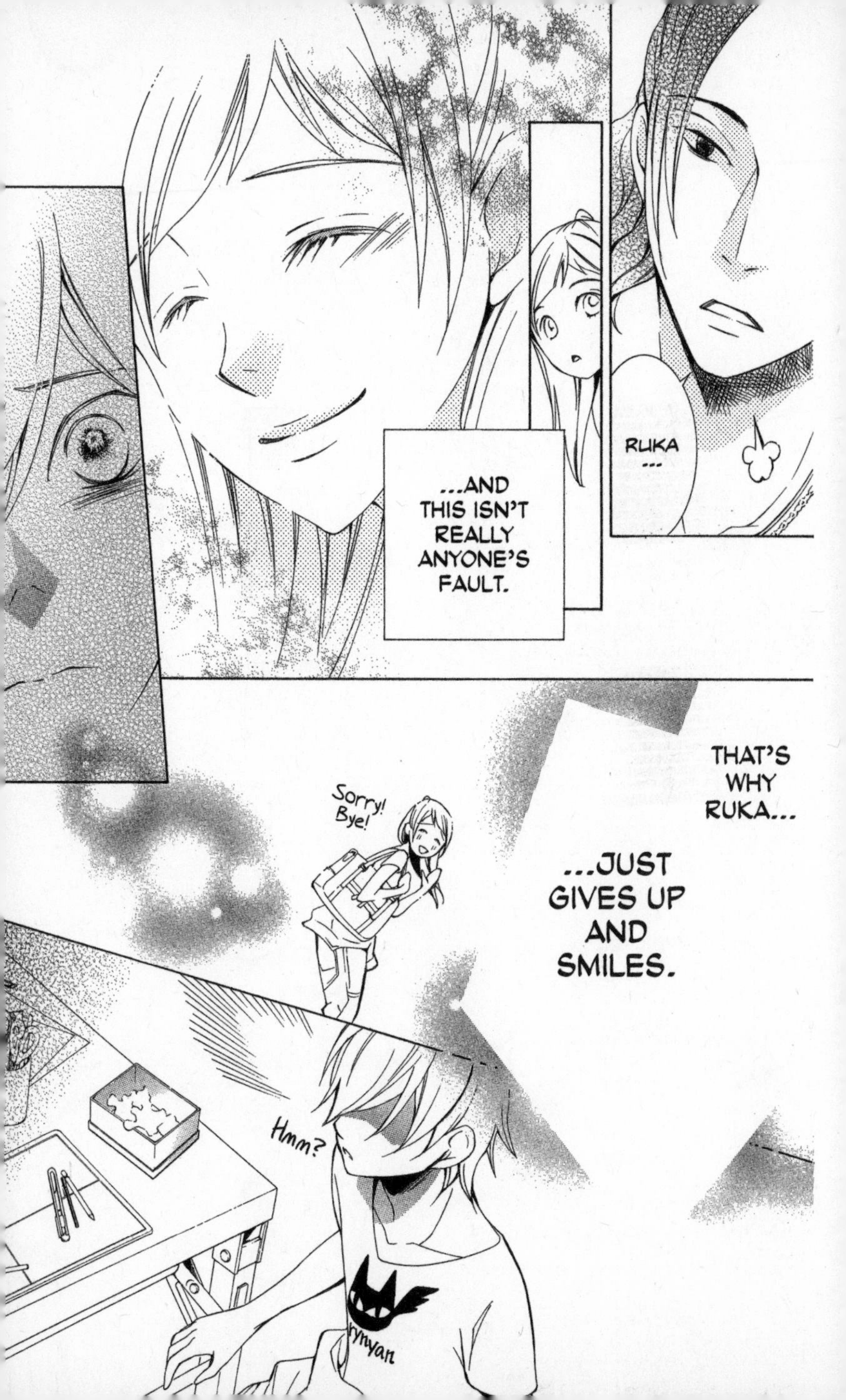
RUKA...
...AND THIS ISN'T REALLY ANYONE'S FAULT.
THAT'S WHY RUKA...
...JUST GIVES UP AND SMILES.
Sorry! Bye!
Hmm?

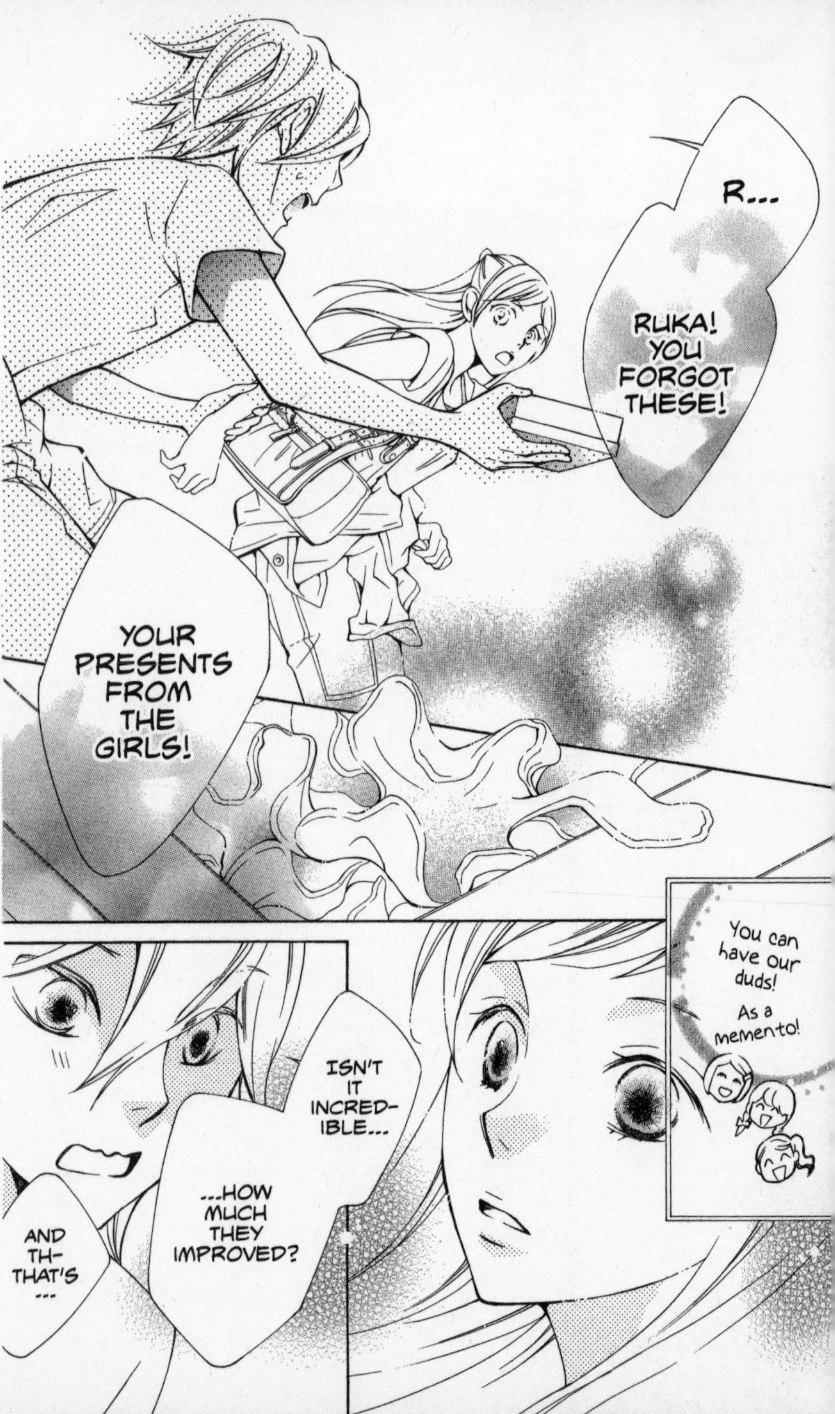
R...
RUKA! YOU FORGOT THESE!
YOUR PRESENTS FROM THE GIRLS!
You can have our duds!
As a memento!
ISN'T IT INCREDIBLE...
...HOW MUCH THEY IMPROVED?
AND TH-THAT'S ...

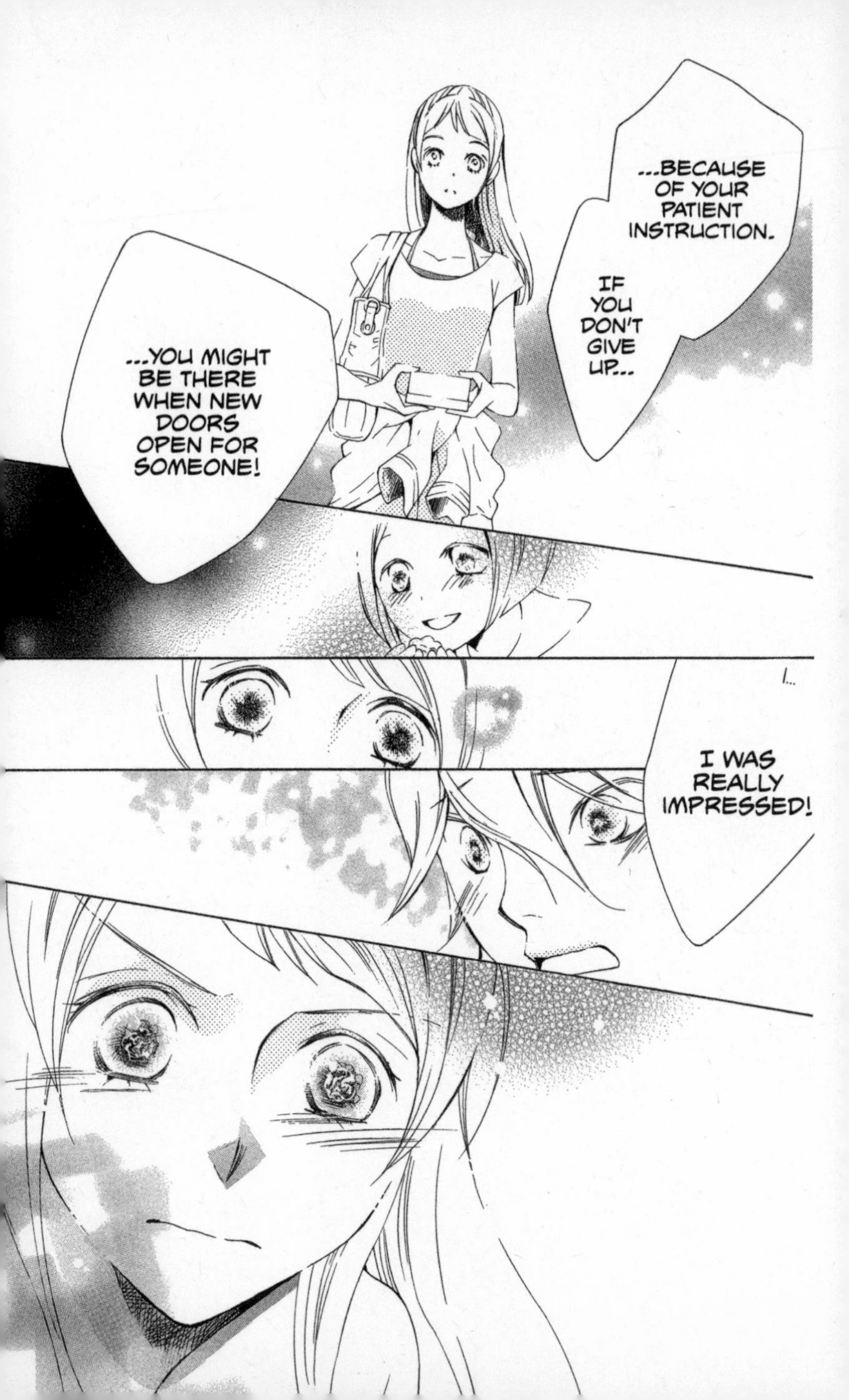
...BECAUSE OF YOUR PATIENT INSTRUCTION.
IF YOU DON'T GIVE UP...
...YOU MIGHT BE THERE WHEN NEW DOORS OPEN FOR SOMEONE!
I...
I WAS REALLY IMPRESSED!

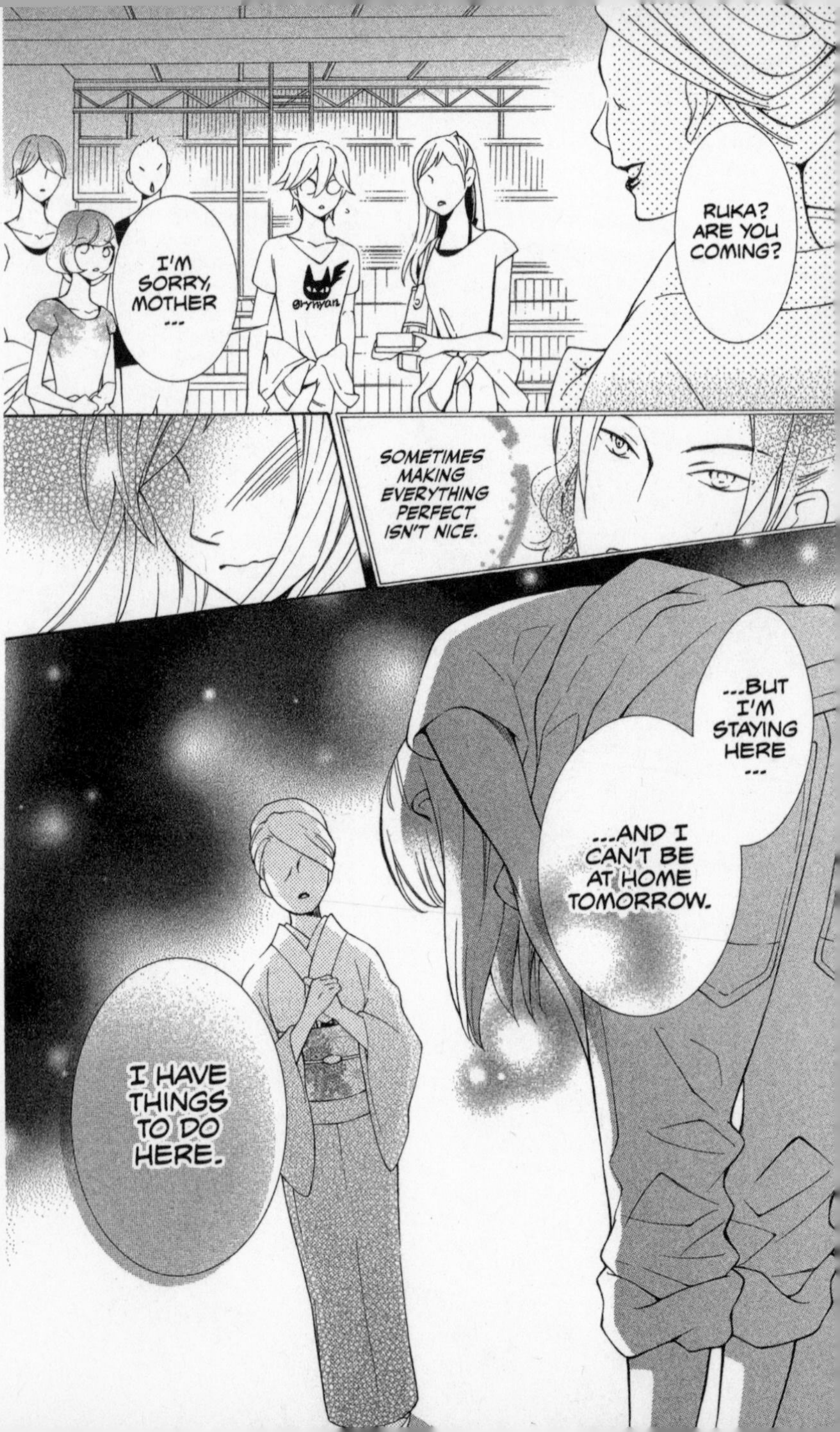
RUKA? ARE YOU COMING?
I'M SORRY, MOTHER ...
SOMETIMES MAKING EVERYTHING PERFECT ISN'T NICE.
...BUT I'M STAYING HERE ...
...AND I CAN'T BE AT HOME TOMORROW.
I HAVE THINGS TO DO HERE.

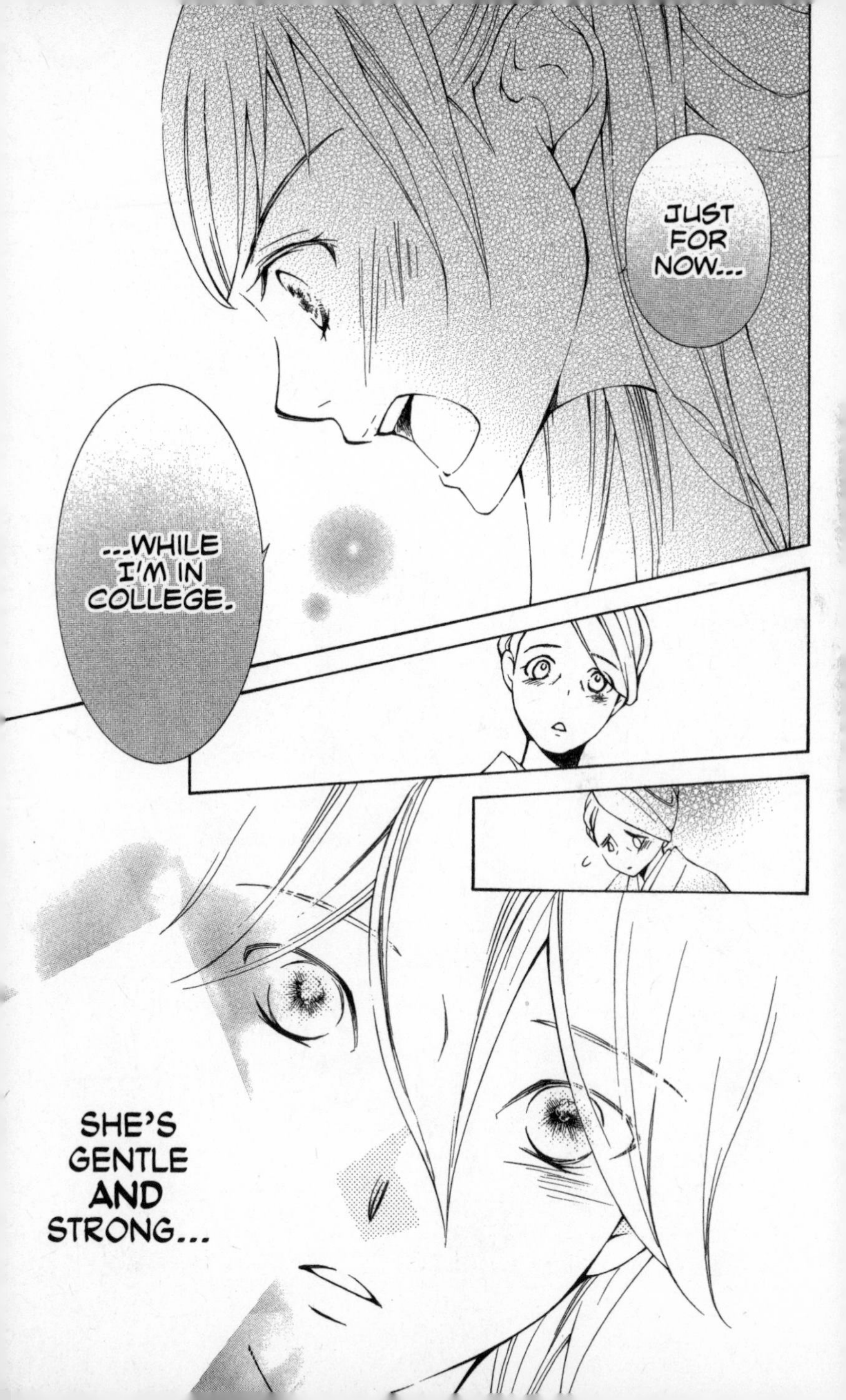
JUST FOR NOW...
...WHILE I'M IN COLLEGE.
SHE'S GENTLE AND STRONG...

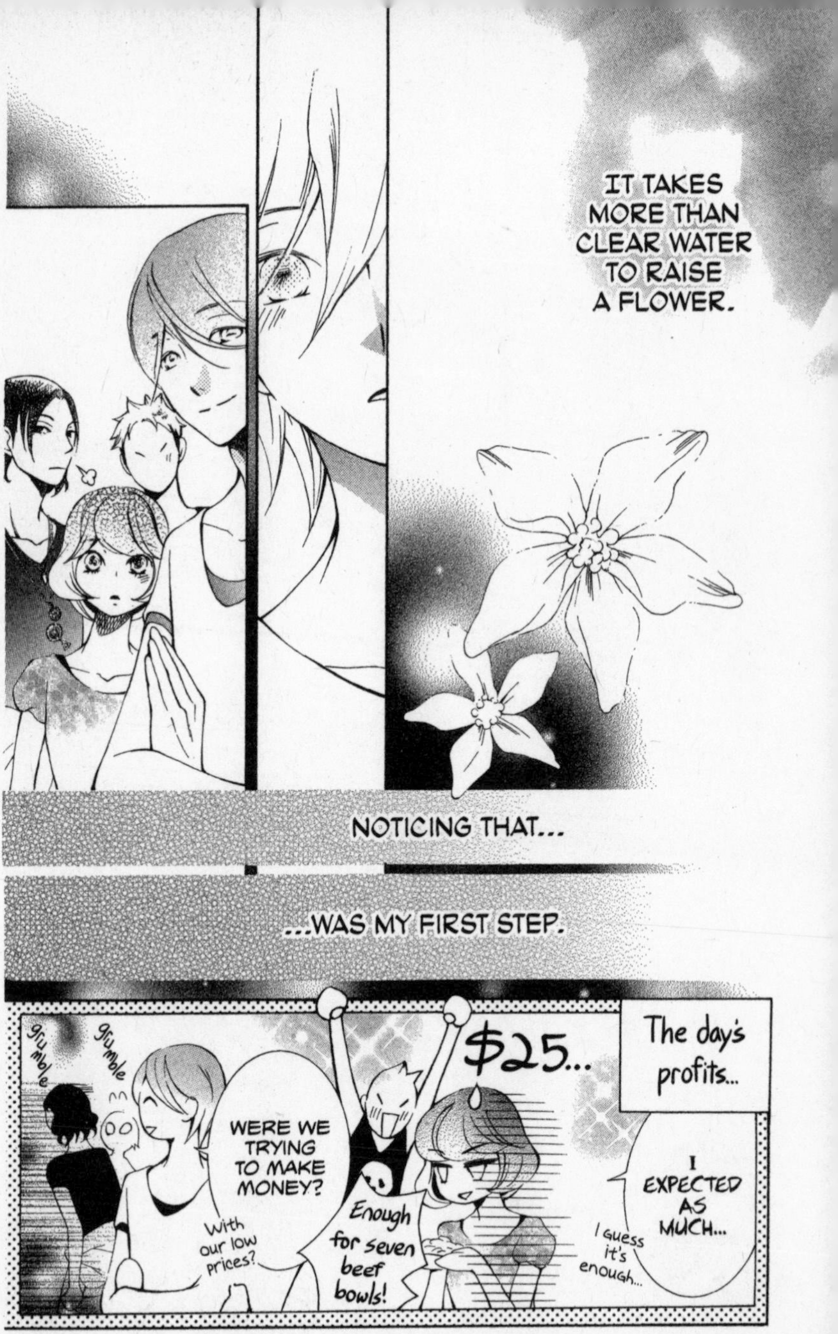
IT TAKES MORE THAN CLEAR WATER TO RAISE A FLOWER.
NOTICING THAT...
...WAS MY FIRST STEP.
The day's profits...
$25...
I EXPECTED AS MUCH...
I guess it's enough...
Enough for seven beef bowls!
WERE WE TRYING TO MAKE MONEY?
With our low prices?
grumble
grumble

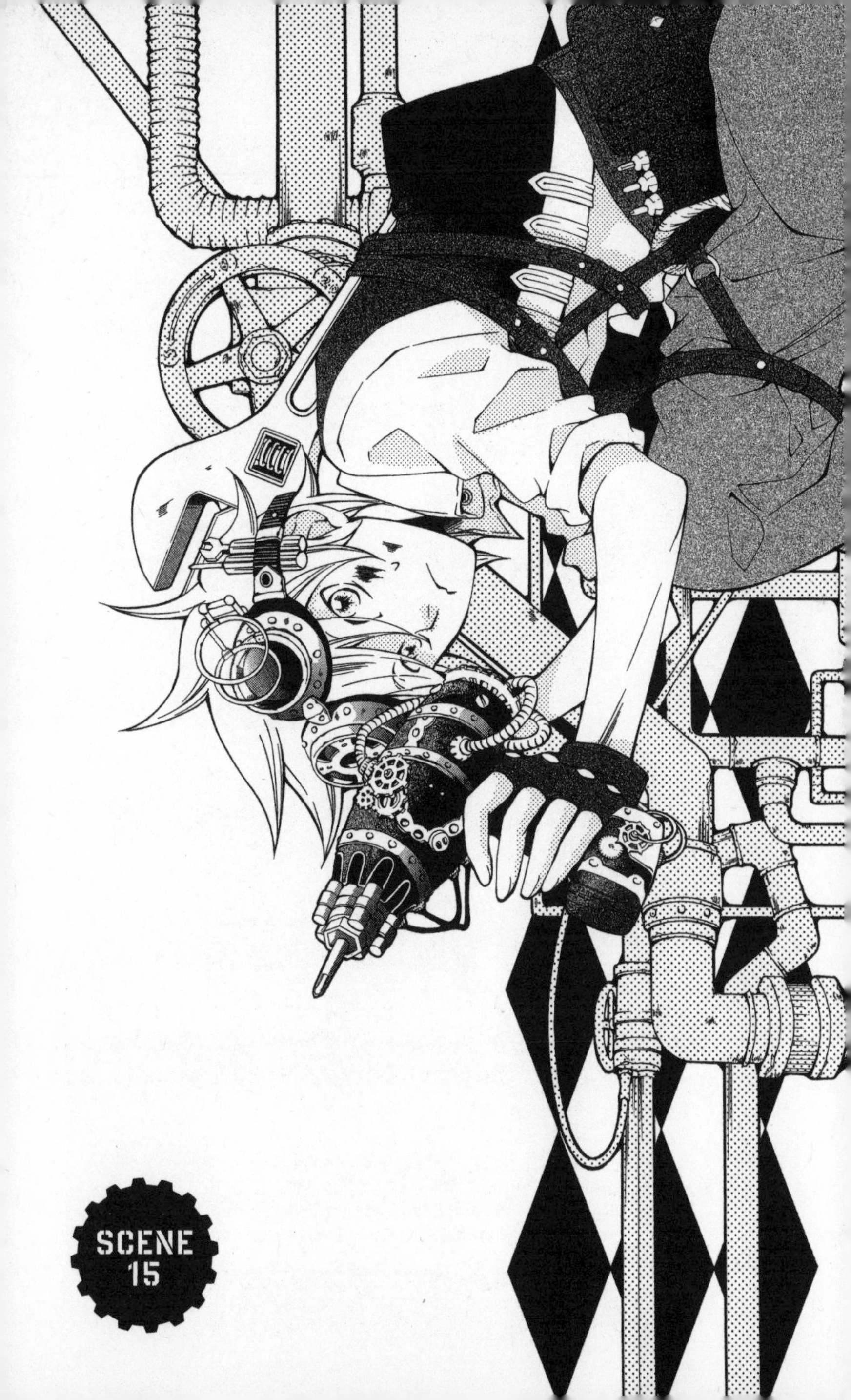
SCENE
15

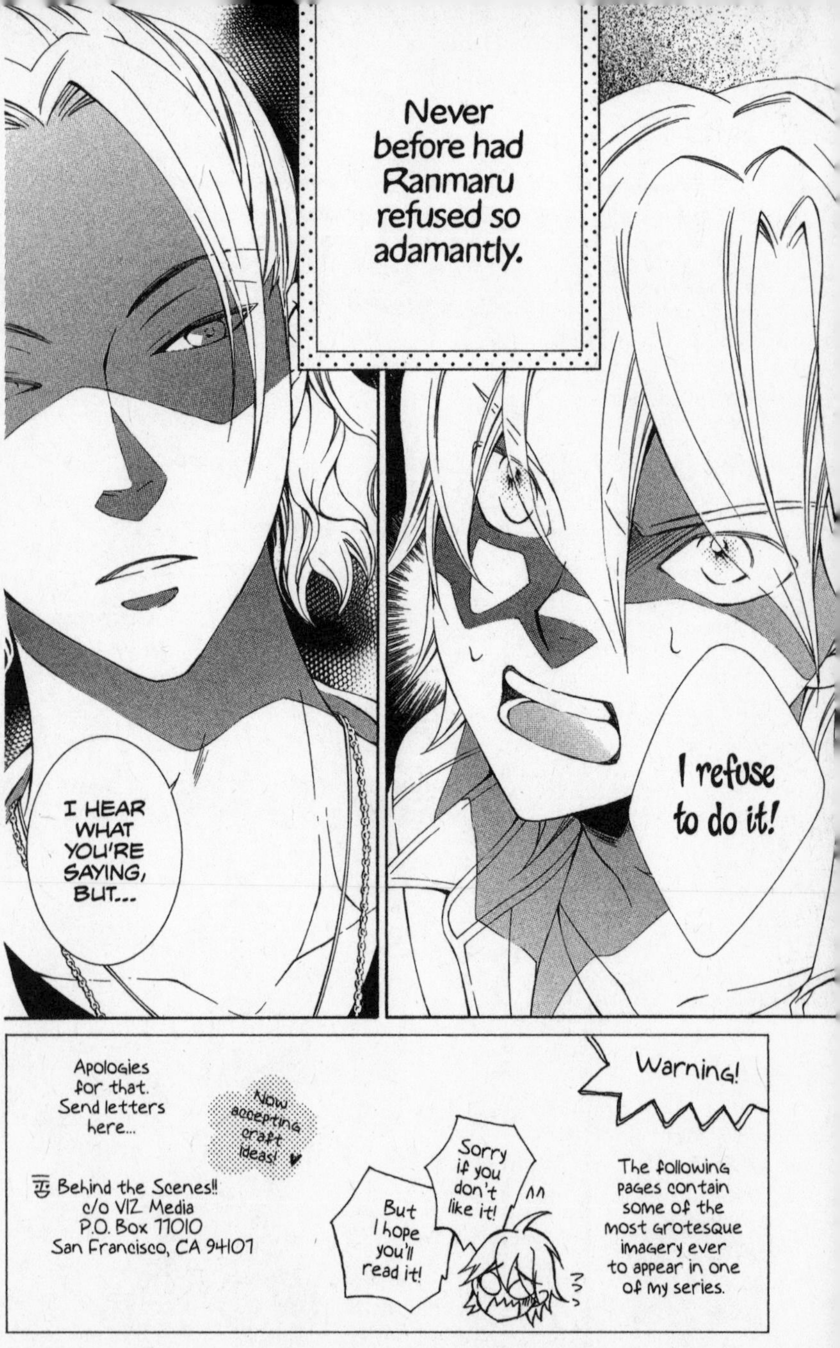
Never before had Ranmaru refused so adamantly.
I refuse to do it!
I HEAR WHAT YOU'RE SAYING, BUT...
Warning!
The following pages contain some of the most grotesque imagery ever to appear in one of my series.
Sorry if you don't like it! ^^
But I hope you'll read it!
Now accepting craft ideas! ♥
Apologies for that. Send letters here...
〒 Behind the Scenes!! c/o VIZ Media P.O. Box 77010 San Francisco, CA 94107

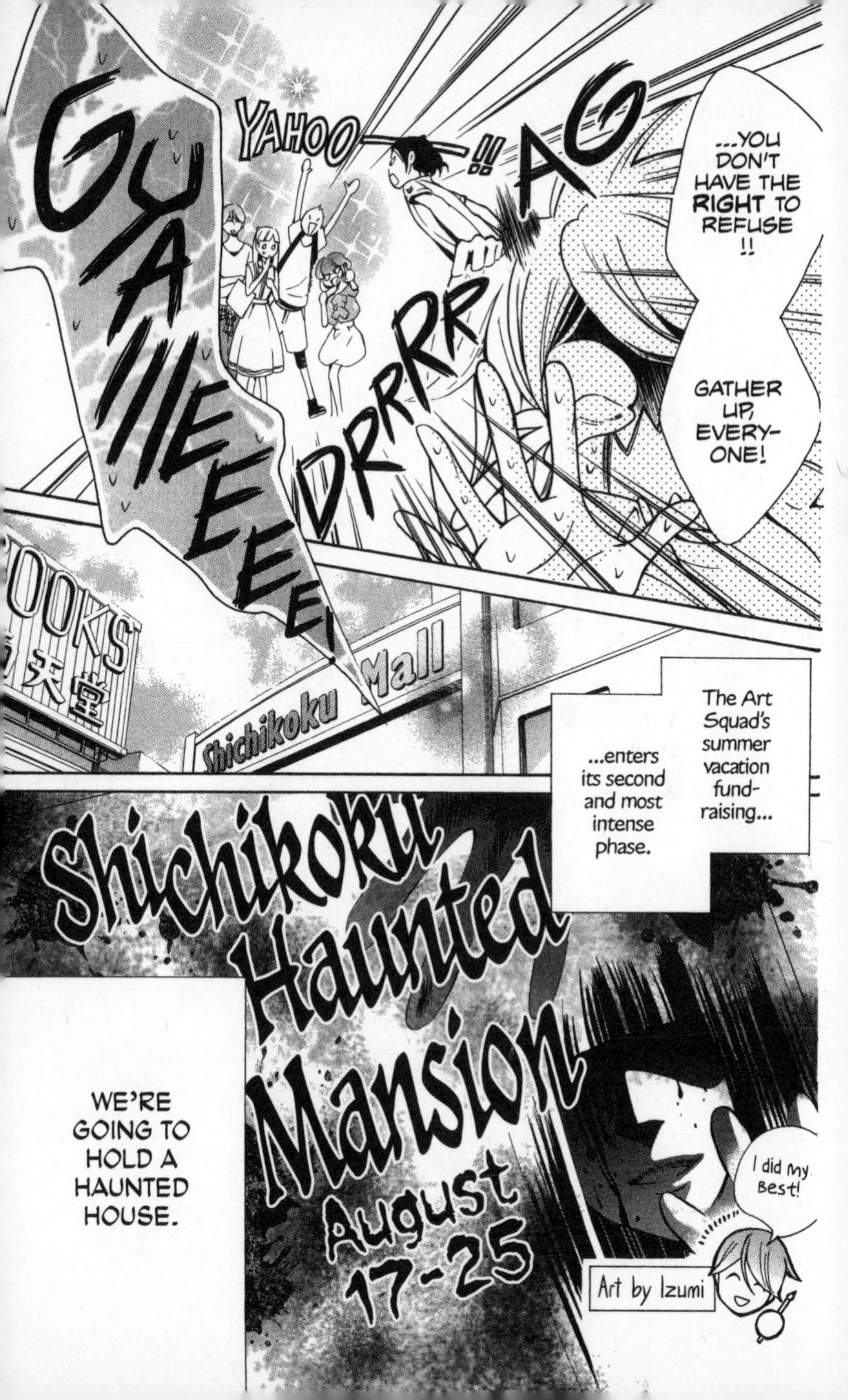
...YOU DON'T HAVE THE RIGHT TO REFUSE !!
GATHER UP, EVERY-ONE!
AG
YAHOO!!
GYAIIEEEE!
DRRRRR
Shichikoku Mall
The Art Squad's summer vacation fund-raising...
...enters its second and most intense phase.
Shichikoku Haunted Mansion
August 17-25
I did my Best!
Art by Izumi
WE'RE GOING TO HOLD A HAUNTED HOUSE.

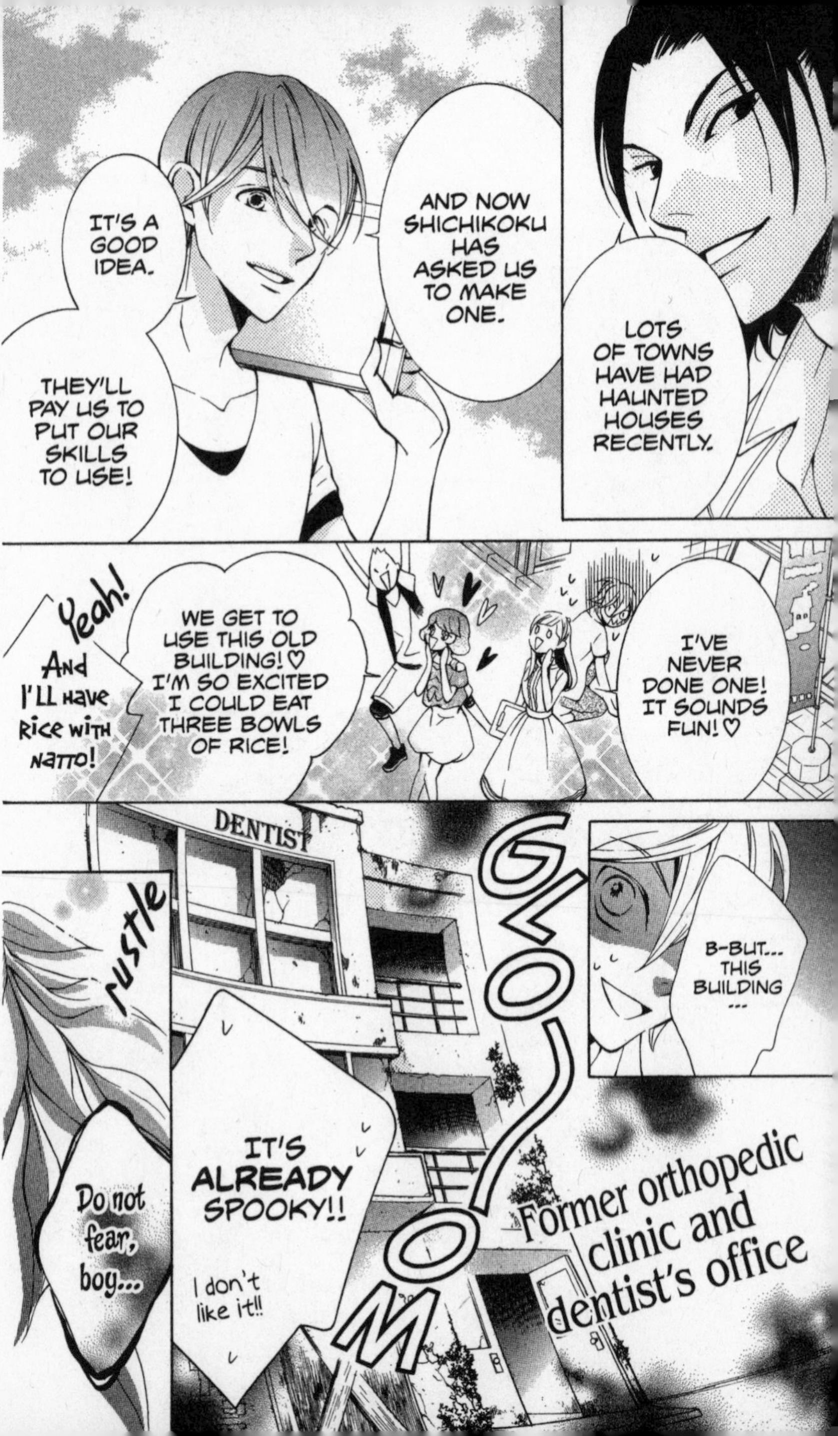
LOTS OF TOWNS HAVE HAD HAUNTED HOUSES RECENTLY.
AND NOW SHICHIKOKU HAS ASKED US TO MAKE ONE.
IT'S A GOOD IDEA.
THEY'LL PAY US TO PUT OUR SKILLS TO USE!
I'VE NEVER DONE ONE! IT SOUNDS FUN! ♡
WE GET TO USE THIS OLD BUILDING! ♡ I'M SO EXCITED I COULD EAT THREE BOWLS OF RICE!
Yeah!
And I'll have rice with natto!
B-BUT... THIS BUILDING ...
GLOOM
Former orthopedic clinic and dentist's office
DENTIST
IT'S ALREADY SPOOKY!!
I don't like it!!
rustle
Do not fear, boy...

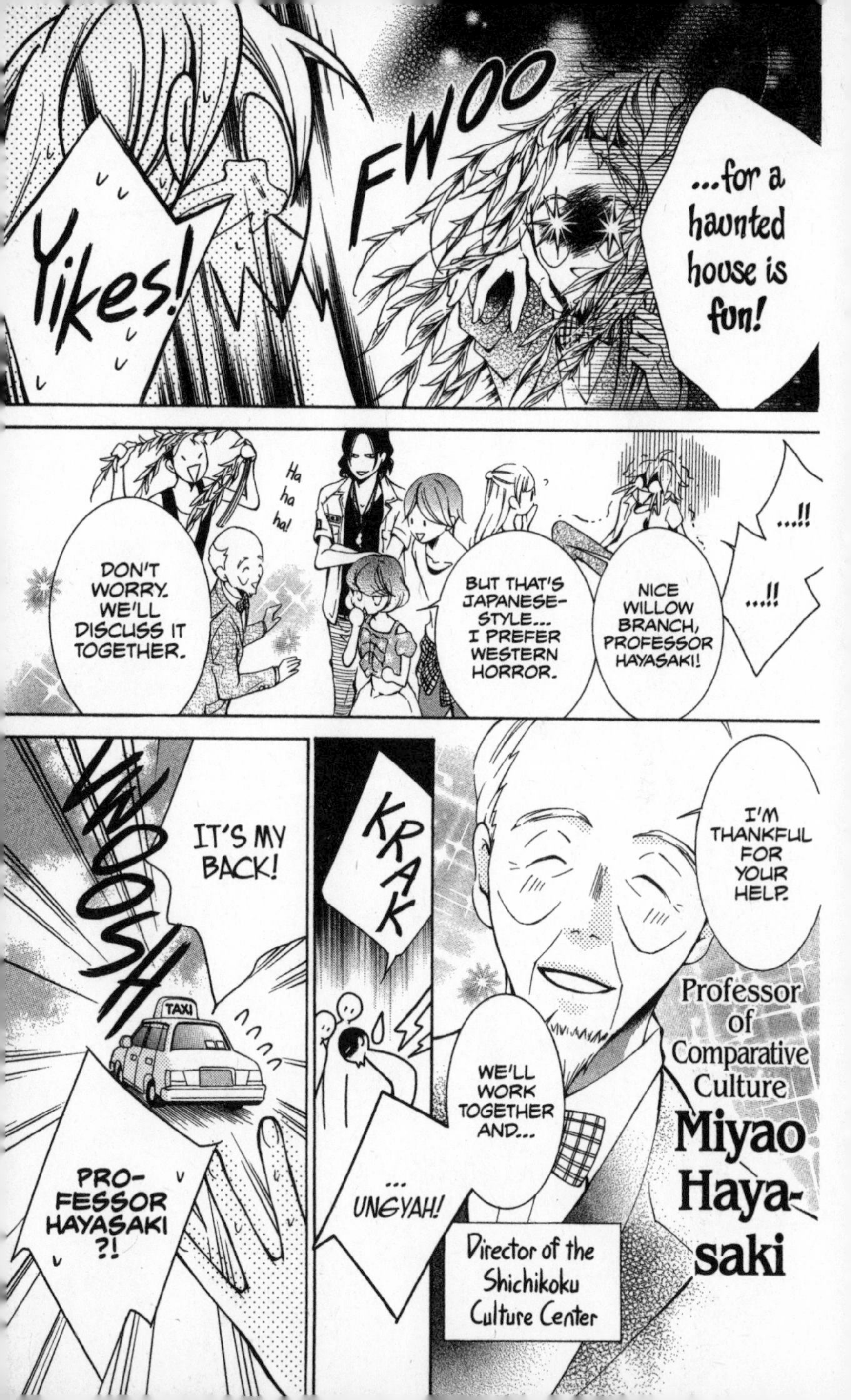
...for a haunted house is fun!
FWOO
Yikes!
...!!
...!!
NICE WILLOW BRANCH, PROFESSOR HAYASAKI!
BUT THAT'S JAPANESE-STYLE... I PREFER WESTERN HORROR.
Ha ha ha!
DON'T WORRY. WE'LL DISCUSS IT TOGETHER.
I'M THANKFUL FOR YOUR HELP.
Professor of Comparative Culture Miyao Hayasaki
WE'LL WORK TOGETHER AND...
Director of the Shichikoku Culture Center
...UNGYAH!
KRAK
WHOOSH
IT'S MY BACK!
TAXI
PROFESSOR HAYASAKI?!

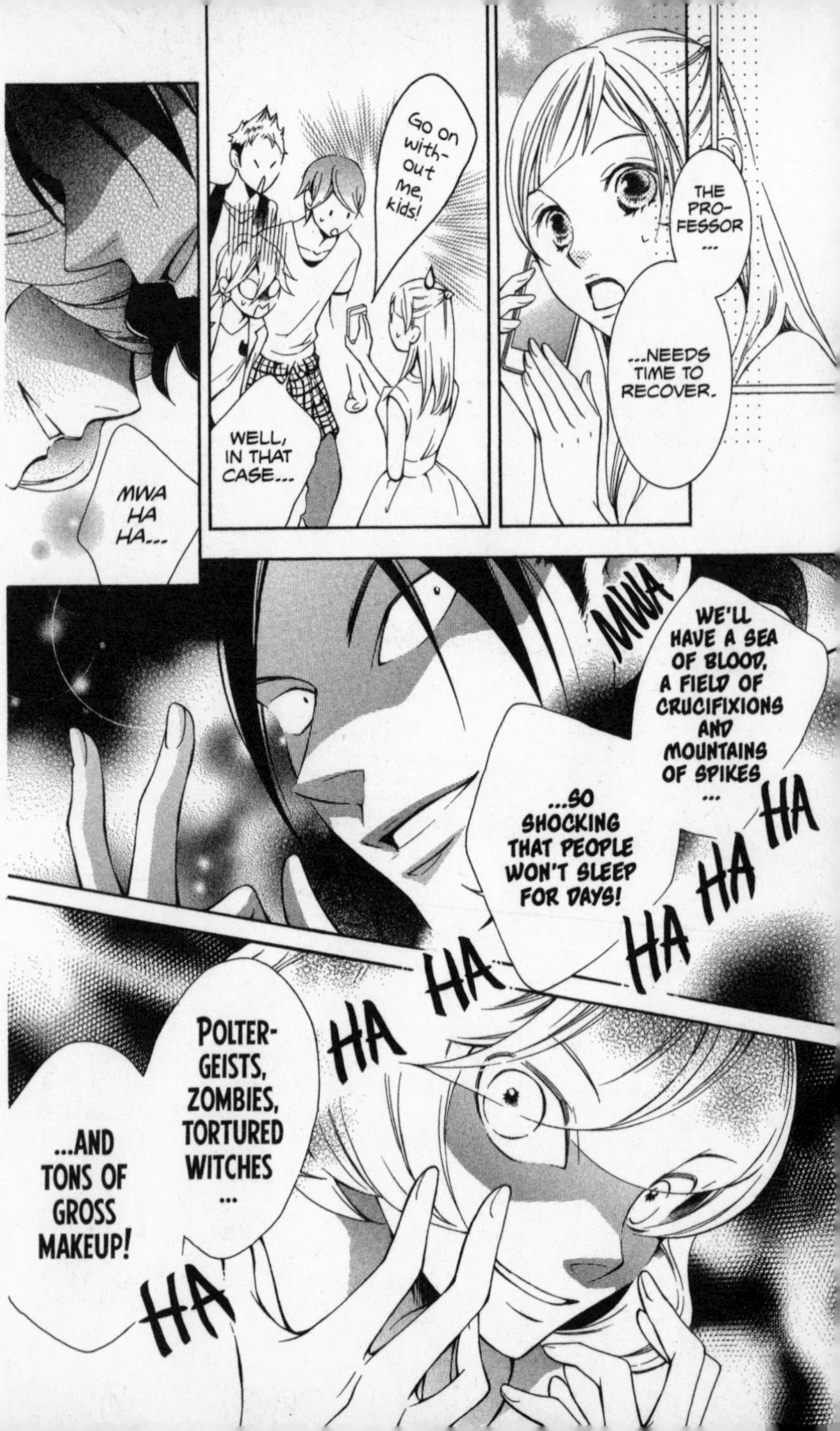
THE PRO-FESSOR ...
...NEEDS TIME TO RECOVER.
Go on with-out me, kids!
WELL, IN THAT CASE...
MWA HA HA...
MWA
WE'LL HAVE A SEA OF BLOOD, A FIELD OF CRUCIFIXIONS AND MOUNTAINS OF SPIKES ...
...SO SHOCKING THAT PEOPLE WON'T SLEEP FOR DAYS!
HA HA HA HA HA HA
POLTER-GEISTS, ZOMBIES, TORTURED WITCHES ...
...AND TONS OF GROSS MAKEUP!
HA

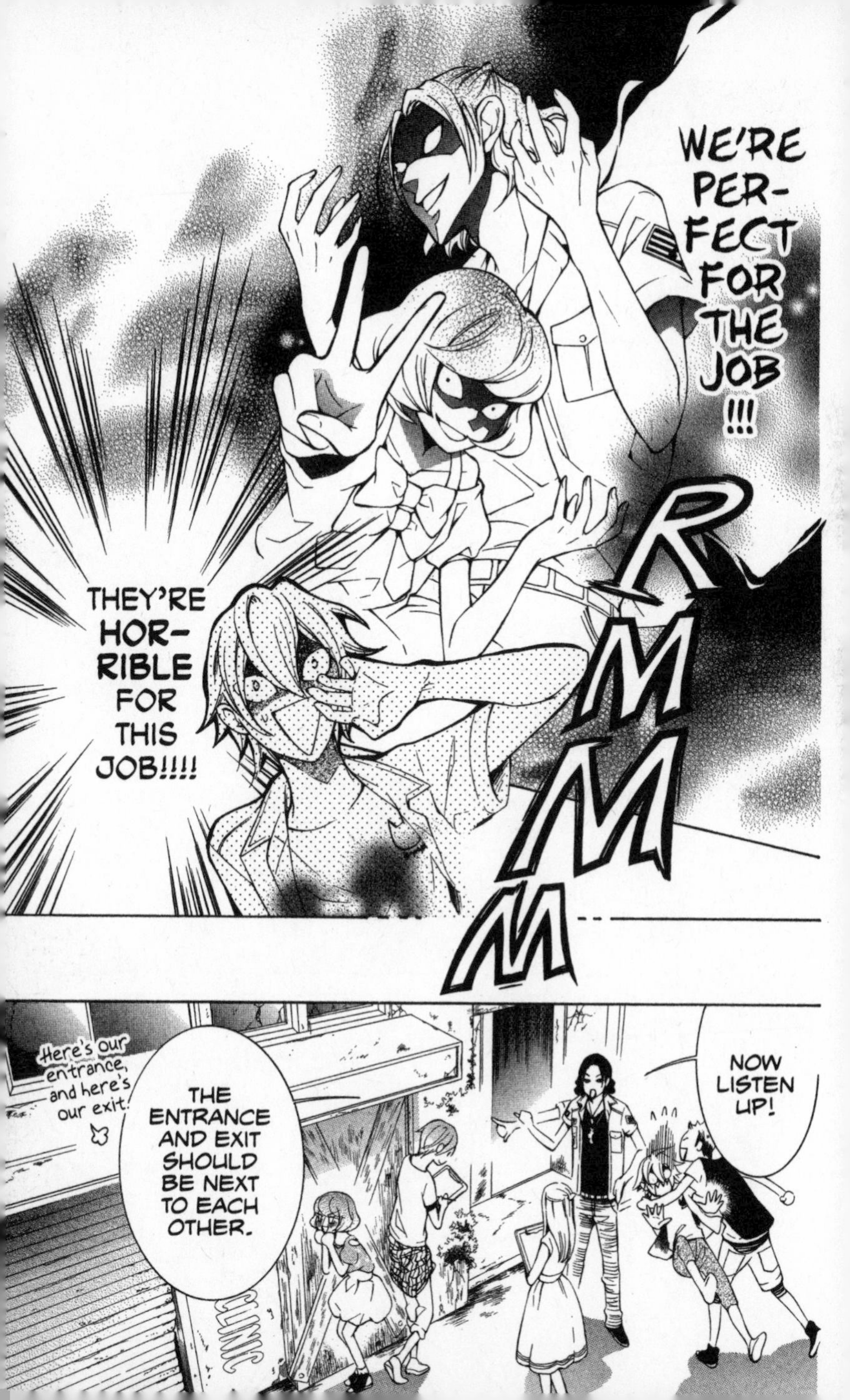
WE'RE PERFECT FOR THE JOB!!!
RMMM
THEY'RE HORRIBLE FOR THIS JOB!!!!
NOW LISTEN UP!
THE ENTRANCE AND EXIT SHOULD BE NEXT TO EACH OTHER.
Here's our entrance, and here's our exit!
CLINIC

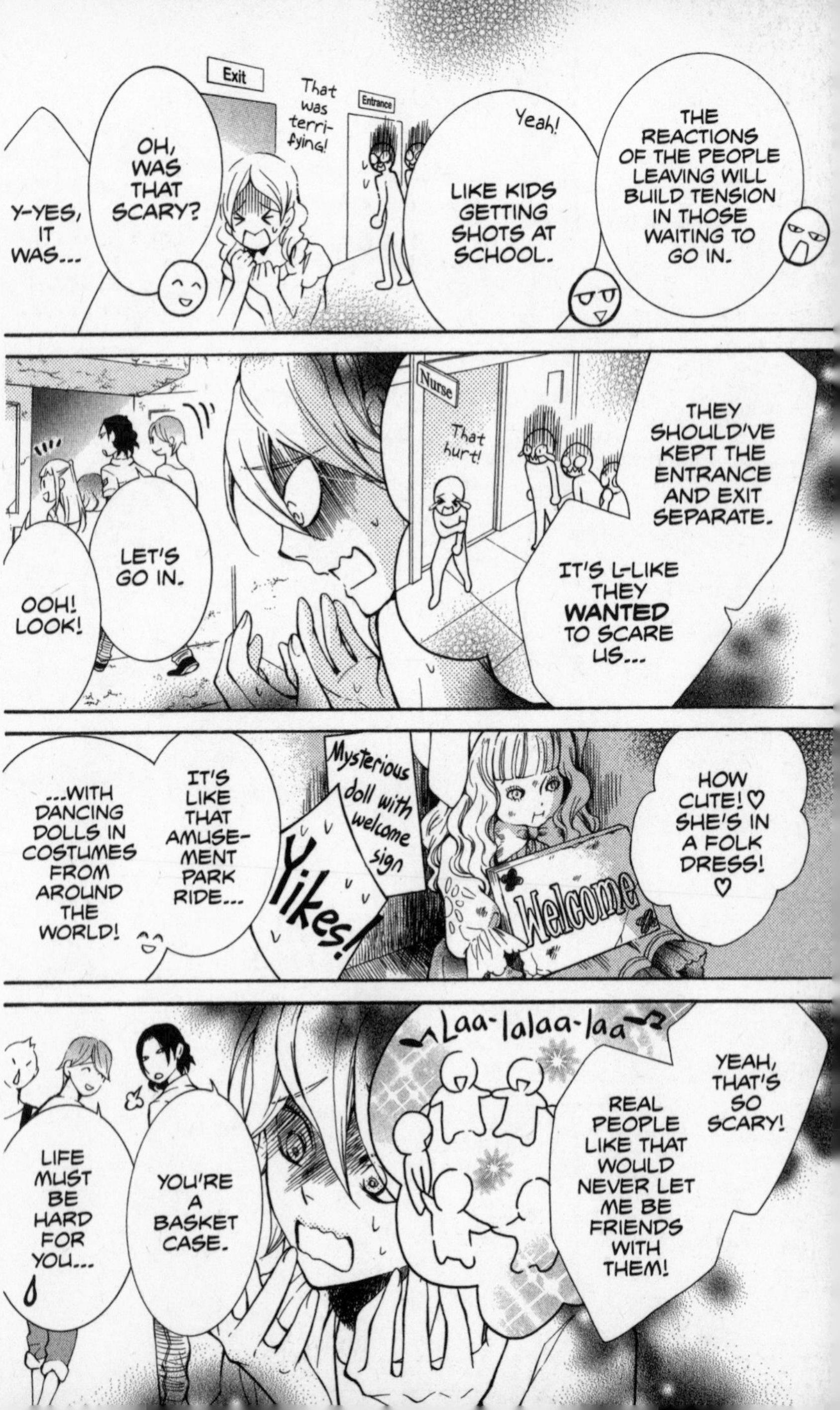
THE REACTIONS OF THE PEOPLE LEAVING WILL BUILD TENSION IN THOSE WAITING TO GO IN.
Yeah!
LIKE KIDS GETTING SHOTS AT SCHOOL.
Entrance
That was terrifying!
Exit
OH, WAS THAT SCARY?
Y-YES, IT WAS...
THEY SHOULD'VE KEPT THE ENTRANCE AND EXIT SEPARATE.
IT'S L-LIKE THEY WANTED TO SCARE US...
Nurse
That hurt!
LET'S GO IN.
OOH! LOOK!
HOW CUTE! ♡ SHE'S IN A FOLK DRESS! ♡
Welcome
Mysterious doll with welcome sign
Yikes!
IT'S LIKE THAT AMUSEMENT PARK RIDE...
...WITH DANCING DOLLS IN COSTUMES FROM AROUND THE WORLD!
YEAH, THAT'S SO SCARY!
REAL PEOPLE LIKE THAT WOULD NEVER LET ME BE FRIENDS WITH THEM!
Laa-lalaa-laa
YOU'RE A BASKET CASE.
LIFE MUST BE HARD FOR YOU...

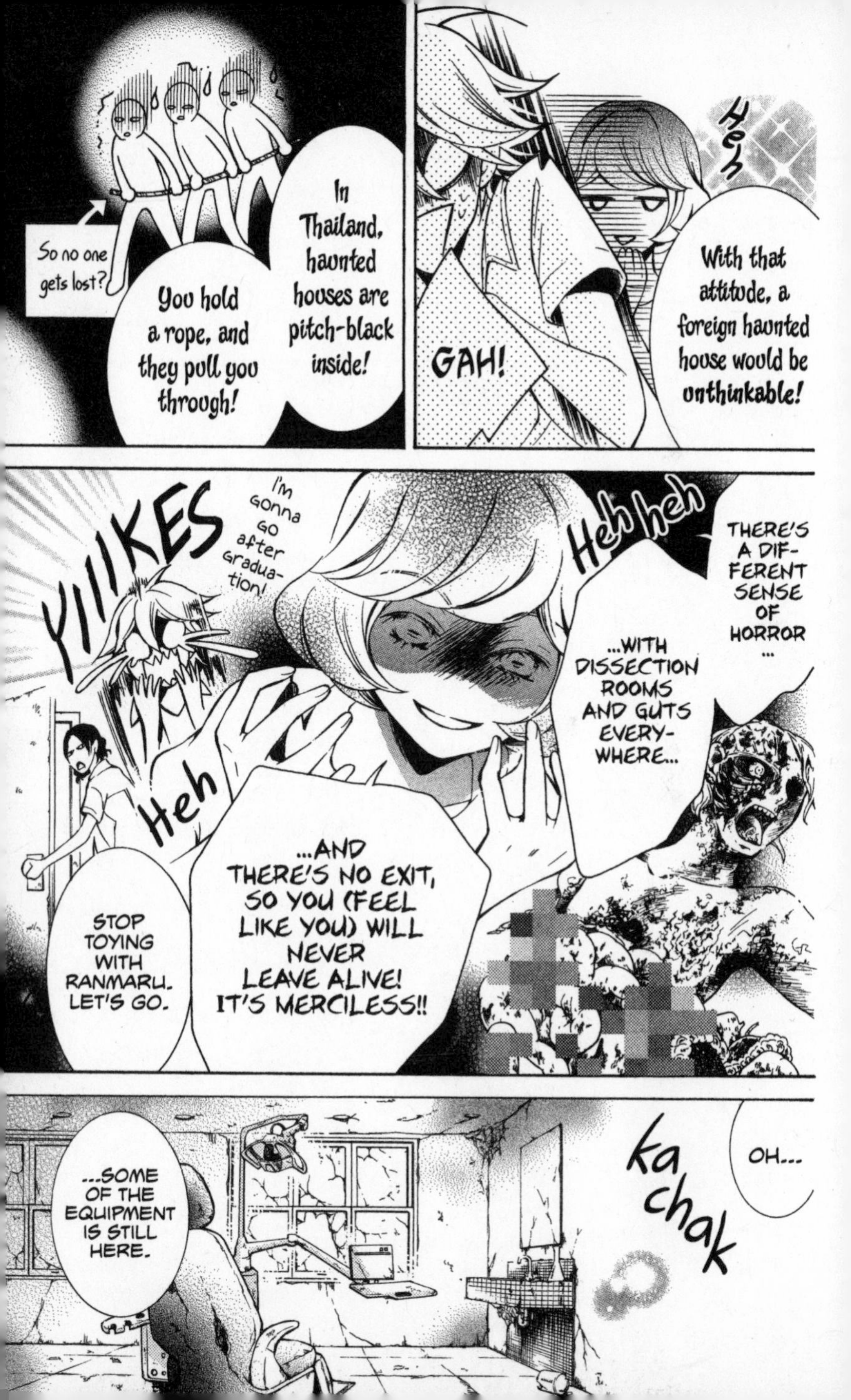
Heh
With that attitude, a foreign haunted house would be unthinkable!
GAH!
In Thailand, haunted houses are pitch-black inside!
You hold a rope, and they pull you through!
So no one gets lost?
THERE'S A DIF-FERENT SENSE OF HORROR...
Heh heh
...WITH DISSECTION ROOMS AND GUTS EVERY-WHERE...
...AND THERE'S NO EXIT, SO YOU (FEEL LIKE YOU) WILL NEVER LEAVE ALIVE! IT'S MERCILESS!!
Heh
YIIIKES
I'm gonna go after gradua-tion!
STOP TOYING WITH RANMARU. LET'S GO.
OH...
ka chak
...SOME OF THE EQUIPMENT IS STILL HERE.

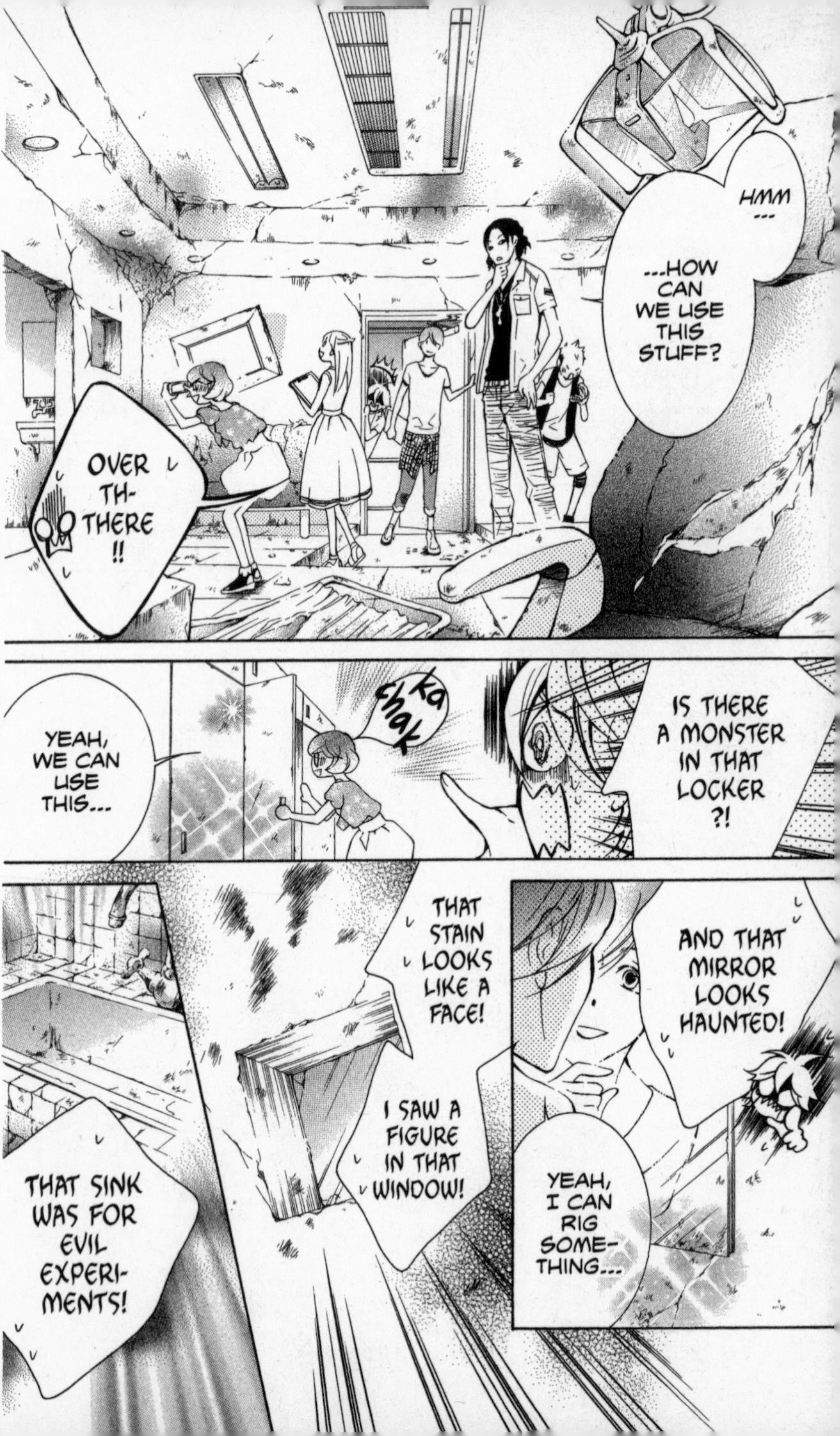
HMM...
...HOW CAN WE USE THIS STUFF?
OVER TH-THERE!!
IS THERE A MONSTER IN THAT LOCKER?!
KA CHAK
YEAH, WE CAN USE THIS...
AND THAT MIRROR LOOKS HAUNTED!
YEAH, I CAN RIG SOMETHING...
THAT STAIN LOOKS LIKE A FACE!
I SAW A FIGURE IN THAT WINDOW!
THAT SINK WAS FOR EVIL EXPERIMENTS!

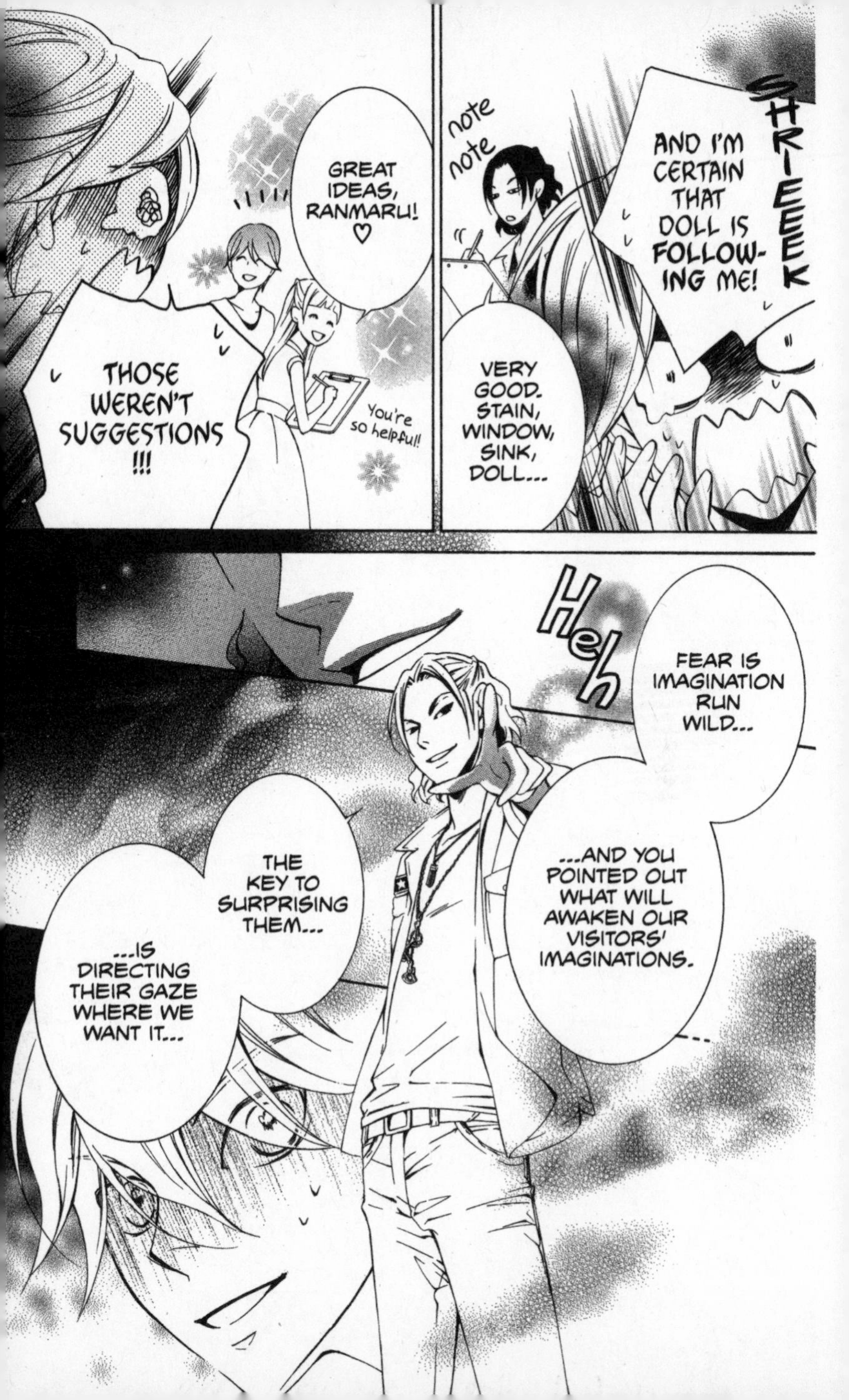
SHRIEEEK
AND I'M CERTAIN THAT DOLL IS FOLLOWING ME!
note note
VERY GOOD. STAIN, WINDOW, SINK, DOLL...
GREAT IDEAS, RANMARU! ♡
You're so helpful!
THOSE WEREN'T SUGGESTIONS!!!
Heh
FEAR IS IMAGINATION RUN WILD...
...AND YOU POINTED OUT WHAT WILL AWAKEN OUR VISITORS' IMAGINATIONS.
THE KEY TO SURPRISING THEM...
...IS DIRECTING THEIR GAZE WHERE WE WANT IT...

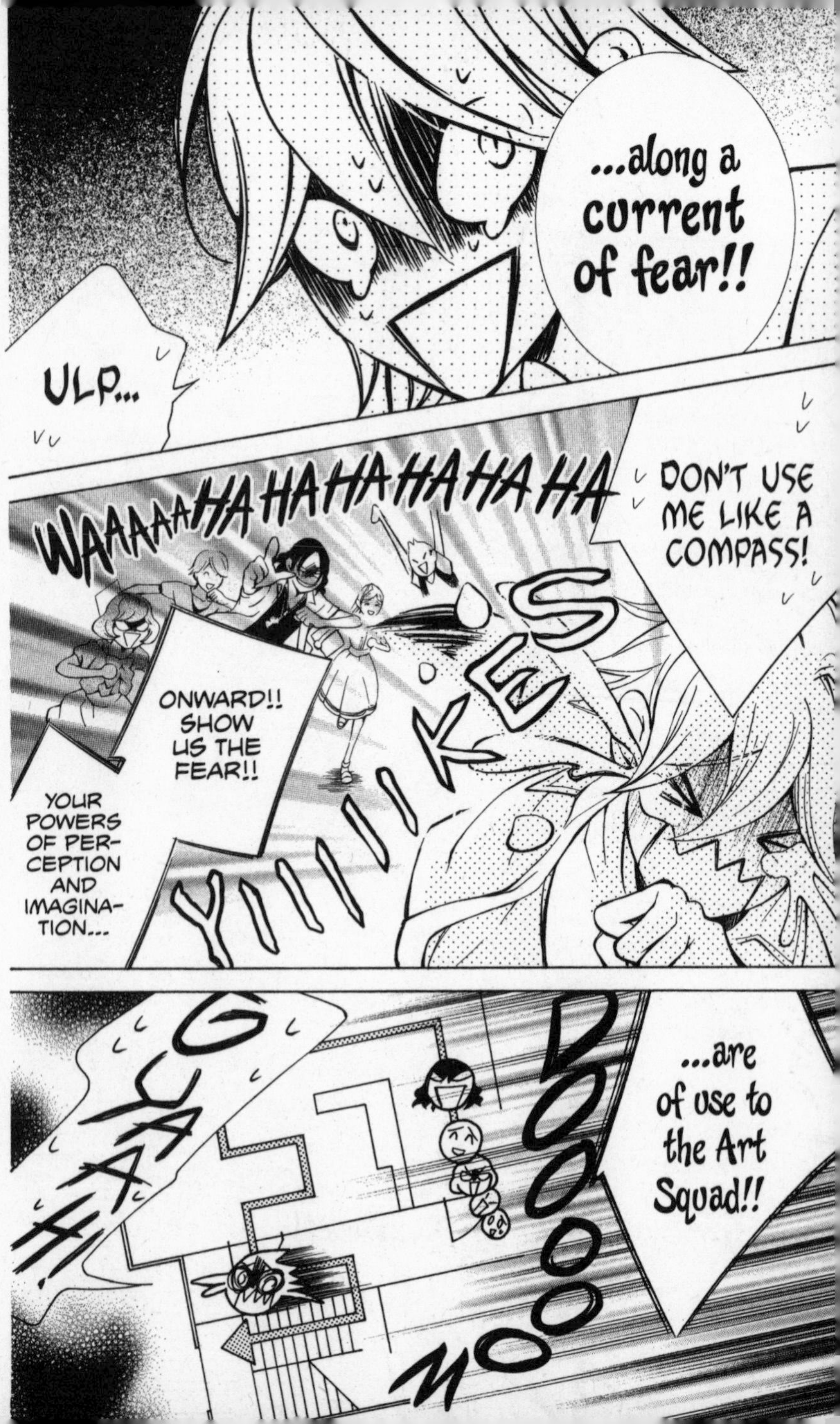
...along a current of fear!!
ULP...
DON'T USE ME LIKE A COMPASS!
WAAAAAHAHAHAHAHAHAHA
YIIIIKES
ONWARD!! SHOW US THE FEAR!!
YOUR POWERS OF PERCEPTION AND IMAGINATION...
...are of use to the Art Squad!!
DOOOOOOM
GUYAAAH!

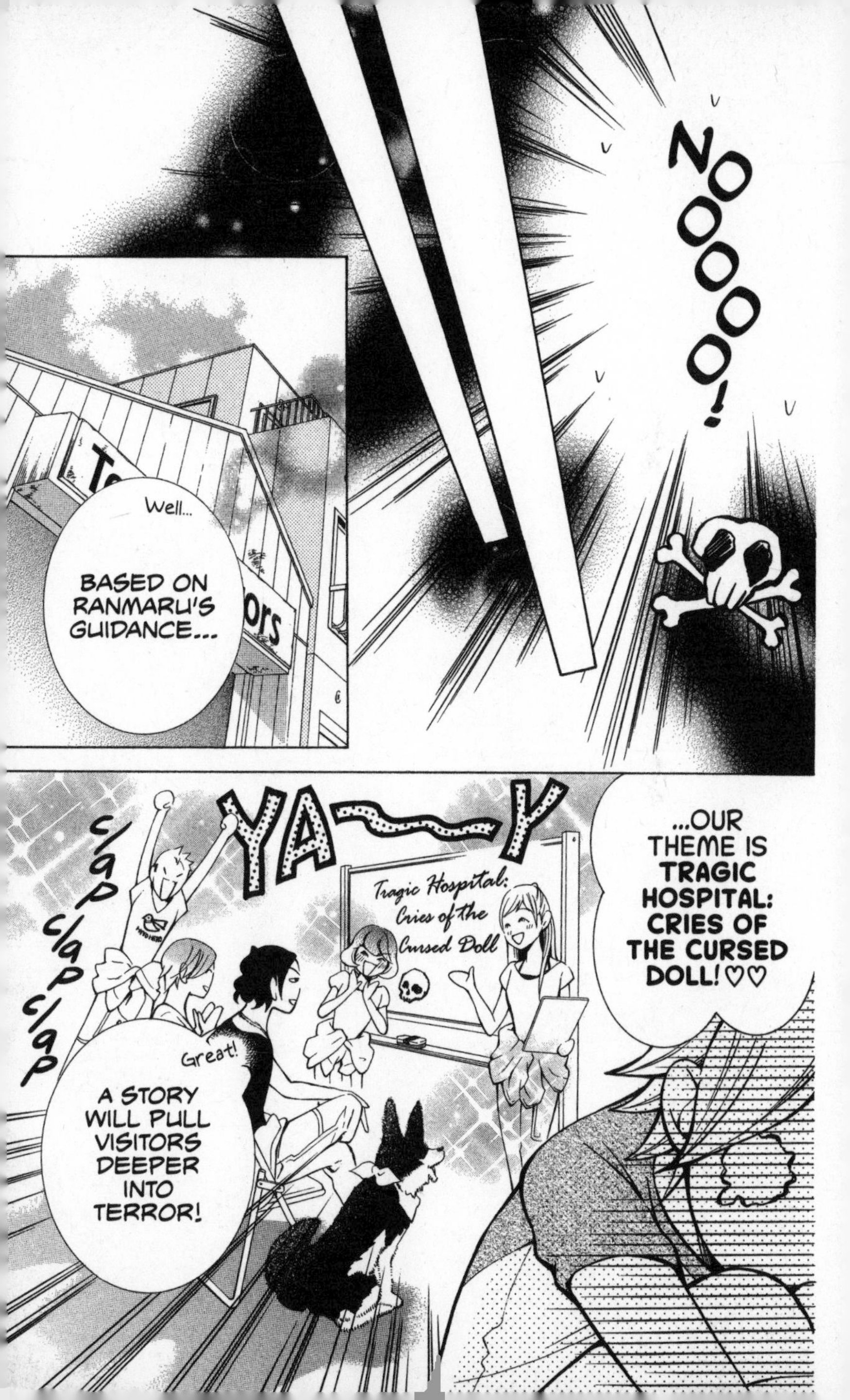
NOOOOO!
Well...
BASED ON RANMARU'S GUIDANCE...
...OUR THEME IS TRAGIC HOSPITAL: CRIES OF THE CURSED DOLL! ♡♡
YA~~Y
Tragic Hospital: Cries of the Cursed Doll
clap clap clap clap
Great!
A STORY WILL PULL VISITORS DEEPER INTO TERROR!

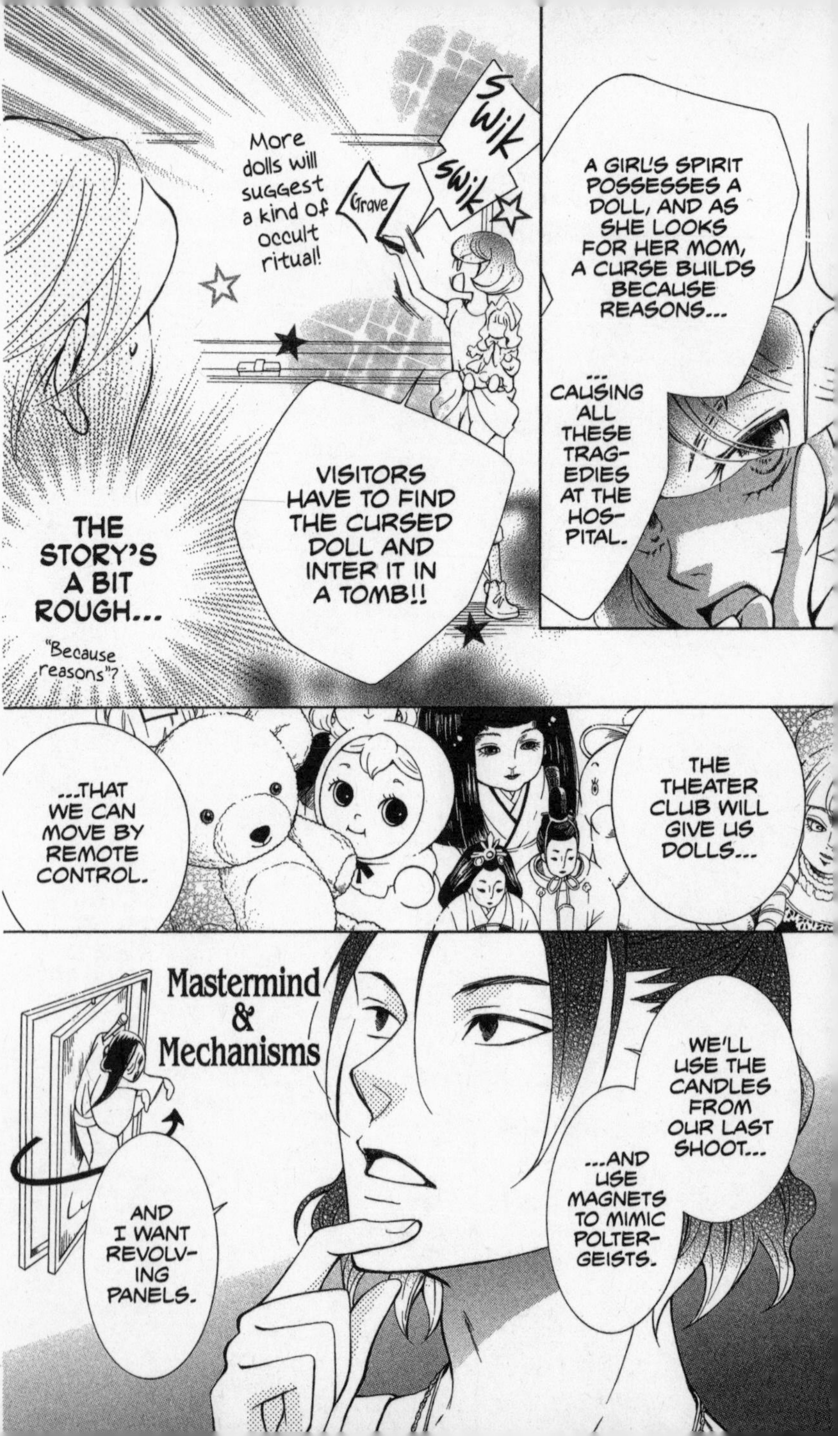
A GIRL'S SPIRIT POSSESSES A DOLL, AND AS SHE LOOKS FOR HER MOM, A CURSE BUILDS BECAUSE REASONS...
...CAUSING ALL THESE TRAG-EDIES AT THE HOS-PITAL.
SWIK
SWIK
More dolls will suggest a kind of occult ritual!
Grave
VISITORS HAVE TO FIND THE CURSED DOLL AND INTER IT IN A TOMB!!
THE STORY'S A BIT ROUGH...
"Because reasons"?
THE THEATER CLUB WILL GIVE US DOLLS...
...THAT WE CAN MOVE BY REMOTE CONTROL.
WE'LL USE THE CANDLES FROM OUR LAST SHOOT...
...AND USE MAGNETS TO MIMIC POLTER-GEISTS.
Mastermind & Mechanisms
AND I WANT REVOLV-ING PANELS.

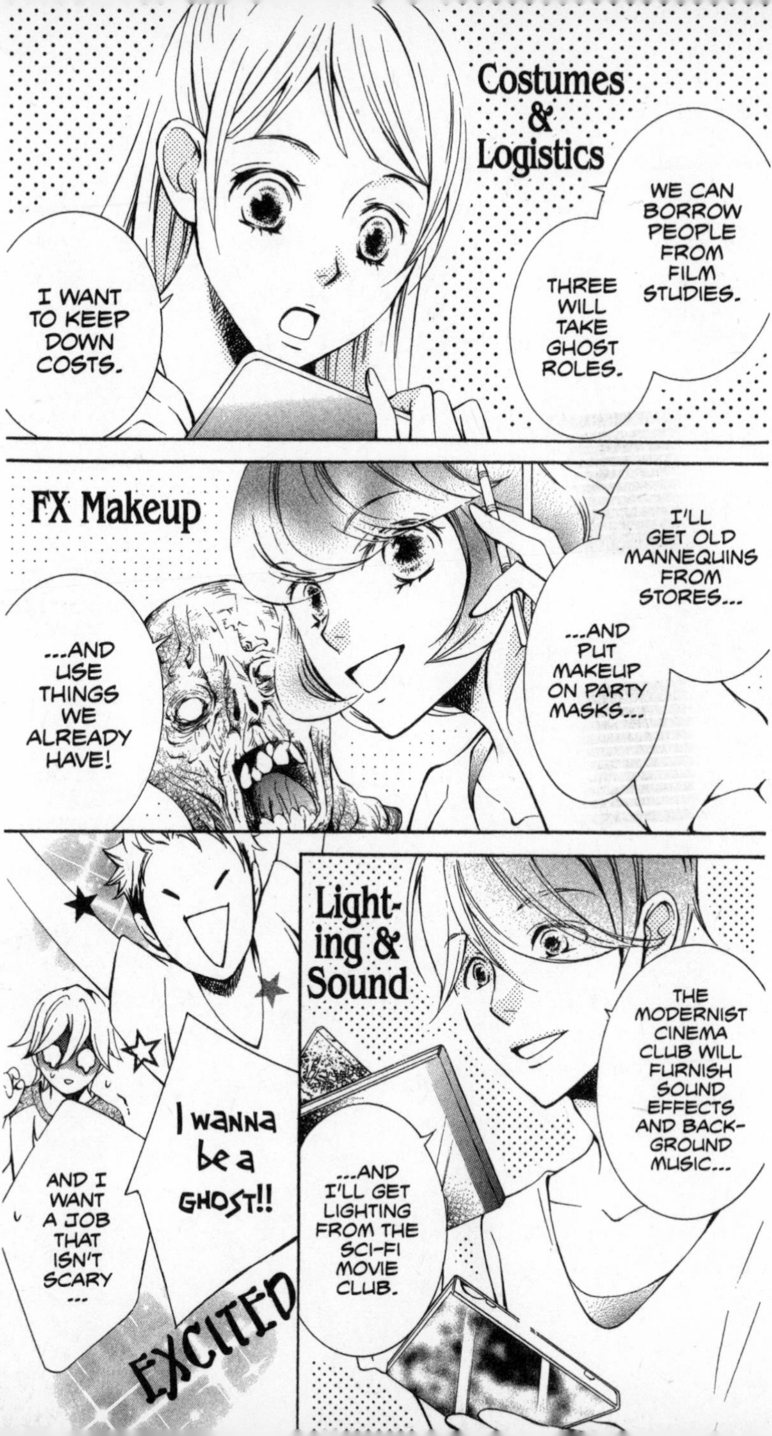
Costumes & Logistics
WE CAN BORROW PEOPLE FROM FILM STUDIES.
THREE WILL TAKE GHOST ROLES.
I WANT TO KEEP DOWN COSTS.
FX Makeup
I'LL GET OLD MANNEQUINS FROM STORES...
...AND PUT MAKEUP ON PARTY MASKS...
...AND USE THINGS WE ALREADY HAVE!
Light-ing & Sound
THE MODERNIST CINEMA CLUB WILL FURNISH SOUND EFFECTS AND BACK-GROUND MUSIC...
...AND I'LL GET LIGHTING FROM THE SCI-FI MOVIE CLUB.
I wanna be a GHOST!!
AND I WANT A JOB THAT ISN'T SCARY...
EXCITED

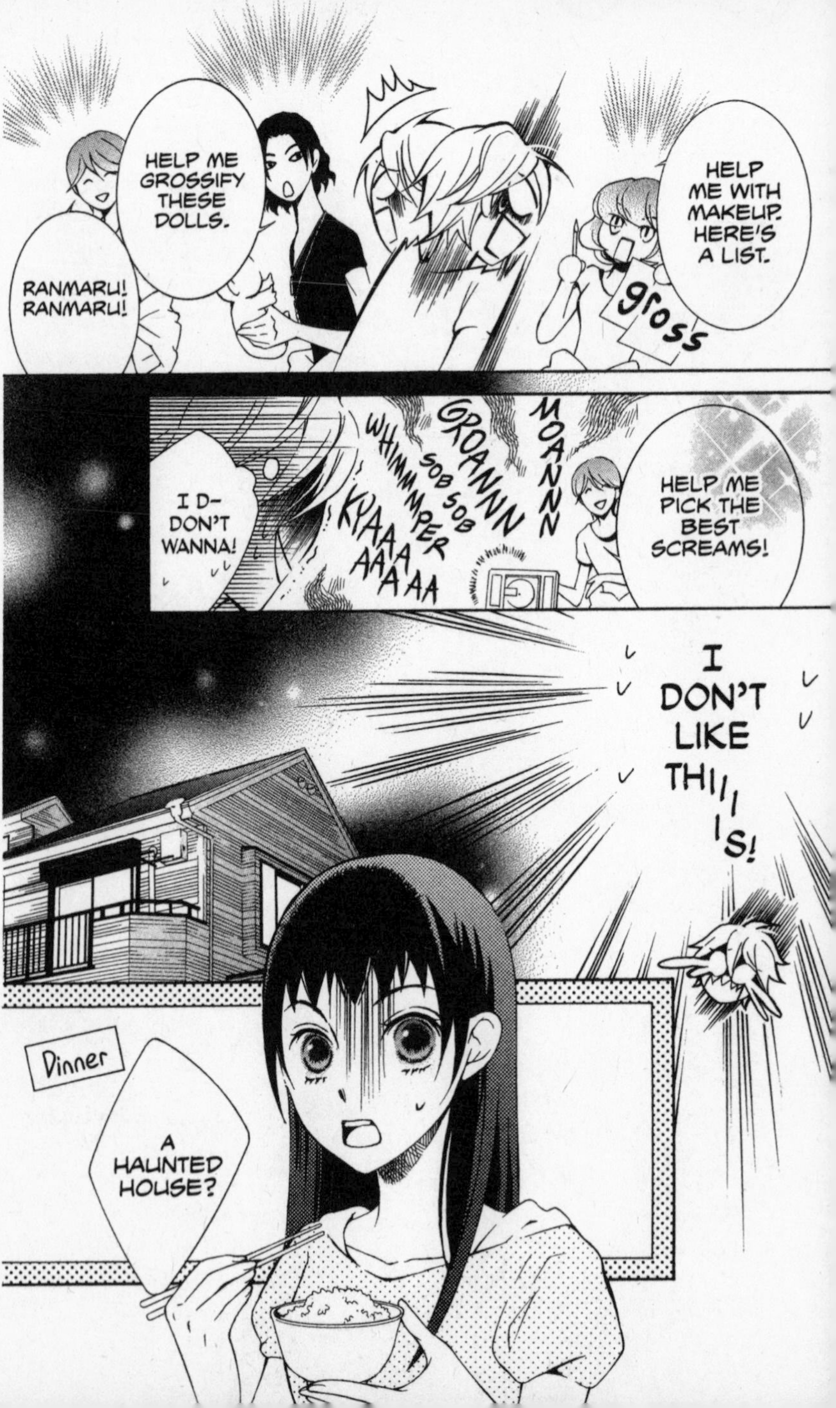
HELP ME WITH MAKEUP. HERE'S A LIST.
gross
HELP ME GROSSIFY THESE DOLLS.
RANMARU! RANMARU!
HELP ME PICK THE BEST SCREAMS!
MOANNNN
GROANNNN
SOB SOB
WHIMMMPER
KYAAAAAAAAA
I D- DON'T WANNA!
I DON'T LIKE THIIIIS!
Dinner
A HAUNTED HOUSE?

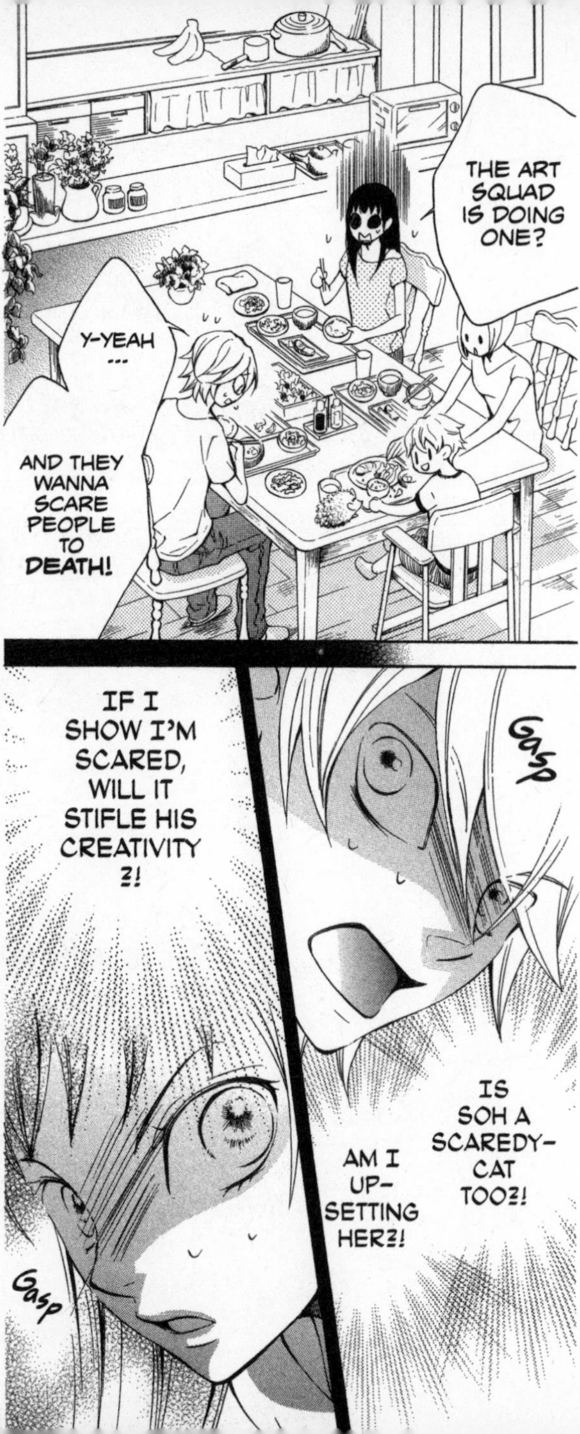
THE ART SQUAD IS DOING ONE?
Y-YEAH ...
AND THEY WANNA SCARE PEOPLE TO DEATH!
Gasp
IS SOH A SCAREDY-CAT TOO?!
AM I UP-SETTING HER?!
IF I SHOW I'M SCARED, WILL IT STIFLE HIS CREATIVITY?!
Gasp

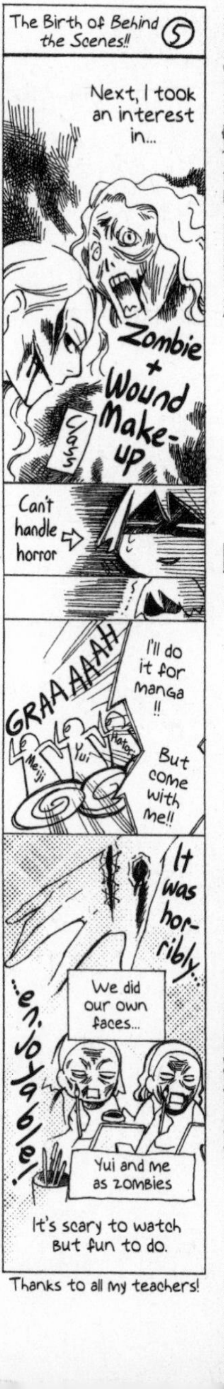
The Birth of Behind the Scenes!! 5
Next, I took an interest in...
Zombie + Wound Make-up
Class
Can't handle horror
GRAAAAAH
I'll do it for manga!!
But come with me!!
Meiji
Yui
Hatori
It was horribly...
...enjoyable!
We did our own faces...
Yui and me as zombies
It's scary to watch but fun to do.

Thanks to all my teachers!

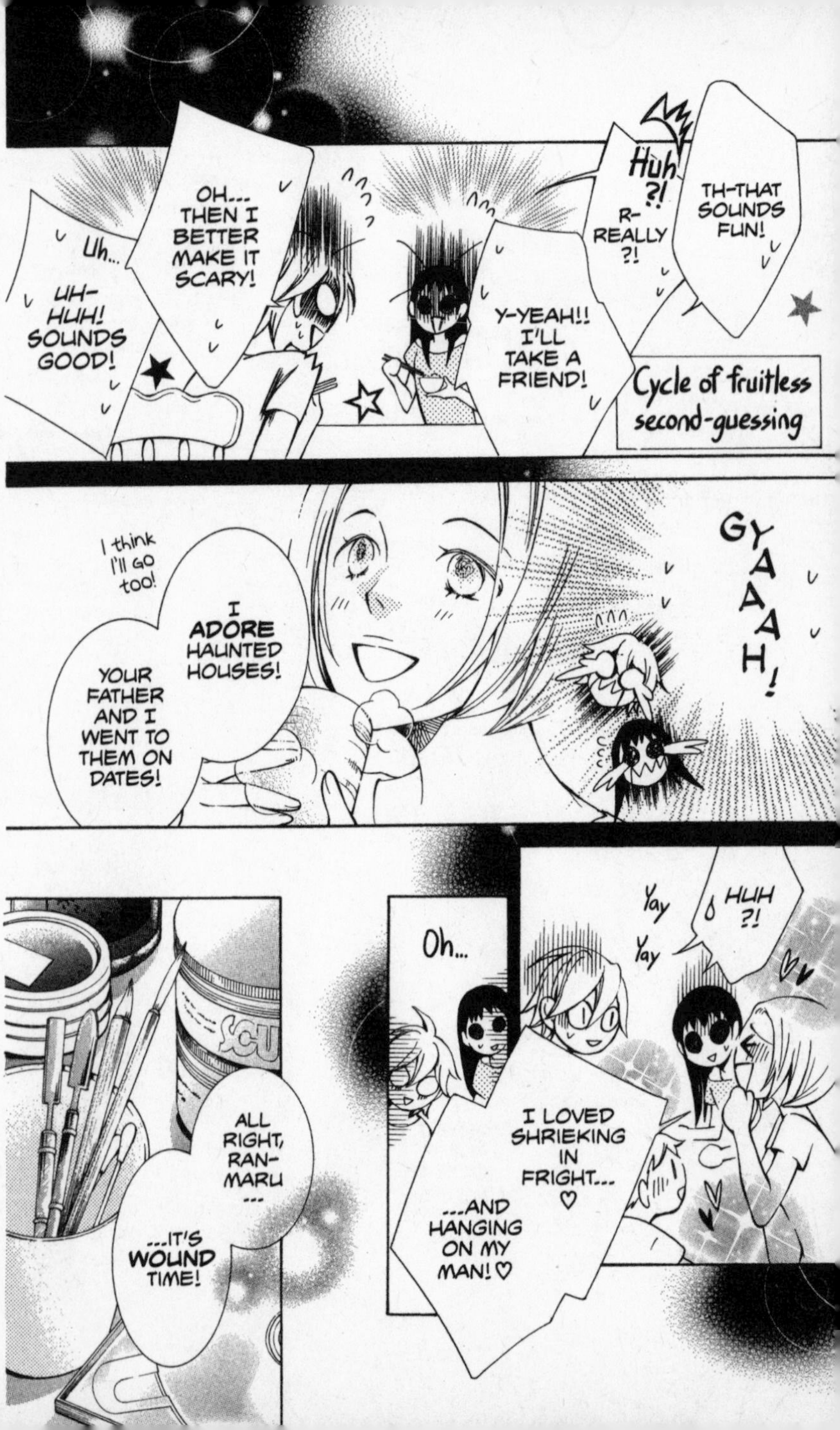
TH-THAT SOUNDS FUN!
Huh ?!
R-REALLY ?!
Y-YEAH!! I'LL TAKE A FRIEND!
Cycle of fruitless second-guessing
OH... THEN I BETTER MAKE IT SCARY!
Uh...
UH-HUH! SOUNDS GOOD!
GYAAAH!
I think I'll go too!
I ADORE HAUNTED HOUSES!
YOUR FATHER AND I WENT TO THEM ON DATES!
HUH ?!
Yay
Yay
Oh...
I LOVED SHRIEKING IN FRIGHT... ♡
...AND HANGING ON MY MAN! ♡
ALL RIGHT, RAN-MARU...
...IT'S WOUND TIME!

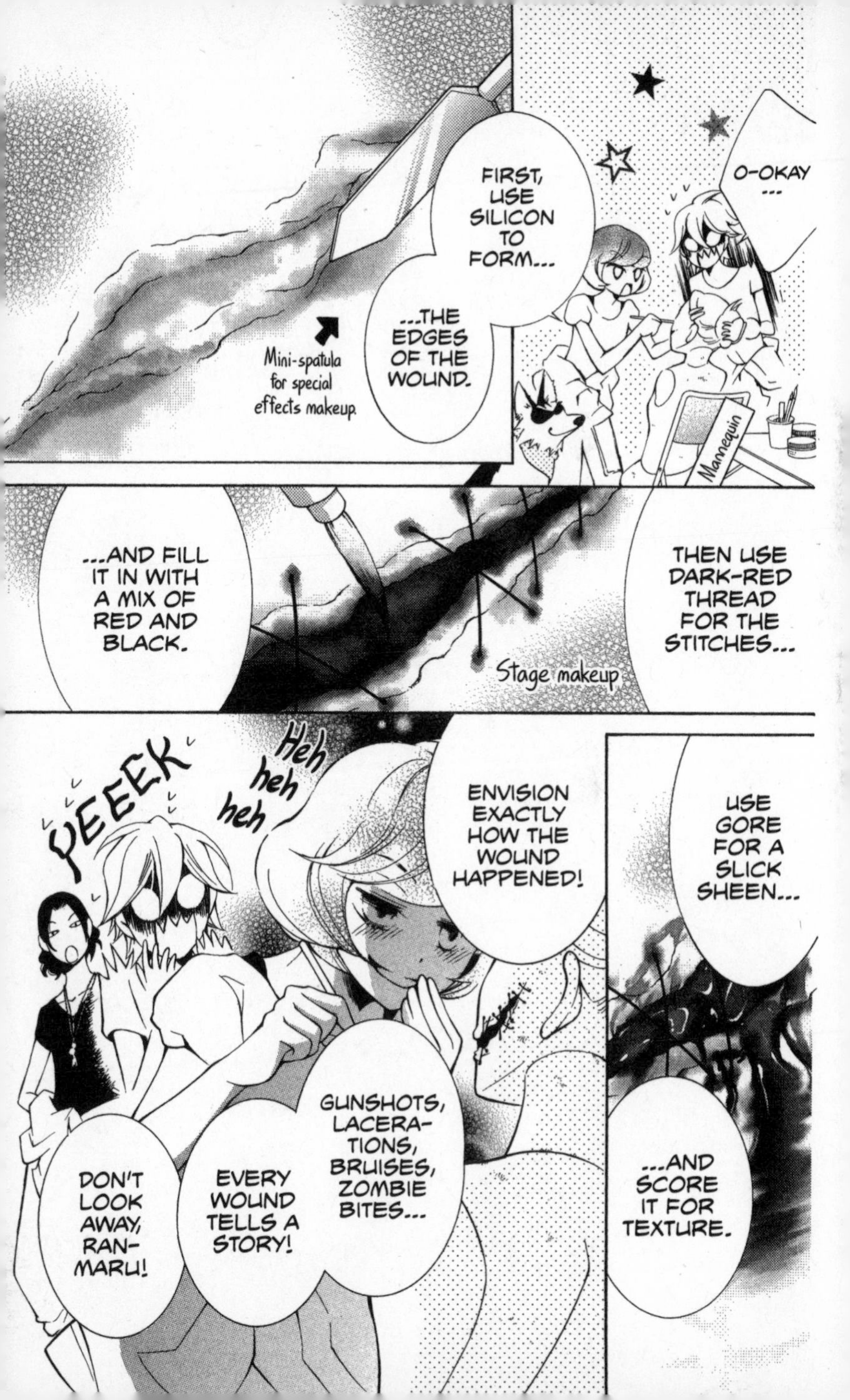
FIRST, USE SILICON TO FORM...
...THE EDGES OF THE WOUND.
O-OKAY...
Mannequin
Mini-spatula for special effects makeup.
THEN USE DARK-RED THREAD FOR THE STITCHES...
Stage makeup
...AND FILL IT IN WITH A MIX OF RED AND BLACK.
USE GORE FOR A SLICK SHEEN...
...AND SCORE IT FOR TEXTURE.
ENVISION EXACTLY HOW THE WOUND HAPPENED!
Heh heh heh
YEEEK
GUNSHOTS, LACERA-TIONS, BRUISES, ZOMBIE BITES...
EVERY WOUND TELLS A STORY!
DON'T LOOK AWAY, RAN-MARU!

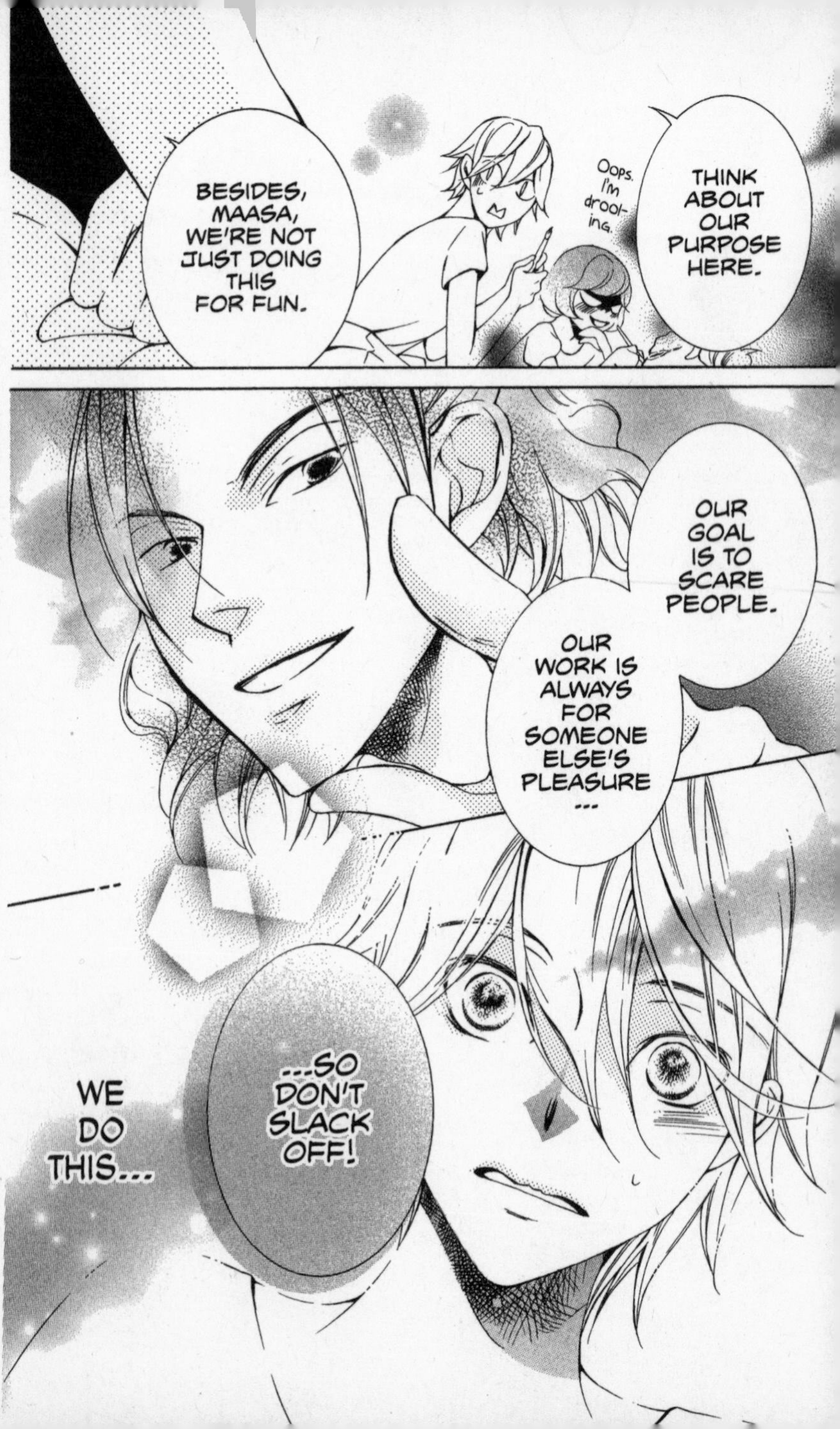
THINK ABOUT OUR PURPOSE HERE.
Oops. I'm drool-ing.
BESIDES, MAASA, WE'RE NOT JUST DOING THIS FOR FUN.
OUR GOAL IS TO SCARE PEOPLE.
OUR WORK IS ALWAYS FOR SOMEONE ELSE'S PLEASURE...
...SO DON'T SLACK OFF!
WE DO THIS...

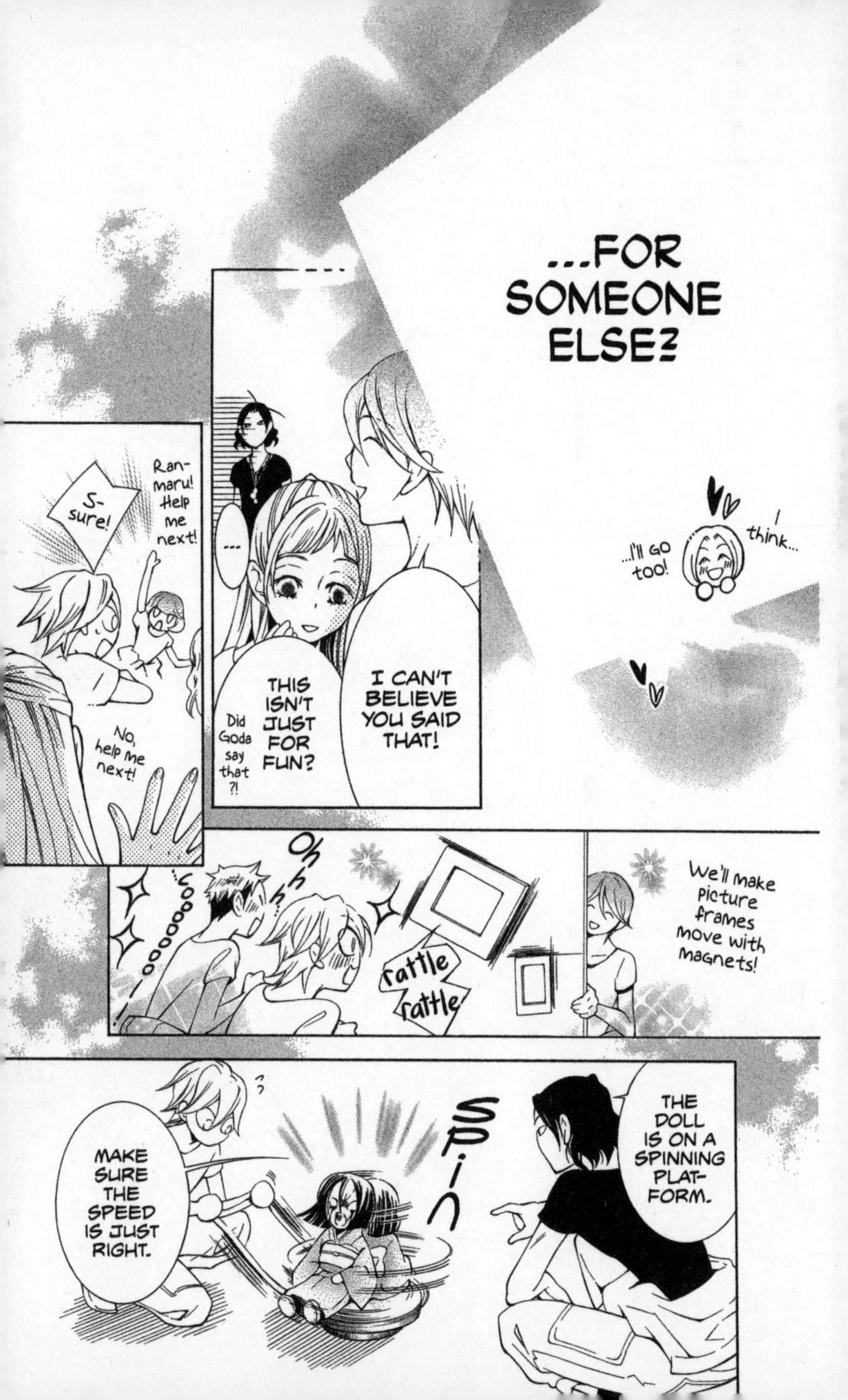

...FOR SOMEONE ELSE?
I think...
...I'll go too!

I CAN'T BELIEVE YOU SAID THAT!
THIS ISN'T JUST FOR FUN?
Did Goda say that?!
Ran-maru! Help me next!
S-sure!
No, help me next!
We'll make picture frames move with magnets!
rattle rattle
Ohhh
Oooooooo...!
THE DOLL IS ON A SPINNING PLATFORM.
SPIN
MAKE SURE THE SPEED IS JUST RIGHT.

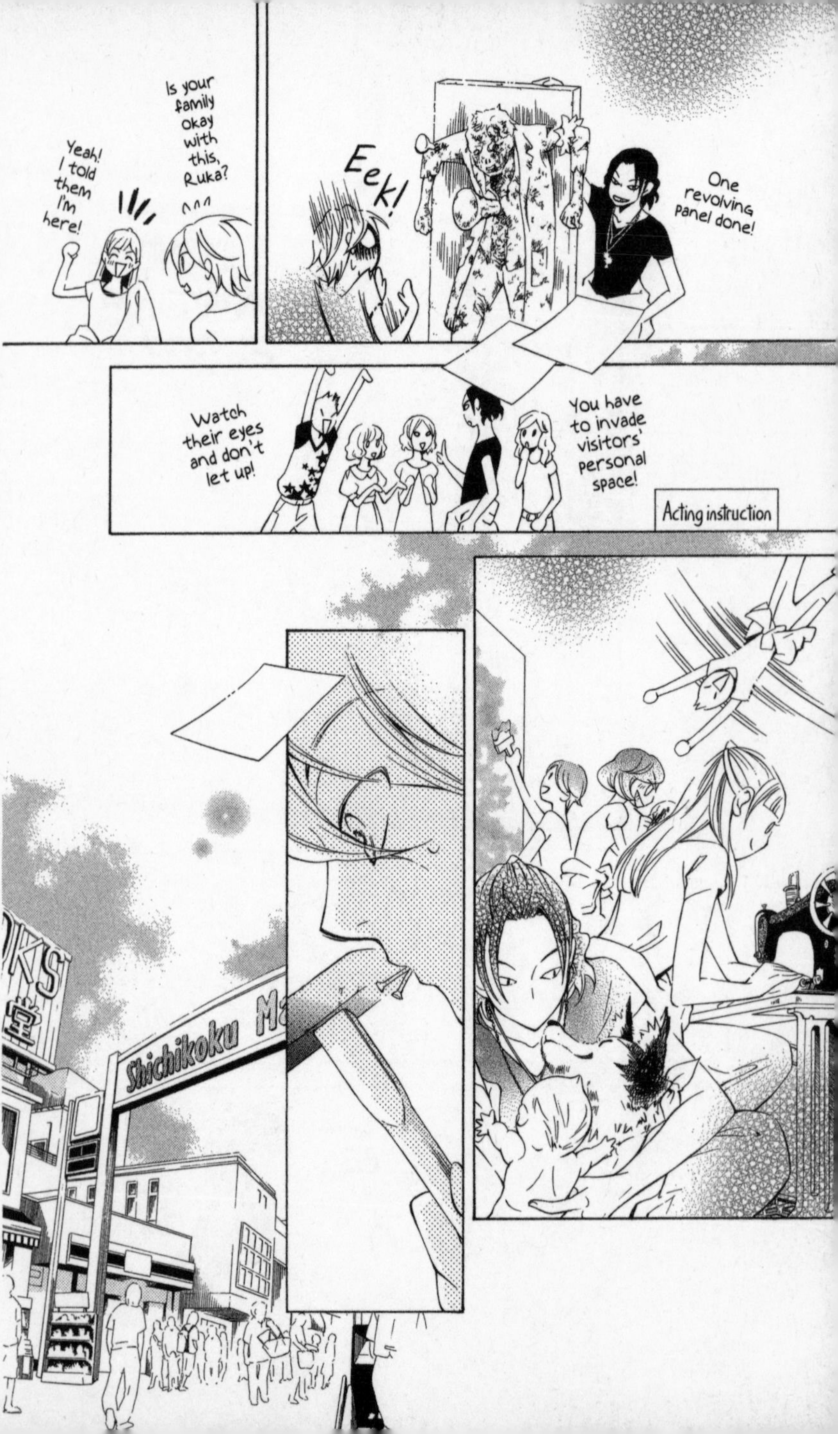
One revolving panel done!
Eek!
Is your family okay with this, Ruka?
Yeah! I told them I'm here!
Acting instruction
You have to invade visitors' personal space!
Watch their eyes and don't let up!
Shichikoku

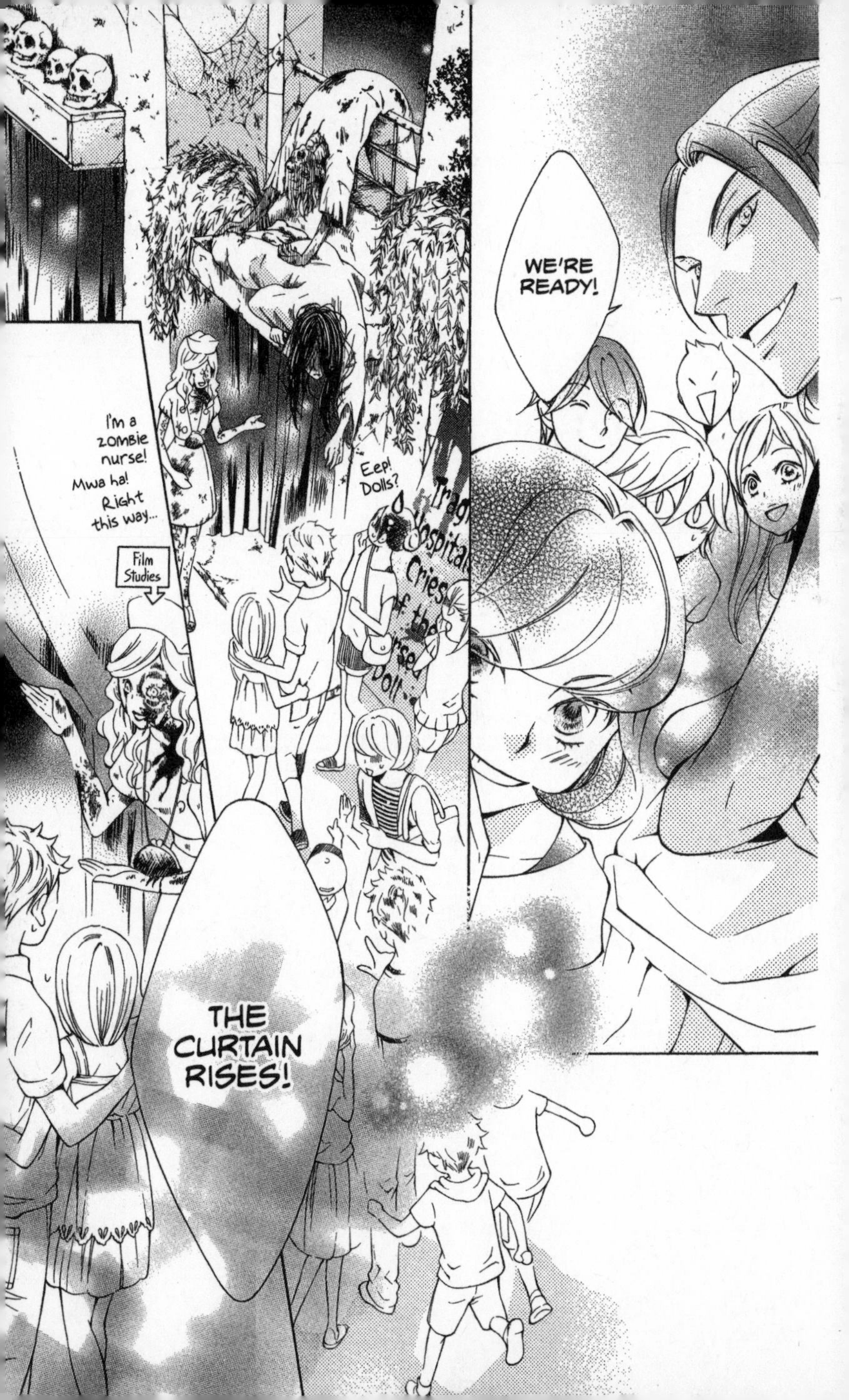
WE'RE READY!
Eep! Dolls?
I'm a zombie nurse! Mwa ha! Right this way...
Film Studies
THE CURTAIN RISES!

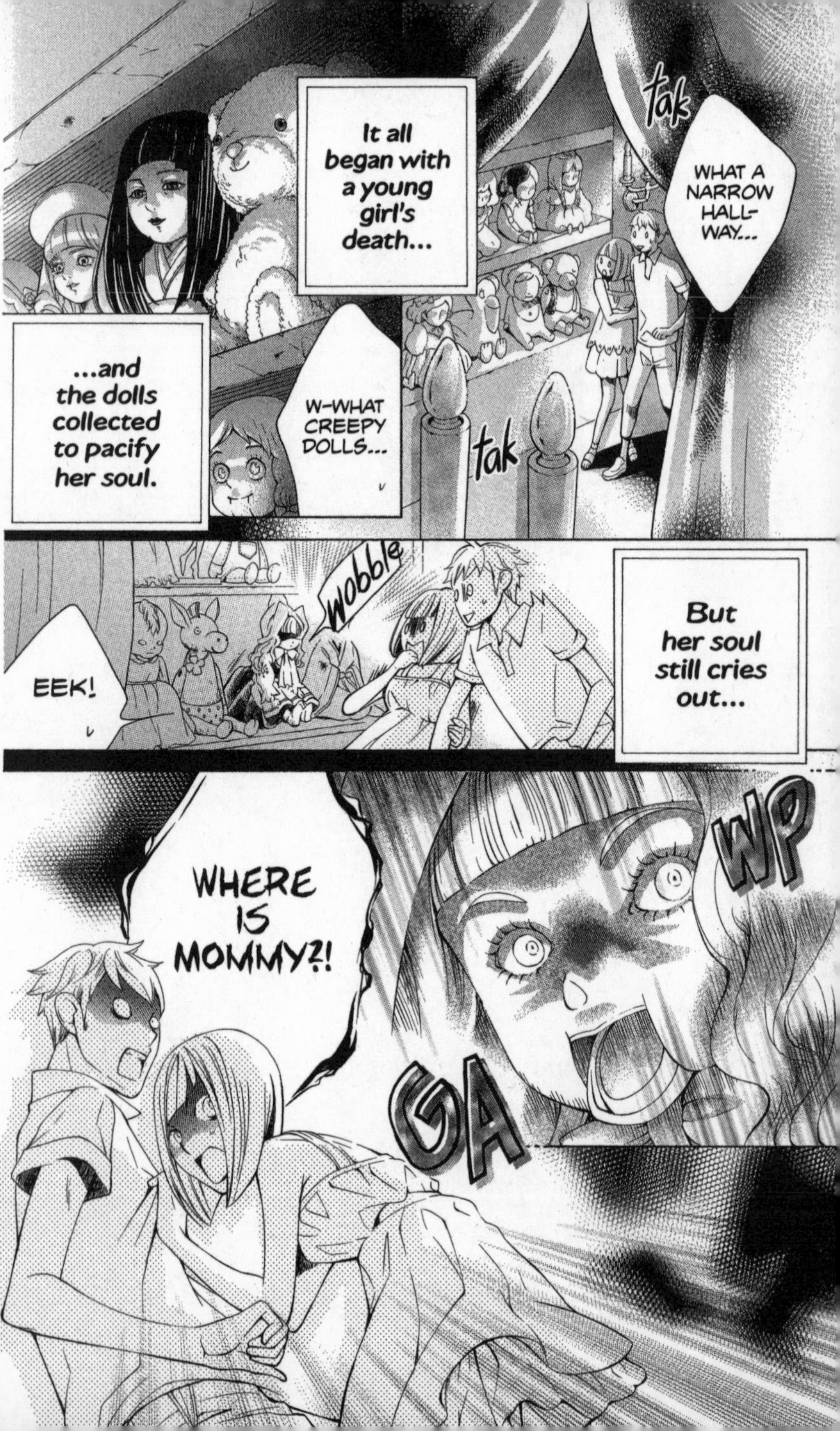
tak
WHAT A NARROW HALL-WAY...
It all began with a young girl's death...
W-WHAT CREEPY DOLLS...
tak
...and the dolls collected to pacify her soul.
But her soul still cries out...
wobble
EEK!
WP
WHERE IS MOMMY?!
GA

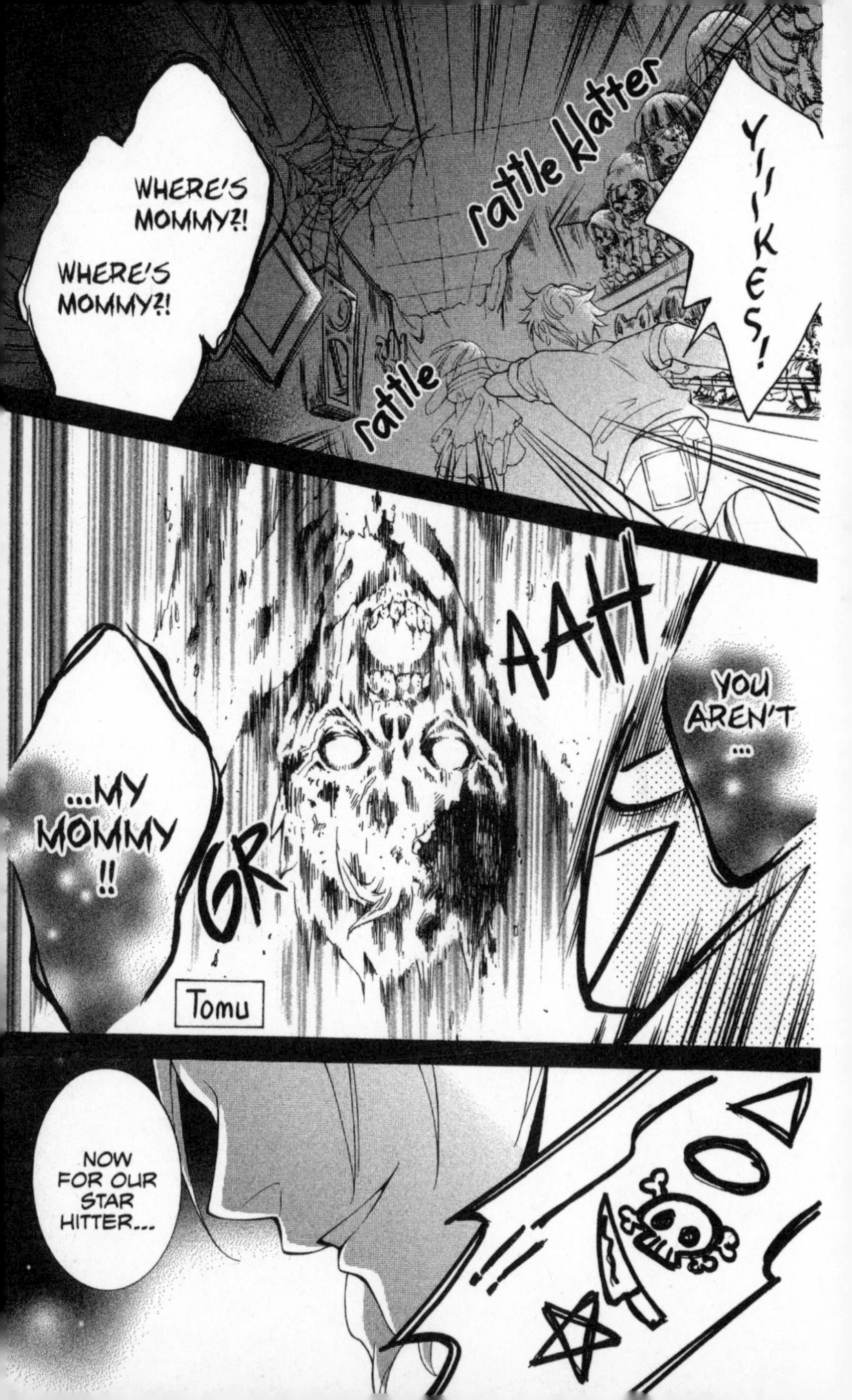
YIIIKES!
rattle klatter
rattle
WHERE'S MOMMY?!
WHERE'S MOMMY?!
YOU AREN'T ...
AAH
GR
...MY MOMMY !!
Tomu
!!
NOW FOR OUR STAR HITTER...

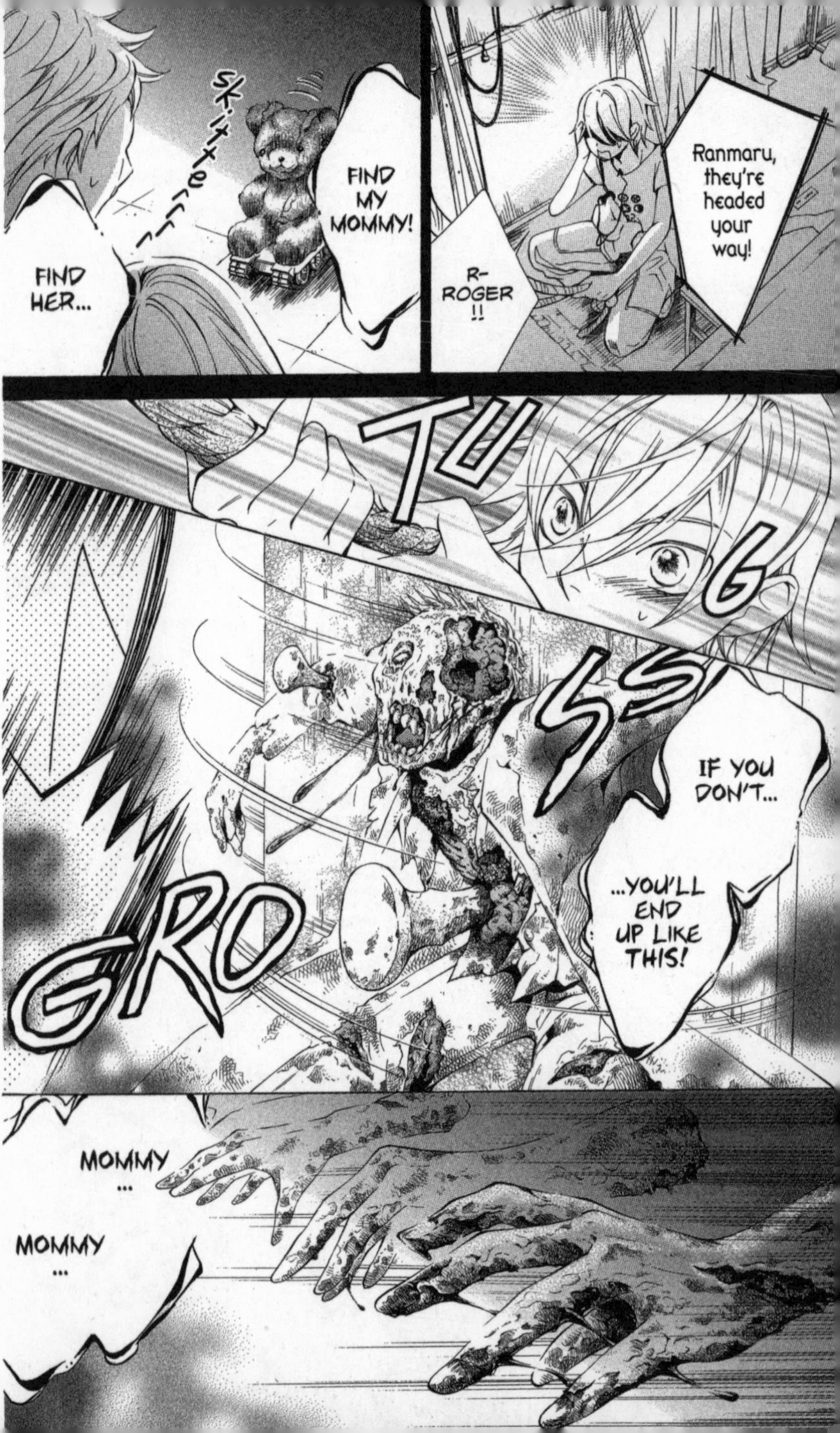
Ranmaru, they're headed your way!
R-ROGER!!
FIND MY MOMMY!
skitterrrr
FIND HER...
TU
G
SS
IF YOU DON'T...
...YOU'LL END UP LIKE THIS!
GRO
MOMMY...
MOMMY...

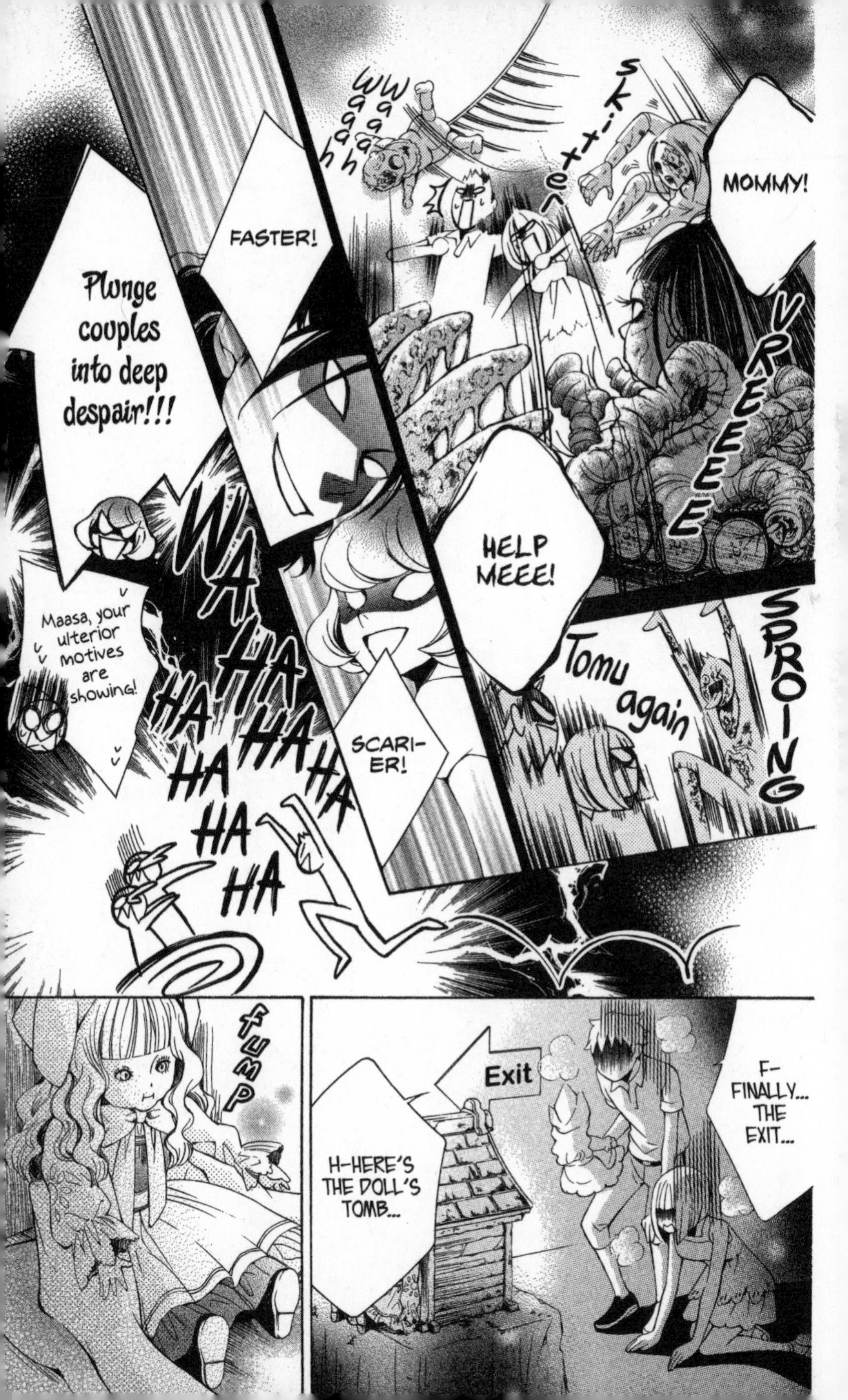
MOMMY!
s-k-i-t-t-e-r
Waaah
Waaah
VREEEEE
HELP MEEE!
SPROING
Tomu again
FASTER!
Plunge couples into deep despair!!!
WAHAHAHAHAHAHAHAHAHA
SCARI-ER!
Maasa, your ulterior motives are showing!
F-FINALLY... THE EXIT...
Exit
H-HERE'S THE DOLL'S TOMB...
FUMP

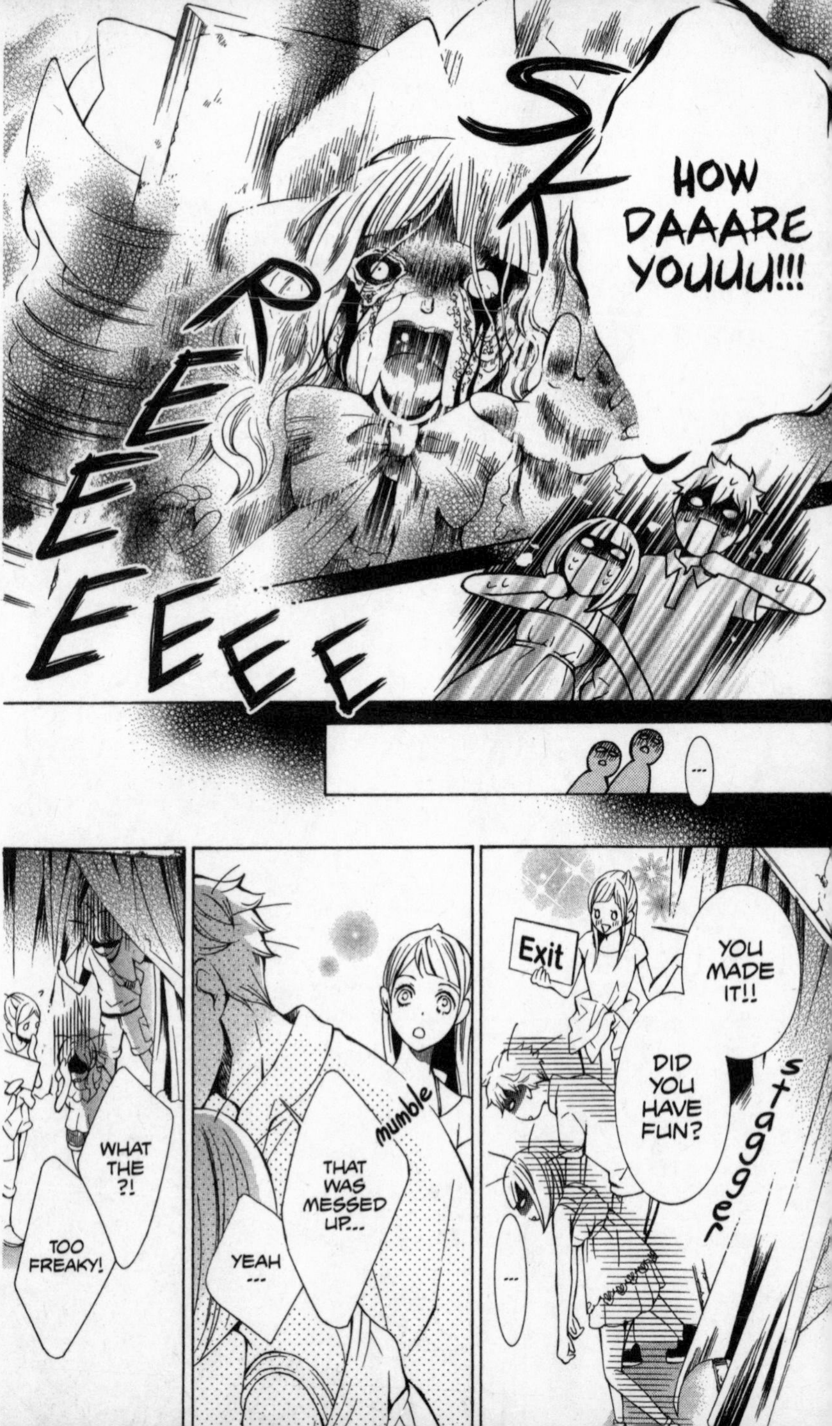
SKREEEEEE
HOW DAAARE YOUUU!!!
...
YOU MADE IT!!
DID YOU HAVE FUN?
stagger
...
mumble
THAT WAS MESSED UP...
YEAH ...
WHAT THE ?!
TOO FREAKY!

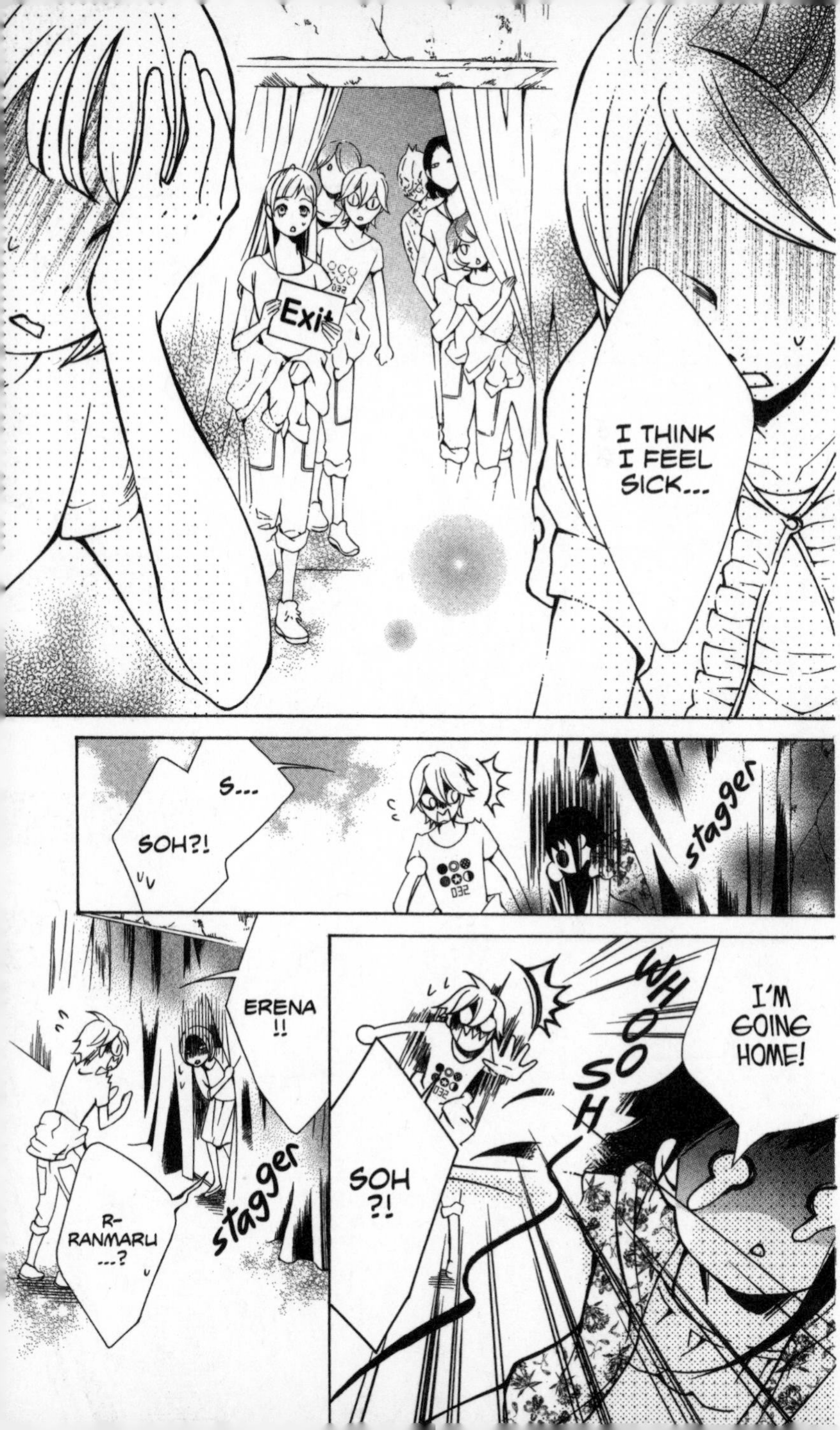
I THINK I FEEL SICK...
stagger
S... SOH?!
I'M GOING HOME!
WHOOOSH
SOH ?!
ERENA !!
stagger
R-RANMARU ...?

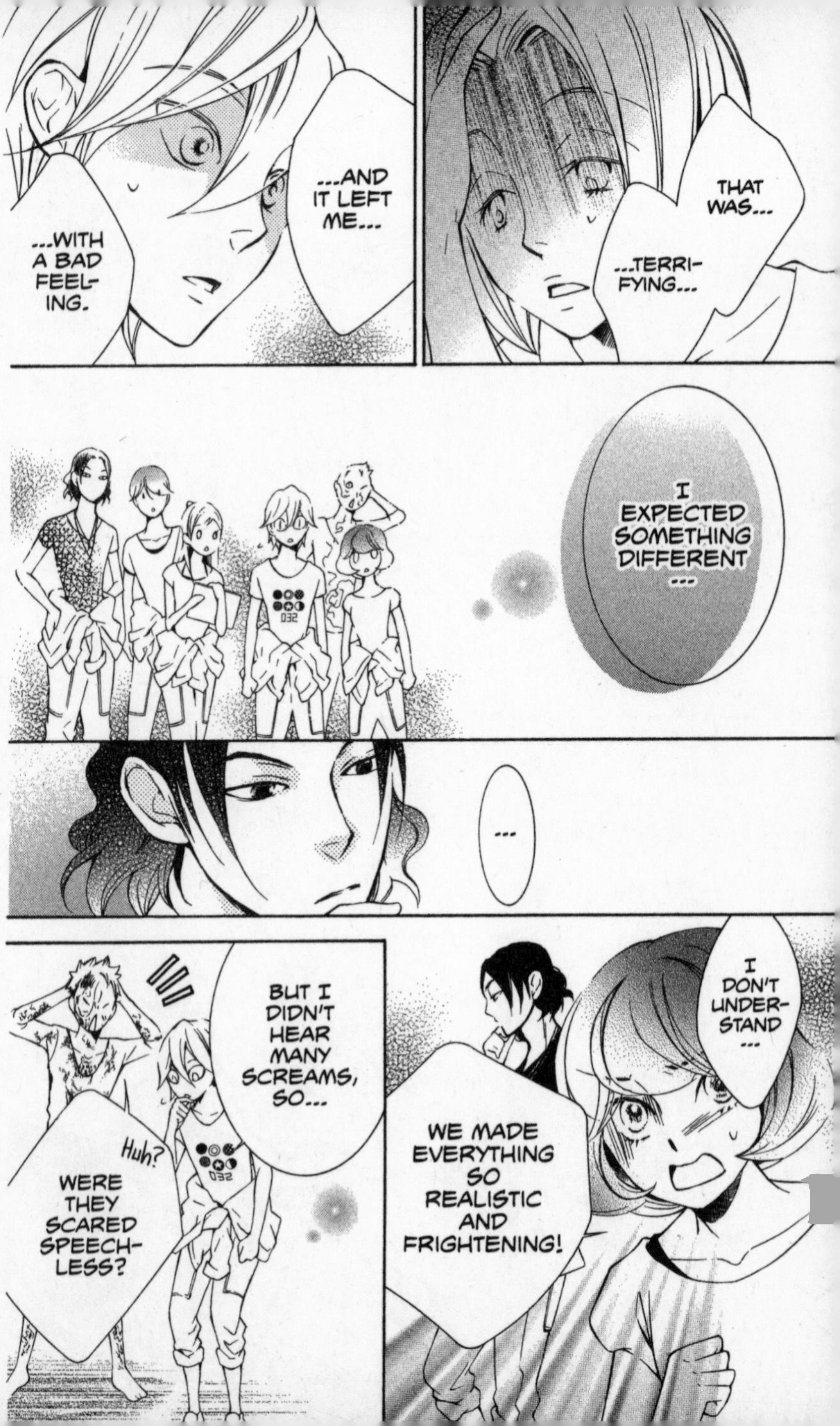
THAT WAS...
...TERRI-FYING...
...AND IT LEFT ME...
...WITH A BAD FEEL-ING.
I EXPECTED SOMETHING DIFFERENT...
...
I DON'T UNDER-STAND...
WE MADE EVERYTHING SO REALISTIC AND FRIGHTENING!
BUT I DIDN'T HEAR MANY SCREAMS, SO...
Huh?
WERE THEY SCARED SPEECH-LESS?

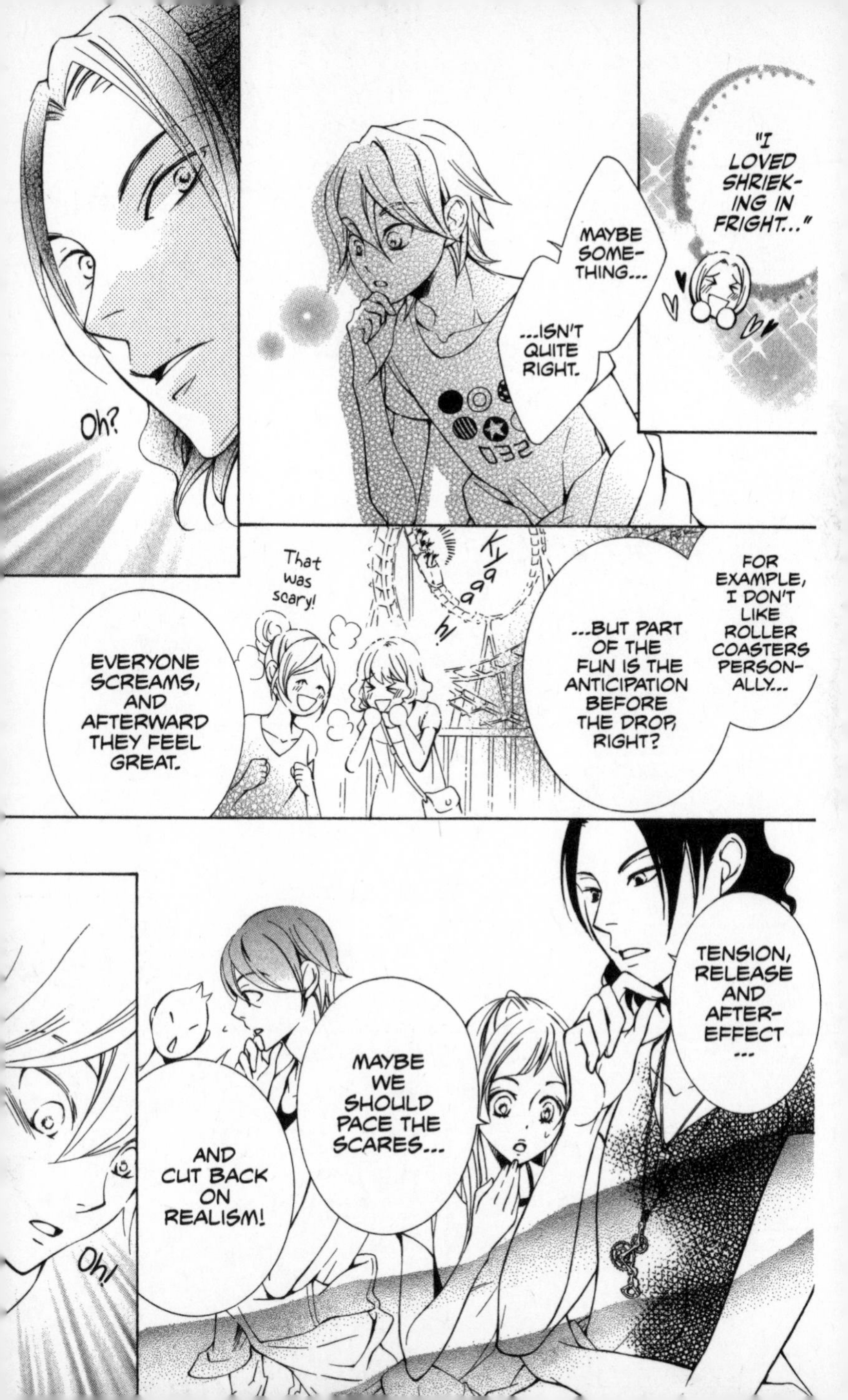
"I LOVED SHRIEKING IN FRIGHT..."
MAYBE SOMETHING...
...ISN'T QUITE RIGHT.
Oh?
FOR EXAMPLE, I DON'T LIKE ROLLER COASTERS PERSONALLY...
...BUT PART OF THE FUN IS THE ANTICIPATION BEFORE THE DROP, RIGHT?
Kyaaaah!
That was scary!
EVERYONE SCREAMS, AND AFTERWARD THEY FEEL GREAT.
TENSION, RELEASE AND AFTER-EFFECT...
MAYBE WE SHOULD PACE THE SCARES...
AND CUT BACK ON REALISM!
Oh!

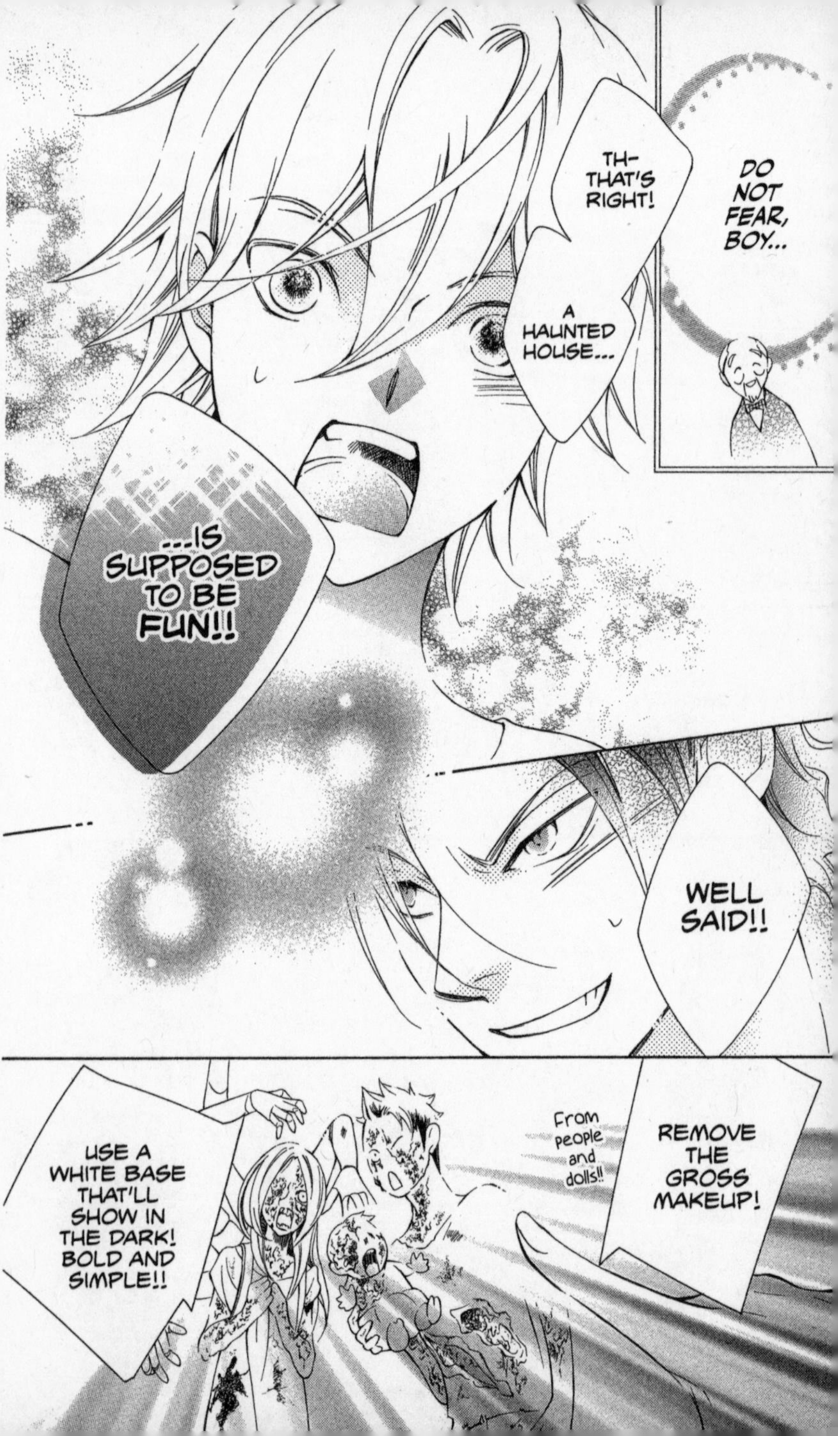
DO NOT FEAR, BOY...
TH-THAT'S RIGHT!
A HAUNTED HOUSE...
...IS SUPPOSED TO BE FUN!!
WELL SAID!!
REMOVE THE GROSS MAKEUP!
From people and dolls!!
USE A WHITE BASE THAT'LL SHOW IN THE DARK! BOLD AND SIMPLE!!

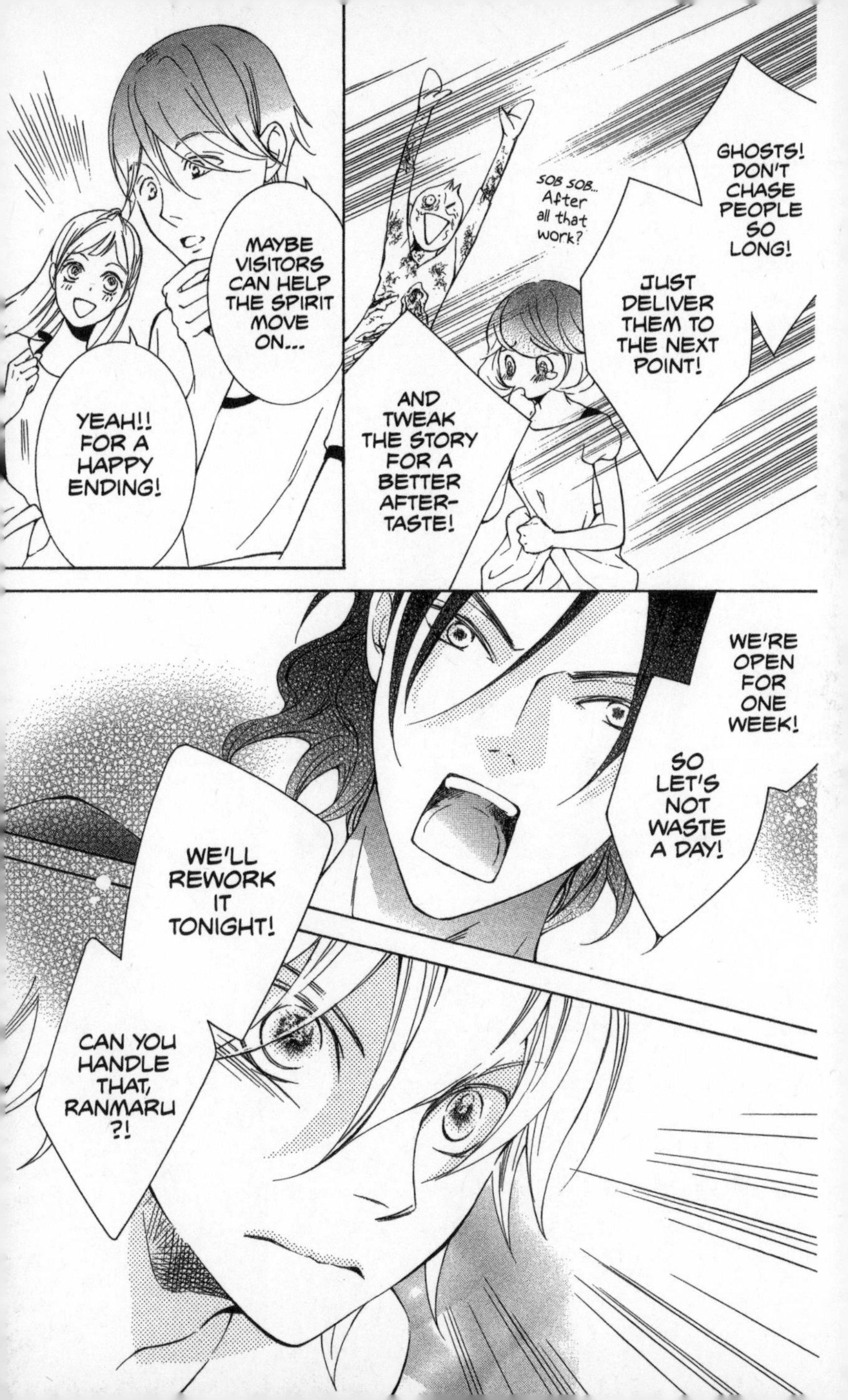
GHOSTS! DON'T CHASE PEOPLE SO LONG!
SOB SOB... After all that work?
JUST DELIVER THEM TO THE NEXT POINT!
AND TWEAK THE STORY FOR A BETTER AFTER-TASTE!
MAYBE VISITORS CAN HELP THE SPIRIT MOVE ON...
YEAH!! FOR A HAPPY ENDING!
WE'RE OPEN FOR ONE WEEK!
SO LET'S NOT WASTE A DAY!
WE'LL REWORK IT TONIGHT!
CAN YOU HANDLE THAT, RANMARU?!

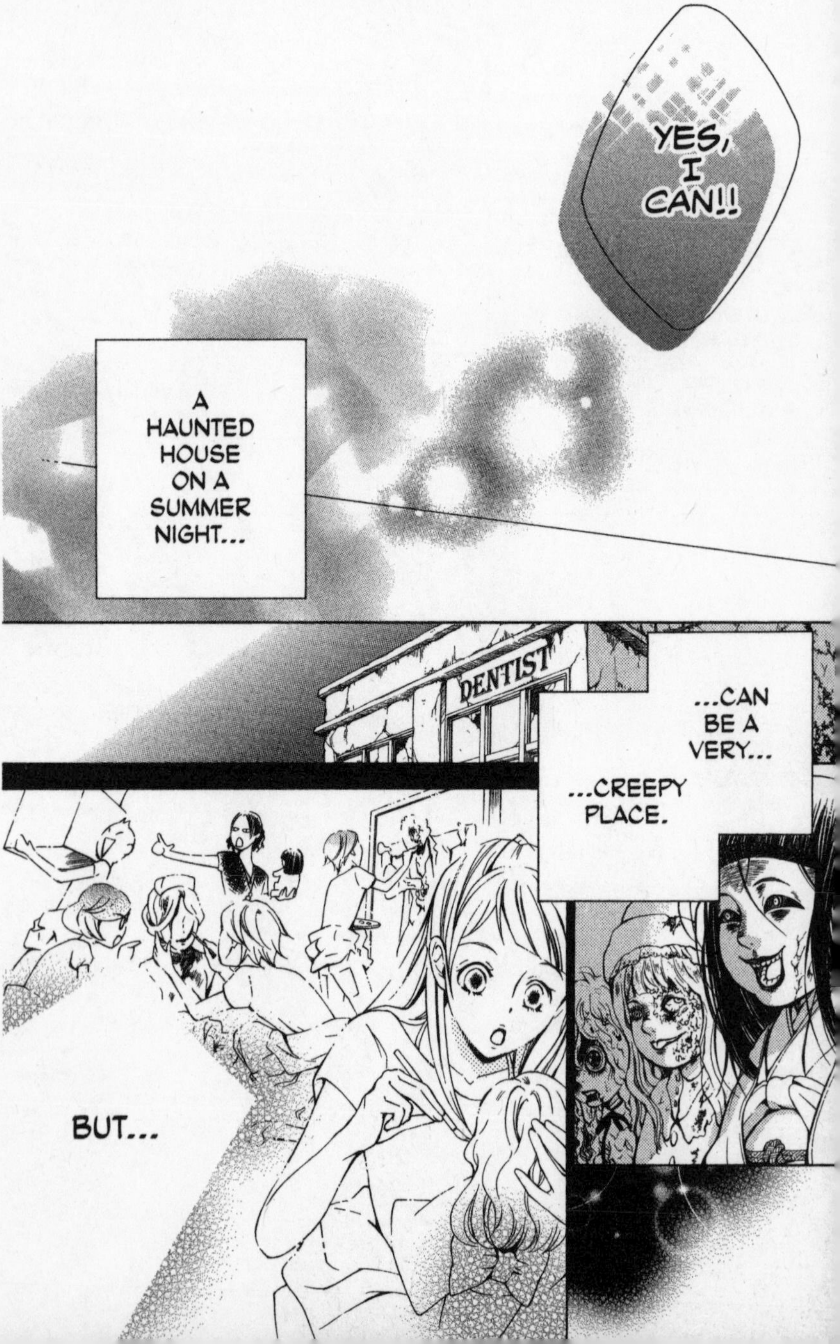
YES, I CAN!!
A HAUNTED HOUSE ON A SUMMER NIGHT...
DENTIST
...CAN BE A VERY...
...CREEPY PLACE.
BUT...

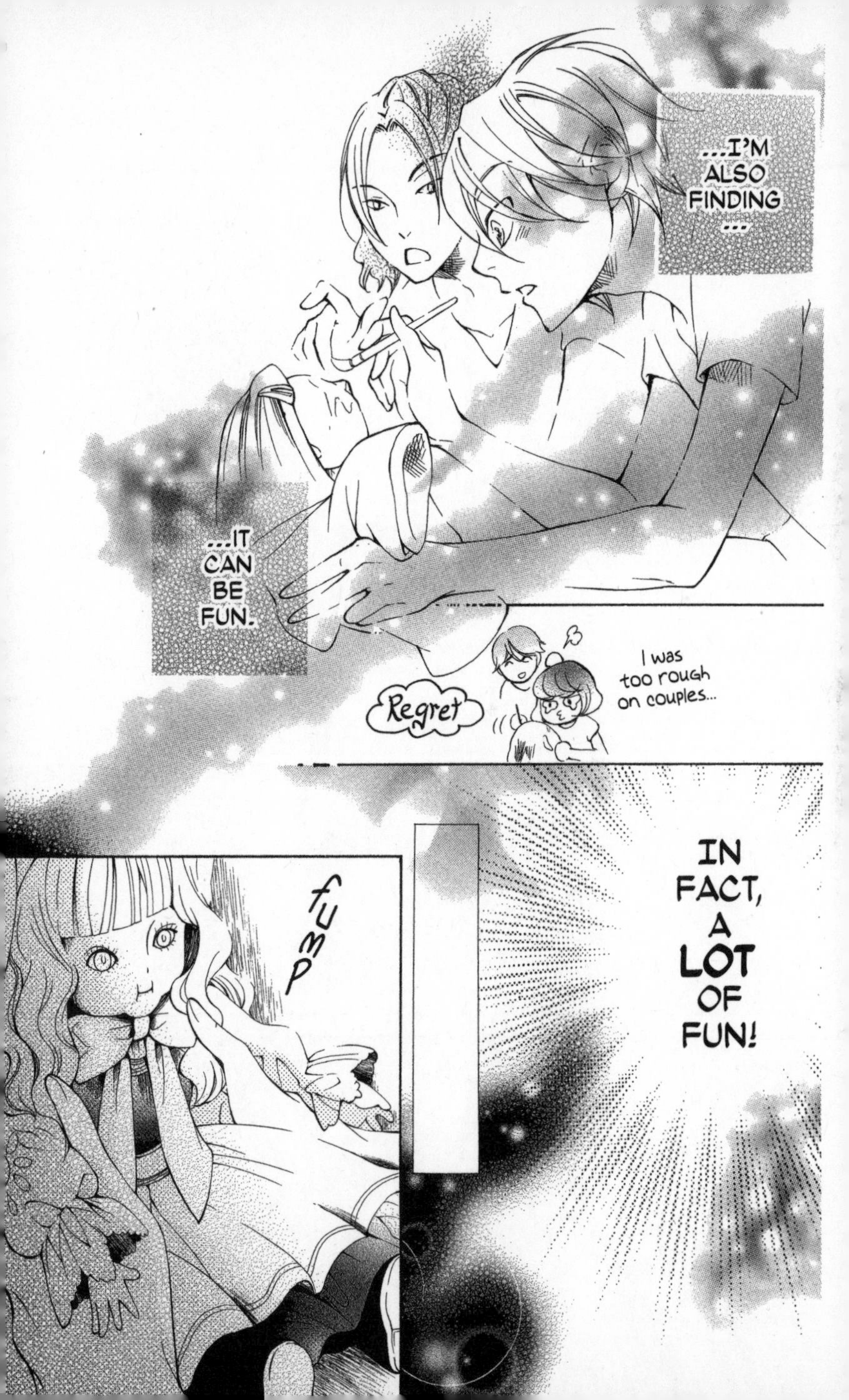
...I'M ALSO FINDING...
...IT CAN BE FUN.
I was too rough on couples...
Regret
IN FACT, A LOT OF FUN!
FUMP

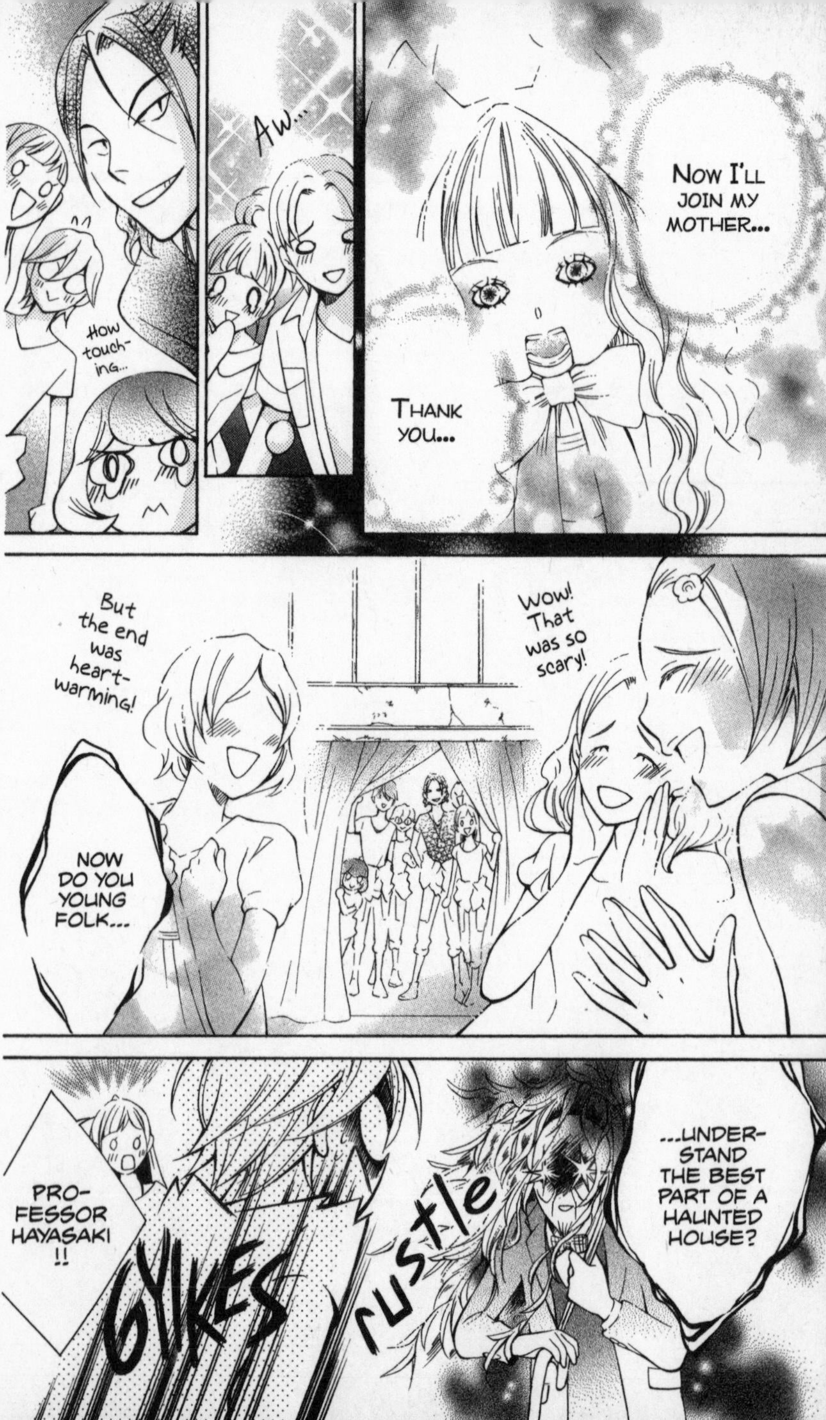
Now I'll join my mother...
Thank you...
Aw...
How touching...
Wow! That was so scary!
But the end was heart-warming!
NOW DO YOU YOUNG FOLK...
...UNDERSTAND THE BEST PART OF A HAUNTED HOUSE?
rustle
GYIKES
PROFESSOR HAYASAKI!!

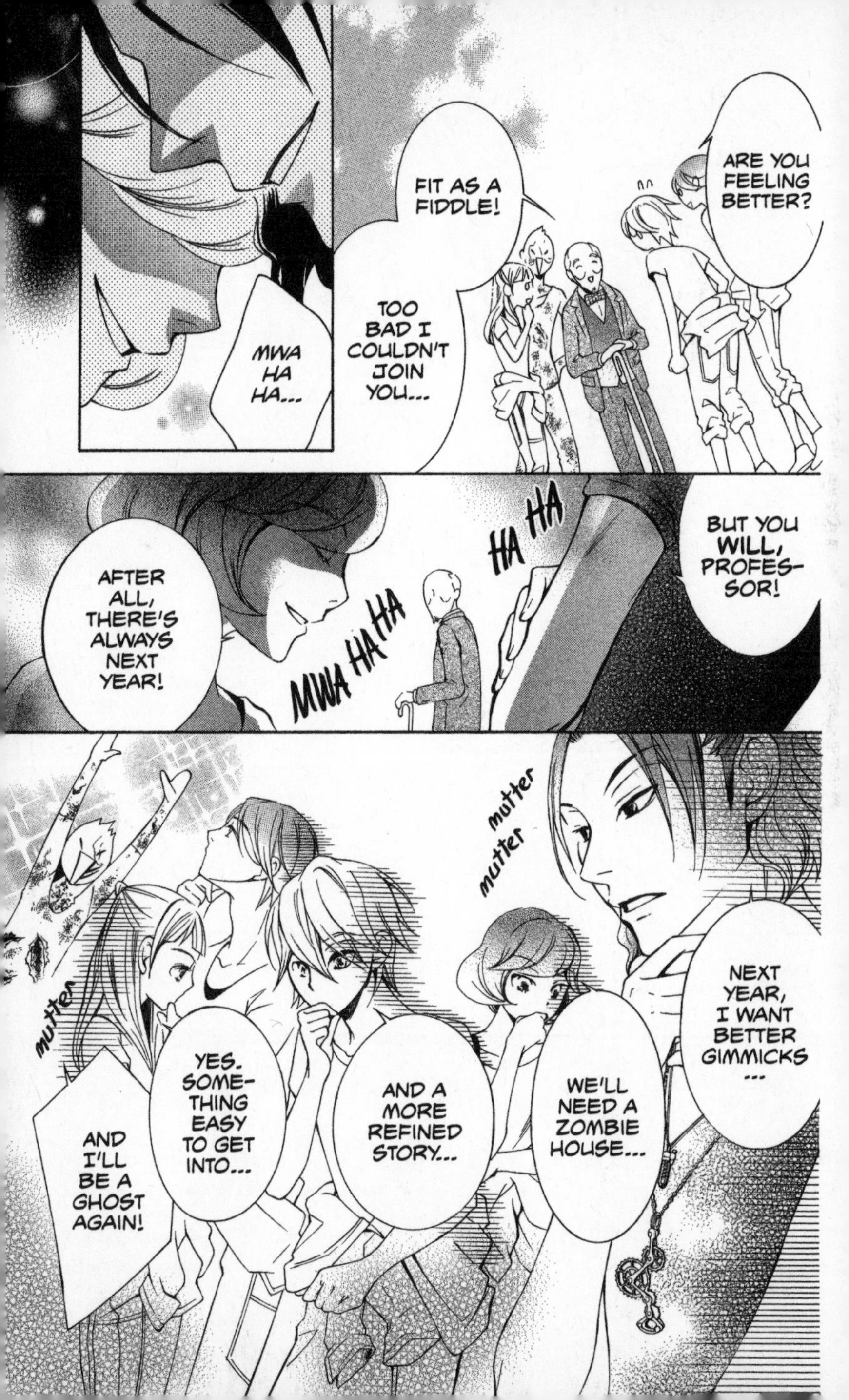
ARE YOU FEELING BETTER?
FIT AS A FIDDLE!
TOO BAD I COULDN'T JOIN YOU...
MWA HA HA...
BUT YOU WILL, PROFESSOR!
HA HA
MWA HA HA
AFTER ALL, THERE'S ALWAYS NEXT YEAR!
mutter mutter
NEXT YEAR, I WANT BETTER GIMMICKS...
WE'LL NEED A ZOMBIE HOUSE...
AND A MORE REFINED STORY...
YES. SOMETHING EASY TO GET INTO...
mutter
AND I'LL BE A GHOST AGAIN!

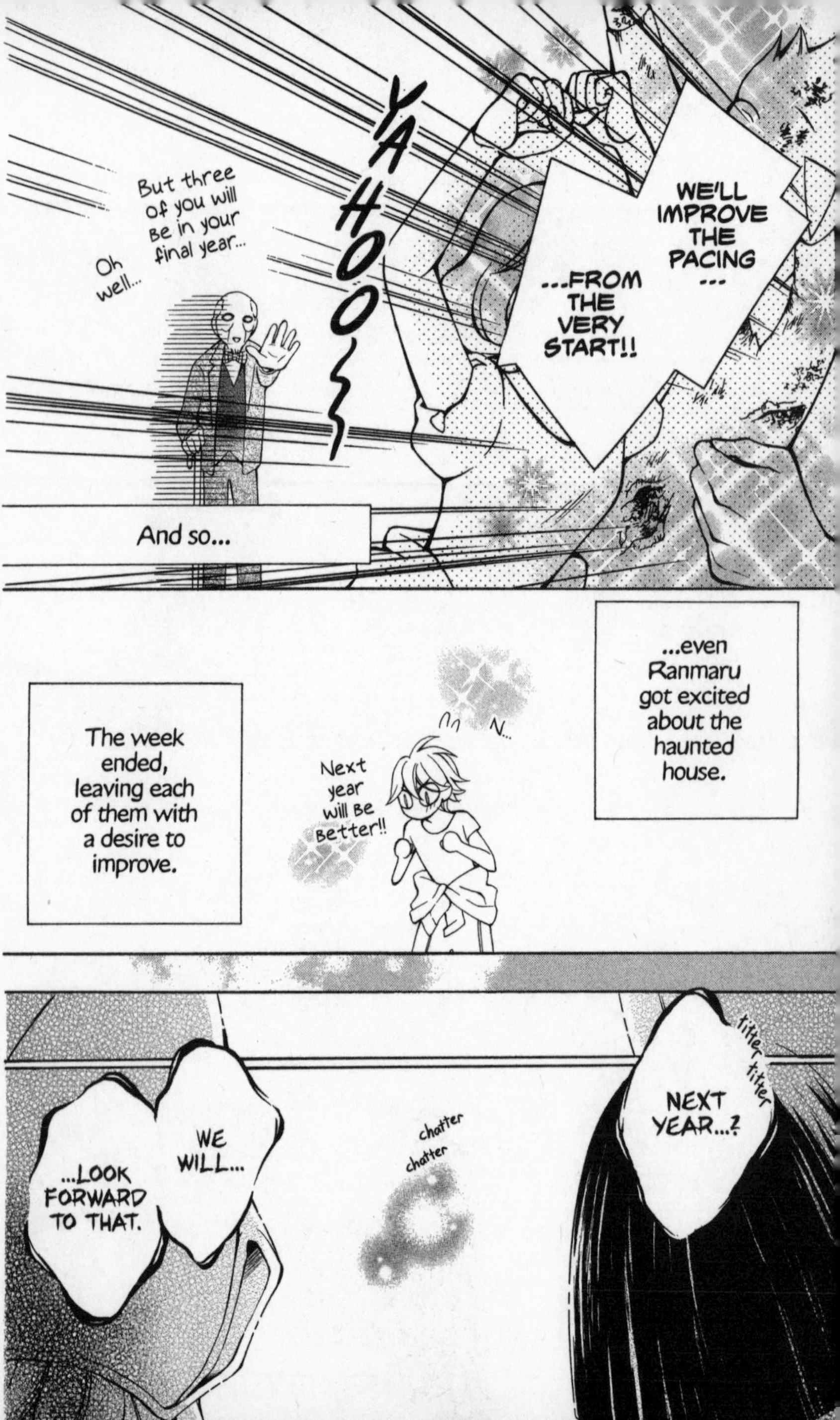
WE'LL IMPROVE THE PACING...
...FROM THE VERY START!!
YAHOOO
But three of you will be in your final year...
Oh well...
And so...
...even Ranmaru got excited about the haunted house.
N...
Next year will be better!!
The week ended, leaving each of them with a desire to improve.
titter titter
NEXT YEAR...?
chatter chatter
WE WILL...
...LOOK FORWARD TO THAT.

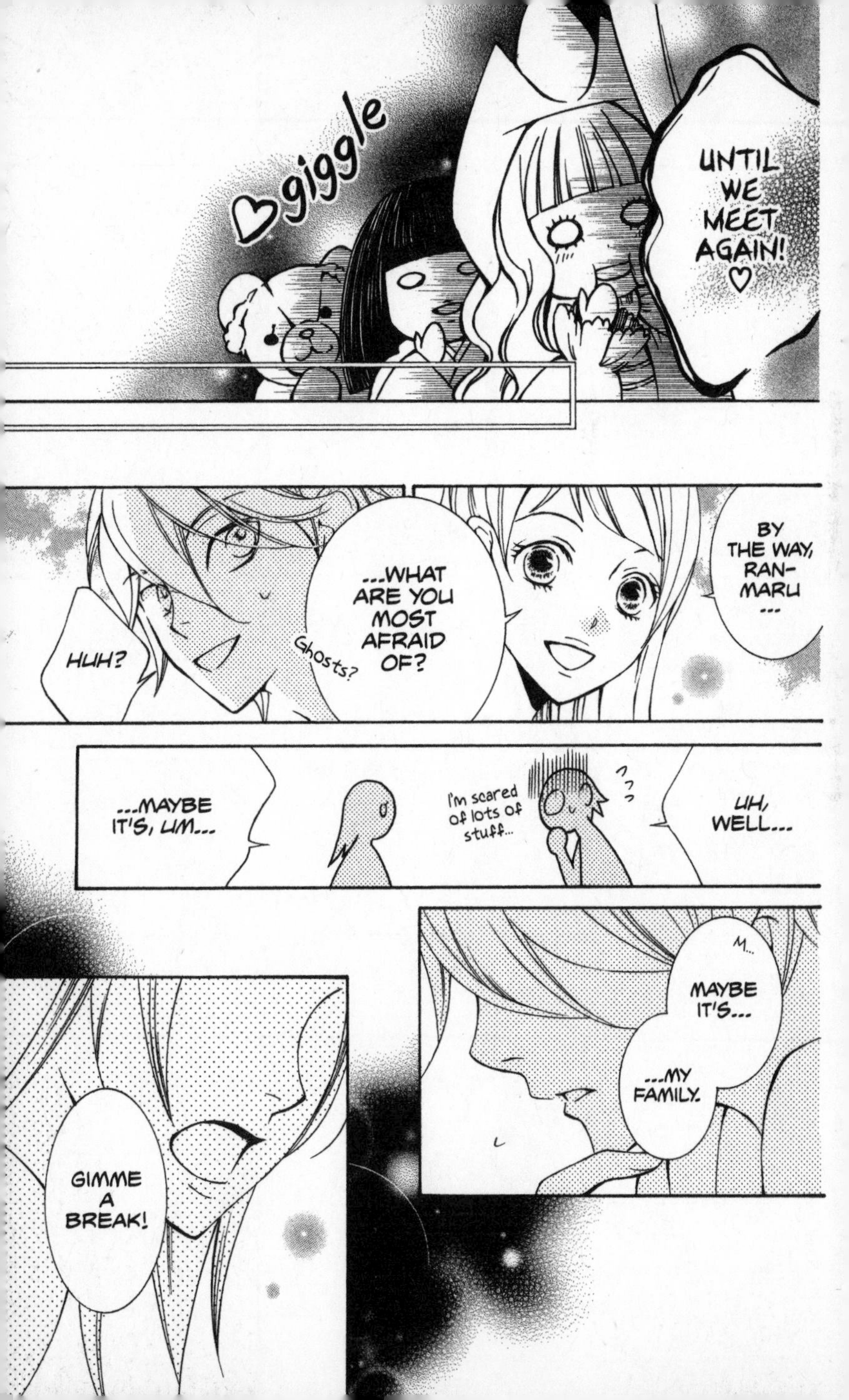
UNTIL WE MEET AGAIN! ♡
♡giggle
BY THE WAY, RAN-MARU...
...WHAT ARE YOU MOST AFRAID OF?
Ghosts?
HUH?
UH, WELL...
I'm scared of lots of stuff...
...MAYBE IT'S, UM...
M... MAYBE IT'S...
...MY FAMILY.
GIMME A BREAK!

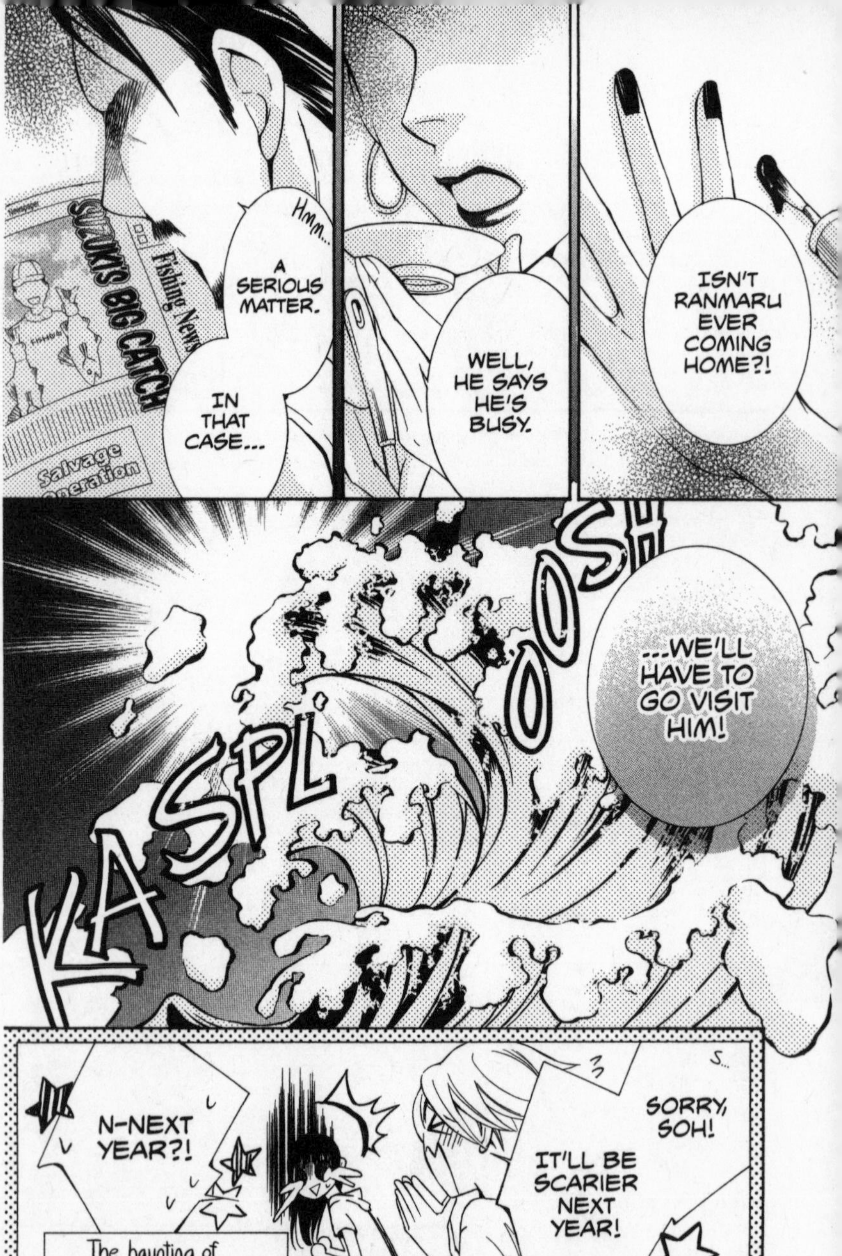
ISN'T RANMARU EVER COMING HOME?!
WELL, HE SAYS HE'S BUSY.
Hmm...
A SERIOUS MATTER.
SUZUKI'S BIG CATCH
Fishing News
Salvage Operation
IN THAT CASE...
...WE'LL HAVE TO GO VISIT HIM!
KASPLOOOSH
S...
SORRY, SOH!
IT'LL BE SCARIER NEXT YEAR!
N-NEXT YEAR?!
The haunting of Soh will continue...

BEHIND THE SCENES!! VOLUME 3 – THE END

ART SQUAD DAILY LIFE

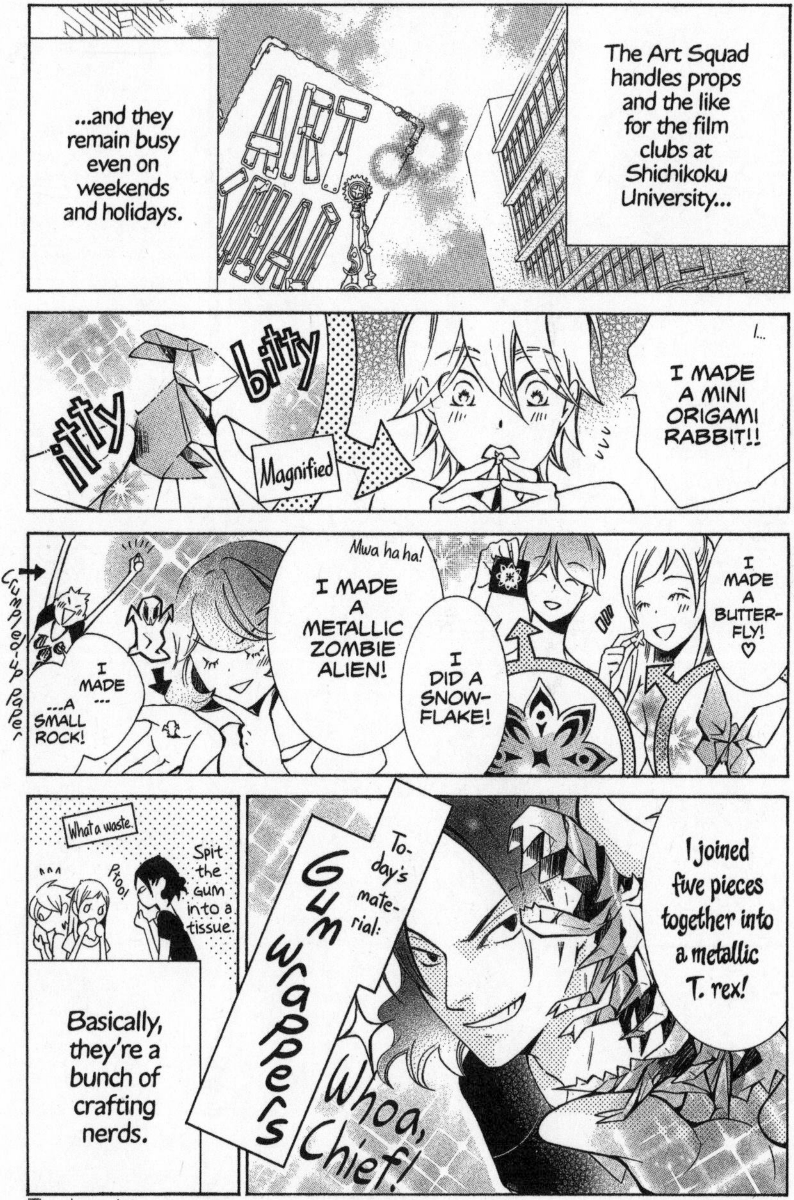

The Art Squad handles props and the like for the film clubs at Shichikoku University...
...and they remain busy even on weekends and holidays.
I...
I MADE A MINI ORIGAMI RABBIT!!
Magnified
itty
bitty
I MADE A BUTTER-FLY! ♡
I DID A SNOW-FLAKE!
Mwa ha ha!
I MADE A METALLIC ZOMBIE ALIEN!
I MADE... ...A SMALL ROCK!
Crumpled-up paper
I joined five pieces together into a metallic T. rex!
To-day's mate-rial:
Gum wrappers
Whoa, Chief!
What a waste.
Spit the gum into a tissue.
Ptoo!
Basically, they're a bunch of crafting nerds.

They also use drinking-straw wrappers and disposable chopstick sleeves.

HANG IN THERE, MR. PESSIMIST!!

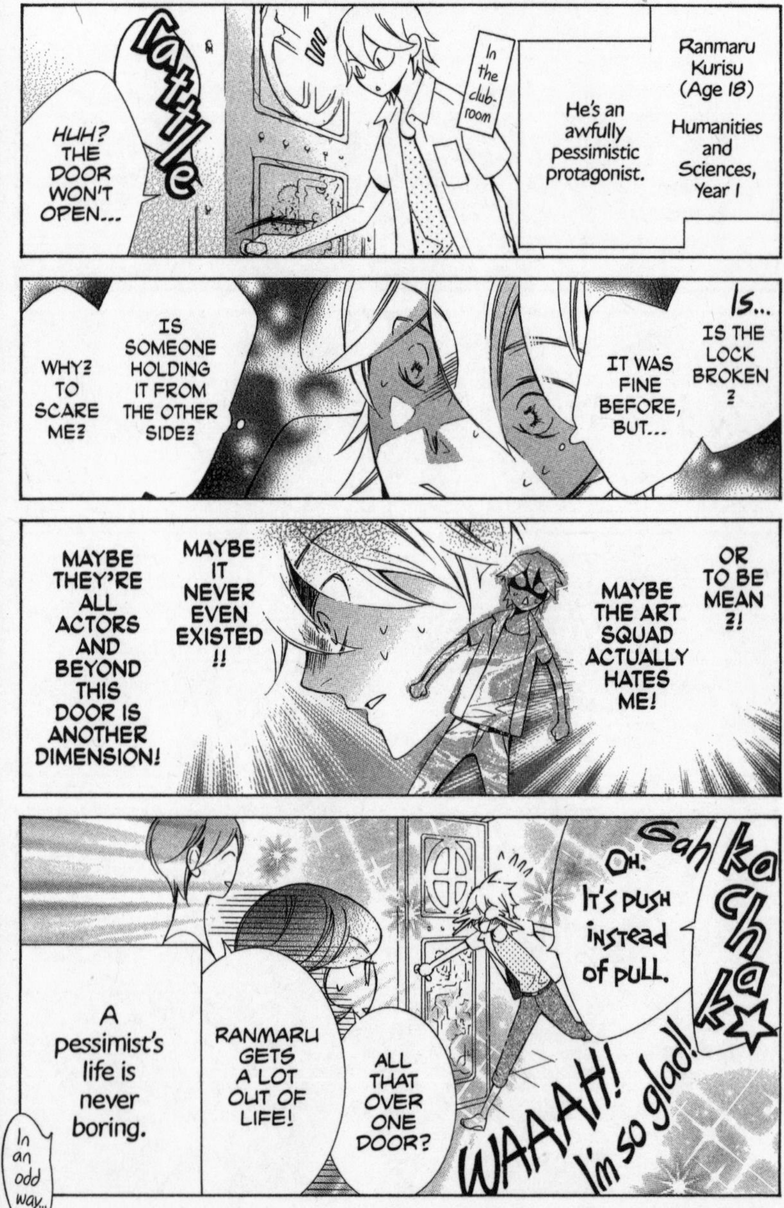
Ranmaru Kurisu (Age 18) Humanities and Sciences, Year 1
He's an awfully pessimistic protagonist.
In the club-room
rattle
HUH? THE DOOR WON'T OPEN...
Is...
IS THE LOCK BROKEN?
IT WAS FINE BEFORE, BUT...
IS SOMEONE HOLDING IT FROM THE OTHER SIDE?
WHY? TO SCARE ME?
OR TO BE MEAN?!
MAYBE THE ART SQUAD ACTUALLY HATES ME!
MAYBE IT NEVER EVEN EXISTED!!
MAYBE THEY'RE ALL ACTORS AND BEYOND THIS DOOR IS ANOTHER DIMENSION!
kachak☆
Gah
OH. It's push instead of pull.
WAAAH! I'm so glad!
ALL THAT OVER ONE DOOR?
RANMARU GETS A LOT OUT OF LIFE!
A pessimist's life is never boring.
In an odd way...

THE CHIEF'S 108 HOBBIES

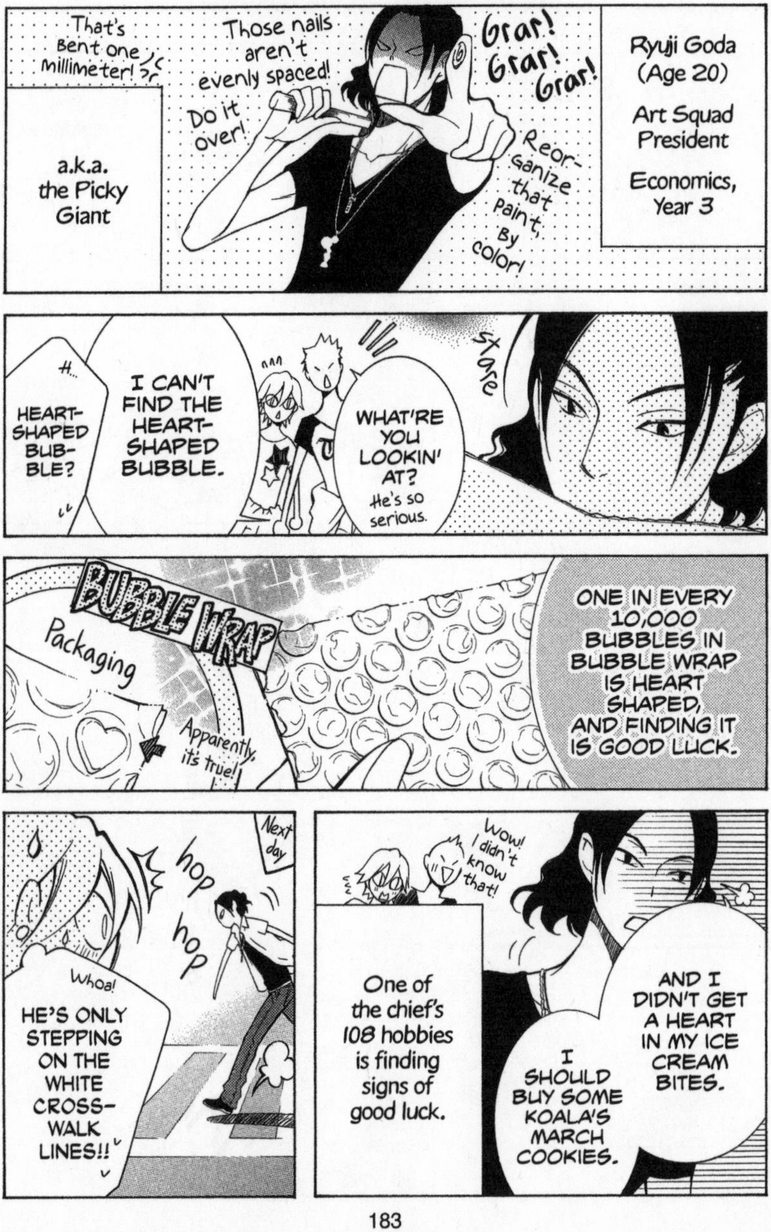
Ryuji Goda (Age 20)
Art Squad President
Economics, Year 3
Grar! Grar! Grar!
Reorganize that paint, By color!
Those nails aren't evenly spaced!
Do it over!
That's Bent one Millimeter!
a.k.a. the Picky Giant
stare
WHAT'RE YOU LOOKIN' AT?
He's so serious.
I CAN'T FIND THE HEART-SHAPED BUBBLE.
H... HEART-SHAPED BUB-BLE?
ONE IN EVERY 10,000 BUBBLES IN BUBBLE WRAP IS HEART SHAPED, AND FINDING IT IS GOOD LUCK.
BUBBLE WRAP
Packaging
Apparently, it's true!
AND I DIDN'T GET A HEART IN MY ICE CREAM BITES.
I SHOULD BUY SOME KOALA'S MARCH COOKIES.
Wow! I didn't know that!
One of the chief's 108 hobbies is finding signs of good luck.
Next day
hop
hop
Whoa!
HE'S ONLY STEPPING ON THE WHITE CROSS-WALK LINES!!

THE ART SQUAD'S CONSCIENCE

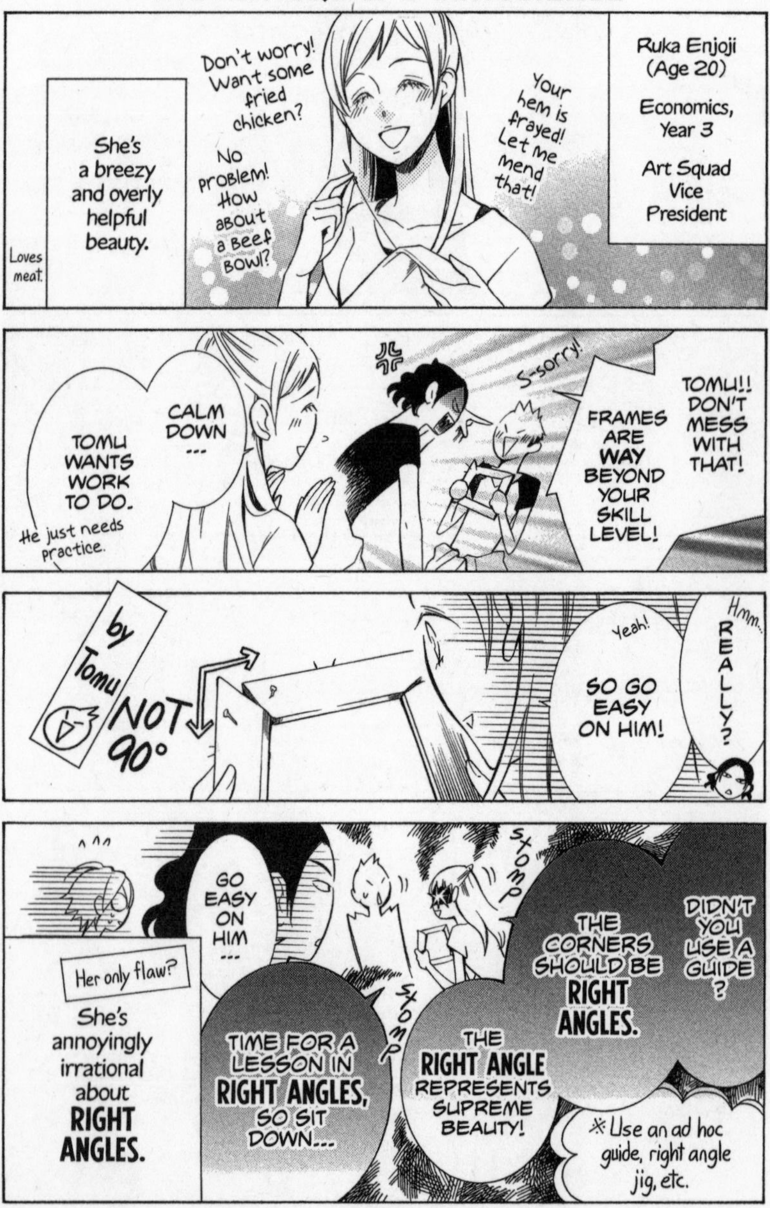
Ruka Enjoji (Age 20)
Economics, Year 3
Art Squad Vice President
Your hem is frayed! Let me mend that!
Don't worry! Want some fried chicken?
No problem! How about a beef bowl?
She's a breezy and overly helpful beauty.
Loves meat.
TOMU!! DON'T MESS WITH THAT!
FRAMES ARE WAY BEYOND YOUR SKILL LEVEL!
S-sorry!
CALM DOWN ...
TOMU WANTS WORK TO DO.
He just needs practice.
Hmm...
REALLY?
Yeah!
SO GO EASY ON HIM!
by Tomu
NOT 90°
DIDN'T YOU USE A GUIDE?
THE CORNERS SHOULD BE RIGHT ANGLES.
STOMP
THE RIGHT ANGLE REPRESENTS SUPREME BEAUTY!
※Use an ad hoc guide, right angle jig, etc.
TIME FOR A LESSON IN RIGHT ANGLES, SO SIT DOWN...
STOMP
GO EASY ON HIM ...
Her only flaw?
She's annoyingly irrational about RIGHT ANGLES.

FULFILL YOUR LIFE! (WITH ZOMBIES!)

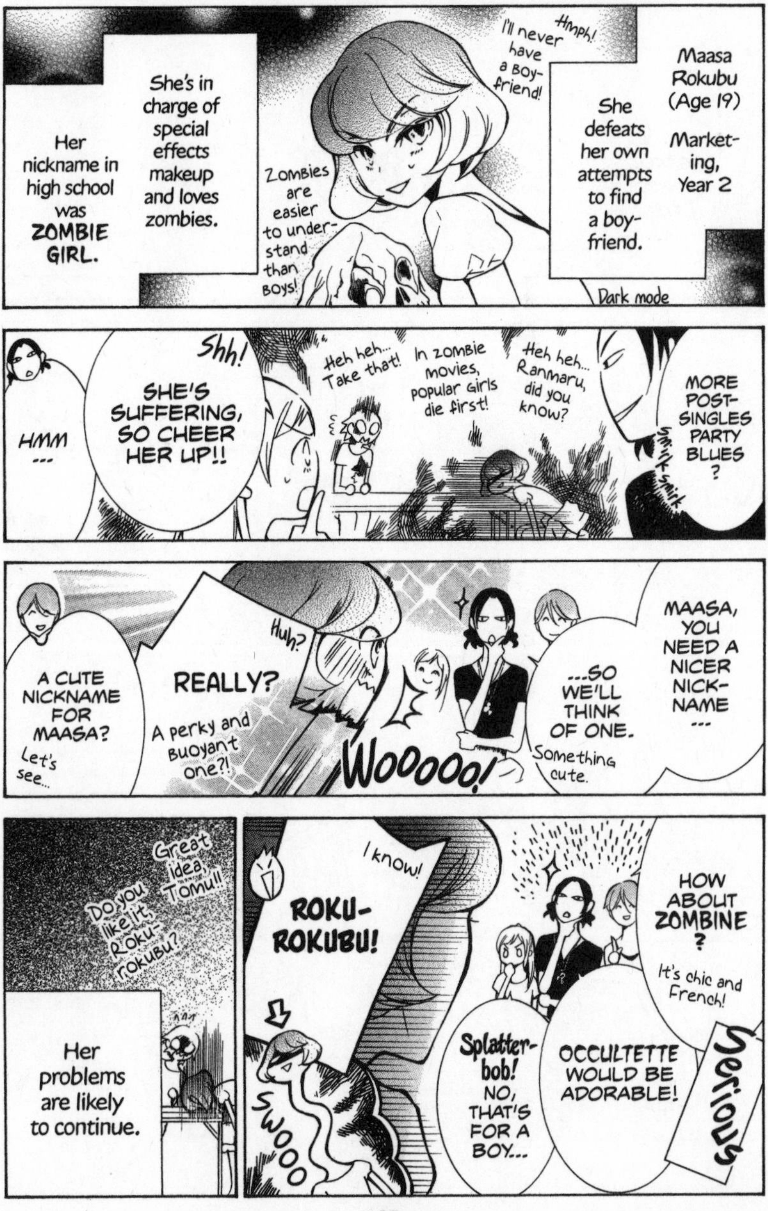
Maasa Rokubu (Age 19)
Marketing, Year 2
She defeats her own attempts to find a boyfriend.
Hmph!
I'll never have a boyfriend!
Dark mode
Zombies are easier to understand than boys!
She's in charge of special effects makeup and loves zombies.
Her nickname in high school was ZOMBIE GIRL.
MORE POST-SINGLES PARTY BLUES?
Smirk smirk
Heh heh... Ranmaru, did you know?
In zombie movies, popular girls die first!
Heh heh... Take that!
Shh!
SHE'S SUFFERING, SO CHEER HER UP!!
HMM...
MAASA, YOU NEED A NICER NICKNAME...
...SO WE'LL THINK OF ONE.
Something cute.
Huh?
REALLY?
A perky and buoyant one?!
WOOOOO!
A CUTE NICKNAME FOR MAASA?
Let's see...
HOW ABOUT ZOMBINE?
It's chic and French!
Serious
OCCULTETTE WOULD BE ADORABLE!
Splatterbob! NO, THAT'S FOR A BOY...
I know!
ROKU-ROKUBU!
SWOOO
Great idea, Tomu!!
Do you like it, Roku-rokubu?
Her problems are likely to continue.

THE ART SQUAD'S PRETTY DUDE

Izumi Samura (Age 20)
Economics, Year 3
Most popular guy in the Art Squad.
Always smiling and a little spacey
Good at design
a.k.a. the Art Squad's Snufkin
Like Snufkin, he's given to wandering around.
WHAT A NICE DAY! SHALL I SKETCH IN THE PARK?
Yeah, Go head!
TOMORROW I WATCH THE BOOKSHOP, AND THE NEXT DAY...
...I MEET SOME LADY FRIENDS AND...
He wanders here...
...and there...
...and brings back treasure.
So no one minds.
GWUMP
A man in the park Gave me some wood and used Books!
And Girls Gave me sweets!
Well done, Izumi!
Wow...
INSTEAD OF SNUFKIN, HE'S MORE LIKE THE STRAW MILLIONAIRE!
Shh!!
THAT DOESN'T FIT HIS LOOKS!!
He's a pretty Boy!!

The Art Squad is poor.

WORK IT, TOMU!!

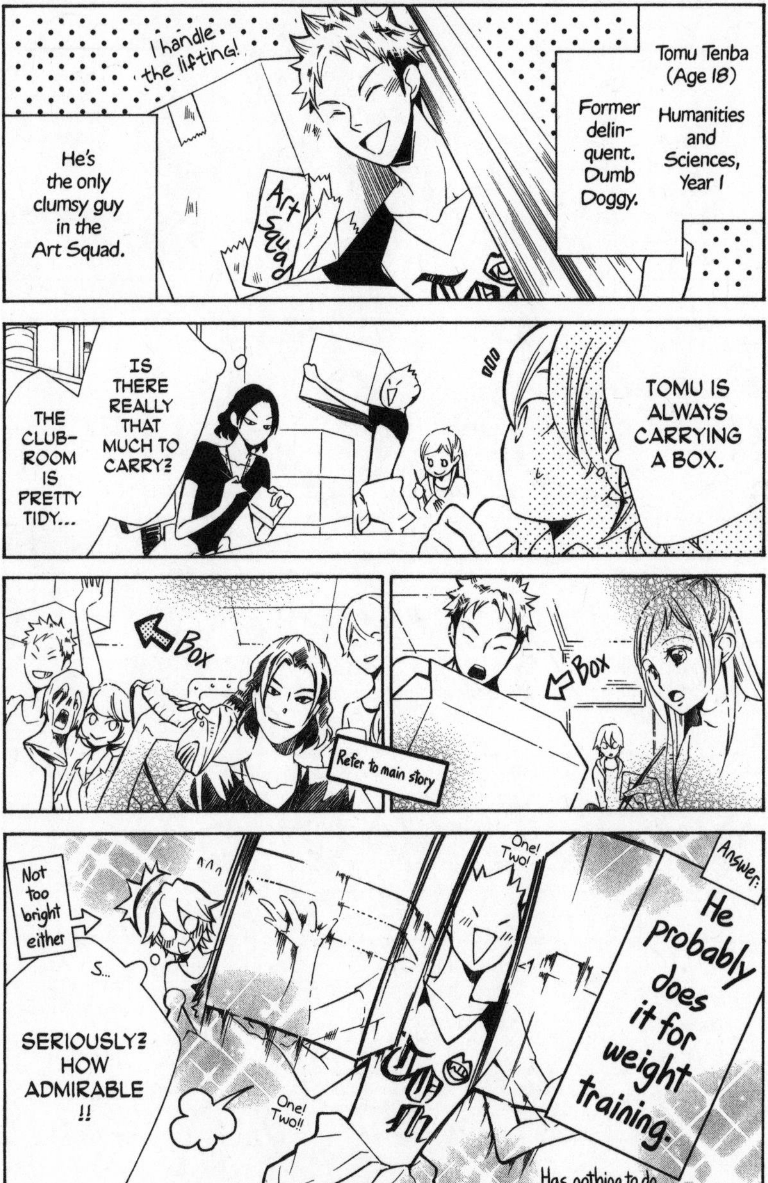
Tomu Tenba (Age 18)
Humanities and Sciences, Year 1
Former delinquent. Dumb Doggy.
I handle the lifting!
Art Squad
He's the only clumsy guy in the Art Squad.
TOMU IS ALWAYS CARRYING A BOX.
IS THERE REALLY THAT MUCH TO CARRY?
THE CLUBROOM IS PRETTY TIDY...
Box
Box
Refer to main story
Answer:
He probably does it for weight training.
One! Two!
Has nothing to do
One! Two!!
SERIOUSLY?! HOW ADMIRABLE!!
S...
Not too bright either

WORK IT, TOMU!! 2

Tomu Tenba (age 18) is the Art Squad's only clumsy guy.
We have to finish these by tomorrow!
Ranmaru, scrape this!
...
Ruka...
Maasa, age that prop!
When everyone else is busy, he has nothing to do.
So he spends the time running!
WHOOOOOOSH
Campus halls
Grah!
Hurry up, Maasa!
Wheew
Huff
ka chak
Ruka, come here.
Izumi, where's that board?
WHOOOOOOOOOSH
FINALLY! WE FIN-ISHED!
TOMU, WHY ARE YOU TIRED?
Wheez
Huff
Wheez
I'm SHOWING my SOLIDAR-ITY!!
Huff
HOW ADMI-RABLE!!
Huh?
Tomu Tenba...
...believes in hard work, victory and friendship!!

BEHIND THE SCENES!! DAILY LIFE – THE END

Special Thanks:

Ms. O
Nakamura-sama

Everyone on the editorial staff
Everyone involved in publishing this book

Yasuhito Tachibana-sama
YANG-sama
Namiko Yokota-sama
Waseda Film Society
Forêt-sama
Rodemu-sama
Kamaty Moon-sama
Nafumi Sasaki-sama
Osamu Hakamada-sama
Myu2-sama
Tsutomu Osanai-sama
Tomo Hyakutake-sama
Akiteru Nakada-sama
Okadaya, Shinjuku
Kana-sama (NIZAKANA)

■ Staff: Yui Natsuki, Aya Aomura, Umeko, Shizuru Onda, Keiko, Yutori Hizakura

■ Staff continued: Miki Namiki-sama, Meiji-sama, Shii Tsunokawa-sama, Sano-sama, Chidori Sawamura-sama, Haruka Sanagi-sama

And to all the readers!!

Bisco Hatori
2016. Feb.

References: *Why Do People Fear?*, Hirofumi Gomi, Media Factory
Conceptual SFX Makeup 2, Graphic-sha Publishing

GLOSSARY

Page 91, sidebar: Tokyu Hands
A chain store in Japan selling crafting supplies and other items.

Page 92, panel 3: Taisho era
The period in Japan spanning 1912–1926.

Page 108, panel 2: Uchu ippin
Uchu ippin means "number one dish in the universe" and is a play on the idea of the best dish under the heavens.

Page 143, panel 3: Haunted house
Haunted houses and other fright events are often held during the hot summer months in Japan because the scares give you chills!

Page 144, panel 3: Natto
A traditional Japanese staple of fermented soybeans. High in protein and other essential nutrients, natto has a rather slimy texture and is an acquired taste.

Page 185, panel 4: Rokurokubu
Rokurokubi is a monster with a long neck, similar to the illustration of Maasa in this panel. Rokurokubu is a combination of this monster's name and Maasa's last name, Rokubu.

Page 186, panel 1: Snufkin
A character from the Finnish series *Moomin*.

Page 186, panel 4: Straw Millionaire
A fairy tale about a man who trades things, always getting something of higher value in return.

AUTHOR BIO

A Japanese-style bar I went to the other day was playing movie soundtracks. Eating sashimi to music from *Back to the Future*, *Indiana Jones* and more...was sort of exciting!

-Bisco Hatori

Bisco Hatori made her manga debut with *Isshun kan no Romance* (A Moment of Romance) in *LaLa DX* magazine. The comedy *Ouran High School Host Club* was her breakout hit and was published in English by VIZ Media. Her other works include *Detarame Mousouryoku Opera* (Sloppy Vaporous Opera), *Petite Pêche!* and the vampire romance *Millennium Snow*, which was also published in English by VIZ Media.

Behind the Scenes!!

VOLUME 3

Shojo Beat Edition

STORY AND ART BY Bisco Hatori

English Translation & Adaptation/John Werry
Touch-Up Art & Lettering/Sabrina Heep
Design/ Izumi Evers
Editor/Pancha Diaz

Urakata!! by Bisco Hatori
© Bisco Hatori 2016
All rights reserved.
First published in Japan in 2016 by HAKUSENSHA, Inc., Tokyo.
English language translation rights arranged with HAKUSENSHA, Inc.,
Tokyo.

Printed in the U.S.A.

Published by VIZ Media, LLC
P.O. Box 77010
San Francisco, CA 94107

10 9 8 7 6 5 4 3 2 1
First printing, January 2017

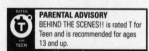

www.viz.com

www.shojobeat.com